In the Flesh

the complete

performance

history

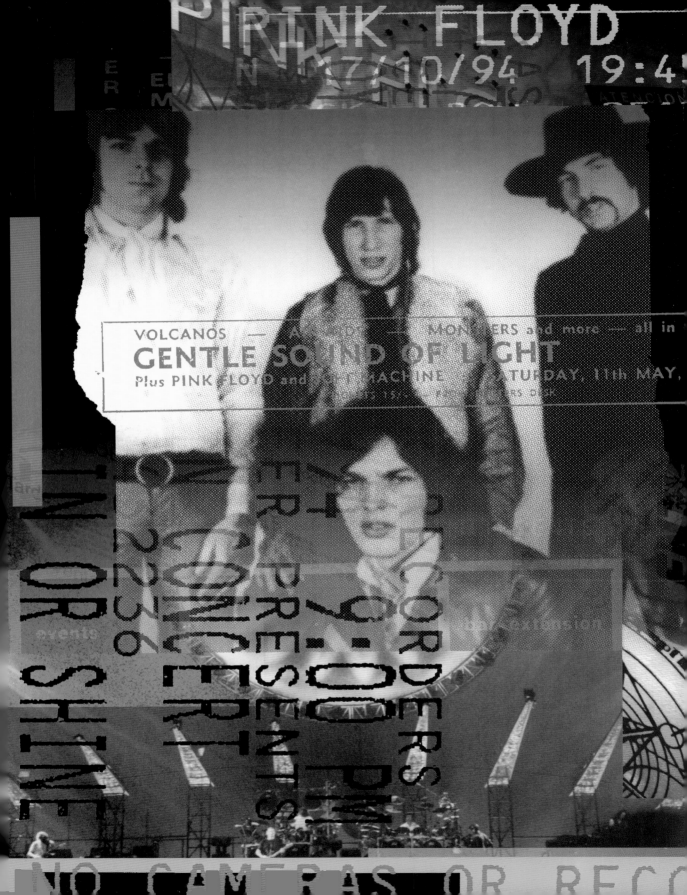

In the Flesh

the complete

performance

history

**GLENN POVEY
AND IAN RUSSELL**

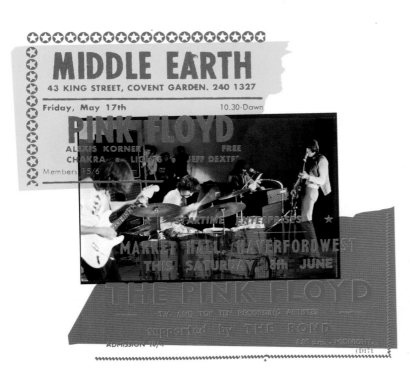

ST. MARTIN'S GRIFFIN
NEW YORK

ISBN 0-312-19175-8

First published in
Great Britain 1997 by
Bloomsbury Publishing Plc.

First U.S. Edition.
10 9 8 7 6 5 4 3 2 1

Designed by
Bradbury and Williams

Edited by Richard Dawes

The authors gratefully welcome
any new information that you
may have, especially any
performance details and set
lists not documented here.
Please write to them c/o
Second Wave Promotions,
PO Box 385, Uxbridge,
Middlesex UB9 5DZ, UK.

*Pink Floyd, January 1967. Left to right: Richard Wright, Roger Waters
(standing), Syd Barrett (seated), Nick Mason*

INTRODUCTION

In the summer of 1993 I organized the first International Pink Floyd Fan Convention at Wembley Conference Centre in London. It was a huge one-day gathering that incorporated a collectors' market, video programmes and live entertainment culminating in a three-hour show by the Australian Pink Floyd – their UK launch.

The event assembled the subscribers and readers of the Pink Floyd magazine *Brain Damage*, which I had edited for many years and through which I met Ian Russell. It was on that day that Ian and I first discussed the idea of documenting all Pink Floyd's live appearances from the earliest days. At that point we hadn't even considered what form the idea would take, let alone approached a book publisher.

Before long our seemingly insane quest began. In our attempt to locate every performance, we searched through masses of national and local newspapers, magazines and the underground press as well as venue and university records – not forgetting the first-hand accounts of Pink Floyd fans the world over.

Ultimately, our efforts led to the first comprehensive list of all Pink Floyd's stage appearances – from tiny clubs to vast stadiums – plus related TV and radio broadcasts, films and videos. We are also pleased to provide, for the first time in print, details of all the Pink Floyd's precursor bands. This is a period that previous writers have at best covered sketchily and at worst ignored entirely. In addition we have compiled an exhaustive listing of Pink Floyd's recorded work, as well as detailing each member's solo career.

We have had the very good fortune to have worked with a highly committed publisher, and a huge debt of thanks is due to Penny Phillips at Bloomsbury for her constant encouragement. Her efforts on our behalf enabled us to travel abroad in order to bring the level of research up to that which we had already achieved in the UK. For this purpose Ian consulted libraries in the Netherlands, Germany and Switzerland and I travelled to the USA.

Since late 1996 the writing of this book has kept me busy through to the small hours and beyond many, many times; as did the final edit, which was an arduous exercise made thankfully less painful with the assistance of Richard Dawes, to whom I am grateful for his commitment to improving the readability of the material. I should also thank the book's designer, Laurence Bradbury.

Looking back, the book has been an act of exorcism. For me, at least, the long-standing obsession with Pink Floyd that initiated the project and fuelled its progress has evolved into a calmer appreciation of the remarkable talents of this enduring band. It was a long haul for both of us, but oddly enough, I suspect that in time Ian and I will miss our years of searching through piles of old newspapers and magazines and rooting around in libraries for snippets of information. Who knows – we may soon find ourselves in the thick of another project no less daunting than this one.

In the meantime, we very much hope you will enjoy reading our book.

Glenn Povey

GLENN POVEY, JUNE 1997
With much love to my wonderful parents,
George and Sylvia

Note: All dates in performance listings are chronological and venue details indicate, in the case of the UK, original locations as they were before the Local Government Reorganisation Act of 1974. All locations of performances which took place in Germany before the amalgamation of West and East Germany are given as West Germany.

Set lists are only listed where the details are certain, whether partial or complete. Intervals in shows are denoted by a double slash (//).

1

1962 - 1965

2

1966 - 1967

3

1968 - 1969

4

1970 - 1971

5

1972 - 1973

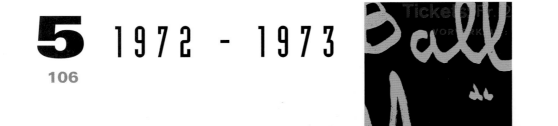

1

Although Pink Floyd didn't enjoy widespread public recognition until 1967, their roots can be traced as far back as the very early sixties and an ever-growing circle of interrelated groups and musicians based in and around the compact and cosmopolitan English university city of Cambridge.

Two of the founder members grew up there: Syd Barrett (born Roger Keith Barrett in Cambridge on 6 January 1946; he acquired the nickname 'Syd' in his late teens) and Roger Waters (born George Roger Waters in Great Bookham, Surrey, on 6 September 1943). It was also the hometown of late-sixties addition David Gilmour (born David Jon Gilmour in Cambridge on 6 March 1946), although only Barrett and Gilmour, in their teens, were active musicians in the city.

The first signs of any constructive activity can be pinpointed to early 1962, at the Barrett family home in Hills Road, which was the venue for a series of Sunday afternoon gatherings of Syd and his friends.

In a back room of this large house the youngsters played along to their latest musical finds, mainly American rock 'n' roll singles, with makeshift instruments and, if they were lucky, their first acoustic guitars. Barrett, as well as being the youngest in the family, was the only child still at home, his two sisters and brother having long since moved away. His mother was tolerant and welcomed the company his friends gave him not only because of this but also because of his father's recent untimely death.

These gatherings are believed to have become a local focus of activity for upwards of thirty teenagers at a time. Among those in regular attendance were local boys Geoff Mott, Clive Welham – a would-be drummer tapping out tunes on a biscuit tin with a knife and fork – and Tony Sainty. After one particular get-together the keen young musicians, including Barrett, decided to form a group and in doing so became the band that started the Pink Floyd family tree. They called themselves Geoff Mott and The Mottoes.

Mott had something of a reputation, having been expelled from school for his outlandish behaviour. His apparent arrogance and imposing stature made him the natural choice of front man for the new band, although they played to an audience only a handful of times. 'We did a lot of work at private parties,' Barrett later recalled. 'Some of our material was original but mostly we stuck to Shadows instrumentals and a few American songs.'[1]

Curiously, Roger Waters cites one of their concerts as his stage debut: the culmination at the Friends Meeting House of a CND march through Cambridge on 11 March 1962. Although he did occasionally drop in on the Barrett gatherings, he was only ever a spectator, not having picked up an instrument to date, so this seems highly unlikely. Waters was completely uninvolved in the Cambridge music scene up to that time. Indeed, it was not until later that year, when he moved away to pursue a seven-year

Architecture Studies course at London's Regent Street Polytechnic, that his interest in becoming a musician began at all – he blew all of his student grant on his first guitar.

As it turned out, The Mottoes' career was extremely brief. Geoff Mott went on to better things with The Boston Crabs, remembered by some as the first Cambridge band to get a record deal and see national chart success, although they split up shortly afterwards.

Drummer Clive Welham went on to form The Ramblers, who picked up from where the Mottoes had left off and enjoyed a successful year together. David Gilmour, in his first band, was recruited as a member of The Ramblers towards the end of their career, following founder member Albie Prior's departure. Welham knew Gilmour

The Ramblers, Cambridge, 1962. Left to right: Richard Baker, Mervyn Marriot, Jim Marriot, Albie Prior, Clive Welham, John Gordon.

already from their time at the Purse Preparatory School for Boys, despite being two years his senior. It was he who introduced Gilmour to Barrett when the pair had just enrolled at the Cambridge College of Art and Technology, Barrett to study Art and Design and Gilmour Modern Languages.

They became good friends in their two years of study: 'We spent a lot of time together listening to the same music,' recalled Gilmour. 'Our influences are probably pretty much the same and I was a couple of streets ahead of him at the time and was teaching him to play Stones riffs.'[2] It is surprising, though, that they never formed a band together. 'There was a bit of rivalry there,' Gilmour's future band mate Ken Waterson noted. 'They would always wind each other up, saying, "Ah, you bastard, I'm better than you." Not offensive or anything, just a bit of a laugh.'[3]

Gilmour was already becoming established with Chris Ian & The Newcomers, whom he had joined in January 1963, when, that summer, Barrett swapped his guitar for a bass and joined a new group. Those Without, who played blues-oriented material, lasted only a few months. Barrett's next band, The Hollerin' Blues, were also short-lived, giving only three shows, all in July 1964. Barrett played guitar at only two of these, while Robert Smith was drafted in for the other one. Ken Waterson recalls the band quite clearly: 'This guy Barney came to me and said can we borrow your amp? and I said OK, so we went up to the Victoria Road Congregational Church and said, right, as it's your amp, you're in the band! We had no bass player – we had Stephen Pyle and this guy Pete Glass on harmonica, me singing and we were playing Bo Diddley. Hollerin' Blues used to play Bo Diddley and then started playing Jimmy Reed stuff. We got hold of this album, *Live at Carnegie Hall*, and started learning stuff off that. We only did three gigs. This one up at the

Footlights Club went out on a blast of "La Bamba" which went on for about half an hour, with me and Barney doing a conga with the audience, stoned out of our heads. That was a bit wild.'[4]

Impromptu sets and mad jam sessions like this went on regularly at the Union Society, a small University basement meeting hall-cum-venue that Waterson remembers fondly: 'Syd, Barney, Alan Sizer and John Gordon all went down and everyone did a spot and they would pat you on the back, they would all give you a boost. They were good old boys – if you fucked up they'd still say well done, mate. They said we've got this Yank coming down, this short, squatty geezer, and they said he's good, and he did four or five numbers, and it was Paul Simon, who was at the University. All the arty-farty lot used to hang out in The Criterion pub. Storm Thorgerson [later the designer of Pink Floyd album sleeves] was one, and someone who later became an actor – they were the more studenty types – and he was quite involved with Syd quite a bit then.'

Barrett's musical career in Cambridge ceased altogether after his successful application to pursue a three-year degree course at the Camberwell School of Art in south London, starting in the autumn of 1964. He travelled down with another Cambridge musician, Bob Klose of Blues Anonymous, and both moved into the house in Highgate, north London, in which Waters was renting a flat.

Meanwhile Chris Ian & The Newcomers had, under successive managers David Hurst and Nigel Smith, been enjoying moderate success on the Cambridge gig circuit, performing cover versions of Beatles and other Liverpool scene numbers. Ken Waterson, the vocalist, recalled: 'We used to support a lot of the Cambridge bands. We never got any money for it. This guy Chris Ian, any money we got he had, it went on equipment. Even with the crap equipment, old Dave

[Gilmour] sounded pretty good, he had a poxy old Burns guitar and a crappy amp but you could see he'd got it even then. He was bloody good.… He was having lessons from Chris Jones, who was in the Hi-Fi's. He was shy, pretty laid back, he didn't like the violence. We'd be up on stage and some bloody great ruck would start in the audience with these American servicemen punching the crap out of each other.'[5]

After Chris Ian's departure, the band, now renamed The Newcomers, had a patchy career. Waterson was dividing his time between them and another act, The Louis Pocrowski 7, which incidentally featured some future Pink Floyd associates, drummer Willie Wilson (of Johnny Phillips & The Hi-Fi's) for some fourteen gigs and saxophonist Dick Parry (of Soul Committee) for one. Even Gilmour signed up for two shows. As 1963 drew to a close, The Newcomers disbanded, but Waterson remained with The Louis Pocrowski 7, whose erratic appearances continued until the autumn of 1964.

It was around this time that a little-known Cambridge outfit called The Four Posters emerged, with David Altham, Tony Sainty and Will Garfitt among its members. 'We had the advantage of having so many members doing different things,' remembers Garfitt. 'One would be at the Cambridge Tech and so we'd get gigs there, another at the Gas Works for their do's, one at the University where we would play at the Pit Club and so on. I just decided my talents lay in painting rather than struggling in a band. One thing I always remember was riding in Syd's car, a Ford Popular or something similar, and I remember asking him if we could go any faster because he was driving so slowly. But he came out with a very strange line, something like, "I'm too young to die, I've got too much to give to the world, so we'll have to drive at my speed or not at all", which was an incredibly … well, I don't know, it was just a very strange thing to say … considering.'[6]

The Four Posters and The Newcomers split at almost the same time, creating a glut of musicians, and out of this came Jokers Wild. They are regarded as one of the Cambridge scene's most successful semi-pro groups, probably because it is the one that Gilmour is most widely associated with. But in their own right they had a very strong following as a result of a series of residencies at the fashionable Dorothy and Victoria ballrooms in the centre of the city.

Jokers Wild, Victoria Ballroom, Cambridge, 1965. Left to right: David Gilmour, David Altham, John Gordon, Tony Sainty, Clive Welham.

CHRIS CHENE
THE JOKERS WILD, one of the town groups, playing at the Victoria Ballroom last Wednesday evening.

Drummer Clive Welham remembers his time with Jokers Wild very well. 'We did R&B, harmony pieces, Beach Boys, Four Seasons, which seemed to appeal to a wide audience. We didn't do any of our own material – no one did in those days. People used to write songs and then get bands to do them. We used to do Beatles numbers as well. We had a chap come down from Liverpool who saw us at the Victoria Ballroom, where we had a residency. He brought some people down to see us, one was the ex-publicity agent for The Beatles, Brian Sommerville. David Altham had been involved in some incident with his girlfriend – he was caught in a compromising position in his room at college with this girl and there was a big stink, and I don't think he was allowed to play at that gig with us. It was in the paper because he was the son of some lord or whatever. Dave went off to do some recording stuff in London but I think they were after some things from him. While he was there he met Lionel Bart. The papers made reference to the fact that he may be leaving Jokers Wild but it came to nothing.'[7]

Around August 1965, in a break from band activities, Barrett returned home and linked up with Gilmour and a group of other Cambridge friends to take off on a brief summer holiday to the south of France, trundling about in a bashed-up Land-Rover. The only remarkable event of their adventures was that while in St Tropez the pair wound up in police custody, for busking.

By autumn 1965 Jokers Wild were hot property on the Cambridge scene and travelled to the Regent Sound Studios in London's Denmark Street, to record some of their repertoire. This material was eventually put on to a privately pressed five-track 12-inch album and a 7-inch EP single and these were distributed among family and friends.

Before the end of the year they were back at the studio, this time recording tracks for a single

for the Decca label under the guidance of an up-and-coming pop impresario and Cambridge graduate, Jonathan King. 'He went to see us one week at the Victoria Ballroom, but he went on the wrong night and saw Hedgehoppers Anonymous, and got them to record a single,' recalled Welham. But they were soon back on track with King: 'A cover of Sam and Dave's "You Don't Know What I Know", with Dave singing the lead. It was much better than our first recording effort. Dave Altham and Dave Gilmour produced it; we got it right that time, we were properly prepared. Decca was very pleased with it but Sam and Dave released it over here and that was it.'[8]

This fact sealed their fate overnight and although they continued to perform, it was a downhill ride. Tony Sainty left the band in early 1966, to be deputized for occasionally by Waterson, and was permanently replaced by Peter Gilmour, one of David's two brothers.

Welham remembers the band progressing to the débutante scene, performing at London society parties and other high-profile gigs: 'We drove to London with two coach-loads of fans from Cambridge and did a gig with the Animals at an art college. It was a sizeable audience, about 800 crammed in. We did two fifteen-minute sets and they did about an hour. We did an Admiralty League at the Dorchester in London, all upper-crust types with Rolls-Royces and Bentleys everywhere.'

But Welham's departure from the group wasn't far behind Sainty's: he suffered a nervous breakdown trying to hold down a full-time job at the same time as travelling to and from venues. Willie Wilson had been deputizing for him on occasion since April, but with Welham's condition worsening he now took over full time.

At the end of 1966 John Gordon, another defector to art college, also quit, leaving the Gilmour brothers, Wilson and Altham, who managed to pick up a series of gigs in Spain and

France. Eventually, though, Altham and Peter Gilmour also broke away and Jokers Wild fell by the wayside.

The following year, during the 'Summer of Love', David Gilmour linked up with Ricky Wills (also of Soul Committee) and together with Wilson they cashed in on the trend by busking around France as The Flowers. They reportedly stayed with starlet Brigette Bardot on their travels and within the year had become Bullit, though little is known of their achievements.

To return to the autumn of 1963, Roger Waters, who by this time had been away from Cambridge for a year, teamed up with fellow students from Regent Street Polytechnic and others to form a beat group called Sigma 6. The line-up included future Pink Floyd members Nick Mason (born Nicholas Berkeley Mason in Birmingham on 27 January 1944) and Richard Wright (born Richard William Wright in Hatch End, Middlesex, on 28 July 1943), who were Waters' flat mates at the time. Wright had graduated from a trad-jazz band as a saxophonist.

The band even boasted its own manager, a former Regent Street Polytechnic student called Ken Chapman, who had cards made up of the 'Available for Weddings and Parties' variety. 'We used to learn his songs and then play

ARCHITECTURAL ABDABS

By BARBARA WALTERS

AN up-and-coming pop group here at the Poly call themselves "The Abdabs" and hope to establish themselves playing Rhythm and Blues. Most of them are architectural students.

Their names are Nick Mason (drums); Rick Wright (Rhythm guitar); Clive Metcalf (bass); Roger Waters (lead); and finally Keith Noble and Juliette Gale (singers).

Why is it that Rhythm and Blues has suddenly come into its own? Roger was the first to answer.

"It is easier to express yourself rhythmically in Blues-style. It doesn't need practice, just basic understanding."

"I prefer to play it because it is musically more interesting," said Clive. I suppose he was comparing it to Rock. Well, how does it compare? Roger was quite emphatic on this point: "Rock is just beat without expression, though admittedly Rhythm and Blues forms the basis of original rock."

It so happens that they are all modern Jazz enthusiasts.

Was there any similarity? I asked.

In Keith's opinion there was. "The Blues is just a primitive form of modern jazz.

The Abdabs, early 1964. Left to right: Nick Mason, Roger Waters, Keith Noble and Clive Metcalf.

them for Gerry Bron [later of the Bronze record label],' recalled Waters. 'They were fantastic songs: "Have You Seen A Morning Rose", to the tune of a Tchaikovsky prelude or something.' [9]

By the spring of 1964 Sigma 6 were known as The Abdabs (or the Screaming Abdabs). They were the only one of these London bands to receive any press coverage, in an early edition of West One, the Polytechnic's student newsletter. Contrary to popular belief, there never was an 'Architectural Abdabs' – this was just the headline under which the piece appeared.

With the arrival of Barrett and Klose, The Abdabs became the short-lived Spectrum Five (one of a number of temporary names that may have included The Meggadeaths). 'I had to buy another guitar,' explained Barrett, 'because Roger played bass – a Rickenbacker – and we didn't want a group with two bass players. So I changed guitars and we started doing the pub scene.'[10]

They were still based in Highgate, where their live-in landlord, Mike Leonard, a lecturer at Hornsey College of Art and of a musical inclination himself, firmly approved of his tenants' activities and allowed rehearsals in his front room. Within a short time the band were calling themselves Leonard's Lodgers. As Wright was taking a sabbatical – having been expelled from the Polytechnic, he was enjoying an extended holiday in the Greek islands – Leonard was invited to stand in on organ for the occasional booking. 'Mike thought of himself as one of the band. But we didn't, because he was too old basically. We used to leave the house to play gigs secretly without telling him,'[11] recalled Mason. Over time they started rehearsing more at the Polytechnic instead of the house, slowly nudging Leonard out in favour of Wright, who was invited back on board.

However, soon it became apparent that the band lacked a front man of any substance. Barrett and Klose fumbled through the vocals as best they could, but neither had the confidence or vocal range to carry it off effectively in the style that the band were aiming for. Therefore, during the Christmas break Barrett was dispatched to Cambridge to try to convince his former band mate Geoff Mott to join them in London. However, there was hardly any incentive for Mott to join a group that had very few gigs, no agency, no manager and, on the face of it, no prospects.

At the same time and by extreme good fortune, Waters and Klose bumped into a face they vaguely knew from Cambridge in a West End music store. Chris Dennis, at that time serving with the Royal Air Force at its Uxbridge base in west London, had until recently been the lead vocalist in a not long disbanded Cambridge group, The Redcaps, and was looking for another band to join. He accepted the offer immediately.

Barrett had less luck, but although he couldn't persuade Mott to join, he didn't return empty-handed, claiming to have found the band its new name: 'Pink Floyd'. In the absence of any better ideas this suggestion was immediately adopted, although initially they called themselves The Pink Floyd Blues Band. Far from coming to him in a blinding flash while in an LSD trance or being beamed to him by passing aliens from space, as some might have it, the name's true origins lay in Barrett's record collection. It is the amalgamation of the first names of two old Carolina bluesmen whose work was very familiar to him: Pinkney Anderson and Floyd 'Dipper Boy' Council. As Waters once put it, if they had opted for the other combination – Anderson Council – it would have sounded like a local authority. There was even a rumour circulating Cambridge, as Ken Waterson remembers, that 'Syd was in this band Pete Floyd, but someone had got that one wrong, and then we heard the band was called The Pink Floyd Sound.'[12]

By the end of January 1965, and with only a handful of gigs to the band's name, Dennis had received a posting to the Persian Gulf, leaving Barrett, as the most charismatic member, to take on what was for him the unnatural role of lead

An early version of Pink Floyd, London, first half of 1965. Left to right: Nick Mason, Roger Waters, Syd Barrett, Bob Klose and Rick Wright.

singer. But Klose was feeling uncomfortable with Barrett's wayward approach. Something of an introvert, he may have been a far more disciplined musician and indeed of greater ability, but he lacked Barrett's spontaneity and raw talent. As Gilmour reflected, 'The thing with Syd was that his guitar playing wasn't his strongest feature. His style was very stiff. I always thought I was the better guitar player. But he was very clever, very intelligent, an artist in every way. And he was a frightening talent when it came to words, and lyrics. They just used to pour out.'[13]

Klose didn't stay much longer and, amid the usual musical differences revolving around a clash of personalities, he left the band in the summer of 1965. Wright in particular had a close affinity with Barrett and says of Klose's departure: 'Before him we'd play the R&B classics, because that's what all groups were supposed to do then. But I never liked R&B very much. I was actually more of a jazz fan. With Syd the direction changed, it became more improvised around the guitar and keyboards. Roger started playing bass as a lead instrument, and I started to introduce more of my classical feel.'[14]

From this point until the following year Pink Floyd remained a sideline for its members, all still pursuing their studies. Their only notable achievement was to compete in the seventh heat of the *Melody Maker* National Beat Contest, but after failing to gain a place in the subsequent heats the band slipped back into obscurity.

Notes
1. *Beat Instrumental*, October 1967
2. *Pink Floyd – A Visual Documentary*, Miles. Omnibus 1980
3–5. Authors' interview with Ken Waterson, September 1996
6. Glenn Povey interview with Will Garfitt, 25.9.96
7-8. Authors' interview with Clive Welham, October 1996
9. *Zig Zag* 32
10. *Beat Instrumental*, October 1967
11. *Mojo*, May 1994
12. Authors' interview with Ken Waterson, September 1996
13–14. *Mojo*, May 1994

Between spring 1962 and the end of 1966 a series of bands containing one or more members of the future Pink Floyd performed in Cambridge, England. Beginning in the first half of 1964, a number of London-based precursors of Pink Floyd were formed.

CAMBRIDGE

GEOFF MOTT & THE MOTTOES

(spring 1962)
Personnel:
Roger (Syd) Barrett: Guitar, vocals
Geoff Mott: Vocals
Tony Sainty: Bass guitar
Clive Welham: Drums
■ **11.3.62**
Friends Meeting House, Cambridge, Cambridgeshire, England.

THE RAMBLERS

(March 1962–October 1963)
Personnel:
Richard Baker: Bass guitar
David Gilmour: Guitar (in performances marked*)
John Gordon: Rhythm guitar
Chris Marriot: Vocals
Mervyn Marriot: Guitar
Albie Prior: Guitar
Clive Welham: Drums
■ **24.3.62**
Free Church Hall, Cambridge, Cambridgeshire, England.
■ **3.5.62**
Guildhall, Cambridge, Cambridgeshire, England.
With The Redcaps.
■ **12.5.62**
Free Church Hall, Cambridge, Cambridgeshire, England.
■ **25.5.62**
City Supporters Club, Cambridge, Cambridgeshire, England
■ **8.6.62**
City Supporters Club, Cambridge, Cambridgeshire, England.
■ **20.10.62**
Free Church Youth Club, Cambridge, Cambridgeshire, England.
■ **13.11.62**
King's Head, Fen Ditton,
Cambridgeshire, England.
■ **1.12.62**
Guildhall, Cambridge, Cambridgeshire, England.
■ **15.12.62**
Fulbourn Hospital, Fulbourn, Cambridgeshire, England.
■ **16.2.63**
Memorial Hall, Great Shelford, Cambridgeshire, England.
■ **7.3.63** **Victoria Ballroom, Cambridge, Cambridgeshire, England.**
■ **15.4.63**
Church Hall, Sawston, Cambridgeshire, England.*
■ **16.5.63**
Victoria Ballroom, Cambridge, Cambridgeshire, England.*
Supporting The Worryin' Kind.
■ **2.8.63**
Rex Ballroom, Cambridge, Cambridgeshire, England.
With Steve Francis and The London Strollers.
■ **17.8.63**
Victoria Ballroom, Cambridge, Cambridgeshire, England.
With Rikki & The Caravelles.
■ **12.10.63**
Village Hall, Harston, Cambridgeshire, England.

CHRIS IAN & THE NEWCOMERS

(January–March 1963)
Personnel:
Barney Barnes: Rhythm guitar
Roger Bibby: Bass guitar
Chris Ian Culpin: Drums
David Gilmour: Guitar, vocals
Ken Waterson: Vocals
■ **26.1.63**
Memorial Hall, Fulbourn, Cambridgeshire, England.
■ **16.3.63**
Guildhall, Cambridge, Cambridgeshire, England.
Supporting Mark Arnold & The Dawnbreakers.
■ **23.3.63**
Village Hall, Dry Drayton, Cambridgeshire, England.

THE NEWCOMERS

(April–October 1963)
Personnel:
Barney Barnes: Rhythm guitar
Roger Bibby: Bass guitar
David Gilmour: Guitar, vocals
Kenny Lennon: Vocals (in performances marked*)
Johnny Philips: Vocals
Ken Waterson: Vocals
Willie Wilson: Drums
■ **4.5.63**
Guildhall, Cambridge, Cambridgeshire, England.
Supporting Johnny Philips & The Swinging Hi-Fi's.
■ **25.5.63**
Village Hall, Trumpington, Cambridgeshire, England.*
■ **27.5.63**
St Andrews Baptist Hall, Cambridge, Cambridgeshire, England.*
■ **8.6.63**
Rex Ballroom, Cambridge, Cambridgeshire, England.*
With the Roy Dennis Orchestra.
■ **3.8.63**
Rex Ballroom, Cambridge, Cambridgeshire, England.
With The Prowlers.
■ **24.8.63**
Rex Ballroom, Cambridge, Cambridgeshire, England.
With Rikki Elwin & The Kobalts.
■ **5.10.63**
Rex Ballroom, Cambridge, Cambridgeshire, England.
With The Johnny Quantrose 5.
In addition to those listed above, and according to Ken Waterson's notes, The Newcomers played concerts at the Rex Ballroom twice more; the Victoria Ballroom twice; Great Shelford Memorial Hall once as support; St Columba's Hall twice; Townley Memorial Hall, Fulbourn twice; Grantchester Village Hall twice; Bottisham Village College twice; the Guildhall once more as support; the Blue Circle Cement Works Social Club twice; the Regent Street Church Hall once; Harston Village Hall once and St Augustus Church Hall twice.

THOSE WITHOUT

(summer 1963)
Personnel:
Roger (Syd) Barrett: Bass guitar

Steve Pyle: Drums
Alan Sizer: Guitar, vocals
Smudge: Guitar
Note: The band were revived in
1964 with Robert Smith on bass
guitar and performed infrequently
until 1965.

■ **16.6.63**
**Congregational Church
Youth Club, Cambridge,
Cambridgeshire, England.**
■ **12.9.63**
**Cheshunt College Lodge,
Cambridge, Cambridgeshire,
England.**

THE HOLLERIN' BLUES
(July 1964)
Personnel:
Barney Barnes: Keyboard,
electric piano, vocals
Roger (Syd) Barrett: Guitar
Pete Glass: Harmonica
Steve Pyle: Drums
Ken Waterson: Vocals, maracas,
harmonica

JOKERS WILD
(October 1964–6)
Personnel:
David Altham: Guitar,
saxophone, keyboards, vocals
David Gilmour: Guitar, vocals
and occasional harmonica
John Gordon: Rhythm guitar,
vocals (to end 1966)
Tony Sainty: Bass guitar, vocals
(to early 1966)
Clive Welham: Drums, vocals (to
mid 1966)
Also: Peter Gilmour: Bass guitar,
vocals (from early 1966); Willie
Wilson: Drums (from mid 1966)

■ **14.10.64**
**Les Jeux Interdits, Victoria
Ballroom, Cambridge,
Cambridgeshire, England.**
Commencement of a weekly
residency. Closing date unknown.
■ **13.1.65**
**Les Jeux Interdits, Victoria
Ballroom, Cambridge,
Cambridgeshire, England.**

Cambridgeshire, England.
■ **13.2.65**
**Dorothy Ballroom, Cambridge,
Cambridgeshire, England.**
■ **19.2.65**
**Caius College Valentine
Ball, Guildhall & Corn
Exchange, Cambridge,
Cambridgeshire, England.**
With Tommy Kinsman and Ivan
Chin's West Indian Band.
■ **22.2.65**
**Old English Gentleman,
Cambridge, Cambridgeshire,
England.**
■ **24.2.65**
**Dorothy Ballroom,
Cambridge, Cambridgeshire,
England.**
■ **26.3.65**
**The Racehorse, Cambridge,
Cambridgeshire, England.**
■ **5.5.65**
**Les Jeux Interdits, Victoria
Ballroom, Cambridge,
Cambridgeshire, England**

**Ballroom, Cambridge,
Cambridgeshire, England.**
■ **5.6.65**
**Dorothy Ballroom, Cambridge,
Cambridgeshire, England.**
■ **15.6.65**
**Peterhouse College May
Ball, Peterhouse College,
Cambridge, Cambridgeshire,
England.**
With Zoot Money's Big Roll
Band, The Paramounts (later
known as Procol Harum), steel
band, dance band and cabaret.
■ **30.6.65**
**Les Jeux Interdits, Victoria
Ballroom, Cambridge,
Cambridgeshire, England.**
■ **3.7.65**
**Dorothy Ballroom,
Cambridge, Cambridgeshire,
England.**
■ **6.7.65**
**Les Jeux Interdits, Victoria
Ballroom, Cambridge,
Cambridgeshire, England.**
■ **1.9.65**
**Les Jeux Interdits, Victoria
Ballroom, Cambridge,
Cambridgeshire, England.**
■ **8.9.65**
**Les Jeux Interdits, Victoria
Ballroom, Cambridge,
Cambridgeshire, England.**
■ **12.11.65**
**Bassingbourn Village
College, Bassingbourn,
Cambridgeshire, England.**
■ **19.11.65**
**Shadow Ball, Victoria
Ballroom, Cambridge,
Cambridgeshire, England.**
With the Riverside Jazz Band
and Ballroom Orchestra.
■ **26.11.65**
**Comberton College,
Comberton, Cambridgeshire,
England.**
■ **??.??.65**
**The Pit Club, Cambridge
University, Cambridge,
Cambridgeshire, England.**
Supporting George Melly.
■ **??.??.65**
**Byam Shaw School of Art,
Campden Hill, Notting Hill
Gate, London, England.**
With Pink Floyd (see Pink Floyd

■ **??.7.64**
**Masonic Hall, Cambridge,
Cambridgeshire, England.**
■ **??.7.64**
**Victoria Road Congregational
Church Hall, Cambridge,
Cambridgeshire, England.**
■ **??.7.64**
**Footlights Club, Cambridge,
Cambridgeshire, England.**

■ **20.1.65**
**Les Jeux Interdits, Victoria
Ballroom, Cambridge,
Cambridgeshire, England.**
■ **28.1.65**
**Les Jeux Interdits, Victoria
Ballroom, Cambridge,
Cambridgeshire, England.**
■ **30.1.65**
Dorothy Ballroom, Cambridge,

■ **12.5.65**
**Les Jeux Interdits, Victoria
Ballroom, Cambridge,
Cambridgeshire, England.**
■ **19.5.65**
**Les Jeux Interdits, Victoria
Ballroom, Cambridge,
Cambridgeshire, England.**
■ **2.6.65**
Les Jeux Interdits, Victoria

entry below for further details).

■ **??.??.65**
Great Shelford, Cambridgeshire, England.

With The Pink Floyd Sound and Paul Simon (see Pink Floyd entry below for further details).

Jokers Wild often performed at dances at RAF and USAF bases around Cambridge, including those at Mildenhall, Lakenheath, Alconbury and Chicksands.

Jokers Wild – Discography

Don't Ask Me/Why Do Fools Fall In Love. Regent Sound Recordings RSR 0031 (7-inch acetate single).

Jokers Wild. Regent Sound Recordings RSLP 007 (one-sided 12-inch mini-album): Why Do Fools Fall In Love/Walk Like A Man/Don't Ask Me/Big Girls Don't Cry/Beautiful Delilah.

The above two pressings were runs of fifty copies distributed to friends and family only.

You Don't Know What I Know/ That's How Strong My Love Is (unreleased recording session tapes). These were produced by Jonathan King for a proposed single release on Decca Records. They are reportedly now in David Gilmour's care.

After Jokers Wild, Gilmour teamed up with Ricky Wills (bass guitar) and Willie Wilson (drums) in two shortlived bands, The Flowers and Bullit, who toured parts of Europe in 1966 and 1967. Gilmour's last band before joining Pink Floyd was The Crew, comprising Gary Wright (keyboards), Alan Reeves (organ) and Archie Legget (bass guitar), who gigged throughout Paris and the south of France

LONDON

SIGMA 6

(autumn 1963)
Personnel:
Nick Mason: Drums
Roger Waters: Guitar
Richard Wright: Rhythm guitar, piano, organ and brass
Clive Metcalf: Bass guitar

Keith Noble: Vocals
Sheilagh Noble: Occasional backing vocals
Vernon (Thompson?): Rhythm guitar
Sigma 6 ('Sigma' was sometimes written as the Greek letter) made a number of informal party appearances.

THE ABDABS

(or The Screaming Abdabs)
(spring–summer 1964)
Personnel:
Juliette Gale: Vocals
Nick Mason: Drums
Clive Metcalf: Bass guitar
Keith Noble: Vocals
Roger Waters: Guitar
Richard Wright: Rhythm guitar

■ **??.??.64**
The Marquee, Soho, London, England.

The band's only appearance at a proper music venue was at The Marquee, as extras in an unidentified film. Other than a couple of private house parties the band continually rehearsed at the Regent Street Polytechnic and at the London home of Mike Leonard, the landlord of Waters, Mason and Wright.

THE SPECTRUM FIVE

(autumn 1964)
Personnel:
Roger (Syd) Barrett: Rhythm guitar, vocals
Bob Klose: Guitar, harmonica, vocals
Nick Mason: Drums
Roger Waters: Bass guitar, vocals
Richard Wright: Keyboards, vocals

■ **2,3.5.64**
Beat City, Oxford Street, London, England.

■ **??.??.64**
Camberwell School of Art, Camberwell, London, England.

'I was attending Camberwell Art School during the mid-sixties at the time Syd Barrett was there (although I seem to remember he was called Roger). He was a couple of years above me. I was the college social secretary and I recall that on one occasion we

were stuck for a group to play at a dance. I was told that there was a sort of in-house group who might play on the night in question. This turned out to be Syd Barrett's band, who were called The Spectrum Five, most of whom went on to be Pink Floyd. They played a mixture of blues and rock. I think we paid them about £20 plus booze!.' (Dick Maunders)

LEONARD'S LODGERS

(winter 1964)
Personnel:
Roger (Syd) Barrett: Rhythm guitar, vocals
Bob Klose: Guitar, harmonica, vocals
Mike Leonard: Occasional keyboards
Nick Mason: Drums
Roger Waters: Bass guitar, vocals

THE PINK FLOYD BLUES BAND/THE TEA SET/ THE PINK FLOYD

(January–winter 1965)
Personnel:
Roger (Syd) Barrett: Rhythm guitar, vocals
Bob Klose: Guitar, harmonica, vocals (until summer only)
Chris Dennis: Vocals (January only)
Nick Mason: Drums
Roger Waters: Bass guitar, vocals
Richard Wright: Keyboards, saxophone, vocals

Alternating their name, the formative Pink Floyd performed only a handful of times. As The Tea Set they recorded a demo tape (unreleased) in a London studio not far from their future recording home of Abbey Road. Around this time they also recorded a recently discovered 7-inch acetate single of Lucy Leave/King Bee.

■ **??.2.65**
Count Down, Palace Gate, Kensington, London, England.

'We played from eight 'til one in the morning with a twenty minute break in the middle. We were paid £15' (Roger Waters, in Michael Wale's *Vox Pop*)

■ **22.5.65**
Summer Dance, Homerton

College, Cambridge, Cambridgeshire, England.
With Geoff Mott's Boston Crabs and Unit 4+2.

■ **26.6.65**
Melody Maker National Beat Contest, Wimbledon Palais, Wimbledon, London, England.

Pink Floyd were entered in the seventh heat of this annual contest, organized by *Melody Maker*, but failed to gain a place in any successive heats.

■ **26.6.65**
Beat Contest, The Country Club, Belsize Park, London, England.

In Pink Floyd's 1974–5 UK/US tour programme mention is made that they lost both this and the above contest on the same night.

■ **??.??.65**
Byam Shaw School of Art, Campden Hill, Notting Hill Gate, London, England.

'There was a big end-of-term party that had a bird-cage theme and we had both Pink Floyd and Jokers Wild play inside this enormous bird-cage we had built with bird mobiles hanging up everywhere and all that psychedelic lighting.' (Will Garfitt)

■ **??.??.65**
Great Shelford, Cambridgeshire, England

'Storm Thorgerson got engaged to Libby January, and Douglas January, her father, who was a local estate agent, put on a party with The Pink Floyd Sound and Jokers Wild, with Paul Simon as the cabaret act. He did a set with classics like "Where Have All The Flowers Gone?" in front of all these rich businessmen. Some songs were quite critical of them, but they had no idea and were applauding wildly. It was in a marquee at the back of this large country house.
I sat on and off the drum kit because of my wrist problems. Willie Wilson sat in on drums and I came to the front on tambourine.' (Clive Welham)

2

By early 1966 the band's fortunes were taking a dramatic turn for the better. The fledgeling Pink Floyd had secured a series of gigs at private events organized by an American entrepreneur, Bernard Stollman (whose brother, Steven, ran the ESP record label, home of The Fugs and many other weird and wonderful acts). The first of these events, all held in the late afternoon on Sundays at the Marquee club in London's Soho, was billed as a 'Giant Mystery Happening', but the subsequent shows have become commonly known as the 'Spontaneous Underground'.

Apart from the first 'Happening', the shows were never advertised in the press. They relied solely on an audience of the performers' friends and a handful of freaks who had heard the word on the street or found handbills at select outlets. There were never more than fifty or so people at any one event and although there were only five shows in total, they did prove to be a turning point in the band's emergence as an original talent. The shows allowed them to get away with almost anything on stage, but more importantly, they brought them to the attention of the people who were beginning to shape 'alternative London'.

Coincidentally, it was at one of these events that would-be pop manager Peter Jenner chanced upon the band he had been dreaming of. At the time he was a bored lecturer at the London School of Economics and he and his friend John 'Hoppy' Hopkins were seeking a way of making their fortune within the booming music industry. They had already formed a loose partnership in the shape of DNA Productions and had signed up a group called AMM. The pair had taken the band to Joe Boyd, an expatriate American and acquaintance of theirs working as Elektra Records' UK representative, but they obtained a painfully small financial return for their trouble.

It is worth noting that AMM were achieving some notoriety in London. They dressed in white laboratory coats and experimented heavily in infant electronics and unconventional amplification methods, creating a unique sound which pre-dated 'Kraut Rock' by several years. They operated out of the Beckenham Arts Lab, not far from Barrett's art school at Camberwell, and they too were regulars on Sundays at the Marquee. Clearly they were an inspiration and in particular for Pink Floyd's more abstract sounds, which were becoming fundamental to their new direction. Nevertheless, their album, *AMM-Music*, now reissued on CD, is an almost continuous drone and one of the most tuneless rackets of all time. Consequently it didn't take DNA long to realize that a more mainstream act would be a wiser investment.

What Jenner heard that day was, for the most part, a very conventional set. 'At that stage they were a blues band who played things like "Louie Louie" and then played wacky bits in the middle. I wandered around trying to work out where the noise was coming from, just what was playing it. I couldn't work out whether it was coming from the keyboards or from the guitar and that was what interested me.'[1] But, as Waters later said, 'We didn't know many songs, so it was a matter of settling on a chord and improvising, if that's the word.'[2]

Jenner may have been rejoicing in his find, but his initial offer to manage the band was met with indifference: they were far more concerned with their impending holidays, unsure if they would even bother resuming on their return. But Jenner tried again a few weeks later, and this time got a more favourable response. As Hopkins was now concentrating on other things, Jenner decided to draft in a new business partner, Andrew King, an old friend. King had time on his hands to book gigs, having recently quit a job at British European Airways, as well as an inheritance with which to buy the band new equipment, and a partnership was forged.

Meanwhile Spontaneous Underground had folded and the party had moved to Notting Hill in west London. It was a fairly run-down, multicultural district at the time; its low rents and the easy availability of drugs attracted its fair share of students and other young people keen to live a bohemian lifestyle.

DNA had fallen by the wayside and Hopkins' interests, after a recent trip to America, now lay in creating a community identity and spirit by setting up an 'anti-university' in the form of an enlightened night school and a citizens' advice bureau for the local population. With substantial help from Hopkins' friends Jenner, King, Boyd and many others, the London Free School (LFS) began life on 8 March 1966.

The LFS was located in a basement flat at 26 Powis Terrace, rented from the notorious Black Power activist Michael X. For all its good intentions, it was fraught with funding problems from the outset and by the following year had degenerated into a dope-smoking haven and rehearsal space for local bands. If one good thing came from the experiment, it was the fact that it led to the now internationally renowned Notting Hill Carnival, which that July was organized by the LFS. Later Boyd recalled above all the 'wild-eyed, slightly condescending idealism, bringing the over educated elite into healthy contact with the working class'.[3] However, the core group of organizers were reluctant to let their talents go to waste and sought to raise cash in order to publish a more informed, London-wide newspaper than the LFS's community newsletter, *The Grove*. They decided to do this by holding 'social dances' at All Saints Church Hall in nearby Powis Gardens. The vicar was willing to allow the hall to be used for this purpose, because, under the auspices of the LFS, the dances would benefit the whole of the local community.

It wasn't long before Jenner and King's newly signed band were invited to perform, accompanied by slide projections to enhance their act, created by Joel and Toni Brown, friends of John Hopkins and visitors to London from Timothy Leary's Millbrook Center in the USA. Word spread on the bush telegraph that something new and exciting was happening in Notting Hill and after only a few appearances by the band the hall was packed to capacity.

Similar lighting effects to the Browns' had been a common feature at concert dances on the West Coast of America for some time, but it is believed that the couple were responsible for introducing the first psychedelic 'light-show' to the UK. Before long, however, the phenomenon would be viewed as more sinister than mere visual entertainment. The media linked it to the growing availability of psychedelic drugs such as LSD, and suggested that the purpose of light-shows was to intensify the multi-sensory effects of hallucinogens.

The London Free School events are where Pink Floyd's colour-and-sound experimentation originated, but soon many more amateur technicians were developing static and moving oil-based slide shows to accompany live and recorded music. When the Browns moved on,

Jack Bracelin took over the duties, founding Five Acre Lights, which during the next year was to provide the environmental lighting at many 'alternative' venues in London. Over the next few months various lighting technicians were used by Pink Floyd. Pip Carter, a friend from Cambridge, was followed by Joe Gannon later that year, who was often regarded as the 'fifth Floyd' in their early months since he was their first full-time technician on the road. The following year Gannon was replaced by John Marsh and Peter Wynne-Wilson, both of whom also did most of the driving between gigs.

Throughout the early autumn Hopkins was busy organizing finance and staff to produce his London-wide newspaper, and in October the first edition of *International Times*, or *IT* as it came to be known, was published. Issued fortnightly as an information centre and non-political broadsheet dealing with musical, literary, artistic and social issues, as well as the drug culture, it was produced in the basement of co-editor Barry Miles' influential alternative bookshop Indica – as in *Cannabis indica*.

A massive launch party was held for *IT* on 15 October, not at All Saints Church Hall, but at the vast Roundhouse in Chalk Farm, north London. As Pink Floyd were regarded as the house band, they topped the bill, playing their biggest show to date while securing valuable mainstream media exposure. Indirectly this gig led to a further string of dates at the Roundhouse and by the end of the year they had even appeared at an Oxfam benefit concert at the prestigious Royal Albert Hall.

Pink Floyd were at last making ripples within the alternative music scene and, although they had no record contract yet, they were building a large and faithful London following. In addition, Barrett was becoming a prolific songwriter and over a period of time the band's covers of blues standards were giving way to his songs of childlike wonder and space rituals, with frenzied feedback overlaid at an ever-increasing volume.

It was shortly after the *IT* launch that Jenner was able to relinquish his post at LSE and join King full-time in their management venture, Blackhill Enterprises. The business was run from Jenner's Paddington town house, with June Child (later the wife of Marc Bolan) as its secretary. A six-way partnership was created and, with enthusiasm prevailing over experience, the pair were able to book a series of shows, primarily based on Jenner's contacts, in the period leading up to Christmas.

However, Blackhill were no experts at booking their band into national venues, which is where they needed to spread their wings. The Bryan Morrison Agency, a small but expanding firm of booking agents, were asked to book Pink Floyd, a band they had never heard of, for the London-based Architectural Association's annual Christmas Ball. The new year was already looking up for Blackhill and Pink Floyd, and a successful

partnership with Bryan Morrison began that lasted, for Pink Floyd at least, until the early 1970s.

Unfortunately, things weren't going so well for Hopkins. *IT* was suffering major cash-flow problems, because insufficient advertising revenue was being generated. At the same time, although the All Saints Church Hall was regularly overcrowded, the London Free School still couldn't pay its bills. Its financial burdens were relieved when Boyd suggested a move from Notting Hill to a more central location which would attract a wider audience and be able to cope with the expected increase in attendance.

In no time at all he had secured the ideal venue: an Irish basement ballroom called the Blarney, conveniently located in Tottenham Court Road in the West End, which the landlord was prepared to hire out on Friday nights until dawn.

Initially two dates were booked, one either side of Christmas, and the very last of the combined Hopkins and *IT* money was invested. On 23 and 30 December 1966 'UFO Presents

Hornsey College of Art, London, 18 November 1966

Opening night of UFO, London, 23 December 1966

Night Tripper' was launched at the Blarney. The gamble paid off: large crowds flocked to see Pink Floyd top the bill on both nights.

The club's name was a matter of some debate, Boyd preferring UFO (Unidentified Flying Object or Underground Freak Out, depending on who was asked) and Hopkins favouring the advertised name. Since Boyd elected to manage the venue, it reverted to UFO. 'A vacuum waiting to be filled,' he remembers. 'Hundreds of freaks looking for a central meeting point.'[4] As Britain's first, and now legendary, psychedelic club, UFO continued to be held on these premises until the end of July 1967, publicized with large dayglo and multicoloured screen-printed posters designed by Michael English and Timothy Weymouth. As well as showcasing a huge variety of new underground acts and established bands, including Soft Machine, Arthur Brown and Tomorrow, it also promoted the recently converted-to-psychedelia Move and Procol Harum. The future of *IT* was at last secure and indeed it went on to outlive UFO by many years.

On 1 February 1967 Pink Floyd turned professional. The vast amount of coverage the band were now receiving in the music press and the pressure of engagements were compromising their studies. Now, with a good London following, it seemed logical that if they were to continue seriously then they should turn their attention to securing a record deal. Despite Jenner and King's attempts at recording them the previous year, Bryan Morrison's advice was that they should re-record them professionally, at greater expense, with the aim of selling a finished master tape to a prospective record company rather than going cap in hand with a rough demo tape.

Since the ubiquitous Boyd had at his disposal the facilities of the Sound Techniques studios in Chelsea, he offered his services as the band's producer and, seeing this as his golden opportunity,

he rather impetuously formed Witchseason Productions to handle their recording affairs. Of the five tracks recorded, 'Arnold Layne' was selected as the stand-out song, because of its catchy tune and lyric.

Offers to sign the band were received from Elektra and Polydor Records, the latter coming close to signing them. However, Morrison clearly had greater influence over Blackhill than Boyd had reckoned on, suggesting they hold out for a label with greater financial clout that could successfully promote the band. Ultimately it was the mighty EMI who signed Pink Floyd, to its then subsidiary label Columbia, for a greater advance and royalty rate than any previous offer.

Much to Boyd's horror, EMI weren't so keen on independent producers and insisted on using their own in-house staff and facilities. His days were numbered. 'I was choked when Morrison persuaded them to wait,' he remembers bitterly. 'EMI were very hostile to indie producers at the time.'[5] In reality the band had little choice because the man responsible for their signing, Sidney Arthur Beecher-Stevens (who, incidentally, as head of sales at Decca in 1962, was one of the many executives to turn down the Beatles), insisted that as part of the deal his own A&R man, Norman Smith, should be responsible for watching over, but not interfering with, Pink Floyd's future recording career. This also allayed certain fears within EMI that some of the more undesirable fringe elements associated with the band would distract them from their professional obligations.

Interestingly, the deal also included album development, which was very unusual for the time, allowing the band free rein in the studio. EMI knew they had something but, since it was unlike anything else they'd heard before, they didn't know quite what. They took the decision to just let the band get on with it, and this has been their general policy over the years (Pink Floyd are

The band at Mike Leonard's house, in Highgate, London, 21 January 1967

in fact we set up this recording to do just that along with other titles. It was an all-night session, and I could see that they weren't too keen in fact to attempt a remake, so in fact we never did have a go at that.'[7]

When it came out in March, Blackhill paid to have the single hyped in order to ensure that it reached a favourable chart position. As a result, it was guaranteed radio airplay, but, although BBC Radio One were happy to oblige, pirate Radio London banned it for being too smutty. Even Pete Murray reviewed it on BBC TV's *Juke Box Jury*, his comments infuriating Waters: 'He said we were a con. He thought it was just contrived rubbish to meet some kind of unhealthy demand.'[8]

Furthermore, a backlash was brewing in certain media circles. It was suggested that Pink Floyd, then spearheading the 'counter-culture', were promoting music sympathetic to certain types of drug abuse. In April EMI were forced to issue a statement to the press to effectively deny

still with the label), proving that Stevens' gamble more than paid off. 'I classed them as weird, but good,'[6] he confessed.

Having heard the tracks on offer, EMI set about re-recording them at their own Abbey Road studio in London's St John's Wood. Although Boyd had been given the nudge, he certainly had the last laugh when his original recording was used after all. As Norman Smith recalled: 'I told the boys I'd like to have another go any rate and all knowledge of this situation and insisted that, to them and the band, the term 'psychedelic' meant the use of light and sound in performance rather than an excuse to take LSD and watch the pretty lights. Even as late as July the band were hampered by the sideswipes they received, which caused Waters to air his frustrations in the *NME*: 'We are simply a pop group. But because we use light and colour in our act a lot of people seem to imagine that we are trying to put across some message with nasty, evil undertones.'

Surprisingly, despite all the LSD connotations of their act, the band were a very straight-laced bunch. It was only much later that drugs featured on the agenda: 'None of them did drugs when I met them,' said Jenner, 'except Syd, and we would only smoke dope. Then with the Summer of Love and all that bollocks Syd got very enthusiastic about acid and got into the religious aspect of it. The others were very straight. Rick would take a puff now and again, but Roger and Nick would never go near it.'[9]

If EMI were worried about the drugs issue, they should have been far more concerned about the band's live performance. Both 'Arnold Layne' and its June follow-up, 'See Emily Play', were as far removed from their stage act as they could possibly be. Their quaint pop songs were ignored completely in favour of high-volume, mind-bending workouts lasting in some cases well over ten minutes. While these were acceptable on their home turf of London, provincial audiences were nonplussed, fully expecting to hear their chart hits. Pink Floyd literally hit the audience with a wall of sound verging on 'white noise'.

This reputation had already spread, as *Melody Maker* pointed out: 'Are the Pink Floyd being quite honest when they make coy and attractive records like "See Emily Play" then proceed to make the night hideous with a thunderous, incomprehensible, screaming, sonic torture that five American doctors agree could permanently damage the senses?'

When word got around that they rarely played their chart successes, some promoters insisted on making the band sign a pre-performance clause to ensure that they did so, to avoid audience unrest. Many of the out-of-London bookings attracted people out for a drink and a dance who would often riot when confronted by this vision from hell. Stories of the reception the band received in some parts of the country are near-legendary. Beer (still in the glasses) was thrown at them, fights broke out and torrents of abuse were hurled, as Nick Mason testified: 'During that period we were working at Top Rank circuits and they hated it. Hated it. We could clear halls so fast it wasn't true. I mean they were outraged by what came round on the revolving stage and they lost very little time in trying to make this clear.'[10] But, he explained, 'We were not demoralised. We rejuvenated every time we came back to London and got that fix of finding that there was an audience for us.'[11]

Such was their determination that not once did they cease trying to win over the masses. There was no way the band were going to make a single compromise. It was their way or not at all, and this was summed up in an ironic comment by Waters at the time: 'We've got the recording side together and not the playing side. So what we've got to do now is get together a stage act that has nothing to do with our records – things like 'Interstellar Overdrive' which is beautiful, and instrumentals that are much easier to play.'[12]

This approach may have paid off in the long run, but at the time, given their then technical ability and set list, forcing this material, rather than their 'hits', on the public was verging on professional suicide.

Nevertheless, Pink Floyd's meteoric rise to success was having an adverse side-effect on

*Press launch at EMI Records, London, 4 March 1967, in
preparation for the release of 'Arnold Layne'*

Barrett, who was starting to show marked signs of
fatigue. The pressure he was under as the band's
leader, coupled with the self-inflicted onslaught of
constant touring, caused him to withdraw into
himself. An increasing use of LSD, both in private
and on stage, offered little escape and indeed
made matters far worse by filling him with
chronic stage fright.

The first hint of something going slightly awry
came in July, at the BBC Studios, where they were
recording 'See Emily Play' for *Top of The Pops*. The
single had sold well, significantly better than their
debut, and, as a result of its chart performance,
secured a remarkable three consecutive weeks on
the show. (The BBC managed to erase these
recordings, along with a substantial amount of
other important archive material, in the 1970s.)
As legend has it, Pink Floyd turned out for their
first appearance in all their supreme psychedelic
Carnaby Street attire. On the second show, Syd's

appearance is less immaculate and by the third
week he is dishevelled, unshaven and in rags, with
a careless attitude, uninterested in performing,
and insisting that if John Lennon didn't have to
appear on the show, then neither did he.

Sadly, this erratic behaviour increased apace,
and a catalogue of disastrous events unfolded
throughout the rest of the year. The first occurred
at the recording studio for the BBC Light
Programme's *Saturday Club*. According to the
engineer's report, Syd just 'freaked out'.[13] The
session was abandoned, but hopes were upheld
for a return performance at UFO that night. Boyd
in particular was looking forward to seeing the
band after a long break, but when he cast his eyes
on Barrett the singer just blanked him. 'It was like
somebody had pulled the blinds, you know,
nobody home.'[14]

At the Love-In Festival June Bolan observed
him on stage: 'Syd just stood there, his arms

hanging down. Suddenly he put his hands on the guitar and we thought he's actually going to do it, but he just stood there, tripping out of his mind.'[15] It was a pitiful transformation and one that greatly frustrated the rest of the band since it was becoming an all too familiar occurrence.

For their part, Jenner and King were quick to defuse the situation and ordered the band to have the rest of the month off, cancelling all of their bookings and insisting they take a well-deserved holiday in Spain. It is ironic that one major music paper greeted the week of their debut album's release date with the headline 'Pink Floyd Flake Out'. Blackhill spent most of the break trying to convince hungry music journalists that the band had not split up but were merely recuperating on doctor's orders as they were suffering from nervous exhaustion.

Amsterdam, 29 April 1967, before playing on Dutch TV

The album, *The Piper At The Gates Of Dawn*, which took its title from a chapter in the Kenneth Grahame novel *The Wind In The Willows*, was a far more attractive affair than their stage performance, in that it was a perfect mix of psychedelic songs and instrumentals. These ranged from the poppy 'Flaming' and 'Lucifer Sam' through the hippie *I-Ching*-style recital of 'Chapter 24' and the whimsical, childlike poetry of 'Gnome' and 'Scarecrow', to the spacey freak-outs of 'Pow R Toc H' and 'Astronomy Dominé' – and, of course, the monumentally thunderous 'Interstellar

Overdrive'. These last three tracks were possibly the closest representation of their stage act – provided you turned your amplifier up to maximum. While the album lost many hard-core UFO followers – at least those who preferred the cacophonous, freak-out element – it gained many more followers and was a fine achievement that is regarded to this day as one of the greatest UK psychedelic albums of the sixties.

Returning to active duty, Pink Floyd plunged straight back into a heavy touring schedule, including their first overseas bookings, in Scandinavia and Ireland. It is noteworthy that, with Barrett effectively no longer fronting the band, Waters acted as spokesman in press and radio interviews of this period and for some time afterwards. It may be that this sudden assumption of responsibility was symptomatic of his already strong sense of leadership.

Blackhill, meanwhile, were keen to break into the lucrative US market. EMI's American sister label, Capitol Records, based in Hollywood, took on the band, assigning them to its subsidiary label, Tower Records, and called for a promotional tour which would include San Francisco, Los Angeles, New York, Chicago and Boston. The debut album was scheduled for release to coincide with the tour, Tower heralding them as 'The Light Kings of England'.

With the band chaperoned by King, the tour was due to start in late October at Bill Graham's Fillmore Auditorium in San Francisco. Much to King's distress, their work permits were delayed and the first set of engagements had to be cancelled. A bad omen indeed, for when the first set of shows did come through, the band were scheduled to support Big Brother and The Holding Company – about as musically incompatible as you could get. If that wasn't bad enough, the revered light-show was far from

Publicity shot, London, early autumn 1967

exceptional. Since most UK light-shows were only ever presented in small clubs or medium-sized theatres, lighting the Fillmore (a large ballroom) and Winterland (a converted ice rink with a circular gallery) was a daunting task for Peter Wynne-Wilson. In all, noted King, 'our lights looked pathetic. The biggest lamp we had was a single kilowatt bulb, but a typical West Coast show had 20. The only things that worked were the more powerful slide projectors.'[16] Although this was a bearable situation, Syd's condition was far from normal. 'Detuning his guitar all the way through one number, striking the strings. He more or less just ceased playing and stood there leaving us to muddle along as best we could,' said Mason.[17]

Two scheduled TV shows were equally catastrophic. On the *Pat Boone Show* the band attempted to mime their way through 'See Emily Play', before facing the horrors of an interview in which Barrett responded with total silence to the questions asked of him. They didn't fare much better on *Dick Clark's American Bandstand*. Here Waters struggled to mime lead vocals through 'Apples And Oranges', since Barrett's attention seemed to be focused on a gaping void and he once again merely returned a mute stare in reply to Clark's questions.

'Syd actually went mad on that first American tour,' said Mason. 'He didn't know where he was most of the time. I remember he de-tuned his guitar on stage at Venice, Los Angeles, and just stood there rattling the strings, which was a bit weird, even for us. Another time he emptied a can of Brylcreem on his head because he didn't like his curly hair.'[18]

This chain of events was far more than Capitol could handle since they were relying on these important TV plugs to push the album. In a final, somewhat embarrassing meeting with Capitol's MD, King had to witness the man break down before his eyes. 'He burst into tears and asked us what he was going to do.'[19] It was the last straw and Pink Floyd were recalled to the UK, very bruised by the whole episode.

However, despite the obvious stress affecting them all, recuperation was definitely out of the question this time. Blackhill had already committed the band to a month of intense touring, on what is generally considered to be the last successful UK pop 'package tour'. Such tours were normally reserved for lightweight entertainment and rock 'n' roll, but this was the first, and probably the last, to showcase 'underground' acts. With The Jimi Hendrix Experience and The Move headlining, and support from Amen Corner, The Nice, The Outer Limits and Eire Apparent, the bands appeared in descending order of importance, with a stage time to match.

The opening night got off to a flying start when Pink Floyd threatened to walk out of the tour during the afternoon rehearsals at the Albert Hall when they were told they could not use their own lighting gear and projection screen.

The band were allocated a twenty-minute set – just about long enough for three numbers, which nevertheless caused some bewilderment to the majority of fans, who had turned out for Hendrix. 'They got a very mixed reaction,'[20] recalled Noel Redding, Hendrix's bassist.

Syd's behaviour was still a cause for concern; often he would sit alone on the tour bus or wander off into town when he should have been on stage. Mitch Mitchell, drummer with the Experience, recalled that: 'It was actually good fun – lunacy most of the time. However, Syd

Barrett didn't talk to anyone during that time.'[21] Indeed, he was often replaced on stage altogether by the young Davy O'List, guitarist with The Nice. 'I used to stand by the side of the stage to watch the Floyd. They only used to play one number in their set and because it was a fairly straightforward guitar thing, I was able to pick it up quite quickly. So when Syd didn't turn up one night, Floyd asked me to go on instead.'[22]

Even Barrett's old pal Dave Gilmour could see little hope: 'It was totally impossible for me to understand the way Syd's mind was working at that time. It was also from having been to two or three of their gigs impossible for me see how they could carry on quite like that, because Syd was quite obviously not up to being in that group at that time.'[23]

Nevertheless, there are clearly a number of

points that don't quite add up in the Barrett story. For instance, Waters recently spoke of that first US trip and the *American Bandstand* incident, recalling how the rehearsal takes had gone just fine and without incident but, come the final transmission take, Barrett just stood there, arms limply hanging by his side. 'He knew of course perfectly well what was going on. He was just being crazy.'[24]

And there is also the footage from BBC's *Tomorrow's World*, repeated, for the first time, as part of the BBC *Omnibus* documentary on Pink Floyd in November 1994. Filmed in December 1967 and broadcast in January 1968, it shows Barrett in fine fettle. Whatever happened between Syd and the others, the real story – if there is one – has been held very tightly to the band's chest.

One theory is that Barrett, his marbles not quite where they used to be, and certainly behaving erratically, was now incapable of continuing to produce the catchy pop songs that the band had previously relied upon to get them into the charts. 'Apples And Oranges', his last single with them, was released in mid-November and failed to gain a good chart placing. But their public had changed too. Their current live set reflected the emergence of Waters' own brand of science-fiction epics, such as 'Set The Controls For The Heart Of The Sun', which was taking them on a new slant altogether. This inevitably clashed with the newer Barrett compositions like 'Vegetable Man' and 'Jugband Blues', which were doing nothing to advance Pink Floyd's career. It seems as if there was a conscious attempt by the band to radically reinvent themselves, in order to survive the collapse of Flower Power.

It is likely that Barrett sensed this redefinition and, aware of the fact he was not going to be a part of their new identity, pre-empted the move. Probably in a state of LSD-induced disorientation, whether he meant to or not, he was making the band's life as awkward as he could. In one particularly well-documented studio session he wilfully teased them with his latest composition, 'Have You Got It Yet?' The song changed with every take, making it impossible to follow. Such tales are legendary and the announcement that he wanted to add a banjo and sax player to the line-up left the rest of the band in little doubt as to where this was all leading. He had to go.

After their last big gig of the year, Christmas on Earth Continued, at London's Olympia, word was put out that an 'additional' guitarist was being sought. Although Davy O'List and Jeff Beck were initially considered, it was David Gilmour who eventually got the call, and since he wasn't doing anything better he accepted without hesitation.

Whether it was done this way to limit the hurt to Barrett's feelings is also open to speculation; perhaps it was thought that the addition of a friend would help to stabilize him.

Notes

1. *Days In The Life* by Jonathon Green. Heinemann 1988
2. *You* magazine, c.1990
3–5. Glenn Povey interview with Joe Boyd, 1987
6. *Pink Floyd* by Rick Sanders. Futura 1976
7. *Pink Floyd Story*, Capital Radio, 17.12.76
8. *Zig Zag 32*
9. *Mojo*, May 1994
10. *Pink Floyd Story*, Capital Radio, 17.12.76
11. *Mojo*, July 1995
12. *Melody Maker*, 5.8.67
13. *In Session Tonight* by Ken Gardiner, BBC 1994
14. *Pink Floyd – A Visual Documentary* by Miles. Omnibus 1980
15. *Days In The Life* by Jonathon Green. Heinemann 1988
16. *Crazy Diamond* by Pete Anderson and Mike Watkinson. Omnibus 1991
17–18. *Mojo*, May 1994
19. *Crazy Diamond* by Pete Anderson and Mike Watkinson. Omnibus 1991
20. Glenn Povey correspondence with Noel Redding, 1996
21. *The Hendrix Experience by Mitch Mitchell*, Pyramid 1990
22. *Space Daze* by Dave Thompson. Cleopatra 1994
23. *Pink Floyd Story*, Capital Radio, 17.12.76
24. *Dancing In The Street*, BBC TV, 20.7.96

1966

PINK FLOYD
(January 1966 - December 1967)
Personnel:
Syd Barrett: Guitar, vocals
Nick Mason: Drums
Roger Waters: Bass guitar, vocals
Rick Wright: Keyboards, vocals

■ **30.1.66**
Giant Mystery Happening, The Marquee, Soho, London, England.
With Donovan, AMM, the Pete Lemer Trio, poets and African singers.
Surprisingly, the then primarily jazz-oriented *Melody Maker* dropped by for this opening night but described it all as 'highly pretentious nonsense' and commented on some very 'substandard beat music', presumably a reference to Pink Floyd.

■ **27.2.66**
Spontaneous Underground, The Marquee, Soho, London, England.
'A Child's Eye View of Madness' shrieked the headline of *Titbits* in a belated account of these happenings: 'What a rave! A man crawling naked through jelly. Girls stripped to the waist. Off-beat poetry. Weird music. It all adds up to Raving London. For the capital no longer swings. It goes berserk!'

■ **11.3.66**
Rag Ball, University of Essex, Wivenhoe Park, Colchester, Essex, England.
With Marianne Faithfull, The Swinging Blue Jeans, Jimmy Pilgrim & The Classics, steel and jazz bands.
The Pink Floyd played their first-ever gig with a moving light-show on the first night of this three-day University rag weekend: films made by students were projected on to a backdrop screen.

■ **13.3.66**
Spontaneous Underground, The Marquee, Soho, London, England.

■ **27.3.66**
Spontaneous Underground, The Marquee, Soho, London, England.

■ **7.4.66**
Spontaneous Underground, The Marquee, Soho, London, England.

■ **30.9.66**
London Free School, All Saints Church Hall, Notting Hill, London, England.
'I was a DJ at a club in West Hampstead called Klooks Kleek playing soul, Motown and R&B. One night a well-dressed guy, probably late twenties, came up to me and said he had a new band playing its first show in Ladbroke Grove the next night; would I take the club record console and some records to play in the interval between two sets, for a fiver? I told him I couldn't take the console, but I had a Dansette-type deck that plugged into a PA system and he said, fine. So when I get there, it turns out to be Pink Floyd. I told them I only had soul and R&B records but they said that's what they wanted.' (Brian Wilcock)

■ **14.10.66**
London Free School, All Saints Church Hall, Notting Hill, London, England.
Set list: Pink/Let's Roll Another/Gimme A Break/Stoned Alone/I Can Tell/The Gnome/Interstellar Overdrive/Lucy Leave/Stethoscope/Flapdoodle Dealing/Snowing/Matilda Mother/Pow R Toc H/Astronomy Dominé. As the above set list indicates, by this time Pink Floyd had developed a great deal of original material but were still experimenting within the framework of R&B standards that would feature in their act until the end of the year. John Hopkins later wrote in *International Times* that at this time the band were playing 'mainly instrumentals and numbers that would sometimes last for half an hour'.

■ **15.10.66**
The Roundhouse, Chalk Farm, London, England.
The launch party for *International Times*, and indeed Pink Floyd, was a festival compressed into one evening. It was billed in the debut issue of *IT* as 'The Greatest Happening of Them All'. This mad gathering was attended by some 2,500 people and *IT* made sure its coming-out ball was given the fair review it deserved: '...Darkness, only flashing lights, people in masks, girls half naked. Other people standing about wondering what the hell was going on. Pot smoke. Now and then the sound of a bottle breaking. The Pink Floyd psychedelic pop group did weird things to the feel of the event with their scary feed-back sounds, slide projectors playing on their skin – drops of paint run riot on the slides to produce outer-space, prehistoric textures – spotlights flashing on them in time with a drum beat... The Soft Machine, another group with new ideas drove a motor bike into the place ... a large car in the middle of it all painted bright pop-art stripes... Simon Postuma and Marijke Koger, the Amsterdam couple, designed an interesting cubicle with coloured screens and nets and within the box one of them, in suitable dress, read palms and told fortunes ... the London Film Co-op gave an all-night film show featuring films like *Scorpio Rising* and *Towers Open Fire* ... famous people turned up: Antonioni and Monica Vitti, Paul McCartney disguised as an Arab, Kenneth Rexroth, Peter Brook, Micky Most and Tony Secunda. We also saw a well-known junkie, a notorious homosexual... A giant jelly made in a bath for the party was unfortunately run over by a bicycle....'

■ **21.10.66**
London Free School, All Saints Church Hall, Notting Hill, London, England.

■ 28.10.66
London Free School, All Saints Church Hall, Notting Hill, London, England.

■ 31.10.66
Thompson Private Recording Studios, Hemel Hempstead, Hertfordshire, England.

It has been documented, but not substantiated, that on the same day as their management company, Blackhill Enterprises, was set up, the band were whisked away to record a demo tape to tout around prospective record companies. The songs 'Let's Roll Another One' and 'I Get Stoned' have been reported as being on this tape but evidently the band would have had little chance of securing a deal by presenting these titles. It has often been speculated that this session reaped a take of 'Interstellar Overdrive' that was utilized by film-maker Anthony Stern for his 'cut and paste' fifteen-minute 'day-in-the-life-of' documentary *San Francisco*.

■ 4.11.66
London Free School, All Saints Church Hall, Notting Hill, London, England.

■ 5.11.66
Wilton Hall, Bletchley, Buckinghamshire, England.
Supported by The Torments.

■ 5.11.66
Five Acres, Bricket Wood, Watford, Hertfordshire, England.
This was one of several caravan parks situated in the area, but the only one that played host to a naturist group. Jack Bracelin, the site manager and later proprietor of Five Acre Lights, who supplied lighting for the Free School, invited Pink Floyd to make a late appearance at the clubhouse. However, as this would probably have been open to the general public there is little chance the audience would have been naked – not in November anyway!

■ 8.11.66
London Free School, All Saints Church Hall, Notting Hill, London, England.

■ 11.11.66
London Free School, All Saints Church Hall, Notting Hill, London, England.

■ 15.11.66
London Free School, All Saints Church Hall, Notting Hill, London, England.

■ 18.11.66
Hornsey College of Art, Hornsey, London, England.
Although the band had rehearsed here many times because of their connection with Mike Leonard, who taught at the college, this was their first documented gig there. Students of the Advanced Studies Group let fly with an array of lighting equipment they had built as part of their course work.

■ 19.11.66
Technical College, Canterbury, Kent, England.
Supported by The Koalas.

■ 22.11.66
London Free School, All Saints Church Hall, Notting Hill, London, England.

■ 29.11.66
London Free School, All Saints Church Hall, Notting Hill, London, England.
'Since I last saw the Pink Floyd they've got hold of bigger amplifiers, new light gear and a rave from Paul McCartney. This time I saw them at Powis Gardens on Tuesday 29th, the last of their regular shows there. Their work is largely improvisation and lead guitarist Sid Barrett shoulders most of the burden of providing continuity and attack in the improvised parts. He was providing a huge range of sounds with the new equipment, from throttled shrieks to mellow feedback roars. Visually the show was less adventurous. Three projectors bathed the group, the walls and sometimes the audience in vivid colour. But the colour was fairly static and there was no searching for the brain alpha rhythms by chopping up the images. The equipment that the group is using now is infant electronics: let's see what they will do with the grown-up electronics that a colour television industry will make available.' (*International Times*)

■ 3.12.66
'Psychodelphia versus Ian Smith', The Roundhouse, Chalk Farm, London, England.
With the Ram Holder Messengers and underground film shows, poets and happenings. This event was promoted by the Majority Rule for Rhodesia Committee and held in protest at Ian Smith, the Governor of Rhodesia (now Zimbabwe), continuing his policy of white minority rule. The show attracted media interest after advertising posters were plastered up featuring Smith made to resemble Hitler. The *NME* reviewed Pink Floyd's current stage act in some detail: 'Last Friday [29.11.66] the Pink Floyd, a new London group, embarked upon their first happening – a pop dance incorporating psychedelic effects and mixed media – whatever that is! The slides were excellent – colourful, frightening, grotesque, beautiful and the group's trip into outer-space sounds promised very interesting things to come. Unfortunately all fell a bit flat in the cold reality of All Saints Hall, but on Saturday night at Chalk Farm's Roundhouse things went better when thousands of people turned up to watch the show. The Floyd need to write more of their own material - "psychedelic" versions of "Louie Louie" won't come off, but if they can incorporate their electronic prowess with some melodic and lyrical songs – getting away from R&B things, they could well score in the near future.'

■ 12.12.66
You're Joking (A Benefit For Oxfam), Royal Albert Hall, Kensington, London, England.
With Peter Cook and Dudley Moore, Paul Jones, The Alan Price Set, Chris Farlowe, Barry Mackenzie, Peter and Gordon, Jackie Trent and Barry Fantoni. In addition to their own short set, Pink Floyd joined in the grand finale: a tongue-in-cheek rendition of 'Yellow Submarine'.

■ 23.12.66
UFO Presents Night Tripper, The Blarney, Tottenham Court Road, London, England.
With Soft Machine.

■ 29.12.66
The Marquee, Soho, London, England.
With Syn.

■ 30.12.66
UFO Presents Night Tripper, The Blarney, Tottenham Court Road, London, England.
With Soft Machine.

■ 31.12.66
New Year's Party, Cambridge Technical College (School of Art), Cambridge, Cambridgeshire, England.
Early show. 'It was so loud it actually hurt. I had to go outside and sit on the steps because it was so painful. They were very

unique though and had all the light-show thing going. I heard later that the college had received complaints of the noise as far away as Newnham.' (Mick Barnet)

■ **31.12.66**
New Year's Rave: All Night Rave, The Roundhouse, Chalk Farm, London, England.
With The Who and The Move. 'The Pink Floyd have a promising sound, and some very groovy picture slides which attract far more attention than the group, as they merge,

commented that it was the first time he saw Pink Floyd play. This ultimately led to his invitation to the band to contribute to his documentary film, *Tonite Let's All Make Love In London.*

1967

■ **5.1.67**
The Marquee, Wardour Street, Soho, London, England.
Supported by Eyes of Blue.

■ **6.1.67**
Freak Out Ethel, Seymour

Peter Whitehead, although segments of silent footage were not released until 1994, as part of the See For Miles video *The Pink Floyd – London 66–67.*

■ **14.1.67**
Great Hall, University of Reading, Whiteknights, Reading, Berkshire, England.
'We would like to express our disgust at the appalling performance given by the Pink Floyd at the "dance" on Saturday. How could people dance to such an offensive din?

■ **16.1.67**
The Clubroom, Institute of Contemporary Arts, London, England.
This was the first time pop music had been allowed at the ICA and *Record Mirror* reported an informal discussion between the band and audience after the show.

■ **17.1.67**
Music In Colour by The Pink Floyd, Commonwealth Institute, Kensington, London, England.
'During the interval between sessions at the Institute there was a performance of NOIT, a mime for paper giants. The creation of artist John Latham, this work is, I'm told, a three dimensional representation of Pink Floyd's state of mind.' (*Kensington Post*)

■ **19.1.67**
The Marquee, Soho, London, England.
Supported by Marmalade.

■ **20.1.67**
UFO, The Blarney, Tottenham Court Road, London, England.
With Spectral Audio Olfactory, Karate, Trip Machine and Government Propaganda.

■ **21.1.67**
The Birdcage, Eastney, Portsmouth, Hampshire, England.

■ **27.1.67**
UFO, The Blarney, Tottenham Court Road, London, England.
With AMM, Five Acre Lights, Dave Brown, Plight of the Erogenius and Chapter 1.
Pink Floyd's performance was filmed on this night and clips of 'Interstellar Overdrive' and 'Matilda Mother' were used in the Granada TV documentary arts programme *Scene Special*, subtitled 'It's So Far Out It's Straight Down' and broadcast on 7.2.67 at 10.25pm. It also included coverage of performance art at the Roundhouse, a 'happening' in

blossom, burst, grow, divide and die.' (*Melody Maker*)

■ **??.12.66**
The Architectural Assocation, Bedford Square, London, England.
Reported in Rick Sanders' Pink Floyd biography. The AA has no records of its Christmas balls.

■ **??.12.66**
Royal College of Art, Kensington, London, England.
This show was also noted in Sanders' book, and although the RCA hadn't retained records, it was confirmed by Peter Whitehead, who, in a recent interview with *Record Collector*,

Hall, Paddington, London, England.
With Ginger Johnson's African Drum Band, Wayward Ellis & The Zone, Rich St John, Alexander Trocchi, belly dancers, light-shows and other happenings.

■ **8.1.67**
The Upper-Cut, Forest Gate, London, England
Unconfirmed appearance.

■ **13.1.67**
UFO, The Blarney, Tottenham Court Road, London, England.
With Marilyn Monroe films and The Giant Sun Trolley.
Pink Floyd's set was filmed by

The Pink Floyd were so cacophonous that the most cunningly random-noise-making machine could hardly have been more oppressive. The only thing we found to console us was that University dances will never be more debased than this; at least we trust not. We very much regret that certain members of the University degraded themselves by applauding such a performance, and we congratulate the element among the few remaining at the end who gave vent to their indignation by boo-ing.' (*Shell*, Reading University student magazine)

Piccadilly Circus and interviews with various celebrities, including Paul McCartney.

■ **28.1.67**
University of Essex, Wivenhoe Park, Colchester, Essex, England.
'The psycho-delic dance was a double triumph. The maximum permitted attendance of 500 was achieved and a profit of about £30 was made. Never before has a dance at Essex been fully supported or shown profit. At a social committee meeting on January 30th Mick Gray [Chairman] reported that the dance was by no means trouble free. Several outsiders arrived, and when turned away, lingered on the campus. At about 1am four students from North Essex Technical College, who had been at the dance, were arrested by a police patrol whilst attempting to remove the engine from a motor cycle in the central car park.' (*Wyvern*, Essex University student magazine)

■ **2.2.67**
Cadenna's, Guildford, Surrey, England.
Pink Floyd's first professional date.

■ **3.2.67**
Queens Hall, Leeds, Yorkshire, England.
With Cream, go-go dancers, a fairground and a barbecue. This rave went on all night and in the morning breakfast was served. The advert announced the release of a live gorilla in the crowd at midnight.

■ **9.2.67**
New Addington Hotel, New Addington, Surrey, England.

■ **10.2.67**
Leicester College of Technology, Leicester, Leicestershire, England.

■ **11.2.67**
University of Sussex, Falmer, Brighton, East Sussex, England.
With The Alan Bown Set, The Wishful Thinking and Russells Clump.

■ **16.2.67**

Guildhall, Southampton, Hampshire, England.
This concert was cancelled because of the local council's concerns over the band's mind-altering light-show and the drugs connection reported in the national press.

■ **17.2.67**
St Catherine's College Valentine Ball, Dorothy Ballroom, Cambridge, Cambridgeshire, England.
With Bob Kidman, Alexis Korner's Blues Inc. and The Pearl Hawaiians.

■ **18.2.67**
California Ballroom, Dunstable, Bedfordshire, England.
Supported by The Equals and Two Of Each.

■ **20.2.67**
Adelphi Ballroom, West Bromwich, Warwickshire, England.

■ **24.2.67**
Ricky Tick, Thames Hotel, Windsor, Berkshire, England.
Early show.

■ **24.2.67**
UFO, The Blarney, Tottenham Court Road, London, England.
Late show with Brothers Grimm and film shows.

■ **25.2.67**
Ricky Tick, Hounslow, Middlesex, England.

28.2.67
Blaises, Kensington, London, England.
Supported by The Majority.

■ **1.3.67**
The Dance Hall, Eel Pie Island Hotel, Twickenham, Middlesex, England.

■ **2.3.67**
Assembly Rooms, Worthing, East Sussex, England.
Supporting Geno Washington.

■ **3.3.67**
Market Hall, St Albans, Hertfordshire, England.
Supported by Tuppence The TV Dancer.

■ **4.3.67**
Poly Rag Ball 1967, Large Hall, Regent Street Polytechnic, London, England.
Supported by The Minor Birds with the Miss Poly Finals and DJ Ed 'Stewpot' Stewart.
'Everyone present at the dance appeared to enjoy themselves but in my opinion the Pink Floyd are not at their best as a "college hop" group. Despite the suggestions of a "freak-out" implied by the dance tickets, the Rag Ball was a glorified "hop". There were more psychedelic effects when the bar flashed the lights on and off to indicate closing time than the rest of the dance put together. The only spontaneous happening I observed was when a young lady who had drunk more than her stomach could bear, had gone out into the cold night air.' (*West One*, Regent Street Polytechnic student magazine)

■ **5.3.67**
Saville Theatre, Shaftesbury Avenue, London, England.
With Lee Dorsey, The Ryan Brothers and Jeff Beck.

■ **6.3.67**
Granada TV Studios, Manchester, Lancashire, England.
The Move were given their own thirty-minute slot on ITV presenting a pop music programme called *The Rave*, which was a proposed replacement for the infamous *Ready Steady Go!* Pink Floyd appeared as their guests on this first episode and previewed their forthcoming single, 'Arnold Layne'. In the same week the band were reported as having prepared a thirty-minute television pilot to show to EMI Records so that the company could decide whether or not to

sponsor a series for broadcast on ITV. The project never came to fruition.

■ **7.3.67**
Malvern Big Beat Sessions, Winter Gardens, Malvern, Worcestershire, England
'The Malvern Winter Gardens has banned the use of the words "It's a freak out, it's a psychedelic happening" in advertising for the appearance of London group, The Pink Floyd. Entertainment's Manager Mr. J.D. Harrison told us that several hundred pamphlets were distributed at Tuesday night's Big Beat session last week advertising the group's appearance in March. After consulting with the chairman of the Winter Gardens and Publicity Committee, Councillor Ron Holland decided that the remaining 20 pamphlets should not be handed out.... Mr. Harrison said, "['Psychedelic' is] a word that should not be used. I think it's a trend to the drug world. It's wrong, completely wrong. I rang up Malvern Public Library to find out the meaning of the word and I was told it related to trances induced by the drug LSD."' (*Malvern Gazette*)

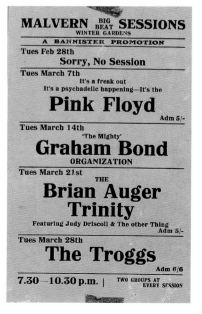

■ **9.3.67**
The Marquee, Wardour Street, Soho, London, England.
With The Thoughts.

■ **10.3.67**
UFO, The Blarney, Tottenham Court Road, London, England.
With Special Guest Robot, films, lights and 'raids'.
Pink Floyd's regular slot at UFO was complemented by a screening of a promotional film they had made for their debut single, 'Arnold Layne'. It has been regularly shown, to the present day, on various UK and European TV shows, and was even used by Roger Waters, on screen, during his 'Radio KAOS' solo tour of 1987.

■ **11.3.67**
Technical College, Canterbury, Kent, England.
Supported by Specta Quin Team.

■ **12.3.67**
The Agincourt, Camberley, Surrey, England.
Supported by Mike Raynor & The Condors.

■ **17.3.67**
Kingston Technical College, Kingston-upon-Thames, Surrey, England.

■ **18.3.67**
Enfield College of Technology, Enfield, Middlesex, England.

■ **23.3.67**
Rotherham College of Technology Dance, Clifton Hall, Rotherham, Yorkshire, England.
Pink Floyd replaced Shotgun Express at short notice.

■ **24.3.67**
Ricky Tick, Hounslow, Middlesex, England.

■ **25.3.67**
Ricky Tick, Thames Hotel, Windsor, Berkshire, England.

■ **26.3.67**
Rex Ballroom, Bognor Regis, West Sussex, England.

■ **28.3.67**
Chinese R&B Jazz Club,

Corn Exchange, Bristol, Gloucestershire, England.

■ **29.3.67**
The Dance Hall, Eel Pie Island Hotel, Twickenham, Middlesex, England.

■ **31.3.67**
Top Spot Ballroom, Ross-on-Wye, Herefordshire, England.
Supported by Group 66.

■ **1.4.67**
The Birdcage, Eastney, Portsmouth, Hampshire, England.

■ **3.4.67**
BBC Playhouse Theatre, Northumberland Avenue, London, England.
A live studio session performing 'Arnold Layne' and 'Candy And A Currant Bun' for the BBC Radio Light Programme *Monday, Monday!* and broadcast at 1.00pm.

■ **6.4.67**
BBC Television Centre, Wood Lane, London, England.
Pink Floyd's first-ever appearance on the UK's most influential pop music show, BBC TV's *Top of The Pops*. 'Arnold Layne' was due for broadcast, but a last-minute change prevented this.

■ **6.4.67**
City Hall, Salisbury, Wiltshire, England.
Supported by The Nite Shift.
Set list included: Untitled instrumental/Arnold Layne/Interstellar Overdrive/Matilda Mother

■ **7.4.67**
Floral Hall, Belfast, County Antrim, Northern Ireland.
Supported by The Jimmy Johnston Showband.

■ **8.4.67**
Rhodes Centre, Bishop's Stortford, Hertfordshire, England.
Supported by The New Generation

■ **8.4.67**
The Roundhouse, Chalk Farm, London, England.
With The Flies, Earl Fuggle, The Electric Poets, The Block, Sandy & Narda dancers and Sam Gopal.

■ **9.4.67**
Britannia Rowing Club, Nottingham, Nottinghamshire, England.

■ **10.4.67**
The Pavilion, Bath, Somerset, England.
'Three electricians should have taken a bow at the Pavilion last night. Instead four people took the applause – four people who had, apparently haphazardly, thumped out music. The four were the Pink Floyd, one of the most intriguing groups to visit the city. The overall effect created by the noise of those on-stage and the lighting from those off-stage was interesting to say the least. Jaundiced blotches ran down mottled multi-coloured backgrounds. Flashing lights transformed the group into ghouls, with giant prancing shadows of distorted beings dwarfing the performers as the lighting changed with the pounding rhythm.' (*Bath & Wilts Evening Chronicle*, reproduced by kind permission of *The Bath Chronicle*)

■ **13.4.67**
Tilbury Railway Club, Tilbury, Essex, England.

■ **15.4.67**
Kinetic Arena – K4 Discoteque, Main Ballroom, West Pier, Brighton, East Sussex, England.
Set list included: Candy & A Currant Bun/Astronomy Dominé/Matilda Mother/Pow R Toc H/Interstellar Overdrive/Lucifer Sam.
Pink Floyd were invited by Hornsey College of Art's Advanced Studies Group to perform in their 'kinetic audio visual environments' – collectively entitled 'K4'. They played in front of a sixty-foot-wide white projection screen with a PA system suspended from the ceiling.

■ **19.4.67**
Bromel Club, Court Hotel, Downham, Bromley, Kent, England.

■ **20.4.67**
Queen's Hall, Barnstaple, Devon, England.
Supported by The Gordon Riots.

■ **21.4.67**
The Starlite, Greenford, Middlesex, England.

■ **21.4.67**
UFO, The Blarney, Tottenham Court Road, London, England.

■ **22.4.67**
Benn Memorial Hall, Rugby, Warwickshire, England.
This show replaced the one scheduled for the 69 Club, Royal York Hotel, Ryde, Isle of Wight.
Set list included: Interstellar Overdrive/Candy & A Currant Bun/Arnold Layne.
'Like mad scientists they wielded their instruments treating each guitar string or drum stick with a fanaticism that rivalled the tantrums of the most despotic dictator. On stage at the Benn Memorial Hall on Saturday was the most weird, frighteningly way-out group fans in Rugby had ever seen – The Pink Floyd. Their experiments went far beyond the realms of pop music…. They displayed a remarkable dedication to a brand of music which may fade into the past, or could be the next progression in the musical annals of the 20th century.' (*Rugby Advertiser*)

■ **23.4.67**
Starlight Ballroom, Crawley, West Sussex, England.

■ **24.4.67**
London, England.
Melody Maker reported that the band were due to start work on a thirty-minute film called The *Life Story of Percy The Ratcatcher*. The project never reached fruition.

■ **24.4.67**
Blue Opera Club, The Feathers, Ealing Broadway, London, England.

■ **25.4.67**
The Stage Club, Oxford, Oxfordshire, England.
Supported by The Vibratones.

■ **28.4.67**
Tabernacle Club, Hillgate, Stockport, Cheshire, England.
■ **29.4.67**
Nederland 1 TV Studios, Zaandam, Netherlands.
The band travelled in their van to the Netherlands to perform 'Arnold Layne' live on the *Fan Club* pop-music show which was broadcast on 5.5.67 at 7.00pm.
■ **29.4.67**
24 Hour Technicolor Dream, Alexandra Palace, Muswell Hill, London, England.
With thirty other groups, including The Move, The Who, The Pretty Things, Soft Machine, Tomorrow, Creation and The Graham Bond Organisation. This was billed as 'The Biggest Party Ever" and every band offered to play for free. In addition there were fairground attractions, igloos dispensing banana-peel joints and the usual giant jellies.
It is regarded as an historic event in rock history but, predictably, has grown rosier with age. Mick Farren, quoted in Jonathon Green's book *Days In The Life*, gives an account of The Social Deviants' performance that accurately sums up the evening (clearly it was best appreciated by those who were bombed out of their minds): 'We were the first band on and we were fuckin' terrible. Nobody had ever played a gig this big. It was a rectangle the size of Paddington station with similar acoustics. Because of the helter skelter we couldn't see the band playing at the other end of the hall, but we could hear it, like a slightly more melodic version of the 3.15 from Exeter pulling in at the platform.' Pink Floyd eventually turned up at 3am on the 30th after a break-neck journey by van from the Netherlands. Regardless of the fact that they probably played like bums (certainly Peter

Jenner remembers he and Barrett took LSD), it is seen by many as a magnificent finale to a night of complete madness, the band taking the stage as the dawn sunlight pierced the huge windows of the main hall.
The event was documented by three BBC TV film crews for inclusion in a *Man Alive* edition entitled *What Is A Happening?* and broadcast on BBC2 on 17.5.67 at 8.05pm. Segments repeated since then have not featured Pink Floyd and it is just possible that they were never filmed. Film-maker Peter Whitehead took cameras to the show, where he spotted John Lennon, among other celebrities, but although he captured the scale of the event as a whole, he failed to pick up Pink Floyd on stage. Segments of Whitehead's work here are also featured on the aforementioned See For Miles 1994 video *The Pink Floyd – London 66–67*.
■ **30.4.67**
Plaza Teen Club, Thornton Lodge, Huddersfield, Yorkshire, England.
Supported by The Match Box and DJ Doc Merwin.
■ **3.5.67**
Moulin Rouge, Ainsdale, Lancashire, England.
Presented by The Southport Technical College and Old Students' Association.
■ **4.5.67**
Locarno, Coventry, Warwickshire, England.
■ **6.5.67**
Kitson College, Leeds, Yorkshire, England.
■ **7.5.67**
King & Queen Mojo A Go-Go, Tollbar, Sheffield, Yorkshire, England.
■ **12.5.67**
Games For May, Queen Elizabeth Hall, South Bank, London, England.
Set list: Dawn (tape recording)/Matilda Mother/ Flaming/Games For May//

Bicycle/Arnold Layne/Candy And A Currant Bun/Pow R Toc H/ Interstellar Overdrive/Bubbles (tape recording)/Ending (tape recording)/encore: Lucifer Sam.
Generally regarded as a turning point for the Pink Floyd, this show included their first public use of an idea developed in the recording studio: additional speakers were placed at the back of the hall to give an effect of 'sound in the round'. A joystick was used to pan pre-recorded sound effects and instruments anywhere within the circle formed by the speakers. The set-up, which was built by technicians at EMI, was stolen after the show. The idea was resurrected for the band's 1969 tour as the 'Azimuth Co-ordinator'. In addition, props were arranged on stage and bubble machines let fly, along with a well-developed light-show which incorporated 35mm film slides and movie sequences. New compositions were also written, including the song 'Games For May', which would form the basis of the band's second single, 'See Emily Play'. The *Financial Times* gave a rave review: 'Pink Floyd have successfully grafted vision on to sound in their performance by the skilful use of projected colours…. They remained largely invisible in the first half, their figures dimly deciphered behind the brilliant colours which flickered over them. On a back-cloth shapes like amoeba under a microscope ebbed and flowed with the glimpse of an occasional human form. The colours were primary and brilliant. Musically the Floyd are not outstanding. There was good organ and drumming but the guitars were rarely allowed to develop a theme. Only on slower numbers was feeling apparent and here the lyrics, which often invoked childhood illusions of unicorns and scarecrows, soothed the mood.

In the more strident songs the words were completely lost, and the sound became just an accompaniment to the colours rather than a partnership. A better balance was achieved after the interval, when the free flow of the psychedelic mind was given its head. In between some pounding instrumental excursions which carried the Floyd close to the new dimension in experience they aim for, the group wandered around the stage playing with friction cars, and water, and blowing bubbles against a recorded cacophony. With the sound at full blast and the colours flashing red, blue, green, those who were at all responsive to the performance succumbed to the illusion. By the end of the evening music disappeared and only electronic sounds remained, filling the hall and the head.'
■ **13.5.67**
St George's Ballroom, Hinckley, Leicestershire, England.
■ **14.5.67**
BBC Television Centre, Wood Lane, London, England.
A live studio recording for the BBC2 TV programme *The Look Of The Week* gave Pink Floyd the chance to perform two non-single tracks to the nation: 'Pow R Toc H' and 'Astronomy Dominé', the second of which has had many repeats on BBC TV over the years. Barrett and Waters were involved in an exchange with the music critic Professor Hans Keller, who considered their music to be 'terribly loud' and a 'regression to childhood'.
■ **19.5.67**
Club A'Go Go, Newcastle-upon-Tyne, Northumberland, England.
This show replaced the one

Right: Sound check, QEH, 12 May 1967

SCARECROW

ARNOLD LAYNE

TAPE DAWN

scheduled for 14.4.67, which was cancelled.

Set list included: Interstellar Overdrive/Astronomy Dominé/Pow R Toc H/Lucifer Sam/Matilda Mother/Chapter 24/Arnold Layne.

■ **20.5.67**

Floral Hall, Southport, Lancashire, England.

Supported by Big Sleep.
Set list included: Interstellar Overdrive/Pow R Toc H/Arnold Layne.

■ **21.5.67**

The Regent, Brighton, East Sussex, England.

Show cancelled.

■ **23.5.67**

Town Hall, High Wycombe, Buckinghamshire, England.

Plus Rod Welling with Top Discs and Prizes.

■ **24.5.67**

Bromel Club, Court Hotel, Downham, Bromley, Kent, England.

■ **25.5.67**

Gwent Constabulary ('A' Division) Dance, Grosmont Wood Farm, Cross Ash, near Abergavenny, Monmouthshire, Wales.

Supported by Volume IV with MC Eddie Tattersall.

■ **26.5.67**

Empress Ballroom, Winter Gardens, Blackpool, Lancashire, England.

Supported by The Koobas, Johnny Breeze & The Atlantics and The Rest. Compered by Jimmy Saville.

■ **27.5.67**

Bank Holiday Beano, Civic Hall, Nantwich, Cheshire, England.

Supported by The SOS.

■ **29.5.67**

Barbecue 67, Tulip Bulb Auction Hall, Spalding, Lincolnshire, England.

With The Jimi Hendrix Experience, Cream, Geno Washington & The Ram Jam Band, Zoot Money & His Big Roll Band and Sounds Force Five.

■ **2.6.67**

UFO, The Blarney, Tottenham Court Road, London, England.

With Hydrogen Jukebox, The Sun Trolley, Tales of Ollin and Soft Machine.

'The Pink Floyd played last week to the largest crowd UFO has ever held. At times queues stretched for yards up Tottenham Court Road, and twice the box office had to close because the floor was packed. The audience included Jimi Hendrix, Chas Chandler, Eric Burdon, Pete Townshend and members of the Yardbirds. Appeals by Suzy Creamcheese and Joe Boyd were made to the rather emotional crowd to prevent them taking any action against John Hopkins' imprisonment, until after his appeal has been heard. It is a pity that with all this happening the Pink Floyd had to play like bums. The Soft Machine also appeared briefly to perform a poem for John Hopkins. The Tales of Ollin dance group played for about 40 minutes and completely captured the audience imagination, also on the bill was the Hydrogen Jukebox.' (*International Times*)

■ **9.6.67**

College of Technology/College of Commerce, Hull, Yorkshire, England.

Supported by The ABC and The Night Starvation.

The show was advertised in such a way that fans had to guess which college was hosting the concert on the night. We have not been able to determine the facts either.

■ **10.6.67**

The Nautilus, South Pier, Lowestoft, Suffolk, England.

■ **11.6.67**

The Immage, Terneuzen, Netherlands.

8.00pm show.

■ **11.6.67**

Concertgebouw, Vlissingen, Netherlands.

11.00pm show.

■ **13.6.67**

Blue Opera Club, The Feathers, Ealing, London, England.

■ **15.6.67**

Free Concert, Abbey Wood Park, Abbey Wood, London, England.

With Episode Six.
Another free concert organized by Greenwich Council, also with Episode Six, had been held the previous evening, on the esplanade in front of the *Cutty Sark* in Greenwich, but we cannot confirm Pink Floyd's appearance.

■ **16.6.67**

Tiles, Oxford Street, London, England.

Supported by Sugar Simone & The Programme.
Pink Floyd's set was filmed for inclusion in a Rediffusion TV documentary entitled *Come Here Often*, a feature on Tiles and its resident DJ, Mike Quinn. The edition was first broadcast on ITV on 18.7.67 at 5.25pm.

■ **17.6.67**

The Ballroom, Dreamland, Margate, Kent, England.

Supported by The Tony Merrick Set.

■ **18.6.67**

Radio London Motor Racing & Pop Festival, Brands Hatch Race Track, Brands Hatch, Kent, England.

With Chris Farlowe & The Thunderbirds, Episode Six, The Shell Shock Show and DJs Mark Roman and Ed Stewart.

■ **20.6.67**

Commemoration Ball, Main Marquee, Magdalen College, Oxford, Oxfordshire, England.

With John Bassett, Georgie Fame, Herbie Goins and Frankie Howerd. Also, in the Old Bursary, The De Quincey Discotheque; in the Cloisters Night Club, The Right Track, Steel Band and The Pooh; and, in the Junior Common Room, the Spike Wells Trio and film shows.
The event began at 10.00pm and ended at 6.00am. Pink Floyd

performed two twenty-minute sets, at 11.00pm and 3.15am.

■ **21.6.67**

Bolton College of Art Midsummer Ball, Rivington Barn, Horwich, Bolton, Lancashire, England.

With The Chasers and Northside Six.

■ **22.6.67**

Bradford University, Bradford, Yorkshire, England.

■ **23.6.67**

Rolls-Royce Ball, The Locarno, Derby, Derbyshire, England.

Supported by Paperback Edition and Thorndyke Mordikai's Imagination.

■ **24.6.67**

Césars Club, Bedford, Bedfordshire, England

■ **25.6.67**

Mister Smiths, Manchester, Lancashire, England.

Mister Smiths was a three-floor nightclub where each room had its own themed décor, and Pink Floyd played two shows that evening – one in the main dance hall and the other in the Drokiweeny Beach Room.

■ **26.6.67**

Warwick University, Coventry, Warwickshire, England.

■ **28.6.67**

The Dance Hall, Eel Pie Island Hotel, Twickenham, Middlesex, England.

■ **??.6.67**

Pink Floyd reportedly appeared three times on BBC TV's *Top of The Pops*, performing 'See Emily Play'. The BBC's archives have been destroyed and we cannot confirm the recording or broadcast dates. In addition, Pathé Pictorial made a colour film of the band built around 'Scarecrow', the B-side of the single 'See Emily Play', for the ABC cinema circuit. It has been shown often on European TV.

■ **1.7.67**

The Swan, Yardley, Birmingham, Warwickshire, England.

THE ★ PINK FLOYD ARE HERE NEXT SUNDAY

DANCE
on Sunday, July 9th
7.30 p.m. at the
ROUND HOUSE
CHALK FARM ROAD
N.W.1
with the
PINK FLOYD
●
MOODY BLUES
●
THE OUTER LIMITS
Admission 12/6

MERCIAN AGENCY presents
Torquay's First
LIGHT & SOUND
HAPPENING '67
PINK FLOYD
with "See Emily Play"
JULY 31st.

Supported by Blend 5.

■ **3.7.67**

The Pavilion, Bath, Somerset, England.

■ **5.7.67**

The Dance Hall, Eel Pie Island Hotel, Twickenham, Middlesex, England.

■ **8.7.67**

Northwich Memorial Hall, Northwich, Cheshire, England.

Supported by Phoenix Sound.

■ **9.7.67**

The Roundhouse, Chalk Farm, London, England.

Supported by The Moody Blues and The Outer Limits.
A BBC2 TV crew were reported as filming the show for the *Man Alive* series, but it was never broadcast. In the *NME* article that reported this, Pink Floyd were said to be representing Britain in the June 1968 Olympic Games in Mexico City by performing at an official youth culture festival of music, although this never happened.

■ **15.7.67**

Stowmarket Carnival, The Cricket Meadow, Stowmarket, Suffolk, England.

With Feel For Soul.

■ **16.7.67**

Redcar Jazz Club, Coatham Hotel, Redcar, Yorkshire, England.

Supported by The Silverstone Set.

■ **18.7.67**

The Palace, Douglas, Isle of Man, England.

■ **19.7.67**

The Floral Hall, Gorleston, Norfolk, England.

Supported by The Alex Wilson Set.
'The crowd, about 800 strong, were subjected to many mind-expanding (trans-psychedelic) influences before the appearance of the group. A BBC2 camera team were there, preparing to record the freak-out, and at the far side of the hall stood a young girl surrounded by slide projectors … preparing

instant colour slides with tints and potions from a portable dispensary…. As the curtains of the stage drew back the Pink Floyd launched themselves into a shuddering opening number, sending the decibels flying round the hall. Flashing green lights, the flashes linked to the rumbles of the guitars, burst around the group from all angles so that at times the different shadows thrown gave the impression that there was a whole crowd of people on the stand…. Visually and soundwise the Pink Floyd are interesting, even exciting, but after the initial effect has worn off, it all seemed a bit thin. As one Floral Hall raver told me, "You've seen one freak-out, you've seen them all."' (*East Anglia Times*)
Any material filmed by the BBC seems not to have been broadcast.

SCOTTISH AND NORTH OF ENGLAND TOUR

■ **20.7.67**

Two Red Shoes Ballroom,

Elgin, Morayshire, Scotland.
Supported by The Copycats.
Set list included: See Emily Play.

■ **21.7.67**

Ballerina Ballroom, Nairn, Nairnshire, Scotland.

Supported by either The Rebel Sounds or The T-Set, according to two different advertisements.

■ **22.7.67**

The Beach Ballroom, Aberdeen, Aberdeenshire, Scotland.

■ **23.7.67**

Cosmopolitan Ballroom, Carlisle, Cumberland, England.

Supported by The Lemon Line and The Cobwebs.

■ **24.7.67**

The Maryland, Glasgow, Lanarkshire, Scotland.

Set list included: Arnold Layne/ Interstellar Overdrive.

25.7.67

Greenock Palladium, Greenock, Lanarkshire, Scotland.

The last night of the tour.

■ **28.7.67**

The BBC Playhouse Theatre, Northumberland Avenue, London, England.

The producer abandoned Pink Floyd's recording session for the BBC Radio Light Programme's show *Saturday Club*, for broadcast on 12 August 1967, when Barrett reportedly 'freaked out'.

■ **28.7.67**

UFO, The Blarney, Tottenham Court Road, London, England.

With Fairport Convention and Shiva's Children.
'In a cacophony of sound played to a background of multi-coloured projected lights the Pink Floyd proved they are Britain's top psychedelic group. In two powerful sets they drew nearly every conceivable note from their instruments but ignored their two hit singles. They included "Pow R Toc H" and a number which received its first hearing called "Reaction in G" which they say was a

reaction against their Scottish tour when they had to do "See Emily Play". Bass player Roger Waters gave the group a powerful depth and the lights played on to them to set an impressive scene. Many of the audience found the Floyd's music too much to sit down to and in more subdued parts of the act the sound of jingling bells from their dancing masters joined in. It is clear that the Floyd prefer playing to UFO type audiences rather than provincial ones and are at their best in an atmosphere more acceptable to them.' (*Melody Maker*)

Sadly, this was the last time UFO opened at these premises. The following Thursday, the landlord gave Joe Boyd one day's notice that he could no longer rent the club to him, having seen a *News of The World* article that revealed the sordid nature of the underground gatherings: 'girls dancing with girls, boys dancing with boys' and implications of drug use. Although Brian Epstein offered Boyd the Champagne Lounge in his Saville Theatre, the club moved to the larger and far less intimate Roundhouse, where it remained until financial troubles forced its closure in October.

■ **29.7.67**
The Wellington Club, The Dereham Exchange, East Dereham, Norfolk, England.
Supported by The Void.

■ **29.7.67**
Love-In Festival, Alexandra Palace, Muswell Hill, London, England.
With Eric Burdon & The Animals, Brian Auger, Julie Driscoll & The Trinity, The Crazy World Of Arthur Brown, Creation, Blossom Toes, Sam Gopal's Dream and Apostolic Intervention.
'... what about one fellow who was stabbed and trailed blood in a path outside the Palace early in the morning? Is this a LOVE-IN? No one had planned the

tense atmosphere, the robbing, looting and violence. In fact the idea had seemed perfect. Only two groups with top billing got any reaction from the icy crowd. The Pink Floyd got a reaction – a bad one. While the Floyd make ridiculously good records, their music can only be termed boring. When the Animals departed, from thence onwards the music, the people, the atmosphere went abruptly downhill. People floated aimlessly around the hall trying to find where something was at. But "it" just wasn't there.' (*Go!*)

■ **31.7.67**
The Town Hall, Torquay, Devon, England.
This was the last engagement the band fulfilled following Barrett's breakdown. The first two weeks of August were set aside for holidays and the following appearances were cancelled: Hamburg, Germany – TV programme *Music For Young People* (2.8); Seagull Ballroom, Ryde, Isle of Wight, England (5.8); Beat Dance, Skyline Ballroom, Hull, Yorkshire, England (10.8); Top Rank, Doncaster, Yorkshire, England (11.8); 7th National Jazz Federation Pop Ballads & Blues Festival, Balloon Meadow, Royal Windsor Racecourse, Windsor, Berkshire, England (12.8); Mecca Ballroom, Grimsby, Lincolnshire, England (1.9).

■ **1.9.67**
UFO Festival, The Roundhouse, Chalk Farm, London, England.
With Arthur Brown, Tomorrow, Fairport Convention and The Nack.

■ **2.9.67**
UFO Festival, The Roundhouse, Chalk Farm, London, England.
With The Move, Soft Machine, Fairport Convention, The Nack and Denny Laine. UFO had attempted to promote a concert in the town centre of Paignton, in Devon, on 1.9.67, staging

bands in a circus marquee, but neither the marquee owners nor the local council liked the idea of a hippie invasion and the event was refused a licence. Instead it moved back to the Roundhouse for the above two dates.

■ 8.9.67
Alexandra Palace, Muswell Hill, London, England.
When Rolling Stones Mick Jagger and Keith Richards were busted on possession charges their manager, Andrew Loog Oldham, proposed a benefit concert to be held at the Alexandra Palace. Pink Floyd were booked among many others to appear but the event was shelved in the early stages of planning following the two Stones' release.

SCANDINAVIAN TOUR
■ 9.9.67
Boom, Århus, Denmark.
Supported by Wishful Thinking, Step By Step, Shaking Phantoms, Barnet And His Dandy-Bublers.
Pink Floyd left some very strong impressions at their first Danish performance in the Boom Dancing Centre. More than 1,000 people attended the show, and at least the same number were unable to get in. After the microphones failed, the band were forced to play a mainly instrumental set.

■ 10.9.67
Gyllene Cirkeln, Stockholm, Sweden.
Supported by The Sleeptones and DJ Errol Devonish.

■ 11.9.67
Starclub, Copenhagen, Denmark.
Supported by The Beefeaters, Peter Belli & B. Brothers, Steppeulvene, The Clan, Hitmakers, Ebonies, The Case and The Defenders.
Set list included: Set The Controls For The Heart Of The Sun.

■ 12.9.67
Starclub, Copenhagen, Denmark.
Supported by The Beefeaters,

Peter Belli & B. Brothers, Steppeulvene, The Clan, Hitmakers, Ebonies, The Case and Melvis.

■ 13.9.67
Starclub, Copenhagen, Denmark.
Supported by The Beefeaters, Peter Belli & B. Brothers, Steppeulvene, The Clan, Hitmakers, Ebonies, The Case and Melvis. The last night of the tour.
Set list: Reaction In G/Arnold Layne/One In A Million/Matilda Mother/Scream Thy Last Scream/Astronomy Dominé.

IRISH TOUR
■ 15.9.67
The Starlite, Belfast, County Antrim, Northern Ireland.
Supported by The Fugitives.

■ 16.9.67
Flamingo, Ballymena, County Antrim, Northern Ireland.
Supported by The Cousins.

■ 17.9.67
The Arcadia, Cork, County Cork, Republic of Ireland.
The last night of the tour.

■ 18.9.67
Brussels, Belgium.
Pink Floyd were widely reported to have flown straight from Cork to Brussels to participate in a 'TV Spectacular'. We have been unable to discover any further details.

■ 19.9.67
Speakeasy, West End, London, England

■ 21.9.67
Assembly Hall, Worthing, West Sussex, England
Set list included: Scream Thy Last Scream/Astronomy Dominé/ Set The Controls For The Heart Of The Sun/Reaction In G/ Interstellar Overdrive.

■ 22.9.67
Tiles, Oxford Street, London, England.
Supported by Roger James Explosion.

■ 23.9.67
Saturday Scene, Corn

Exchange, Chelmsford, Essex, England
■ 25.9.67
BBC Playhouse Theatre, Northumberland Avenue, London, England
A live recording session for BBC Radio One in which the band performed 'Flaming', 'Apples And Oranges', 'Scarecrow', 'The Gnome', 'Matilda Mother', 'Set The Controls For The Heart Of The Sun' and 'Reaction In G'. It was first broadcast on *Top Gear* on 1.10.67 at 2.00pm, except 'Apples And Oranges', which was broadcast on *Top Gear* on 5.10.67 at 2.00pm.

■ 27.9.67
Fifth Dimension, Leicester, Leicestershire, England.

■ 28.9.67
Skyline Ballroom, Hull, Yorkshire, England.
Supported by The Dimples, The Rats, The Disturbance and DJ Rikki Dobbs.

■ 30.9.67
The Imperial, Nelson, Lancashire, England.
Supported by The Atlantics and The Beatovens.

■ 1.10.67
Saville Theatre, Shaftesbury Avenue, London, England.
Supported by Tomorrow, The Incredible String Band and Tim Rose, compered by Joe Boyd. Two shows, at 6.00pm and 8.30pm.
Set list at the second show: Astronomy Dominé/Flaming/ Lucifer Sam/Matilda Mother/ Pow R Toc H/Scarecrow/ Candy And A Currant Bun/ Interstellar Overdrive.
'The beautiful people and hippies turned up in their shawls, embroidered jackets, Indian head-bands and beads to see the Pink Floyd at the Saville on Sunday night. Even the compere, Joe Boyd, was from UFO. The Pink Floyd were one of the first groups to experiment with weird effects and they now have it down to a fine art, or

rather their lighting man has. The flashing patterns and weaving silhouettes are an integral part of their music, which was very loud and mainly instrumental.' (*NME*)

■ 6.10.67
Miss Teenage Brighton Contest, Top Rank Suite, Brighton, East Sussex, England.
Compered by Mike Aherne.
Set list included: Arnold Layne/See Emily Play/Matilda Mother/Astronomy Dominé.

■ 7.10.67
***Record Mirror* and *NME*, London, England.**
In a joint report *Record Mirror* and the *NME* stated that Pink Floyd were planning to stage a series of 'Spectaculars' in March 1968 with a 100-piece choir and a small chamber orchestra. Provisional dates were even announced: Free Trade Hall Manchester (2), Philharmonic Hall Liverpool (9), Royal Albert Hall London (15), Town Hall Birmingham (16), but nothing came of these plans.
The *NME* also reported that Pink Floyd would be recording for television in Germany and Belgium between 17 and 20.10.67 and giving shows in Paris between 22 and 26.10.67, but we are unable to confirm this. Reported additional dates in the Netherlands between 8 and 12.11.67 were cancelled because of the extension of the band's US tour.

■ 7.10.67
Victoria Rooms, Bristol, Gloucestershire, England.

■ 9.10.67
BBC Radiophonic Workshops, London, England.
Pink Floyd were reported as visiting the workshops to co-write a soundtrack for a new TV series.

■ 13.10.67
The Pavilion, Weymouth, Dorset, England.
Supported by Freddy Mack & The Mack Sound and Denise

Scott & The Soundsmen.
Set list: Astronomy Dominé/
Reaction In G/Set The Controls
For The Heart Of The Sun/
Matilda Mother/Interstellar
Overdrive/Pow R Toc H.
■ **14.10.67**
**César's Club, Bedford,
Bedfordshire, England.**
Supported by The Tecknique.
■ **16.10.67**
**The Pavilion, Bath,
Somerset, England.**
■ **21.10.67**
**University of York,
Hesslington, York, Yorkshire,
England.**
■ **28.10.67**
**Dunelm House, University
of Durham, Durham,
County Durham, England.
NORTH AMERICAN TOUR**
The following advertised
appearances by Pink Floyd were
cancelled because the US
Immigration authorities delayed
the issue of their work permits:
Whisky A Go Go, Los Angeles
(23,24.10); Fillmore Auditorium,
San Francisco, California
(26–28.10); KPFA Radio Benefit
Halloween Costume Ball,
Fillmore Auditorium, San
Francisco, California (30.10);
Tower Night Out, Pacific West
High School, San Jose, California
(31.10). Other scheduled dates
that were cancelled included
shows in Chicago and Boston
and a longer residency in New
York City.
■ **30,31.10.67 and 1.11.67**
**Whisky A Go Go, Sunset
Strip, Los Angeles,
California, USA.**
■ **2.11.67**
**Fillmore Auditorium, San
Francisco, California, USA.**
With Richie Havens and Big
Brother & The Holding Company.
■ **3,4.11.67**
**Winterland Auditorium, San
Francisco, California, USA.**
With Richie Havens and Big
Brother & The Holding Company.
■ **5.11.67**
USA TV Broadcast.
A live TV recording session for

the *Pat Boone Show*, miming to
'See Emily Play'. In a brief
interview afterwards, Barrett
merely returned a mute stare.
■ **5.11.67**
**Cheetah Club, Venice, Santa
Monica, Los Angeles
California, USA.**
Two shows: matinée and
evening.
'Pink Floyd, another mind-
bending group from England,
made its only local appearance
last weekend at Santa Monica's
Cheetah. Even the seaweed
was swinging at the end of their
first set. The unbelievable sound
of Pink Floyd was first heard
through a hurricane of colour,
bringing total sensual
involvement of audience and
performers, each absorbed in
the creation of aural/visual
experience. The creation
belonged to Pink Floyd, but
there was ample room for all of
us to share their visions, their
feelings. At the end, the
audience might have been
another creation of the facile,
collective mind of Pink Floyd. To
quote their press release,
"There can be no barriers, there
can be no predictions."' (*Los
Angeles Free Press*)
■ **6.11.67**
**ABC TV Center, Los
Angeles, California, USA.**
Pink Floyd's second US TV
recording session, this time for
ABC's *Dick Clark's American
Bandstand*, was equally
disastrous. The recording was
first broadcast on 16.12.67 and
featured the band miming to
'Apples & Oranges' and 'See
Emily Play' and again included a
brief interview.
■ **9.11.67**
**Fillmore Auditorium, San
Francisco, California, USA.**
With Procol Harum and HP
Lovecraft.
■ **10,11.11.67**
**Winterland Auditorium, San
Francisco, California, USA.**
With Procol Harum and HP
Lovecraft at both shows.

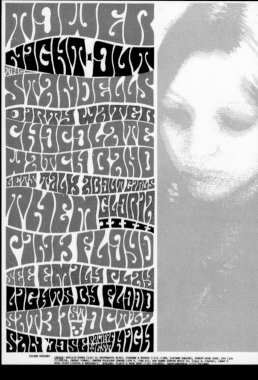

repeatedly warned the noisier teenagers as they brandished stools and shouted in the bar. In the hall, youths hurled abuse at performers. There was more weird music by the Pink Floyd and The Nice. Between them they beat up an electric organ, shattered a couple of thousand eardrums and lost themselves in a swirling cloud of coloured lights.' (*Bristol Evening Post*)

■ **25.11.67**
The Opera House, Blackpool, Lancashire, England.
Two shows, at 6.10pm and 8.20pm.
Set list at early show included: See Emily Play/Set The Controls For The Heart Of The Sun.
Set list at late show: Take Up Thy Stethoscope And Walk/ Set The Controls For The Heart Of The Sun/Interstellar Overdrive.

■ **26.11.67**
Palace Theatre, Manchester, Lancashire, England.
Two shows, at 6.10pm and 8.15pm.

■ **27.11.67**
Festival '67, Whitla Hall, Queens College, Belfast, County Antrim, Northern Ireland.
Two shows, at 7.00pm and 9.15pm.

■ **1.12.67**
Central Hall, Chatham, Kent, England.
Two shows, at 6.15pm and 8.45pm.

■ **2.12.67**
The Dome, Brighton, East Sussex, England.
Two shows, at 6.15pm and 8.40pm.
Set list at late show: Astronomy Dominé/Set The Controls For The Heart Of The Sun/Interstellar Overdrive.
It is said that David Gilmour made his first appearance with Pink Floyd at this show to replace an absent Syd Barrett. Whether his involvement went beyond this date is uncertain, but Mitch Mitchell's book *The*

■ **12.11.67**
Cheetah Club, New York City, New York, USA.
The last night of the tour.

■ **13.11.67**
Hippy Happy Fair, Oude Ahoy Hallen, Rotterdam, Netherlands.
This show was rescheduled from 12.11.67.
Set list: Reaction In G/Pow R Toc H/Scream Thy Last Scream/ Set The Controls For The Heart Of The Sun/Interstellar Overdrive.

THE JIMI HENDRIX TOUR

■ **14.11.67**
The Alchemical Wedding, Royal Albert Hall, Kensington, London, England.
One show at 8.00pm. (Times given on this and other dates of the tour are commencing times of the show and not of Pink Floyd's performance.)
'Possibly the most interesting act was the Pink Floyd's, fresh from playing hippie emporiums on America's West Coast, with what must be the best light-show yet seen in this country and very inventive music … were greeted by silence while most of the audience tried to grasp the 'meaning' behind their music – although they played hard rock based material with

drummer Nick Mason laying down some beautiful rhythms and guitarist Syd Barrett hitting some incredible flights of fantasy… They won rapturous applause, though from an audience which could have not been in the most part Pink Floyd fans. A very satisfying set.' (*Disc & Music Echo*)

■ **15.11.67**
Winter Gardens, Bournemouth, Hampshire, England.
Two shows, at 6.10pm and 8.30pm.
Set list at late show included: Set The Controls For The Heart Of The Sun.

■ **17.11.67**
City Hall, Sheffield, Yorkshire, England.
Two shows, at 6.20pm and 8.50pm.

■ **18.11.67**
Empire Theatre, Liverpool, Lancashire, England.
Two shows, at 6.00pm and 8.35pm.
Set list at late show included: Interstellar Overdrive/Pow R Toc H.

■ **19.11.67**
Coventry Theatre, Coventry, Warwickshire, England.
Two shows, at 6.00pm and 8.30pm.
'Jimi Hendrix fans were

unmoved – and I guess somewhat bewildered – by the Pink Floyd, a group of whom the new wave is more of a spring tide. The Floyd's extended instrumental/electronic experiments were fascinating, almost hypnotic, but unappreciated by an audience probably expecting their hit tunes.' (*Coventry Evening Telegraph*)

■ **22.11.67**
Guildhall, Portsmouth, Hampshire, England.
Two shows, at 6.30pm and 8.50pm.

■ **23.11.67**
Sophia Gardens Pavilion, Cardiff, Glamorgan, Wales.
Two shows, at 6.15pm and 8.35pm.

■ **24.11.67**
Colston Hall, Bristol, Gloucestershire, England.
Two shows, at 6.30pm and 8.45pm.
'There was guitar smashing on-stage at the Colston Hall – and glass smashing off-stage last night. Over boisterous Welsh teenagers were ejected after incidents in the hall bars in the auditorium. Teenagers from over the Severn Bridge came to yell for Welsh group the Amen Corner. Hall officials

Hendrix Experience states that he joined the tour halfway through.

■ **3.12.67**

Theatre Royal, Nottingham, Nottinghamshire, England.

Two shows, at 5.30pm and 8.00pm. David O'List, of The Nice, stood in for Barrett at the first show.

Set list at late show included: Set The Controls For The Heart Of The Sun.

■ **4.12.67**

City Hall, Newcastle, Northumberland, England.

Two shows, at 6.15pm and 8.30pm.

■ **5.12.67**

Green's Playhouse, Glasgow, Lanarkshire, Scotland.

Two shows, at 6.15pm and 8.45pm. The last night of the tour. Set list at late show included: Interstellar Overdrive/Set The Controls For The Heart Of The Sun.

■ **6.12.67**

Royal College of Art, Kensington, London, England.

With The Bonzo Dog Doo Dah Band, The Marmalade and Blue Rivers & His Maroons.

■ **8.12.67**

Chislehurst Caves, Chislehurst, Kent, England.

■ **9.12.67**

Central Office of Information, London, England.

Members of the band and their managers are reported in *Melody Maker* as viewing a colour film clip of the newly recorded 'Jugband Blues' for inclusion in a cultural exchange magazine programme that was networked throughout North America. The track was widely reported to be the band's next single.

■ **13.12.67**

Flamingo Ballroom, Redruth, Cornwall, England.

Presented by the Cornwall Technical College. Supported by P.P. Arnold.

■ **14.12.67**

The Pavilion, Bournemouth,

Hampshire, England.

Presented by Poole College Students Union. Supported by The Clockwork Motion and Caxton.

■ **15.12.67**

Middle Earth, Covent Garden, London, England.

Supported by Fusion Fluff and DJ John Peel.

■ **16.12.67**

Ritz Ballroom, Kings Heath, Birmingham, Warwickshire, England.

Early show. Supported by Gospel Garden, The Rare Breed and DJ Dave Terry.

■ **16.12.67**

Saturday Spectacular, The Penthouse, Constitution Hill, Birmingham, Warwickshire, England.

Late show. Supported by Gospel Garden, The Rare Breed and DJs Dave Terry and Haig.

■ **20.12.67**

BBC Maida Vale Studios, Maida Vale, London, England.

A live BBC Radio One session in which the band performed 'Vegetable Man', 'Scream Thy Last Scream', 'Pow R Toc H' and 'Jugband Blues'. It was first broadcast on *Top Gear* on 31.12.67 at 2.00pm.

■ **21.12.67**

Speakeasy, West End, London, England.

■ **22.12.67**

Christmas On Earth Continued, The Grand Hall, Olympia Exhibition Halls, Olympia, London, England.

With The Jimi Hendrix Experience, Eric Burdon & The Animals, The Who, The Move, Graham Bond Organisation, Soft Machine, Sam Gopal's Dream, Paper Blitz Tissue, Keith West & Tomorrow, DJ John Peel and Jeffrey Shaw & The Plastic Circus and many others. Pink Floyd took the stage at 5.00am.

'It will be one of the most ambitious pop projects ever undertaken in Britain with an incredible line up of top groups.

By using two large specially erected stages at either end of the Grand Hall it is ensured that their music will continue throughout the night non-stop. A cinema in the National Hall will show top vintage films on one screen while a light show is going on on two other screens. In all more than a hundred projectors are being used throughout the building to make up a spectacular display of various lighting effects. In the centre of the hall will be a pool surrounded by sand where one can laze in a tropical atmosphere

to watch the film shows. Fun-fair attractions will be assembled around the two halls and there will be an arcade of boutiques and stalls in the West Hall called "Portobello Road, Continued". Here the strolling steel band will provide music. Two 30-feet high light towers with three projection levels incorporating a dozen radio-controlled follow spots are the centre feature of the spectacular light show. It is expected that 15,000 young people will be at Olympia tomorrow night.' (*Kensington Post*)

3

Clearly Syd Barrett was never going to come back to the real world, and his role within Pink Floyd was all but over. One solution the band thought of was to use him as an off-stage songwriter in the same way that The Beach Boys retained Brian Wilson. But almost at once they realized that this was an impossibility. To further complicate matters, at that time Barrett was living in the same flat as Rick Wright in Richmond. 'I had to say things like, 'Syd, I'm going out to get some cigarettes', and go off and do a gig and come back the next day. It was awful; a terrible time.'[1]

Even so, the five-piece Floyd did play a handful of shows together throughout January. There are no reliable witness reports or press reviews of these final and fraught performances, but Gilmour does have some recollection of them: 'Sometimes Syd sang a bit and sometimes he didn't. It became very obvious that it wasn't going to continue for very long like that and on the sixth one that we would have done together, which I think was at Southampton University, we just never picked him up. Someone said, "Shall we bother to pick up Syd?", and someone said,

The short-lived five-piece
Pink Floyd, January 1968

The band in early 1968, after Syd Barrett's departure

"Nah, let's not bother", and that was the end.'[2]

The subsequent guilt, frustration, anger and hopelessness of the situation has haunted the band ever since, deeply affecting Waters, who, Gilmour has said, 'was the one who had the courage to drive Syd out, because he realised that as long as Syd was in the band, they wouldn't keep it together. The chaos factor was too great. Roger looked up to Syd and he always felt very guilty about the fact he'd blown out his mate.'[3] Consequently, and despite Barrett's relatively short spell in the group, his spectre has hung over Pink Floyd ever since. There are unmistakable allusions to him in various songs, in particular the haunting 'Shine On You Crazy Diamond' from the 1975 album *Wish You Were Here*. In many respects he has never really left the band.

And, just as the remaining members could no longer see a future with Barrett, their managers, Andrew King and Peter Jenner, could no longer

see a future in a Pink Floyd without him. Blackhill Enterprises chose to dissolve the agreement with the band in April 1968 but continued to represent Barrett, who, they felt, would fare better as a solo artist. In the event, Wright very nearly departed at the same time: 'Peter and Andrew thought Syd and I were the musical brains of the group, and that we should form a break-away band, to try to hold Syd together. And believe me, I would have left with him like a shot if I had thought Syd could do it.'[4] Given the lack of offers at the time, and the debts the band had accumulated, to Wright this seemed a not unreasonable option. Blackhill were in the same boat financially and had even sought an Arts Council grant for about £5,000 to assist a stage production featuring Pink Floyd. But this was clearly a thinly disguised veil to try to pay off the bills. It was at this point, Mason told *Zig Zag* magazine some years later, that their debts reached a peak, Waters adding that 'cheques were bouncing all the time because there wasn't enough money to pay everybody, so whoever got their cheque first got their money'.

Nevertheless, Wright decided to stay on board and the Bryan Morrison Agency took over the management of Pink Floyd. In later years Blackhill would be accused of making their biggest business error, but Jenner takes a philosophical view: 'We didn't have the resources to do anything more for them. They needed someone bigger to look after them. I suspect if they'd stayed with us we'd probably have bogged ourselves down in a trough of doom, which was very much in the air at the time.'[5]

Immediate plans were now put into play to revive the band's flagging career. Remarkably, despite this turmoil, the new line-up composed and recorded some new music at Sound Techniques studios for Peter Sykes' film *The Committee*, which starred Paul Jones and featured Arthur Brown.

A projected release in May was cancelled and the film has remained in the archives ever since, as does the band's soundtrack, which is purely instrumental and includes the earliest known version of 'Careful With That Axe Eugene'. With the film's non-appearance the only option left open to Morrison, in order to push the band up a few rungs and secure more bookings, was to release another single.

However, the release in April of 'It Would Be So Nice', penned by Wright and backed by a new Waters composition, 'Julia Dream', was typically dogged with disaster. For EMI and Morrison the single was a failure in almost every respect. This was partly thanks to BBC Radio One, which banned it for the inclusion of the phrase '*Evening Standard*' in the lyrics. Reluctantly, and at a cost of £750 to the band, replacement acetate discs were cut strictly for their benefit and the 'controversial' reference amended to the fictitious 'Daily Standard'. Nevertheless, this change made little difference, for the lapse between its release and airplay promotion had grounded the single. The band weren't entirely convinced this was the only reason – they hated it from the start: 'Nobody ever heard it because it was such a lousy record!' remarked Waters.'6

The last single the band were to release in the UK for some eleven years, December's 'Point Me At The Sky', did no better, fuelling their

I.C.A. & Blackhill Ents.
present
MIDSUMMER HIGH WEEKEND

Saturday, June 29th, noon
MORNING RAGA AT I.C.A.

Saturday, June 29th, 3 p.m.
THE PINK FLOYD TYRANNOSAURUS REX
Free concert at Hyde Park
(The Cockpit)

Saturday, June 29th, 9 p.m.
BONZO DOG DOO-DAH BAND
plus
THE NICE
plus
JUNIOR'S EYES at I.C.A.

Sunday, June 30th, 7.30 p.m.
Evening RAGA with USTAD IMRAT KAHN
West Indian writers at I.C.A.

Tickets from: I.C.A., Nash House
The Mall, S.W.1.   WHI 6393
or at the door
Weekend tickets £2, or for individual events

conviction that singles were a waste of time, money and effort. Nevertheless, Morrison believed that Pink Floyd's struggles in Britain need not inevitably be repeated in the largely unexplored European market. Having performed very little outside the UK in their first professional year, they now had the ideal opportunity to strike out in different territories at the same time as tackling their home ground on their own terms. Nineteen sixty-eight saw Pink Floyd undertake an immense amount of promotional work for European TV channels which slowly built up for them a large and faithful following who were largely unaware of the earlier psychedelic hysteria. Few of them knew who Syd Barrett was, so presenting the band to a fresh audience required little explanation of a change in line-up or style. It was the perfect remedy, and before long, by some bizarre quirk of fate, Pink Floyd were being placed high up the billing at major European pop festivals.

By the summer Blackhill were slowly dragging themselves out of the mire of insolvency by representing Tyrannosaurus Rex, and announced that they were to stage the first Hyde Park free concert on 29 June 1968, having been granted a licence by the Royal Parks and the Ministry of Works. Naturally they chose Pink Floyd as their headline act and the concert is very often regarded as the moment the band successfully relaunched themselves in Britain. Their spellbinding performance was as well received by the press as it was by the assembled crowds. Although the band performed some older numbers, these were now greatly reworked to suit their current style. Belated thanks are due to the highly influential broadcaster and journalist John Peel, who, after seeing the show, championed the band for the next few years.

Coincidentally their second album, A *Saucerful Of Secrets*, was released in that same week, with a sleeve designed by their old Cambridge chum and graphic designer Storm Thorgerson, who was then studying at the Royal College of Art. Thorgerson's work with the renowned seventies design team Hipgnosis would become a trademark of Pink Floyd, and his relationship with the band has endured to the present day.

The album fared well in the charts despite some mixed reactions – *IT*, for example, described the title track as 'too long and boring'. But although it was an album that had no particular formula or real direction, and one that had its fair share of *Piper* leftovers, it nevertheless marked a complete departure from psychedelic pop.

Indeed Barrett's contribution to A *Saucerful of Secrets* is minimal. He had penned the sadly prophetic 'Jugband Blues' just before his departure. Characteristically, he had invited members of a Salvation Army band who were also recording at Abbey Road to Pink Floyd's studio to play whatever they wanted – with no instructions, music or direction and, judging by the resultant track, not entirely the same piece at the same time.

The only indication of any other contribution by Barrett came in a surprisingly coherent response to a reader's letter published in *Melody Maker* on 7 June. In his reply he stated that he played only on 'Remember A Day'. He added that there had been complications regarding the album, but hid the fact that his former band mates had made this concession merely to compensate him for the long hours he had spent in the recording studio's reception area waiting to be invited inside.

Since the album was already in progress during the autumn of 1967 Gilmour's involvement was also minimal and he reportedly received a flat fee for his performance as well as a quarter share in the publishing rights of the title track. 'I contributed what I could but I was, quite honestly, a little on the outside through it all. I certainly didn't feel like a full member and I wasn't up front contributing all the way on it.'[7]

There was probably never any clear definition of the extent to which Gilmour was expected to inject his ideas. While there could be no doubting his ability, his playing style and vocal range were far removed from Barrett's and it took him some time to find his feet – even more so in the recording studio. 'I don't think they – the rest of the band – had fixed ideas of what I should do or how I should do it. I mean I just played rhythm to help it all along. For a good six months – maybe more – I didn't do a single thing. I was pretty paranoid.'[8] His suspicions about the band being a pretty weird bunch were confirmed when he saw Waters and Mason 'draw out A *Saucerful Of Secrets* as an architectural diagram, in dynamic form rather than in any sort of musical form, with peaks and troughs'.[9]

In time, however, Gilmour would introduce his own ideas and unique style. Wright was already regarded as the most talented musician, whereas Waters and Mason were far more concerned with the structure, presentation and overall concept of the band – the 'big picture'. Fortunately this unique relationship worked exceptionally well and over time it became clear that neither element could work without the other.

Surprisingly, their prospects were now looking promising in the USA. The 1967 tour had been a disaster, but Tower kept pushing out singles, despite limited chart success, at a greater frequency than in Britain. As a result the band was gaining a cult following, and a tour of America, mainly on the West Coast, was rather haphazardly arranged for August to tie in with *Saucerful*'s release.

A flood of rave reviews from these shows appeared right across the board, from the underground press to the highly influential industry magazine *Billboard*. The band hated the experience of having to hire all of their equipment rather than take their own with them, but with so much favourable press and Tower's renewed faith in them, the tour was extended to early September.

By the end of the year their presence in Europe, too, was consolidated by further appearances. They were developing a unique style that advanced their career at an impressive pace. Moreover, their finances were stabilizing and for the first time in months they were able to pay themselves more than their roadies.

Come the new year a more mature stage presentation had developed and the Barrett compositions had all but disappeared from the band's repertoire. In addition, most of their earnings from performances now began to be invested in upgrading sound equipment rather than supporting the high costs of a permanent light-show. From now on visual effects, if used at all, were provided by the venues or local promoters. 'Our main thing,' Gilmour said at the time, 'is to improve and we are trying all the time. We are striving to improve our amplification, on stage and in the studios, we want to clean-up the sound equipment.'[10]

At the same time it was becoming clear from the pattern of bookings that no one was ever going to dance to the band's music, so it was fortunate that a new audience was prepared to take them on board: the university and college

Steve Paul's The Scene club, New York City, July 1968, during Pink Floyd's second US tour

circuit. This 'intellectual' crowd, who revelled in their technology and the construction of the songs as pieces of music, would sit down and listen intently. This suited the band just fine, making a welcome change from the initial months of touring to constant heckling and torrents of abuse. Now, during one of their performances you could almost hear a pin drop right up until the very last fading note of a song.

Pink Floyd's press had also improved dramatically and at last they were being taken seriously as pioneers of a new and exciting movement capable of pushing back the boundaries. The experimentalism wasn't so much a free-form muddle as it had been in the past, but something more readily defined by the press, which labelled it – ghastly as the term now sounds – 'Progressive Rock'.

The band's big breakthrough came at a spectacular event held on 14 April 1969 at the Royal Festival Hall, big sister to the Queen Elizabeth Hall (from which they had been banned two years earlier when their bubble machine had soiled the upholstery and carpets). Billed as 'The Massed Gadgets Of Auximenes – More Furious Madness From Pink Floyd', the

Plumpton Festival, Streat, East Sussex, 8 August 1969

event, much to everyone's surprise, sold out well in advance. The show was a high point in Pink Floyd's ability to mix performance, stage and theatrics. The 'Azimuth Co-ordinator', their new 360-degree surround-sound system, made its debut, as did many new and reworked tracks grouped as two suites, 'The Man' and 'The Journey'.

'The Man' opened with 'Daybreak', an alternative title for 'Grantchester Meadows', performed here as an acoustic instrumental piece that would later appear on the *Ummagumma* album with lyrics. This flowed into 'Work', a Mason-fuelled percussion workout during which the others sawed and nailed pieces of wood to make a table; it closed with a bombardment, from speakers all around the hall, of tape-recorded clanking machinery, after which the band's roadies served tea on stage. 'Afternoon' followed, enabling Wright to display his ability on trombone; this is a piece that was later known as 'Biding My Time' and later appeared on the *Relics* compilation album. This was followed by 'Doing It' (a crude reference to sex), an instrumental of percussion and taped voices reminiscent of 'The Party Sequence' on the imminent album *More*. Next came 'Sleeping', an electronic instrumental of ethereal keyboards and slide guitars, merging into 'Nightmare', which incorporated tapes of heavy breathing, ticking clocks and alarm bells. (In the clock sequence on the pre-recorded tapes, a voice yelled in a mock-Scottish accent, 'If you don't eat your meat, you can't have any pudding', which was to appear on *The Wall* album some ten years later.) A reprise of 'Daybreak' ended the cycle and the first half of the show.

After a fifteen-minute intermission tapes of crashing waves and seagulls heralded 'The Journey'. The opening section, 'The Beginning', was later called 'Green Is The Colour', on *More*. This was followed by 'Beset By Creatures Of The Deep', a reworking of 'Careful With That Axe

Eugene'. 'The Narrow Way' would feature as 'Part 3' of the same track, again on *Ummagumma*. This was followed, as the stage lights dimmed and the band came off stage, by a long taped sequence of footsteps circling the auditorium and doors opening and closing, allowing the audience to appreciate the Azimuth Co-ordinator in all its glory. On their return, 'The Pink Jungle', an instrumental, brought the stage back to explosive life, before giving way to the grand finale of the three-part sequence 'The Labyrinths Of Auximenes', 'Behold The Temple Of Light' and 'The End Of The Beginning' – the latter piece taken from the closing section of 'A Saucerful Of Secrets' – dramatically displayed by Wright as he took controls of the grand Festival Hall pipe organ.

Waters, in a later interview, explained the band's goal at this time: 'We wanted to throw away the old format of the pop show standing on a square stage at one end of a rectangular room and running through a series of numbers. Our idea is to put the sound all around the audience with ourselves in the middle. Then the performance becomes much more theatrical.'[11] In fact, Pink Floyd had toyed with the idea of offering their audiences a theatrical experience as long ago as 1967, with plans to take an orchestra on the road for a series of one-off spectaculars which would have incorporated a screen 100 feet high and fifty feet wide on which to project films, slides and oil projections. In one of his last band interviews for *Melody Maker*, on 9 December that year, Barrett predicted that 'in the future, groups are going to have to offer much more than just a pop show. They'll have to offer a well-presented theatre show.'

The overall sound quality at the trial run in the Royal Festival Hall disppointed the band. Furthermore, some press reports saw it as no more than a good rehearsal, although the reviewers could at least understand what was being aimed at. On the other hand, the attendance at the concert boosted confidence among venue promoters and remarkably, although there was no new product to promote, the band were booked for their first headline tour of the UK in June, playing not at the usual round of clubs but at large civic halls.

One of the most important shows of this tour was at the Fairfield Halls in Croydon – an auditorium renowned for its excellent acoustics and atmosphere. The venue issued its own press release, which explained very clearly the feelings aroused by the band at that time: 'As groups go, the Pink Floyd are a strange case. You either love them or hate them. Few past their mid-twenties can tolerate them. For the Pink Floyd were one of Britain's first psychedelic groups, placing almost as much importance on their light-show as their musical side. Their concert at Croydon's Fairfield Halls on Friday, May 30, promises to be a sell out, and if their past concerts are a guide, the Croydon show will include, give or take a song, two numbers. The Floyd – if all goes well – will also be introducing their new concept in audience mind blowing, with a new electronic scheme to fill the concert hall with stereo sound from every angle. And to carry off a show based on a 360 degree stereo system, the Floyd have decided to include far more than a mere selection of songs. They plan to assault their unsuspecting audience by hurling music, lights, poetry and melodrama in furious succession. He who leaves the concert on steady feet will be constitutionally superhuman.'

Such enthusiasm confirmed that Pink Floyd were becoming very much an 'overground' phenomenon and before long they were in meetings with both the Royal and Boston Philharmonic Orchestras to discuss the possibility of joint recordings and performance. 'Not that we are such a successful group,' explained Waters,

'it's just that our name has got about to people who want to do strange things.'[12]

The tour culminated in a concert at the prestigious Royal Albert Hall in London, with the Royal Philharmonic joining the band to close the show. It was a spectacular moment – such a large and grand environment was the perfect vehicle for encapsulating the full splendour of Pink Floyd's theatrics and their remarkable new sound system, which has made them, through years of constant refinement, the world's leading exponents of concert sound production.

In fact the band had been gaining recognition outside their usual circles for some time: French director Barbet Schroeder commissioned them to score his new film, *More*, with the soundtrack album of the same name due for release in July 1969. It told a sorry tale of love and drug addiction on the then hippy island retreat of Ibiza.

Recorded at the Pye Studios in London, and without the band seeing the finished film, the score was written, recorded and mixed in just eight days during late January and early February. Although what is heard on the album is very different from that on the film – most of the songs are very incomplete or played in the background – there are at least two tracks, an unidentified instrumental and one other, 'Seabirds', that only ever appeared in the film. The recordings also featured Nick Mason's then wife, Lindy, on penny whistle. Overall it is a delicate, almost entirely acoustic album that is much overlooked and very underrated.

Cinema release in Britain never came, which is just as well, given lines like 'Groovy man, let's get high', although the album did reach a healthy No.9 in the charts. However, the film went down well in America and also did wonders for the band's profile in France, without doubt paving the way for many successful concert appearances there in the coming year.

ldge,

r 1969

Although the band failed in their ultimate goal to compose the soundtrack for a film that really inspired them, *2001: A Space Odyssey*, their music was unarguably influenced by scenes from outer space, as Wright explained: 'I don't know how conscious that is – I suppose a lot of it is, because Roger is fairly well into science fiction. I suppose much of what gives our music a space-like quality is that it's very free-form – especially on stage. We work out basic formats but it's all improvisation on known themes. A lot of people seem to think that on stage we work with tapes - but that's just not true. We spend a lot of time looking for new sounds especially when we're in the recording studios. A lot of it happens spontaneously, random sounds that happen when we're on a gig – then we remember the sound and use it afterwards.'[13]

By now the band's ability to create an extraterrestrial sound world had led the BBC and several other major European TV stations to invite them to compose music for their coverage of the Apollo 11 moon landings. The publicity this gained for them was staggering, for countless TV viewers heard their music accompanying the culmination of NASA's historic mission.

In addition, the band were working on the music for an American children's cartoon by Alan Aldridge (of *Yellow Submarine* fame), called *Rollo*, about a character who travels through outer space collecting animals for his zoo. The project, which would have involved recording the music for twenty-six half-hour instalments, was never concluded except for an unbroadcast pilot film containing some previously recorded material.

Throughout this burst of activity Pink Floyd pressed on with the recording of their next album, the official follow-up to *A Saucerful Of Secrets*. Called *Ummagumma* – Cambridge slang for copulation – it was to be released at the beginning of November on Harvest, EMI's newly formed

subsidiary label specializing in progressive rock.

Ummagumma was a double album, with one disc consisting of live concert recordings and the other of new studio compositions. Significantly, it was also the last album Norman Smith would produce for Pink Floyd. Smith and the band had been drifting apart for some time, for he favoured the old pop songs and since they were getting to grips with recording studio technology they now needed his help much less.

For the purposes of the live set recordings were made during a series of concerts that followed on from the Festival Hall appearance of 14 April and just before the start of the UK tour. These were made at Bromley Technical College, Mothers in Birmingham – a favoured alternative venue of the time – and the College of Commerce in Manchester. The recordings the band selected were made up entirely of old audience favourites in the belief that they would soon be dropped from their repertoire. Each track on the finished album was of an almost equal length, allowing two per side. The result was respectable versions of 'Astronomy Dominé', 'Careful With That Axe Eugene', 'Set The Controls For The Heart Of The Sun' and 'A Saucerful Of Secrets'.

'The live part of the album we had to record twice,' explained Rick Wright. 'The first time, at Mothers in Birmingham, we felt we'd played really well, but the equipment didn't work so we couldn't use nearly all of that one. The second time, at Manchester College of Commerce, was a really bad gig but as the recording equipment was working really well, we had to use it. Parts of 'Saucer' came from the Birmingham gig which we put together with the Manchester stuff but the stuff on the album isn't half as good as we can play.'[14] For some reason the Bromley show has never been mentioned, but in any event a large part of the vocals was overdubbed at a later date at Abbey Road. It is also worth noting that the album sleeve lists incorrect recording dates.

The studio album was an altogether different affair, comprising, unusually, four equal solo pieces. Best described as experimental, it was developed from existing, or developing, live performance pieces. Wright nearly makes the grade with his four-part concerto 'Sysyphus', while Waters' 'Grantchester Meadows' had lyrics added from its earlier incarnation as a live acoustic instrumental – a nostalgic recollection of his youth and lazy summer days spent by the River Cam. He also penned the ridiculously titled 'Several Species Of Small Furry Animals Gathered Together In A Cave And Grooving With A Pict', in which he rants away in a mock-Scottish accent, bridging the two tracks with an amusing sequence involving a fly being swatted – in full stereo!

Mason's contribution is no more than an experimental space-filler as well, not dissimilar to the percussion bashing sequence of 'Work' that was incorporated into 'The Man' sequence and, like Wright's piece, it has no lyrics. Gilmour, in contrast, produced the enchanting 'Narrow Way', which was also used as a live piece from early on in the year. Along with 'Grantchester Meadows', it is the strongest material on the studio album.

In fact, the whole idea of this flawed project came from Gilmour, who suggested, 'it was down to a lot of paranoia amongst each other, and thinking we would have a good time doing things on our own for a change, just for a laugh'.[15] Although the idea may have been suggested with good intentions, it probably alerted Waters to a weakness he could exploit to his own advantage and thus assert himself, in the long term, as the band's chief lyricist. 'I'd never written anything before,' confessed Gilmour, 'I just went into the studio and started waffling about tacking bits and pieces together. I rang up Roger at one point to ask him to write me some lyrics. He just said, "No."'[16] It was the first noticeable friction in a

catalogue of disputes between the pair that would continue throughout their career together. Although it was by no means a serious matter it does highlight Gilmour's ability to produce worthwhile material under pressure.

The overall impression created by the studio album is one of missed opportunity and self-indulgence. Waters admitted himself, with hindsight, that the album could have been improved with group effort. 'It would have been a better album if we'd gone away, done the things, come back together, discussed them and people could have come in and made comments. I don't think it's a good idea to work in total isolation.'[17]

Mason's summation reinforces this view: 'I think what this demonstrates, is that our sum is always better than our parts.'[18]

On a more positive note, the album displayed the band's preference to preview new material on stage and develop it to their satisfaction, gauging their own performance as well as the audience reaction, before committing themselves to recording. Although this approach undoubtedly improved many recorded works, it had the unwelcome side-effect of attracting the attentions of an ever-expanding army of bootleggers.

Notes

1–2. BBC TV *Omnibus*, 15.11.94

3. *Pink Floyd Story*, Capital Radio, 17.12.76

4–5. *Mojo*, May 1994

6. *Pink Floyd*, Rick Sanders. Futura 1976

7. *Pink Floyd Story*, Capital Radio, 24.12.76

8. *Sounds*, 6.10.73

9. *Mojo*, May 1994

10. *Disc & Music Echo*, 22.11.69

11. *Great Speckled Bird*, 25.5.70

12. *Melody Maker*, c.1969

13–14. Unidentified press articles, c.1970

15. *Beetle*, May 1973

16. *Mojo*, May 1994

17. *Disc & Music Echo*, 8.8.70

18 *Mojo*, May 1994

1968

PINK FLOYD
(January–March 1968)
Personnel:
Syd Barrett: Guitar, vocals
David Gilmour: Guitar, vocals
Nick Mason: Drums
Roger Waters: Bass guitar, vocals
Richard Wright: Keyboards, vocals

■ **12.1.68**
University of Aston, Aston Triangle, Birmingham, Warwickshire, England.
It is widely accepted that this was the first show that Pink Floyd performed as a five-piece with David Gilmour as a permanent member.

■ **13.1.68**
Saturday Dance Date, Winter Gardens Pavilion, Weston-super-Mare, Somerset, England.
Supported by The Ken Birch Band and The 3 of Spades Plus.

■ **19.1.68**
Town Hall, Lewes, East Sussex, England.
Two evening shows.

■ **20.1.68**
Hastings Pier, Hastings, West Sussex, England.
Supported by Beaufords Image. Compered by Pete Drummond. This was almost certainly Barrett's final appearance with Pink Floyd.

■ **26.1.68**
University of Southampton, Highfield, Southampton, Hampshire, England.
Supporting Tyrannosaurus Rex and The Incredible String Band.

■ **27.1.68**
***Melody Maker*, London, England.**
The *Melody Maker* was the first of the international music papers to announce that David Gilmour had joined Pink Floyd, increasing its line-up to five. It stated that he had rehearsed with the band for several weeks and would join them on their first European tour, beginning in February 1968.

■ **27.1.68**

Leicester College of Technology, Leicester, Leicestershire, England.

■ **10.2.68**
The Imperial Ballroom, Nelson, Lancashire, England.
Supported by The Forth Coming and The Atlantics.

■ **16.2.68**
ICI Fibres Club, Pontypool, Monmouthshire, Wales.
Unconfirmed appearance.

EUROPEAN TOUR

■ **17.2.68**
Concertgebouw, Vlissingen, Netherlands.
Supported by Dragonfly, Edatteme Jugband and Living Kick Formation.
Set list included: Encore: Interstellar Overdrive.

■ **18,19.2.68**
Brussels, Belgium.
David Gilmour made his film debut with Pink Floyd by recording a series of promotional clips for Belgian TV. The numbers included: Astronomy Dominé/ Set The Controls For The Heart Of The Sun/Apples And Oranges/Corporal Clegg/ Paintbox/Scarecrow/See Emily Play. The first four numbers appear to have been shot in a large hall or part of a TV studio, with 'Apples And Oranges' in a mock-up of a greengrocer's shop. The latter three were all shot in and around the Parc de Laekan, with the Brussels Atomium clearly visible in the background. All of the tracks were mimed over the original recordings, except for 'Corporal Clegg', which, although mimed, is noticeably different in its earlier incarnation in having a completely different verse ending from that which later appeared on their second album, *A Saucerful Of Secrets*.
'See Emily Play' is the only clip from these sessions that has ever been officially released, appearing on the 1989 compilation video *Rock & Roll – The Greatest Years – 1967*

(Video Collection VC 4058).

■ **20.2.68**
ORTF TV Studios, Buttes Chaumont, Paris, France.
A live TV studio recording session in which the band performed 'Astronomy Dominé', 'Flaming' and 'Set The Controls For The Heart Of The Sun' for the music programme *Bouton Rouge*. It was first broadcast on ORFT2 on 24.2.68 at 6.15pm.

■ **21.2.68**
ORTF TV Studios, Buttes Chaumont, Paris, France.
A live TV studio recording session in which the band performed 'The Scarecrow' and 'Let There Be More Light' for the music programme *Discorama*. It was first broadcast on ORTF2 on 17.3.68 at 12.30pm.

■ **22.2.68**
Rij-School, Leuven, Belgium.
As part of the city carnival, students organized an all-night event featuring, among others, Pink Floyd and The Crazy World of Arthur Brown.

■ **23.2.68**
Pannenhuis, Antwerp, Belgium.
Supported by The Mike Stuart Span.
'400 youngsters experienced "the psychedelic thing" at the Pannenhuis, which only holds 200 people! This beat-mecca in Antwerp was literally shaking on the very ground it was built on. A mind-expanding experience that lasted for two hours was given by Pink Floyd and the Mike Stuart Span. Everything was perfectly enhanced by a primitive "sensual laboratory" that provided light and colour explosions all over the stage while keeping up with the devilish rhythms of the music, equalling a volcano-like outburst of sight and sound. Pink Floyd merely used the lyrics as excess baggage and most of the time did not bother with vocals at all. They let their incredible electronic organ improvisations,

coupled with wonderful guitar effects and supersonic drum solos, do the talking for them. The whole show was proof of a "total communication through light and sound", a concept that left a beat-loving teenage audience stunned at first but in the end succeeded in drawing everybody into a whirlpool of music, sounds and multi-coloured light effects.' (*Het Laatste Nieuws*)

■ **24.2.68**
Cheetah Club, Brussels, Belgium.
The last night of the tour.

■ **??.2.68**
Frankfurt-am-Main, West Germany.
The German music press reported that Pink Floyd were to appear at a Frankfurt club in February but no show took place.

■ **26.2.68**
Domino Club, Lion Hotel, Cambridge, Cambridgeshire.
Pink Floyd replaced the advertised Wages of Sin.

PINK FLOYD
(March 1968–79)
Personnel:
David Gilmour: Guitar, vocals
Nick Mason: Drums
Roger Waters: Bass Guitar, vocals
Richard Wright: Keyboards, vocals

■ **2.3.68**
London, England.
On or around this date Barrett's departure from Pink Floyd was made official, although he continued to be managed by Blackhill as a solo artist.

■ **9.3.68**
Faculty of Technology Union, Manchester Technical College, Manchester, Lancashire, England.

■ **14.3.68**
Whitla Hall, Belfast, County Antrim, Northern Ireland.
Presented by Queens University Students Union.
With Spencer Davis, The Taste and The Freshmen.

■ **15.3.68**
The Stage Club, Oxford,

Oxfordshire, England.

■ **16.3.68**
Crawdaddy, Taggs Island, Hampton Court, Surrey, England.
Early show.

■ **16.3.68**
Middle Earth, Covent Garden, London, England.
Late show. Supported by Juniors Eyes with the Explosive Spectrum Light Show.

■ **20.3.68**
New Grafton Rooms, Liverpool, Lancashire, England.

■ **22.3.68**
Woolwich Polytechnic, Woolwich, London, England.
At this all-night event Pink Floyd took to the stage at 2.00am in front of an audience of fewer than fifty.

■ **6.4.68**
Blackhill Enterprises, London, England.
On or around this date Blackhill

Enterprises dissolved its management agreement with Pink Floyd and the band's affairs were transferred to the Bryan Morrison Agency.

■ **12–14.4.68 Brussels, Belgium.**
Pink Floyd were reported to be recording material for Belgian TV.

■ **20.4.68**
Raven Club, RAF Waddington, Lincolnshire, England.
Supported by The Delroy Williams Show (with go-go girls) and The Individual Set.

■ **3.5.68**
Westfield College, Hampstead, London, England.
With Grand Union.

■ **4,5.5.68**
Brussels, Belgium.
Pink Floyd were reported to be recording material for Belgian TV.

■ **5.5.68**
First International European Pop Festival, Palazzo Dello Sport, Rome, Italy.
Set list: Astronomy Dominé/Interstellar Overdrive/Set The Controls For The Heart Of The Sun/Pow R Toc H. This ambitious festival was first announced for 19–25.2.68 and later for 4–10.5.68 but on both occasions the event failed to take place, one of the main problems being the fact that many of the bands were advertised before agreeing to appear. Only 400 people attended Pink Floyd's show in the huge Palazzo dello Sport. A documentary of the festival, including parts of Pink Floyd's set, was broadcast in colour in the UK in *Rome Goes Pop*, part of BBC2 TV's *Release* series, on 18.5.68 at 9.55pm. The programme also featured

Donovan, Julie Driscoll and groups from Czechoslovakia, Italy and Japan.

■ **11.5.68**
Brighton Arts Festival – The Gentle Sound of Light, Falmer House Courtyard, University of Sussex, Falmer, Brighton, East Sussex, England.
Set list included: Let There Be More Light/Set The Controls For The Heart Of The Sun/Interstellar Overdrive/It Would Be So Nice. A large audience of 1,400 attended this ill-fated concert at which 'Technical troubles started almost immediately after the start of the show when one of the giant 35mm projectors burst into flame. Several fuses burned out and very few if any of the mechanical effects worked. When at about 10.15pm the evening first looked like failing it was arranged that the Pink Floyd who were originally to have appeared for two half hour spots were to go on at 10.30pm for an hour. This should have solved some problems since this group had stated that they did not wish the University's lights to operate while they were on stage preferring to use just their own. The light crews therefore had an hour in which to organise the rest of the show starting with the air raid sequence as Pink Floyd finished. This, when it came, could not be described as successful as somehow the volume of the sirens had been turned down and the two search lights were lost in the glare of the other lights which were left on. Two young girls were mesmerised by the lights and music and had to be treated by the first aid unit.' (*Wine Press*, Sussex University student magazine)

■ **17.5.68**
Middle Earth, Covent Garden, London, England.
12.30am show. With Alexis Korner, Free, DJ Jeff Dexter and Chakra.

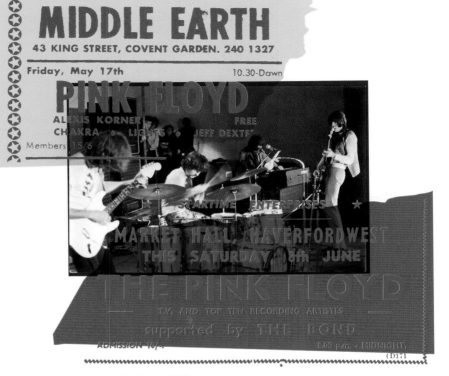

Inset photograph: Netherlands, June 1968

■ **23.5.68**
Paradiso, Amsterdam, Netherlands.
Two evening shows. These replaced a single show scheduled for 30.4.68, which was cancelled.
Set list at early show: Let There Be More Light/Interstellar Overdrive/Set The Controls For The Heart Of The Sun/A Saucerful Of Secrets.
Set list at late show: Keep Smiling People*/Let There Be More Light/Set The Controls For The Heart Of The Sun/Flaming/A Saucerful Of Secrets.
*'Keep Smiling People' is an unrecorded instrumental similar to 'Careful With That Axe Eugene'.

■ **24.5.68**
The Punch Bowl, Lapworth, Warwickshire, England.

■ **25.5.68**
Mayfair Suite, The Belfry Hotel, Wishaw, Sutton Coldfield, Warwickshire, England.
Supported by Young Blood and Pineapple Incident.

■ **26.5.68**
OZ Benefit, Middle Earth, Covent Garden, London, England.
This was one of a series of benefit shows for *OZ* magazine, which was going through its usual difficulties with the authorities.

NETHERLANDS TOUR
■ **1.6.68**
Lijn 3, Amsterdam, Netherlands.
7.00am show.

■ **1.6.68**
Eurobeurs, Apeldoorn, Netherlands.
Early evening show. Supported by The Mozarts, Les Copains and Outlook.

■ **1.6.68**
De Kentering, Rosmalen, Netherlands.
Late evening show.

■ **2.6.68**
Concertgebouw, Vlissingen, Netherlands.
Supported by Dragonfly.
Set list included: Let There Be More Light/Flaming.

■ **3.6.68**
De Pas, Heesch, Netherlands.
Supported by Chockfull, Blaze and The Bubbles.
The last night of the tour, which included unconfirmed shows at the Fantasio and Kosmos in Amsterdam.

■ **8.6.68**
Market Hall, Haverfordwest, Pembrokeshire, Wales.
Supported by The Bond.

■ **12.6.68**
May Ball, King's College, Cambridge, Cambridgeshire, England.
With Soft Machine, Ed Leo Trio, Trevor Hall and a steel band. At this concert Pink Floyd reportedly made use of a mind-blowing light-show supplied by Cambridge band White Unicorn.

■ **14.6.68**
Midsummer Ball, University College London, Gower Street, London, England.
'The big surprise to everyone when the Pink Floyd appeared was how little they missed their recently departed leader Syd Barrett. Now led by bass player Roger Waters they are far and away the best psychedelic blues band in the land and frequently play at Middle Earth (this is a cellar opposite Covent Garden Market – a den where you can dance, sit, listen, eat or even attend more pleasing matters. John Peel is often the compere and makes splendid jokes about drugs and ever present police in fluent Scouse which no one can hear, much less understand).'
(*Pi*, UCL student magazine)

■ **15.6.68**
The Magic Village, Manchester, Lancashire, England.
Supported by Purple Stone and The Alchemist, Jack Lancaster/Bruce Mitchell Quartet with the Inner Light Show.

■ **21.6.68**
Commemoration Ball, Balliol College, Oxford, Oxfordshire, England.
Early show.

■ **21.6.68**
Middle Earth, Covent Garden, London, England.
Late show. With Hurdy Gurdy, Easy Moses and Dexasterous.

■ **22.6.68**
The 1st Holiness Kitch Garden For The Liberation of Love & Peace in Colours, Houtrusthallen, The Hague, Netherlands.
Daytime show. With The Small Faces, The Pretty Things, Dirty Underwear, Group 1850, Chemical Explosions Of Death and War, Living Kick and the Trancedental [sic] Aurora Lightshow among others. This

was a poorly attended event at which Pink Floyd performed only three songs before departing.

■ **22.6.68**
University of East Anglia, Norwich, Norfolk, England.
Evening show.

■ **26.6.68**
Sheffield Arts Festival, Students Union, Sheffield University, Sheffield, Yorkshire, England.
Supported by Jethro Tull.

■ **28.6.68**
Students Celebration Dance – The End of It All Ball, Music Hall, Shrewsbury, Shropshire, England.
Plus the Miss Shropshire Student Contest.

■ **29.6.68**
Midsummer High Weekend, The Cockpit, Hyde Park, London, England.
The first Hyde Park free concert, organized by Blackhill Enterprises. With Tyrannosaurus Rex, Roy Harper and Jethro Tull.
Set list: Let There Be More Light/Set The Controls For The Heart Of The Sun/A Saucerful Of Secrets/Interstellar Overdrive.
'I always claim that the best outdoor event that I've ever been to was the Pink Floyd concert in Hyde Park, when I hired a boat and rowed out, and I lay on the bottom of the boat, in the middle of the Serpentine, and just listened to the band play and their music then, I think, suited the open air perfectly. It was – it sounds ludicrous now – it's the kind of thing you can get away with saying at the time and which is now, in these harsher times sounds a bit silly – but I mean it was like a religious experience. It was marvellous. They played "A Saucerful Of Secrets" and things. They just seemed to fill the whole sky and everything. And to coincide perfectly with the lapping of the water and the trees and everything. It just seemed to be the perfect event.

I think it was the nicest concert I've ever been to.' (*John Peel*, Capital Radio)

■ **29.6.68**
Town Hall, Torquay, Devon, England. Evening show.
Supported by Phydeaux Lime and The Phaze.

NORTH AMERICAN TOUR
The band arrived in the US on 4.7.68, but there were problems with their work permits and they had to stay in Canada until their application was processed. They were also scheduled to perform in Boston during this tour, but their appearance there remains unconfirmed.

■ **8.7.68**
Kinetic Playground, Chicago, Illinois, USA.

■ **12.7.68**
Grande Ballroom, Detroit, Michigan, USA.
Supported by Thyme and Jagged Edge.
Set list: Interstellar Overdrive/A Saucerful Of Secrets/Set The Controls For The Heart Of The Sun/Astronomy Dominé/Flaming.

■ **15–17.7.68**
Steve Paul's The Scene, New York City, New York, USA.
Set list on 15.7.68: Interstellar Overdrive/Set The Controls For The Heart Of The Sun/Astronomy Dominé/Flaming/A Saucerful of Secrets.

■ **24.7.68**
Philadelphia Music Festival, John F. Kennedy Stadium, Philadelphia, Pennsylvania, USA.
With The Who, The Troggs, The Mandala of Canada, Joshua Light Show and Friends Of The Family.

■ **26,27.7.68**
Shrine Exposition Hall, Los Angeles, California, USA.
With Blue Cheer and Jeff Beck.
Set list on 26.7.68: Interstellar Overdrive/Matilda Mother/Set The Controls For The Heart Of The Sun/Saucerful of Secrets.
'The Shrine Hall was so

sweltering sticky hot that had you been in some vague bummer frame of mind you might have taken one look at Single Wing Turquoise Bird's light-show, heard Pink Floyd's "Interstellar Overdrive", and imagined you were in some fundamentalist tent-show evangelist's version of hell. What I hadn't counted on was that the Jeff Beck group, sandwiched between the other two, would put both Pink Floyd AND Blue Cheer to shame. Pink Floyd on record is one thing: live, they're something else. Disappointing.... "Overdrive" came off as listless and muddled, sadly lacking in spark and distinction. Maybe it's Rick Wright's organ which saves the Floyd's concerts from disaster. He wanders into some strange things – hypnotic arabesques in "Matilda Mother", labrynthian flights in "Set The Controls For The Heart Of The Sun", and mystical mazes in "A Saucerful Of Secrets". "Heart Of The Sun" is an object lesson in the disparity between recorded and live Floyd.... In concert much of the ethereality is lost. The organ almost obliterates Syd Barrett's [mistaken for Gilmour] guitar, and Roger Waters, the bassist-vocalist tries to imitate gulls and breakers vocally. The result is almost embarrassingly inadequate.' (*LA Free Press*)

■ **2–4.8.68**
Avalon Ballroom, San Francisco, California, USA.
Supported by Crome Syrcus and The Holy Modal Rounders.

■ **9–11.8.68**
Eagles Auditorium, Seattle, Washington, USA.
With Blue Cheer and lights by the Retina Circus Light Company.

■ **16,17.8.68**
Sound Factory, Sacramento, California, USA.
Supported by Initial Shock and AB Skhy Blues Band.

■ **23,24.8.68**

The Bank, Torrance, Los Angeles, California, USA.
Supported by Black Pearl.

■ **31.8.68**
Sky River Rock Festival and Lighter Than Air Fair, Betty Nelson's Organic Raspberry Farm, Sultan, Washington, USA.
With Kaleidoscope, Muddy Waters, Peanut Butter Conspiracy, Santana, Country Joe & The Fish, John Fahey, HP Lovecraft, Steppenwolf and The Youngbloods and many others. Pink Floyd performed on the opening day of this three-day event (31.8–2.9.68), which, despite making heavy losses due to bad organization and fence-jumping, saw every advertised band appear.
'Gate estimates ranged up to 10,000 before nightfal based on an 11.30am count of 7,000 admissions as young people converged from the four corners of the nation. More than 40 bands made it the largest festival ever held in America. The festive throngs trooped in, filling a five-acre pasture to parking capacity.... Rock lovers seemed to pay little attention to the performing bands, but "hippies" and "straights" alike relaxed.' (*Seattle Post Intelligencer*)

■ **1.9.68**
Oakland Pop Festival, Baldwin Pavilion, Oakland University, Rochester, Michigan, USA.
With Procol Harum, Howlin' Wolf, Chris Chrysalis, Rationals, SRC Thyme, MC5, Jagged Edge, Psychedelic Stooges and The Frost Children. The last night of the tour.

■ **24.8.68**
Royal Lido, Central Beach, Prestatyn, Clwyd, Wales.
Show cancelled because of the extension of the US tour.

■ **4.9.68**
Middle Earth, The Club House, Richmond Athletic Club, Richmond, Surrey, England.

Roger Waters, Hyde Park, 29 June 1968

Pink Floyd's first UK date after their return from the USA.

■ **??.9.68**
Bilboquet, Luxembourg, Paris, France.
Set list included: Let There Be More Light/Interstellar Overdrive.

■ **??.9.68**
Psychedelic Club, Elysée, Paris, France.

■ **8.9.68**
Châtelet, Belgium.
Pink Floyd cancelled their appearance at this festival because of problems with the customs authorities. It reportedly ended in violence, although The Kinks, among other bands, were able to perform.

■ **13.9.68**
Mothers, Erdington, Birmingham, Warwickshire, England.

■ **17.9.68**
BBC Television Centre, Wood Lane, London, England.
Pink Floyd were reported in the music press as viewing a pilot film that included their music.

■ **20.9.68**
Bristol, Gloucestershire, England.
This date was published in a fan-club circular of the time, but remains unconfirmed.

■ **21.9.68**
ORTF TV Studios, Buttes Chaumont, Paris, France.
A live TV recording session in which the band performed "Let There Be More Light" and "Flaming" for the music programme *Samedi et Compagnie*. It was broadcast on ORTF2 on 12.10.68 at 4.15pm.

■ **27.9.68**
Queens Hall, Dunoon, Argyllshire, Scotland.
Supported by The Poets and DJ Tam Ferrie.
Brian Wilson, now a Labour minister, organized the concert, and recalls: 'Pink Floyd had gone to great lengths to get there, because of the terrible weather. The band had to hire their own boat from Gourock. It meant they were late and the audience were getting restless. When the audience of 400 heard their futuristic music, the response was less than ecstatic. Although they died on stage, a few people loved it and couldn't believe they were seeing Pink Floyd in Dunoon.'

■ **28.9.68**
The International Essener Song Tage, Gruga Halle, Essen, Germany.
After the previous evening's fiasco, Pink Floyd cancelled their appearance at this festival and stayed in Scotland until 2.10.68.

■ **1.10.68**
The Maryland, Glasgow, Lanarkshire, Scotland.
Pink Floyd made an impromptu appearance on their last night in Scotland, supporting local band Mind Excursion.

■ **3.10.68**
Thames TV, London, England.
The *NME* reported the broadcast on this day of the first programme in a new and nationally syndicated children's series, *The Tyrant King*. It featured music by Pink Floyd, The Nice, The Moody Blues, Cream and Tyrannosaurus Rex.

■ **4.10.68**
Mothers, Erdington, Birmingham, Warwickshire, England.

■ **6.10.68**
The Country Club, Belsize Park, London, England.

■ **16.10.68**
Théâtre du Huitième, Lyon, France.
With psychedelic light-show by the London Arts Lab.

■ **19.10.68**
Salford University, Salford, Lancashire, England.
This booking was reported early in the term at the University but was cancelled in favour of shows in Belgium.

■ **19.10.68**
Theatre 140, Brussels, Brabant, Belgium.

■ **20.10.68**
Theatre 140, Brussels, Brabant, Belgium.
Two shows, at 3.30pm and 8.30pm.

■ **21,22.10.68**
West Germany.
It was widely reported in the music press that Pink Floyd were in West Germany on these dates to record for TV shows, but we have been unable to discover further details.

■ **25.10.68**
The Boat House, Kew, London, England.

■ **26.10.68**
Union Hall, Imperial College, Kensington, London, England.
Early show.

■ **26.10.68**
Middle Earth, The Roundhouse, Chalk Farm, London, England.
Late show 10.30pm until dawn with Gary Farr, July and DJ Jeff Dexter. Pink Floyd were originally scheduled to appear on 18.10.68.

■ **31.10.68**
L'Antenne du Chapiteau du Kremlin-Bicêtre, Paris, France.
A live TV audience recording session in which the band performed "Let There Be More Light" and "Flaming" for the music programme *Tous en Forme*. It was broadcast on ORTF2 on 26.11.68 at 9.30pm.

■ **1,2.11.68**
Fillmore East, New York City, New York, USA.
Two shows, at 8.00pm and 11.30pm, were scheduled for each night with Richie Havens and Quicksilver Messenger Service. Pink Floyd cancelled at one week's notice and were replaced by the McCoys. Pink Floyd had also intended to return to the USA to complete a tour with Tyrannosaurus Rex, but this plan never came to fruition.

■ **2.11.68**
Student Union Bar, Farnborough Technical College, Farnborough, Hampshire, England.

■ **3.11.68**
BBC TV broadcast, London, England.
BBC1 broadcast, in black and white, a pre-recorded Omnibus special entitled *All My Loving* at 10.40pm. It was a fifty-five-minute film of pop music clips and contained interviews with The Beatles, Donovan, The Who, Jimi Hendrix, Frank Zappa, Lulu and many others. Pink Floyd were represented with a film clip of 'Set The Controls For The Heart Of The Sun' which is thought to have been filmed on the balcony of The Tabernacle, a community hall close to All Saints Church Hall, in Notting

Hill. The programme was first repeated in colour on BBC2 on 18.5.69 at 9.30pm.

■ **7.11.68**
Porchester Hall, Bayswater, London, England.
With Barclay James Harvest and The Edgar Broughton Band. Later Pink Floyd jammed with Alexis Korner and Arthur Brown.

■ **8.11.68**
Fishmonger's Arms, Wood Green, London, England.
Supported by Closed Cell

– was amazing. The hall was absolutely packed – not with the usual sort of kid fans but with a seriously-attentive and wildly appreciative crowd. The customers there at a London suburban pub were the most vivid proof of the existence of an increasingly large, new-type audience for intelligent and imaginative pop.' (*Record Mirror*)

SWISS TOUR
■ **16.11.68**
Restaurant Olten-Hammer,

Chuck and The Ponny's with the Miss Coca-Cola Competition.

■ **17.11.68**
2nd Swiss Rhythm and Blues Festival, Hazyland, Kongresshaus, Zurich, Switzerland.

??.11.68
Blow Up Club, Munich, West Germany.
Two evening shows. These probably took place on 18.11.68 after the brief Swiss tour, which was sponsored by Coca-Cola.

■ **24.11.68**
The Country Club, Belsize Park, London, England.
Supported by Andromeda.

■ **27.11.68**
University of Keele, Newcastle-under-Lyme, Staffordshire, England
Set list: Astronomy Dominé/ Flaming/Careful With That Axe Eugene/Interstellar Overdrive/ Let There Be More Light/Set The Controls For The Heart Of The Sun/A Saucerful Of Secrets.

■ **29.11.68**
Hanover Lodge, Bedford College, Regent's Park, London, England.
Supported by Blonde On Blonde.

■ **30.11.68**
Psychedelic Club, Elysée, Paris, France.
A live audience TV recording session in which the band performed 'Let There Be More Light' and 'Flaming' for the music programme *Surprise-Parti*e. It was broadcast on ORTF2 on 31.12.68 at 10.30pm.

■ **2.12.68**
BBC Maida Vale Studios, Maida Vale, London, England.
A live studio recording session in which the band performed 'Point Me At The Sky', 'Careful With That Axe Eugene' (announced as 'Baby Blue Shuffle In D Major'), 'The Embryo' and 'Interstellar Overdrive' for BBC Radio One. It was broadcast on *Top Gear* on 15.12.68 at 3.00pm and repeated on *Top Gear* on 19.1.69 at 3.00pm.

■ **5.12.68**
Bournemouth College Students Union Xmas Dance, Royal Arcade Ballrooms, Boscombe, Bournemouth, Hampshire, England.
With Status Quo and Mouse & The Kats.

■ **15.12.68**
City Hall, Newcastle-upon-Tyne, Northumberland, England.

Publicity shot for 'Point Me At The Sky', late 1968

Sponge and Stranger Than Yesterday with DJ Jerry Floyd and The Saffron Rainbow Light Show.
Set list included: Careful With That Axe Eugene/A Saucerful Of Secrets.
'The turnout – for what was probably a little-advertised event

Olten, Switzerland.
Early show. Pink Floyd's first-ever Swiss show was reportedly attended by over 400 fans.

■ **16.11.68**
Grosse Tanzparty, Coca-Cola Halle, Abtwil, Switzerland.
Late show supported by The Blues Club, The Axis, The Wood

■ **22.11.68**
Crawdaddy, Club House, Richmond Athletic Club, Richmond, Surrey, England.
Supported by Arcadium.

■ **23.11.68**
Regent Street Polytechnic, London, England.
With Bobby Parker.

otterdam organiseert in samenwerking met "de doelen" –rotterdam op:

Supported by The Pretty Things, Aynsley Dunbar Retaliation, The Deviants and Gordon Snaith. Two shows were scheduled but the earlier one was cancelled because Pink Floyd were delayed on the motorway. They played two numbers in half an hour until, at 10.30pm, the management turned off the power, sparking off a near riot in the audience.

■ **20.12.68**
BBC Paris Cinema, Regent Street, London, England.
A live audience broadcast session in which the band performed 'Let There Be More Light', 'Set The Controls For The Heart Of The Sun', 'Point Me At The Sky' and 'Careful With That Axe Eugene' for the BBC Radio One's *Radio One Club*, commencing at midday.

■ **27.12.68**
Grote Zaal, De Doelen, Rotterdam, Netherlands.
With The Outsiders, Barber Green's Fantastic Collection, The Misfits, R&B Ltd.4, Eye's Blues Formation, The Only's, Joseph Guy, The Heads, Panique, The WW Dance Girls and featuring The Provadya Lightshow.

■ **28.12.68**
Flight to Lowlands Paradise II, Margriethal-Jaarbeurs, Utrecht, Netherlands.
With The Bonzo Dog Doo Dah Band, Tyrannosaurus Rex, Eire Apparent, The Pretty Things and The McKebba Mendelssohn Main Line.
Set list: Astronomy Dominé/ Careful With That Axe Eugene/ Interstellar Overdrive/Set The Controls For The Heart Of The Sun/A Saucerful Of Secrets.

■ **??.??.68**
The Birdcage Club, Harlow, Essex, England.
Unconfirmed appearance.

■ **??.??.68**
Watford Technical College, Watford, Hertfordshire, England.
Unconfirmed appearance.

1969

■ **10.1.69**
Fishmonger's Arms, Wood Green, London, England.
Pink Floyd replaced Jimi Hendrix at short notice.

■ **11.1.69**
Kink Pop Festival, Zwijndrecht, Netherlands.
Show cancelled.

■ **12.1.69**
Mothers, Erdington, Birmingham, Warwickshire, England.
With DJ John Peel.

■ **17.1.69**
Royal Albert Hall, Kensington, London, England.
Pink Floyd were listed, with Ten Years After and Family, on the bill of the Uxbridge Brunel University Rag Week Ball, but did not appear.

■ **18.1.69**
London College of Printing, Elephant and Castle, London, England.
Early evening show.

■ **18.1.69**
Homerton College, Cambridge University, Cambridge, Cambridgeshire, England.
Late evening show. With Armageddon, Saffron Knight, discotheque, The Southside Jazz Band, Fab-Cab and others.

■ **18.1.69**
Middle Earth, The Roundhouse, Chalk Farm, London, England.
Early morning show. With Arcadium, Jimmy Scott & His Band, DJ Jeff Dexter and The Explosive Spectrum Lightshow.
'A large queue began forming outside the Roundhouse from about eleven o'clock at night and by half past one in the morning most of the assembled masses were inside. Under the large central dome there was a large circular floor area. Most of the audience sat on the floor, but late comers sat on the colonnaded promenade. To brighten things up a bit the back of the stage, the roof of the

dome, and a circular strip all the way round under the dome, were draped with white sheets which were used as projection screens for the lights. An hour of recorded music preceded the band's stage entry. At a quarter past two a tentative probing of the immense gong heralded 'Set The Controls For The Heart Of The Sun'. A sixty five minute set followed which included the breaking of a milk bottle in a rubbish bin and the frying of eggs, and more gong beating.' (unidentified press report)
Pink Floyd's set was followed by excerpts from the Tiny Tim film *You Are What You Eat*. The band reportedly attended the premiere of the film on 29.1.69 at the Windmill Theatre, London.

■ **22.1.69**
ORTF Studios, Buttes Chaumont, Paris, France.
A live studio recording session in which the band performed 'Set The Controls For The Heart of the Sun' for the music programme *Samedi et Compagnie*. It was broadcast on ORTF1 on 15.2.69 at 4.00pm.

■ **25.1.69**
69 Club, Royal York Hotel, Ryde, Isle of Wight, England.
Supported by The Cherokees.
Set list included: Set The Controls For The Heart Of The Sun.

■ **7.2.69**
University of Hull, Hull, Yorkshire, England.
Show cancelled after heavy snow delayed the arrival of the band and their equipment.

■ **14.2.69**
University of Warwick, Coventry, Warwickshire, England.
Supported by Bobby Parker.

■ **17–22.2.69**
Royal Lyceum Theatre, Edinburgh, Lothian, Scotland.
Pink Floyd wrote and recorded 'Pawn To King Five', an improvised instrumental piece, to accompany a ballet sequence performed by The Ballet Rambert on these dates.

■ **18.2.69**
Manchester & Salford Students' Shrove Rag Ball, Main Debating Hall, Manchester University, Manchester, Lancashire, England.
With Fairport Convention. Also appearing, in the Open Lounge, were The John Dummer Blues Band and Bakerloo; in the Lesser Debating Hall, The Liverpool Scene, Bridget St John and DJ John Peel; and at the Burlington Street site, The Foundations and Simon Dupree.

■ **21.2.69**
Alhambra, Bordeaux, France.
Supported by Roland Kirk.

■ **24.2.69**
The Dome, Brighton, East Sussex, England.
Supported by The Pretty Things and The Third Ear Band.
Set list included: Interstellar Overdrive/Set The Controls For The Heart Of The Sun/A Saucerful Of Secrets/encore: Let There Be More Light.
'On Monday of last week Jimi Hendrix played his second concert at London's Royal Albert Hall. And the Pink Floyd appeared at The Dome. They did not play their "Symphony In Sixteen Parts". It did not matter…. The group are at their best on the two long instrumentals "Interstellar Overdrive" and "A Saucerful Of Secrets".… "Saucerful" is the title track of their last album. Their version of this was simply incredible – superb drumming from Mason leading onto the centrepiece of polyphonic chaos, news from the quasars. Waters prowled the stage like a captain on the observation deck of a star ship, penetrating ever deeper into the heart of darkness. At their most brilliant, the group go where no man has gone before. The beautiful organ solo leading to the conclusion of the work, showed Rick Wright to be the best organist in Britain. The group finished with "More

Light" – great speed-freak guitar from Gilmore, great bass playing from Waters. This number together with "Set The Controls" shows Roger Waters to be an even better song writer than Sid Barrett, whose departure has not harmed the group, probably helped them. Waters' vocal style is curiously hushed; menacing – too quiet to hear the words, loud enough to generate the meaning. What of the future? The next album will not be their symphony, about which they are unenthusiastic at the moment. They will perform it again some time in another form. Set music holds no appeal to them.' (*Wine Press*, Sussex University student magazine)

■ **25.2.69**
Marlowe Theatre, Canterbury, Kent, England.
'Pink Floyd began their performance with impromptu coughs into the microphones, building up into the opening number. They used electric organ, grand piano, vibes and two large Chinese gongs as well as guitars and drums, and the music (or rather sounds) definitely attacked the senses as advertised. In the second half the musicians wandered about the stage, playing each other's instruments, and generally seeming to have a good time. Some brilliant piano and organ work came from Rick Wright, and the drums were played magnificently by Nick Mason, who kept the group stable with his good sense of rhythm. On stage, without the flashing lights for which they are renowned, they were informal and obviously musically talented.' (*Kent Herald*)

■ **26.2.69**
New Cavendish Ballroom, Edinburgh, Lothian, Scotland.
Pink Floyd performed in aid of Shelter, in an event organized by the University of Edinburgh.

■ **27.2.69**
Glasgow Arts Lab Benefit,

The Maryland, Glasgow, Lanarkshire, Scotland.
Supported by The Jimmy Mullen Jazz Group.

■ **28.2.69**
Commemoration Ball, Queen Elizabeth College, Kensington, London, England.
With The Moody Blues and The Settlers.

■ **1.3.69**
University College London, Gower Street, London, England.

■ **3.3.69**
Bristol University Rag Ball, Victoria Rooms, Clifton, Bristol, Gloucestershire, England.
Supported by East of Eden.

■ **8.3.69**
Rag Ball, New Union, University of Reading, Whiteknights, Reading, Berkshire, England.
With The Pretty Things, The Gods, discotheque, folk singing, blues, and The Sound Kitchen light-show.

■ **11.3.69**
Lawns Centre, Cottingham, Yorkshire, England.
Presented by Huddersfield University.

■ **14.3.69**
Van Dike, Devonport, Plymouth, Devon, England.
Supported by Afterwards.

■ **15.3.69**
Kee Club, Bridgend, Glamorgan, Wales.

19.3.69
Going Down Ball, The Refectory, University College, Singleton Park, Swansea, Glamorgan, Wales.
Set list: Astronomy Dominé/ Careful With That Axe Eugene/ Set The Controls For The Heart Of The Sun/ Interstellar Overdrive/ encore: A Saucerful Of Secrets.

■ **21.3.69**
Blackpool Technical College & School of Art and St Annes College of Further Education Arts Ball, Empress Ballroom, Winter Gardens, Blackpool, Lancashire, England.

With The Love Affair, P.P. Arnold, Carnaby Square, DJ Gary Wild and cabaret.

■ **27.3.69**
St James' Hall, Chesterfield, Derbyshire, England.
Presented by the Students' Union of Chesterfield College of Technology. Supported by King Mob Echo and Gandalf's Garden. Set list: Astronomy Dominé/ Careful With That Axe Eugene/ Interstellar Overdrive/ Set The Controls For The Heart Of The Sun/A Saucerful Of Secrets.

■ **14.4.69**
Royal Festival Hall, South Bank, London, England.
Set list: The Man//The Journey/encore: Interstellar Overdrive.
The programme for this concert gave a listing of Pink Floyd's forthcoming appearances that included the following shows that remain unconfirmed: Sweden (9.6), France (16.6) and Netherlands (18.6).

■ **19.4.69**
SDR TV Broadcast, Stuttgart, West Germany.
Pink Floyd had previously recorded original material for the SDR TV programme *Pink Floyd mit einen neuen Beat Sound*. This show has since been erased from the station's archives and the date of the recording cannot be confirmed.

■ **26.4.69**
Bromley Technical College,

Bromley Common, Kent, England.
With East of Eden. Pink Floyd's set was recorded for the *Ummagumma* album.

■ **27.4.69**
Mothers, Erdington, Birmingham, Warwickshire, England.
With DJ John Peel.
Set list: Astronomy Dominé/ Careful With That Axe Eugene/Interstellar Overdrive/Set The Controls For The Heart Of The Sun/A Saucerful Of Secrets.
Pink Floyd's set was recorded for the *Ummagumma* album. John Peel's ecstatic review for *Disc & Music Echo* was quoted in the 'Pseuds Corner' column of the satirical magazine *Private Eye* 'At one moment they are laying surfaces of sound one upon another in symphonic thunder; at another isolated, incredibly melancholy sounds which cross one another sounding like cries of dying galaxies lost in sheer corridors of time and space.'

■ **2.5.69**
College of Commerce, Manchester, Lancashire, England.
With Roy Harper, Pete Brown & His Battered Ornaments, Principal Edward's Magic Theatre, White Trash, The Edgar Broughton Band, Smokey Rice, The Groundhogs, Nova Express Lightshow and a film theatre. A fairground was also set up on the grounds.

Set list: Astronomy Dominé/ Careful With That Axe Eugene/ Interstellar Overdrive/Set The Controls For The Heart Of The Sun/A Saucerful Of Secrets. Pink Floyd's set was recorded for the *Ummagumma* album.

■ **3.5.69**
Queen Mary College, Mile End, London, England.
Supported by Watch Us Grow. Set list included: Astronomy Dominé/Set The Controls For The Heart Of The Sun/A Saucerful Of Secrets.

■ **9.5.69**
Camden Fringe Festival Free Concert, Parliament Hill Fields, Hampstead Heath, London, England.
With Roy Harper, The Pretty Things, Pete Brown's Battered Ornaments and Jody Grind. Set list: Astronomy Dominé/Set The Controls For The Heart Of The Sun/Careful With That Axe Eugene/A Saucerful Of Secrets.

■ **9.5.69**
University of Southampton, Highfield, Southampton, Hampshire, England.
Late evening show. Supported by Bridget St John and Quintessence.
Set list: Astronomy Dominé/ Careful With That Axe Eugene/ Interstellar Overdrive/The Beginning/Beset By Creatures Of The Deep/A Saucerful Of Secrets.

■ **10.5.69**
Nottingham's 1969 Pop & Blues Festival, Notts County Football Ground, Nottingham, Nottinghamshire, England.
With Fleetwood Mac, The Tremeloes, Marmalade, Georgie Fame, Love Sculpture, Keef Hartley, Status Quo, Duster Bennett, The Dream Police and Van Der Graaf Generator.

■ **12.5.69**
BBC Paris Cinema, Regent Street, London, England.
A live radio recording session in which the band performed 'Daybreak', 'Cymbaline', 'The Beginning', 'Beset By Creatures

Of The Deep' and 'The Narrow Way Pt.3' for BBC Radio One. The BBC archives show that this session was broadcast on *Night Ride* on 14.5.69, but *Radio Times* lists this as a live broadcast session for *Radio One Club* 9.4.69 at midday.

■ **15.5.69**
City of Coventry College of Art May Ball, Locarno Ballroom, Coventry, Warwickshire, England.
With Spooky Tooth and Free.
UK TOUR
■ **16.5.69**
Town Hall, Leeds, Yorkshire, England.
This was the opening show of Pink Floyd's first official UK tour, which was interspersed with one-off engagements both at home and abroad. They performed material previewed the previous month at the Festival Hall in London. Some fine-tuning was required and as a result 'Nightmare' now incorporated 'Cymbaline', with an additional middle section of pre-recorded quadraphonic sequence of footsteps and doors opening and closing, which was heard throughout the auditorium. 'The Pink Jungle' was also extended to include a reworking of 'Pow R Toc H'. As at the Festival Hall show, a costumed 'creature' would often lumber around the hall during the set.

■ **17.5.69**
Paradiso, Amsterdam, Netherlands.
■ **18.5.69**
Concertzaal de Jong, Groningen, Netherlands.
■ **24.5.69**
City Hall, Sheffield, Yorkshire, England.
Set list: The Man//The Journey/ encore: Interstellar Overdrive.
■ **25.5.69**
Benefit for The Fairport Convention, The Roundhouse, Chalk Farm, London, England.
With Blossom Toes, Deviants,

Ecclection, Family, Mick Fleetwood, Mimi & Mouse, Jack Moore, The Pretty Things and DJ John Peel. This concert was not part of the tour, but a hastily arranged benefit to help pay for the care of members of Fairport Convention who were injured in a serious accident on the M1 in which drummer Martin Lamble and a female passenger, Gene Franklin, were killed. However, the show was a far from peaceful event, marred by crowd violence.

■ **30.5.69**
Fairfield Halls, Croydon, Surrey, England
■ **31.5.69**
Commemoration Ball, Main Marquee, Pembroke College, Oxford, Oxfordshire, England.
An off-tour engagement. With Juniors Eyes and Dark Blues.
NETHERLANDS TOUR
The following three-show tour remains unconfirmed:
Provinciale Korenbeurs, Groningen (6.6), Paradiso, Amsterdam (7.6), Meerpaal, Dronten (evening show 8.6).

■ **8.6.69**
Rex Ballroom, Cambridge, Cambridgeshire, England.
2.30pm show.
■ **10.6.69**
Ulster Hall, Belfast, County Antrim, Northern Ireland.
■ **13.6.69**
Van Dike, Devonport, Plymouth, Devon, England.
An off-tour engagement.
■ **14.6.69**
Colston Hall, Bristol, Gloucestershire, England.
'The Pink Floyd unleashed the power of modern electronics, modern pop ideas and modern violence at their concert in Bristol. Electronically the show was brilliant. The Floyd played over recorded tapes which smashed four channel stereo sounds across, around and under the Colston Hall. The ideas were also exciting. A pop concert by a single group with the guts to drop the package tour format and a concert which

followed a musical storyline which wasn't difficult to trace. The concert had its moments. An exciting blues solo by the lead guitarist which Hendrix would have been proud of, nervous organ solos and some weirdly vicious rock and roll climaxes. But the Floyd pulled the punches and the music played on stage didn't live up to the interesting ideas they have created. The music was only intermittently good. For the Floyd it was a surprise, because they usually play immaculately – and the show had its silly moments. In one weirdo number an unnecessary Caliban staggered on to the stage and went into a music hall lavatory joke routine.' (*Bristol Evening Post*)

■ **15.6.69**
Guildhall, Portsmouth, Hampshire, England.
■ **16.6.69**
The Dome, Brighton, East Sussex, England.
'There was this small guy dressed up in a grey-green, warty-skinned costume with a cock that would give a donkey a complex and cause serious damage to a mare. I swear the guy was playing this cock, musically, as he moved, cat-like, around the stage after first stealing around the front and sides of the stalls. My eyes were watering at the sight of this enormous chopper being waved around, so my vision could have been impaired.' (Peter Towner)

■ **20.6.69**
Town Hall, Birmingham, Warwickshire, England.
■ **21.6.69**
Royal Philharmonic, Liverpool, Lancashire, England.
■ **22.6.69**
Free Trade Hall, Manchester, Lancashire, England.
Set list: The Man//The Journey/ encore: Set The Controls For The Heart Of The Sun.

■ 24.6.69
Commemoration Ball, Main Marquee, Front Quad, Queen's College, Oxford, Oxfordshire, England.
An off-tour booking. With Ten Years After.

■ 26.6.69
The Final Lunacy!, Royal Albert Hall, Kensington, London, England.
The last night of the UK tour. Set list: The Man//The Journey (with brass and choir)/encore: Set The Controls For The Heart Of The Sun.
The climax to 'The Journey' saw the group joined on stage by the brass section of the Royal Philharmonic and ladies of the Ealing Central Amateur Choir, conducted by Norman Smith. One of Pink Floyd's more experimental concerts, it featured a member of their crew dressed up as a gorilla, a cannon that fired and even members of band sawing wood on stage. A huge pink smoke bomb was let off at the finale.

■ 29.6.69
Saturday Dance Date,

Winter Gardens Pavilion, Weston-super-Mare, Somerset, England.
Supported by The Ken Birch Band and The Mike Slocombe Combo.

■ 30.6.69
President's Ball, Top Rank Suite, Cardiff, Glamorgan, Wales.
Presented by the Llandaff Technical College. Supported by Stop Watch.

■ 4.7.69
Selby Arts Festival, St James Street Recreation Ground, Selby, Yorkshire, England.
Pink Floyd headlined at this open-air concert staged by art students of Bradford University to mark the end of the week-long festival. It was attended by 2,000 fans.

■ 10.7.69
BBC Television Centre, Wood Lane, London, England.
A live TV recording session for the one-hour BBC1 TV *Omnibus* special entitled *So What If It's Just Green Cheese* – one of many programmes covering the Apollo 11 moon landing. It was broadcast on 20.7.69 at 10.00pm and featured Judi Dench, Ian McKellern, Michael Horden, Roy Dotrice, Marian Montgomery, Dudley Moore and The Dudley Moore Trio. Pink Floyd performed a five-minute improvisation which has become known as 'Moonhead'.

■ 22.7.69
SDR TV Villa Berg Studios, Stuttgart, West Germany.
A TV recording session in which the band performed 'Corporal Clegg' and 'A

Saucerful Of Secrets' for the children's programme *P–1*. It was broadcast on German network TV on 21.9.69 at 5.15pm.

■ 24.7.69
Nederland 1 TV Studios, Zaandam, Netherlands.
A live TV recording session was performed for Nederland 1's coverage of moon-landing week, Apollo 11 – *Een Man op De Maan* (One Man on The Moon).

■ 1.8.69
Van Dike, Devonport, Plymouth, Devon, England.
This show replaced the one scheduled for 27.6.69 but cancelled when the band's equipment failed to arrive.

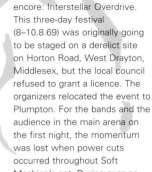

■ 8.8.69
9th National Jazz Pop Ballads & Blues Festival, Plumpton Race Track, Streat, East Sussex, England.
With Soft Machine, Keith Tippett, East Of Eden, Bonzo Dog Band, Roy Harper, The Who and many others.
Set list: Set The Controls For The Heart Of The Sun/ Cymbaline/The Journey/

encore: Interstellar Overdrive.
This three-day festival (8–10.8.69) was originally going to be staged on a derelict site on Horton Road, West Drayton, Middlesex, but the local council refused to grant a licence. The organizers relocated the event to Plumpton. For the bands and the audience in the main arena on the first night, the momentum was lost when power cuts occurred throughout Soft Machine's set. During over an hour of silence the crowd became restless, although most had fallen asleep by the time Pink Floyd came on.

■ 9.8.69
Paradiso, Amsterdam, Netherlands.
Set list: Interstellar Overdrive/ Set The Controls For The Heart Of The Sun/Careful With That Axe Eugene/A Saucerful Of Secrets.
Hilversum 3 Radio were recording this show for a future broadcst but after a microphone failure early in the show the band were forced to perform an instrumental set and as a result the show was never broadcast.

■ 13.9.69
Sam Cutler Stage Show – Rugby Rag's Blues Festival, Rainsbrook, Ashlawn Road, Rugby, Warwickshire, England.
With The Nice, Taste, Free, The Edgar Broughton Band, The Third Ear Band, Roy Harper, Ralph McTell and others.
This huge three-day (13–15.9.69), open-air festival offered one day of Blues, one of

Pop and one of Folk. It was attended by more tham 3,000 people despite heavy downpours of cold rain throughout, and was policed peacefully by the Hell's Angels. Pink Floyd appeared on the Pop day and, remarkably, given the weather conditions, were accompanied by an impressive light-show.

BENELUX TOUR

■ **17.9.69**

Concertgebouw, Amsterdam, Netherlands.

Supported by Dream with the Khamphalous Lightshow.

Set list included: The Man//The Journey.

Pink Floyd's set was this time successfully recorded by Hilversum 3 Radio and an edited version was later broadcast.

■ **19.9.69**

Grote Zaal, De Doelen, Rotterdam, Netherlands.

Supported by Dream.

■ **20.9.69**

Concertzaal de Jong, Groningen, Netherlands.

Two evening shows, the second at midnight. Supported by Dream.

Set list at second show included: Astronomy Dominé/Green Is The Colour – Careful With That Axe Eugene/Interstellar Overdrive/Set The Controls For The Heart Of The Sun/A Saucerful Of Secrets.

■ **21.9.69**

Het Kolpinghuis, Nijmegen, Netherlands.

Afternoon show.

Supported by Dream and the Khamphalous Lightshow.

■ **22,23.9.69**

RTB Studios, Brussels, Belgium.

Unconfirmed TV recording session.

■ **25.9.69**

Stadsschouwburg, Maastricht, Netherlands.

■ **26–28.9.69**

Theatre 140, Brussels, Belgium.

The show of 28.9.69 was the last night of the tour.

■ **3.10.69**

Debating Hall, Birmingham University, Edgbaston, Warwickshire, England.

Supported by Pegasus and Barnabas.

Set list included: Interstellar Overdrive/Set The Controls For The Heart Of The Sun/A Saucerful Of Secrets.

■ **4.10.69**

New Union, Reading University, Whiteknights, Reading, Berkshire, England.

Supported by Quintessence.

■ **10.10.69**

University of Loughborough, Loughborough, Leicestershire, England.

Supported by Jimmy Powell and Arrival.

■ **11.10.69**

Internationales Essener Pop & Blues Festival '69, Grugahalle, Essen, West Germany.

With Fleetwood Mac, The Pretty Things, Yes, Muddy Waters, Alexis Corner, The Nice, Deep Purple and others. Pink Floyd played on the last night of this three-day festival (9–11.10.69).

Set list: Astronomy Dominé/Green Is The Colour – Careful With That Axe Eugene/Interstellar Overdrive/A Saucerful Of Secrets.

■ **18.10.69**

University College London, Gower Street, London, England.

With The Edgar Broughton Band and Majority.

■ **22.10.69**

The Ballroom, University of Nottingham, Beeston, Nottinghamshire, England.

Pink Floyd were mistakenly listed as appearing by both NME and Time Out.

■ **24.10.69**

Fillmore North, Locarno Ballroom, Sunderland, County Durham, England.

Supported by Stone The Crows with DJ John Peel.

Set list: Astronomy Dominé/Green Is The Colour – Careful With That Axe Eugene/Interstellar Overdrive/Set The Controls For The Heart Of The Sun/A Saucerful Of Secrets.

■ **25.10.69**

Actuel Festival, Mont de l'Enclus, Amougies, Belgium.

Set list: Astronomy Dominé/Green Is The Colour – Careful With That Axe Eugene/Interstellar Overdrive/Main Theme from More/Set The Controls For The Heart Of The Sun/A Saucerful Of Secrets. This massive five-day festival was originally intended to be held in St Cloud, Paris, as the First Paris Music Festival (24–28.10.69) but the French police refused to grant the event a licence, as did the authorities in Pelouses de Reuilly, Vincennes when the organizers, Byg Records, tried to relocate it there. They were left with little option but to move it out of France altogether, to the tiny Belgian village of Amougies. Pink Floyd topped the bill on the main stage, which was housed in a massive marquee, playing to an audience of over 2,000. Melody Maker reported: 'Pink Floyd – at last something to compare with "2001". They had to battle against a few crackles from the amplifiers, but came over clear and well balanced. Frank Zappa accepted their challenge to join in on "Interstellar Overdrive" and a few new galaxies were discovered.'

Two documentary films were made of the festival, directed by Gérome Laperrousaz, entitled European Music Revolution and Music Power, the latter featuring Pink Floyd, and these were released on the French cinema circuit in June 1970. There are unconfirmed reports of a radio station in Lille broadcasting parts of Pink Floyd's show on 1.11.69.

■ **31.10.69**

Black Magic & Rock &

Roll, Olympia Stadium, Detroit, Michigan, USA.
Because of contractual difficulties, Pink Floyd, like some of the other acts billed to appear, did not perform.

■ **1.11.69**
Main Debating Hall, Manchester University, Manchester, Lancashire, England.
Supported by Stone The Crows with Nova Express Lightshow. Set list: Astronomy Dominé/ Green Is The Colour – Careful With That Axe Eugene/ Interstellar Overdrive/Cymbaline/ Set The Controls For The Heart

theatre of darkness – a goldmine of sound effects. The removal of the light-show from their act accentuates the sophistication of their sound.' (*Manchester Independent*, Manchester University student magazine)

■ **7.11.69**
Main Hall, Waltham Forest Technical College, Walthamstow, London, England.
Supported by Jan Dukes de Grey. Set list: Astronomy Dominé/ Interstellar Overdrive/Green Is The Colour – Careful With That Axe Eugene/Set The Controls

Centre, Dunstable, Bedfordshire, England.
With DJ Andy Dunkley and Optic Nerve Superlights.

■ **27.11.69**
Mountford Hall, Liverpool University, Liverpool, Merseyside, England.
Set list:: Astronomy Dominé/ Green Is The Colour – Careful With That Axe Eugene/The Man/ Sysyphus/Interstellar Overdrive/ Set The Controls For The Heart Of The Sun/encore: A Saucerful Of Secrets.
'The Floyd gave superb

Uxbridge, Middlesex, England.
Supported by Gracious and The Explosive Spectrum Lightshow. Set list included: Astronomy Dominé/Green Is The Colour – Careful With That Axe Eugene/A Saucerful Of Secrets/encore: Cymbaline.

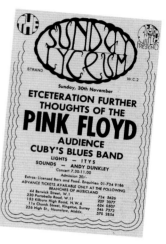

Pink's pop pulls in 800 fans

PLAYING their own brand of progressive pop, Pink Floyd attracted students from as far away as Brighton when they topped the bill at a Waltham Forest Tech dance on Friday.
More than 800 youngsters crammed into the hall and organisers were forced to turn late-comers away.
"It was more of a concert than a dance" said union president Eamon Everatt. "People came to listen to the music."
And obviously they liked what they heard because there was no trouble during the evening—a rare achievement these days—and the union ended up with a small profit to plough back into its next venture.
                                                                                            * (226)

Of The Sun/A Saucerful of Secrets/Pow R Toc H.
'It is difficult to imagine the Pink Floyd who played the Free Trade Hall last term fitting their sound into MDH. The Azimuth co-ordinator should compete fairly strongly with the disco in the open lounge. The Floyd are certainly one of the most technically accomplished groups around, even if flying drumsticks are a feature of their act – their drummer's fingers are notoriously slippery. A packed MDH should prove an interesting animal with creaking doors and ominous footsteps all around it. Their performances are not just musical, but an initiation into the

For The Heart Of The Sun/A Saucerful Of Secrets/encore: Let There Be More Light.

■ **8.11.69**
Refectory Hall, University Union, Leeds University, Leeds, Yorkshire, England.
Supported by The Idle Race.

■ **21.11.69**
***NME*, London, England.**
A tour of Germany with The Pretty Things was announced, but Pink Floyd pulled out at the last minute and were replaced by Fat Mattress. Fans were not informed of the change until they were inside the venues and, in some cases, violence reportedly broke out as a result.

■ **26.11.69**
Queensway Hall, Civic

renderings of "A Saucerful Of Secrets" and "Set The Controls For The Heart Of The Sun", Richard Wright giving an excellent piano solo in "Sysyphus", and we all enjoyed the chair-breaking and stage-bashing of Roger Waters which did seem to make some sense in the context of the musical violence. It was amazing, too, seeing him making those weird sounds with his mouth, when it might be thought that the Floyd sound is composed of electronic gimmickry. They are an experience of the sixties, and will still lead the way for progressive music into the seventies.' (*Guild Gazette*, Liverpool University student magazine.)

■ **28.11.69**
Brunel
University Arts Festival Weekend, Refectory Hall, Brunel University,

■ **30.11.69**
The Lyceum, Strand, London, England.
Supported by Audience and Cuby's Blues Band.

■ **6.12.69**
Afan Festival of Progressive Music, Afan Lido Indoor Sports Centre, Port Talbot, Glamorgan, Wales.
Supporting Pentangle, with East of Eden, Sam Apple Pie, Samson, Daddy Long Legs and Solid State.
Set list included: Green Is The Colour – Careful With That Axe Eugene/Set The Controls For The Heart Of The Sun/Interstellar Overdrive/A Saucerful Of Secrets/Cymbaline.

■ **??.??.69**
University of North Wales, Bangor, Gwynedd, Wales.
Unconfirmed appearance.

■ **??.??.69**
Town Hall, Watford, Hertfordshire, England.
Unconfirmed appearance.

4

1970 – 1971

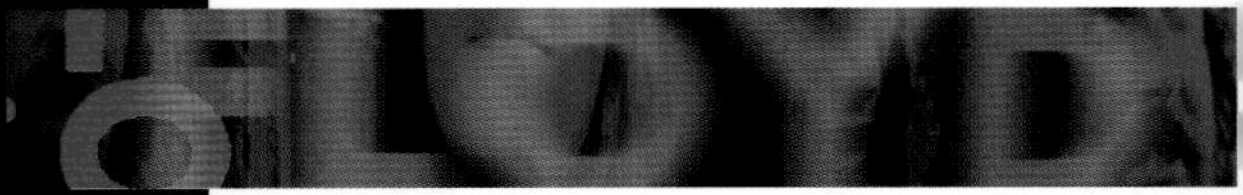

FLOYD

On 5 February 1970 Michelangelo Antonioni's film Zabriskie Point was premiered in New York City. It received extensive press coverage and was propelled to great heights partly because it was Antonioni's eagerly awaited follow-up to the cult classic *Blow Up* and partly because of its focus on American student rebellion – a topic of much concern to the media of the day. While it has not aged well in cinematic terms, it has achieved elevated status in rock music circles for one reason alone: Pink Floyd recorded some unique and otherwise unavailable music for its soundtrack.

The band were invited by Antonioni to write, record and mix the entire film at a studio in Rome in two weeks in December 1969. The director was present throughout the sessions and, according to Nick Mason, was an impossible man to work for: 'We'd start work at about nine [in the evening]. The studio was a few minutes walk down the road, so we'd stagger down the road. We could have finished the whole thing in about five days because there wasn't too much to do. Antonioni was there and we did some great stuff, but he'd listen and go, and I remember he had this terrible twitch, he'd go, "Eet's very beauteeful but eet's too sad" or "eet's too strroong." It was always wrong consistently. There was always something that stopped it being perfect. You'd still change whatever was wrong and he'd still be unhappy. It was hell. Sheer hell. He'd sit there and fall asleep every so often, and we'd go on working till about seven or eight in the morning.'[1]

'What our theory is,' reckoned Gilmour, 'is that he thought our music was too powerful and would have taken over from the film.'[2]

Eventually Antonioni called a halt to the sessions and settled for just three of the eight tracks they had completed: 'Heart Beat Pig Meat', an acoustic number reminiscent in style of the material found on *More*; 'Crumbling Land', an odd country-rock style number; and 'Come In Number 51 Your Time Is Up', a reworking of 'Careful With That Axe Eugene'. This last track appeared to have been Antonioni's prime motive for choosing the band in the first place and he used the revamped version in the film's climax, when the heroine visualizes a TV set and an expensive villa in Death Valley blowing up.

Like the band's previous soundtrack work, the released versions are quite different from those that are heard in the film, which for the most part appear as convenient edits: for instance, when a radio is switched on Pink Floyd comes blaring out. They also experienced a studio leak for the very first time, when three out-takes appeared on a bootleg album, *Omayyad*, under the assumed titles 'Oneone', 'Fingal's Cave' and 'Rain In The Country'. A further track, referred to by the band as 'The Violent Sequence', penned for a riot scene and unreleased in any form, was incorporated into their live set as an acoustic piano piece in the early part of the year. It was a forerunner to the melody of 'Us and Them', which featured on their 1973 album Dark Side Of The Moon.

Ultimately, their efforts were largely wasted, as Antonioni chose to fill the remaining soundtrack with a variety of previously released studio recordings by US artists, including The Grateful Dead, The Youngbloods and Kaleidoscope.

Nevertheless, the film sparked off a massive wave of interest in Pink Floyd. Since *More* had already been a big hit in America, this new exposure led to their first countrywide US tour.

Meanwhile, back in England the Bryan Morrison Agency was in some turmoil, and Morrison sold the business to the NEMS organization. Luckily for Pink Floyd, their representative at the Morrison Agency, Steve O'Rourke, in his new role at NEMS was able to guide them through this unexpected shake-up. He had been involved with the band since early 1967, and during their tours together they had developed a strong bond of trust. Indeed, when he and the band later left NEMS he became their full-time manager, a position he has retained to this very day.

It was also during this time that Waters embarked on his first solo project outside of Pink Floyd, collaborating with the avant-garde performer-composer Ron Geesin on a bizarre experimental documentary film called *The Body*. They were introduced by Nick Mason, who had met Geesin through a mutual friend, Sam Cutler, earlier in the year and had enjoyed socializing together. When Mason introduced Geesin to Waters, they hit it off instantly – both were ideas men, and in a short space of time they became good friends and golfing partners. It was a natural choice for Geesin to turn to Waters when a lyricist was required for his next project.

'It was intended to be a new style of making a documentary feature,' recalled Geesin, 'a stimulatory film. The idea in a fundamental way was to get something good with not very much, the ideal was that if you can express everything in a single melody, and variations, that would be very good. But I don't know what they replaced it with because I never actually saw it. The distributors had had an early sight and said it was too radical for their market, to tame it down, so they added

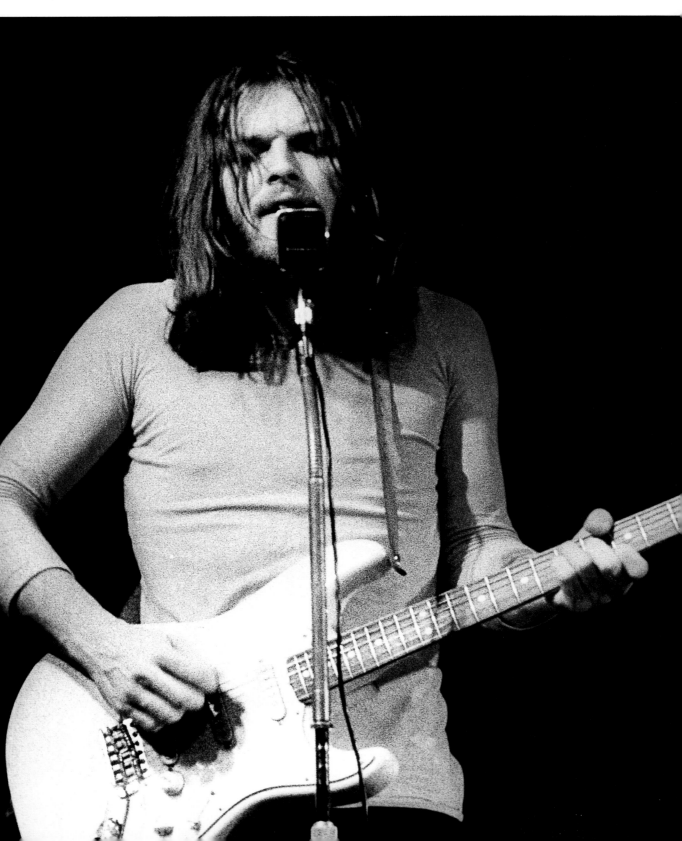

Left: David Gilmour,
Théâtre des Champs-Elysées,
Paris, January 1970

some commentary, so Roy Battersby, the director, was forced to get his mate Vanessa Redgrave, who was in the Workers Revolutionary Party, and they did lots of pansy, posey stuff over it, poems and things, that took the whole heat out of it.'[3]

It is not widely known that the other members of Pink Floyd also appear on the album – on the final track, 'Give Birth To A Smile' – for which they were paid as session musicians and remain uncredited. Waters and Geesin both wanted a four-piece band, and the others willingly obliged. '"You want a big sound,"' Geesin remembers them saying, '"well here we are!"'[4]

Back on the touring circuit, during the early months of 1970 the band had begun to tour with the aforementioned out-take from *Zabriskie Point*, 'The Violent Sequence'; some reworked tracks from the studio half of *Ummagumma*; and two new numbers, one of which was called 'The Embryo'. This had first been worked on in the studio during the latter part of 1968 and a version had been recorded for a BBC session in December of that year. The track is surrounded by a certain amount of controversy since it was never officially sanctioned by the band for release, although it is said that a studio recording was unwittingly authorized by the then Harvest label manager, Malcolm Jones, for inclusion on the sampler album *Picnic*. Except for its appearance on the 1983 Capitol Records Pink Floyd compilation *Works*, the track has remained unreleased, and *Picnic* is now something of a rarity. Surprisingly, given their reluctance to see it released, the band often played the song live during the early seventies.

The other number the band had started to work on in the early part of 1970 was an untitled instrumental which in later months became known as 'Atom Heart Mother'. The track was initiated entirely in the studio and would eventually fill one side of their new album of the same title, where it would feature a ten-piece brass section, a solo cello and a twenty-voice choir.

In its earliest live performance it incorporated a lengthy drum solo and featured Gilmour and Wright vocalizing on what would develop into the familiar choral section. By March, a basic studio recording had been made at Abbey Road, featuring Waters and Mason on bass and drums.

At this stage Geesin was invited to help out with the track. 'Roger proposed to me that I should help Floyd with their next album. He said he would like me to write the brass and choir pieces.... Floyd were off to the States then, and Roger left me with a skeleton tape of rhythm and chords. It was to be a twenty-five-minute piece – and that's a hell of a lot of work.... Nobody knew what was wanted, they couldn't read music.'[5]

With time running short, and a second US tour scheduled for the autumn, the number had to be recorded fast. As Geesin recalled: 'Dave proposed strict ideas for melodies, and then we did the choir section together, both at keyboards collaborating with Rick. We all had sleepless nights, worrying about what was going on.... Well, it got done, but then the thing had to be recorded with the brass band, orchestra and choir.'[6]

It was here that Geesin ran into trouble and came close to a complete breakdown. The pressure of work was piling up and the cantankerous nature of some of the orchestral musicians was driving him to despair. 'I could see the orchestra tuning up and the band playing in all bloody directions, playing different tunes, because I'm not a conductor, simply because I'm self-taught. Conductors are now essential in modern music. I was incapable of telling them what to do. Things were looking terrible, nobody

Technische Universität, West Berlin, 13 March 1970

knew what was going to happen. But then John Aldiss, who was in charge of the best modern choir in the classical area, came to collect the choir parts, and saw our plight. I became adviser, and he the conductor.'[7]

Even Gilmour couldn't help but notice the problems Geesin was facing with the orchestra. 'In the studio they were pretty annoying sometimes, they always used to rush off to the canteen whenever they had the chance, and split right on the dot when the session was over. Towards the end of recording the album it all seemed to get a bit warped. Some of it seems a bit messy, when I listen to it now little things jump out at me and I think, "shouldn't have done that."'[8]

Although Pink Floyd had been performing the piece for some months, the official premiere of 'Atom Heart Mother' took place at the Bath Festival in June, with, for the first time on stage, a full orchestra and choir. This was one of only a handful of occasions over the next year when a brass and choir section would accompany the band live.

The piece was announced as 'The Amazing Pudding' since they still hadn't figured out a suitable title. When the time came to choose one it was all done in the usual rush. The band were previewing a performance of the piece for a live John Peel BBC Radio One concert session at the Paris Cinema before their Hyde Park concert two days later and the title had to be registered for royalties and the DJ had to have an official title by which to introduce it. Geesin explained: 'We were sitting in the control room and John Peel had his newspaper [the *Evening Standard*] and we were sitting round with Nick, Roger and the others. I think they were all there saying, "We haven't got a title for this", and I said, "If you look in there you'll find a title", and then Roger picked up the paper and said, "Atomic Heart Mother" and the others said, "Yeah, that sounds good."'[9]

Gilmour spoke at the time of the problems in taking the new work on the road: 'Something on the scale of "Atom Heart Mother" really takes a lot of getting together. The problem is that we've never done it more than twice with the same people. The choir is usually all right because they're used to working together, but some of the brass people have been really hopeless. We had problems with the sound equipment, getting it miked up and balanced and stuff. The trouble was also not having enough rehearsal time everywhere we did it, because we used a different brass and choir group in Europe than the one we used on the East Coast, and another one on the West Coast. So we used three completely different sets of people performing it. We tried to hire musicians from local symphonies, if possible. Often we couldn't get them all from local symphonies, so we'd just get session musicians. We found our conductor, Peter Phillips, by coming over and looking for someone a couple of months before the tour...'[10]

The album *Atom Heart Mother* is well balanced, with contributions from each member of the band except Mason, who is only a part-composer of the title track. There are only four other numbers on the album, three of which have a very summery, bluesy feel to them: Waters' 'If' (performed rarely at this time, but more frequently on his solo tours); Wright's 'Summer

'68'; and Gilmour's 'Fat Old Sun', which was performed live throughout the year, and had been written at the same time as Waters' 'Grantchester Meadows'.

The closing track, 'Alan's Psychedelic Breakfast', is typical Floyd experimentation. As Waters explained: 'It was the usual thing of an idea coming out of the fact that we'd almost finished an LP but not quite and we needed another so many minutes. We were all frantically trying to write songs, and initially I thought of just doing something on the rhythm of a dripping tap, then it turned into this whole kitchen thing. On the record it's a carefully set up stereo picture of a kitchen with somebody coming in, opening a window, filling a kettle and putting it on the stove. But instead of the gas lighting, there's a chord, so he strikes a match and there's another chord, and so on until it finally goes into a piece of music.'[11]

The kitchen sounds, along with an amusing conversation with Alan Stiles, one of the roadies, were recorded for the most part in Mason's kitchen. The music was added at Abbey Road. Because of its novelty, the track was rarely performed live – only a handful of UK shows in the run-up to Christmas featured it. Waters was anticipating the problems it would cause when he spoke to *Sounds* about it shortly before the tour: 'The logistics of doing it live are quite difficult – we can't obviously take a set of a kitchen round with us and do it all, but we'll have to have some table arrangement to fry eggs on and boil kettles and everything.' This was a task eventually left to the roadies, who, to the accompaniment of broadcaster and DJ Jimmy Young's trademark 'Oft we jolly well go', fried eggs and bacon and made tea on stage. To round off the festive spirit, Mason often dressed up as Father Christmas.

The album's title track caught the attention of Stanley Kubrick, who wanted to use the music in his adaptation of Anthony Burgess's novel *A Clockwork Orange*. 'He wanted to use "Atom Heart Mother",' said Waters, 'and chop and change it about. He just phoned up and said that he wanted it and we said, "well, what do you want to do?" and he didn't know, he just said he wanted to use it, "how I want – when I want". And we said right away, "right, you can't use it."'[12] It is difficult to imagine the film carrying this music – maybe it is just as well it wasn't used after all.

Atom Heart Mother, with its striking sleeve picture of a cow, was in keeping with Pink Floyd's already established sense of the absurd. Posters for the album depicted herds of cattle on The Mall in London (which was closed at dawn to create the image). The success of the promotion played a part in gaining the band their very first number one in the UK's album chart.

With 1971 barely started there was already mounting pressure on Pink Floyd to release new product hot on the heels of the success of *Atom Heart Mother*. Losing little time, they entered the studio in early January for their usual round of brainstorming sessions. It was the first time they were not contractually obliged to use EMI's facilities at Abbey Road and much of the recording of the new album, Meddle, took place at Air, Command and Morgan Sound studios.

Recognizing how long it would take the band to record the album, not least because of their heavy touring commitments, EMI decided to sate the appetite of eager fans in the meantime by releasing a budget-priced compilation album entitled *Relics - A Collection Of Bizarre Antiques And Curios*. Released in May, this stop-gap, with a cover

Poster for Pink Floyd at Pepperland, 16–17 October 1970

illustration by Mason, contained a collection of works from the band's early years, single tracks available for the first time since their deletion and a previously unreleased number, 'Biding My Time'.

The initial *Meddle* sessions at Abbey Road produced some remarkable work. Extending the ideas they had applied on 'Alan's Psychedelic Breakfast', the band put together a whole album without using any musical instruments whatsoever.

It was a complicated process involving the use of kitchen utensils, bottles, cutlery, glasses, lampshades and even sawing up bits of wood, to replicate conventional sounds.

But the 'household objects' project, as it is often referred to, was never to come to fruition. Despite efforts to revive the idea in late 1973, Gilmour felt that it just wasn't worth the time and trouble required to complete even the most basic of sequences: 'We actually built a thing with a stretched rubber band this long [about two feet]. There was a g-clamp this end fixing it to a table and this end there was a cigarette lighter for a bridge. And then there were a set of match-sticks taped down this end. You stretch it and you can get a really good bass sound. Oh, and we used aerosol sprays and pulling rolls of sellotape out to different lengths — the further away it gets the note changes. We got three or four tracks down. It'd be very hard to make any of them really work as a piece of genuine music.'[13]

In addition, the sounds were almost impossible to reproduce live, so it is hardly surprising that the band finally shelved their work on the project.

Over the next few weeks their collective brain developed an epic twenty-minute track with the working title 'Nothing – Parts 1 to 24'. Collecting together twenty-four completely unconnected pieces of music, and using many ideas from the previous sessions, they worked it into shape and performed it live for the first time in April as 'Return Of The Son Of Nothing'. The piece had this title for some months until, when released as a full side of *Meddle*, it was retitled 'Echoes'.

Many fans regard this track as Pink Floyd's masterpiece – a calling card for legions of stoned freaks, the ultimate stereophonic blast-off into inner space both in concert and on vinyl. The band's last great outing into the realms of science-fiction fantasy, it was to prove a live favourite for many years to come and was used in the surfing film *Crystal Voyager* to accompany spectacular underwater shots and wave tunnels.

Only one other track remains a stand-out: 'One Of These Days'. Another live stalwart, this pounding, bass-driven instrumental was developed from a studio experiment that originally featured a vocal tape loop of the venerable Jimmy Young and the BBC Radiophonic Workshop's theme to *Dr Who*. The track features Mason's first and last lead vocal, a garbled one-liner: 'One of these days I'm going to cut you into little pieces', before launching into slide-guitar mayhem. Incidentally, Young was again the butt of Pink Floyd's stoned humour when they chopped up tape recordings of his *Family Favourites* show to make hilarious and nonsensical introductions to their shows throughout the early seventies.

By comparison, the remaining tracks are subdued and very reminiscent of the material on *Atom Heart Mother*, none of which was ever performed live. 'Fearless' is a successful experiment which segues a football crowd singing the terrace anthem 'You'll Never Walk Alone' into the last few seconds of the song – a reminder of Pink Floyd's collective passion for the sport.

To close side one of the album, another throw-away number, typical of the band's sense of humour when it came to improvisation, was added. This time they used a howling dog for lead vocals. 'Dave was looking after Seamus while Steve Marriott [the dog's owner, who was on tour with Humble Pie] was in the States, and he used to bring him into the sessions,' explained Waters, 'and one day he said, "There's something I meant to show you – this dog sings", and he got a harmonica out and blew it at the dog, and as soon as the dog hears a harmonica it starts howling. So we all thought we'd do a short 12-bar and stick him on it.'[14]

Meddle was released in November and featured

Roger Waters, Palais des Sports, Lyon, 12 June 1971

another Hipgnosis sleeve design. It featured a close-up photograph of an ear slightly submerged in rippling water, while the inner sleeve shows a group portrait – the last time the band would be visually identified on an album for some sixteen years, an absence which was to increase their mystique with the public.

With *Meddle* only recently wrapped up and their second US tour of the year just around the corner, the band linked up with Adrian Maben, a French film director backed by German money, who planned to film them in concert. Keen to avoid the usual 'rockumentary'-style presentation, together they hit upon the idea of the band performing without an audience against the spectacular backdrop of the ancient Roman amphitheatre at Pompeii in Italy.

Filming for *Pink Floyd Live At Pompeii* took place between 4 and 7 October 1971 in weather that was still fairly warm. The entire stage set-up was located inside the dusty ruined amphitheatre and complete concert run-throughs, performed day and night, were successfully filmed.

The most popular numbers from the band's current repertoire were used. These included 'Echoes' (split into two halves to open and close the film), 'Careful With That Axe Eugene', 'A Saucerful Of Secrets', 'Set The Controls For The Heart Of The Sun', 'One Of These Days (I'm Going To Cut You Into Little Pieces)' and 'Mademoiselle Nobs'. This last track, a retitling of 'Seamus', is an hilarious sequence in which Wright holds the microphone up to the infamous howling dog while Gilmour blasts away on his harmonica.

Some additional live sequences were shot at a TV studio in Paris between 13 and 20 December and further material was added from an early 1972 recording session at Abbey Road which featured the band at work on the album *Dark Side Of The Moon*. Finally, and to much surprise, the film opened with the album's prelude, 'Speak To

Me', which sets the scene by combining images of the ruined city and the band's road crew assembling their array of equipment. Interspersed throughout the film are brief candid interviews with the band.

Pink Floyd Live At Pompeii was previewed at the Edinburgh Film Festival in the summer of 1972, to rave reviews, and given general cinematic release a year later. A scheduled preview at London's Rainbow Theatre on 25 November 1971 was cancelled because the owners of the theatre, the Rank Organisation, gave the promoter just one day's notice of a previously ignored clause in the lease forbidding the showing of cinematic films at the venue. Rank backed up its decision by claiming that the film had not yet been given a certificate by the British Board of Film Censors, and all 3,000 ticket holders had to be turned away.

As 1971 drew to a close, Pink Floyd's touring schedule was already stretching well into 1973. However, they were very aware that their stage material was becoming rather stale – a point that hadn't escaped the music press – and decided to apply themselves to the task of composing an entirely new set of numbers for their imminent UK tour. Free for the moment from pressure to record a new album, they could perfect new material on the road more extensively than they had been able to do in the past, before going into the studio.

Notes
1. *Disc*, 23.8.75
2. *Beetle*, May 1973
3–7. Authors' interview with Ron Geesin, 16.7.94
8. Unidentified press article
9. Authors' interview with Ron Geesin 16.7.94
10. *Music Now*, 28.11.70; *Beetle*, May 1973
11. *Sounds*, 10.10.70
12. *Great Lake*, April 1973
13. *Sounds*, c.1974
14. *NME*, December 1971

1970

■ 10.1.70
The Ballroom, University of Nottingham, Beeston, Nottinghamshire, England.
Set list: Astronomy Dominé/ Green Is The Colour-Careful With That Axe Eugene/Set The Controls For The Heart Of The Sun/A Saucerful Of Secrets.

■ 17.1.70
Lawns Centre, Cottingham, Yorkshire, England.
Presented by Hull University. Set list included: Astronomy Dominé/Green Is The Colour – Careful With That Axe Eugene/ Atom Heart Mother*/Set The Controls For The Heart Of The Sun/encore: A Saucerful Of Secrets.
*This number has been titled retrospectively for identification purposes; the title was not formally adopted until 16.7.70.

■ 18.1.70
Fairfield Halls, Croydon, Surrey, England.
Set list: Careful With That Axe Eugene/The Embryo/Main Theme from *More*/Biding My Time/Astronomy Dominé/The Violent Sequence/Set The Controls For The Heart Of The Sun/Atom Heart Mother/encore: A Saucerful Of Secrets.
'There was a standing ovation, there was an encore.... Make no mistake, Pink Floyd are good. More than that, they are originals, and have been so since earlier days when they practically invented psychedelia. They are individually adept as musicians and command a range of instruments, Rick Wright for instance played organ, piano, trombone and vibraphone at Sunday's concert. Anything can be legitimately used in creating the atmosphere: recourse to heavy timpani, violent assault on cymbal, flogging a gargantuan gong and insistent thumping of fingers on microphones. Pink Floyd are obsessed with the mystery of outer space – "Set

The Controls For The Heart Of The Sun" and "Interstellar Overdrive" are two titles – and portray it with imagination. Yet the fact remains that their concert on Sunday was marred by repetitive phrasing, by long unmelodic passages, by monotony.... Perhaps with the lighting effects they have abandoned the sterile patches would not have been so noticeable.... Still it was a long concert – nearly three hours – for Messrs. Waters, Wright, Mason and Gilmore to fill. I liked particularly, the contributions of Wright, including funereal excursions of organ playing in the traumatic "Saucerful Of Secrets" and his unhurried, halcyon piano in "Niagara Dellof"*, which was like a respite from a storm – and which was deservedly applauded. Drummer Nick Mason has said: "People have the confidence that if we do something extraordinary, it's quite likely not to be a giant con and there's some purpose or meaning behind it." Certainly not a "con" – but the end product was lamentably, just lacking.' (*Croydon Advertiser*, reproduced by kind permission of the Croydon Advertiser Group)
*This title has not appeared in any other reference to the band's output. Although the piece may have been introduced as such at this concert we suspect it was 'The Violent Sequence'.

■ 19.1.70
The Dome, Brighton, East Sussex, England
Set list included: Careful With That Axe Eugene/The Embryo/Main Theme from *More*/Atom Heart Mother/Astronomy Dominé/Set The Controls For The Heart Of The Sun/A Saucerful Of Secrets.

FRENCH TOUR
■ 23.1.70
Théâtre des Champs-Elysées, Elysée, Paris, France.
Set list: Green Is The Colour –

Careful With That Axe Eugene/ The Violent Sequence/Biding My Time/Atom Heart Mother/ Daybreak/ Sleeping/Main Theme from *More*/A Saucerful Of Secrets.

■ 24.1.70
Théâtre des Champs-Elysées, Elysée, Paris, France.
Set list included: The Man/Set The Controls For The Heart Of The Sun.

■ 2.2.70
Palais des Sports, Lyon, France.
Set list included: The Man// Astronomy Dominé/The Violent Sequence/Set The Controls For The Heart Of The Sun. The last night of the tour. It may have been recorded for radio and broadcast in part on France's Europe 1.

■ 5.2.70
Cardiff Arts Centre Project Benefit Concert, Sophia Gardens Pavilion, Cardiff, South Glamorgan, Wales.
With Quintessence, Daddy Longlegs, Gary Farr, Heaven, Ron Geesin, Tea & Symphony and Black Sabbath.

■ 7.2.70
Royal Albert Hall, Kensington, London, England.

Set list: The Embryo/Main Theme from *More*/Careful With That Axe Eugene/Sysyphus//The Violent Sequence/Atom Heart Mother/Set The Controls For The Heart Of The Sun/encore: A Saucerful Of Secrets.

■ **8.2.70**
Opera House, Manchester, Lancashire, England.
Set list: The Embryo/Careful With That Axe Eugene/Main Theme from *More*/Sysyphus/ Atom Heart Mother/Set The Controls For The Heart Of The Sun/Astronomy Dominé.

Heart Mother.

■ **14.2.70**
King's Hall, The Town Hall, Stoke-on-Trent, Staffordshire, England.
Presented by North Staffordshire Polytechnic.

■ **15.2.70**
Empire Theatre, Liverpool, Lancashire, England.
The Embryo/Careful With That Axe Eugene/Main Theme from *More*/Atom Heart Mother/Astronomy Dominé/Interstellar Overdrive/ Set The Controls For The Heart Of The Sun/A Saucerful Of

Secrets/Set The Controls For The Heart Of The Sun.

■ **23.2.70**
McEwan Hall, University of Edinburgh, Edinburgh, Lothian, Scotland.

■ **28.2.70**
Refectory Hall, University Union, Leeds University, Leeds, Yorkshire, England.
Supported by Heavy Jelly.
Set list: The Embryo/Careful With That Axe Eugene/Set The Controls For The Heart Of The Sun/Atom Heart Mother/A Saucerful Of Secrets/encore:

Set list included: Atom Heart Mother/Set The Controls For The Heart Of The Sun/A Saucerful Of Secrets.

■ **7.3.70**
University of Bristol Arts Festival – Timespace, Colston Hall, Bristol, Gloucestershire–Somerset, England.
'Tea-time at the week-end isn't exactly the right moment to suffer the violence and intensity of a Floyd concert [it began at 3.00pm]. Their music's so involving, sometimes overpowering, that the time of day should have been a positive disadvantage. It didn't matter too much however. They somehow generated the right enthusiasm and turned a lazy afternoon into a full, now and again, frightening experience. This show had its faults. The volume on a couple of their disturbing destructive numbers was quite terrifying, enough to make you feel physically ill. Maybe that's what they were after. But in their melancholy numbers – particularly the "Main Theme" from "More" – they created a sumptuous atmosphere of sadness and regret. The music was effective and it was a thoughtful, worthwhile show.' (*Bristol Evening Post*)

■ **8.3.70**
Mothers, Erdington, Birmingham, Warwickshire, England.
Set list: The Embryo/A Saucerful of Secrets/Set The Controls For The Heart Of The Sun/Careful With That Axe Eugene/Astronomy Dominé/Atom Heart Mother/encore: Blues*.
*Where 'Blues' appears in a set list it indicates an improvised twelve-bar blues intrumental, a common addition to Pink Floyd's set throughout the next couple of years.

■ **9.3.70**
City (Oval) Hall, Sheffield, Yorkshire, England.

Robert Shearer presents

PINK FLOYD

at the
OPERA HOUSE, MANCHESTER

SUNDAY, FEBRUARY 8th, at 7.30 p.m.

Tel. Box Office 061 BLA 1787

PINK FLOYD IN CONCERT
Progressive Pop from London
AUDITORIUM MAXIMUM (Von-Melle-Park)
KLEINER SAAL links
Donnerstag, 12. März 1970, 20 Uhr
12.
März
DM 8.— 12 3
20 Uhr

■ **11.2.70**
Town Hall, Birmingham, Warwickshire, England.
Set list: The Embryo/Main Theme from *More*/Careful With That Axe Eugene/Sysyphus/The Violent Sequence/Set The Controls For The Heart Of The Sun/Atom

Secrets.

■ **17.2.70**
City Hall, Newcastle, Northumberland, England.

■ **22.2.70**
The Electric Garden, Glasgow, Lanarkshire, Scotland.
Set list included: A Saucerful Of

Interstellar Overdrive.

■ **6.3.70**
Great Hall, College Block, Imperial College, London, England.
Supported by Juicy Lucy with Tom & Jerry cartoons shown between bands.

EUROPEAN TOUR

■ **11.3.70**
Stadthalle, Offenbach, West Germany.
Set list: Astronomy Dominé/Green Is The Colour – Careful With That Axe Eugene/Cymbaline/A Saucerful Of Secrets/Interstellar Overdrive/Set The Controls For The Heart Of The Sun/Atom Heart Mother.

■ **12.3.70**
Kleiner Saal, Auditorium Maximum, Hamburg Universität, Hamburg, West Germany.
Set list: Astronomy Dominé/Careful With That Axe Eugene/Cymbaline/A Saucerful Of Secrets/The Embryo/Interstellar Overdrive/Set The Controls For The Heart Of The Sun/Atom Heart Mother.

■ **13.3.70**
Konzert Saal, Technische Universität, West Berlin, West Germany.
Set list: Astronomy Dominé/Careful With That Axe Eugene/Cymbaline/A Saucerful Of Secrets/The Embryo/Interstellar Overdrive/Set The Controls For The Heart Of The Sun/Atom Heart Mother/encore: Blues.

■ **14.3.70**
Meistersinger Halle, Nuremberg, West Germany.
Set list: Astronomy Dominé/Careful With That Axe Eugene/Cymbaline/A Saucerful of Secrets/The Embryo/Interstellar Overdrive/Set The Controls For The Heart Of The Sun/Atom Heart Mother.

■ **15.3.70**
Niedersachsenhalle, Hannover, West Germany.
Set list: Astronomy Dominé/Careful With That Axe Eugene/Cymbaline/A Saucerful Of Secrets/The Embryo/Interstellar Overdrive/Set The Controls For The Heart Of The Sun/Atom Heart Mother (announced as 'Consequently').

■ **19.3.70**
Konserthuset, Stockholm, Sweden.
This show replaced one scheduled for the previous day at Gothenburg which was cancelled.
Set list included: Interstellar Overdrive/Main Theme from *More*/A Saucerful Of Secrets/Atom Heart Mother.

■ **20.3.70**
Akademiska Föreningens Stora Sal, Lund, Sweden.
Set list: Astronomy Dominé/Careful With That Axe Eugene/Cymbaline/A Saucerful of Secrets/The Embryo/Interstellar Overdrive/Set The Controls For The Heart Of The Sun/Atom Heart Mother.

■ **21.3.70**
Tivolis Koncertsal, Copenhagen, Denmark.
The last night of the tour.
Set list included: A Saucerful Of Secrets/Interstellar Overdrive/Set The Controls For The Heart Of The Sun.

■ **30.3.70**
Le Festival Musique Evolution, Le Bourget – Aéroport de Paris, France.
With, among others, Ginger Baker's Airforce, Procol Harum, Kevin Ayres And The Whole World, Keith Relf's Renaissance, Hawkwind, The Edgar Broughton Band, Skin Alley and Le Voyage.
This, the first officially sanctioned music festival in France, was staged in an aircraft hangar. It promised to be quite an event, with many top name bands performing, film shows, light-shows, cheap food, camping and a 'pop village' with market stalls. As it turned out, two adjoining stages accommodated the live entertainment, but little else materialized. Repeatedly, groups were not ready to play, leaving an audience that was far smaller than anticipated listening to impromptu jams by roadies and stray musicians. In addition, food prices were inflated and no authorization was given for camping, so that those who did try to pitch tents were evicted by the police. Cold winds blasted through the hangar, which now doubled as accommodation.
RTL radio and French TV crews covered the event with live transmissions and commentary and almost certainly broadcast parts of Pink Floyd's set, although the transmission dates cannot be confirmed.

NORTH AMERICAN TOUR

■ **9.4.70**
Fillmore East, Manhattan, New York City, New York, USA.
The band took the Azimuth Co-ordinator to the USA for the first time.

■ **10.4.70**
Aragon Ballroom, Chicago, Illinois, USA.
With Rotary Connection, Mason Proffit and Litter.

■ **11.4.70**
State University of New York, Stony Brook, Long Island, New York, USA.
Set list: Astronomy Dominé/Careful With That Axe Eugene/Cymbaline/Atom Heart Mother/Set The Controls For The Heart Of The Sun/A Saucerful of Secrets.

■ **16.4.70**
Fillmore East, Manhattan, New York City, New York, USA.
Set list: Grantchester Meadows/Astronomy Dominé/Main Theme from *More*/The Violent Sequence/Atom Heart Mother/Set The Controls For The Heart Of The Sun/encore: A Saucerful Of Secrets.

■ **17,18.4.70**
Electric Factory, Philadelphia, Pennsylvania, USA.
Two shows, at 8.00pm and 11.00pm. Supported by Insect Trust.

■ **22.4.70**
Capitol Theatre, Port Chester, New York, USA

■ **24,25.4.70**
Eastown Theatre, Detroit, Michigan, USA. With The Frost and The Up.

■ **29.4.70**
KQED TV Studios, San Francisco, California, USA.
Set list: Atom Heart Mother/Cymbaline/Grantchester Meadows/Green Is The Colour – Careful With That Axe Eugene/Set The Controls For The Heart Of The Sun.
This was a live concert performance recorded before the evening show with no audience. It was filmed for future broadcast on the US PBS network and video effects and miscellaneous library footage were added.

■ **29.4.70**
Fillmore West, San Francisco, California, USA.
Evening show.
Set list: Grantchester Meadows/Astronomy Dominé/Cymbaline/Atom Heart Mother/The Embryo/Green Is The Colour – Careful With That Axe Eugene/Set The Controls For The Heart Of The Sun/encore: A Saucerful of Secrets.

■ **1.5.70**
Civic Auditorium, Santa Monica, Los Angeles, California, USA.
Set list: Grantchester Meadows/Astronomy Dominé/Cymbaline/Atom Heart Mother/The Embryo/Set The Controls For The Heart Of The Sun/encore: Interstellar Overdrive.

■ **6.5.70**
Royce Hall, University of California Los Angeles, Los Angeles, California, USA.
In early May, UCLA, like many student campus sites, saw anti-government protests, and in the wake of rioting at Kent State University, Ohio, was preparing for battle itself.
Melody Maker reported that Pink Floyd played a free concert for some 10,000 students which even the National Guardsmen, complete with helmets, riot shields and rifles, seemed to enjoy.

Overleaf: Pink Floyd, 1970

TICKETS:
$4.00

■ 9.5.70
Terrace Ballroom, Salt Lake City, Utah, USA.
Supported by Blue Mountain Eagle.
■ 12.5.70
Municipal Auditorium, Atlanta, Georgia, USA.
Supporting The Guess Who.
■ 16.5.70
The Warehouse, New Orleans, Louisiana, USA.
With The Allman Brothers Band and Country Funk.
The band had $40,000 worth of equipment stolen out of their hired truck while they slept after the gig. The entire contents were taken: four electric guitars, an electric organ, a 4,000-watt sound system with twelve speaker cabinets, five Italian echo units, microphones, two drum kits and ten miles of cable.
'We sat down at our hotel thinking – well that's it. It's all over. We were pouring out our troubles to a girl who worked at the hotel and she said her father worked for the FBI. The police hadn't helped us much, but the FBI got to work and four hours later it was found.' (Nick Mason,

Melody Maker)
■ 22.5.70
Houston Music Theatre, Houston, Texas, USA.
Two shows, at 7.00pm and 10.00pm. Supporting Grand Funk Railroad. Both shows were cancelled on the day.
■ 23.5.70
State Fair Music Hall, Dallas, Texas, USA.
Supporting Grand Funk Railroad. The last night of the tour.
At some stage during the tour Pink Floyd had been invited to perform at a voodoo and science-fiction convention but the American Musicians' Union vetoed their participation.
■ 27.6.70
Bath Festival of Blues & Progressive Music '70, Bath & West Showgound, Shepton Mallet, Somerset, England.
With Led Zeppelin, Canned Heat, Steppenwolf, Johnny Winter, It's A Beautiful Day, Fairport Convention, Colosseum, Keef Hartley, Jefferson Airplane, Frank Zappa And The Mothers of Invention,

The Moody Blues, The Byrds, Flock, Santana, Dr John, Country Joe and Hot Tuna, and comperes John Peel and Mike Raven.
Set list: Green Is The Colour – Careful With That Axe Eugene/A Saucerful of Secrets/Set The Controls For The Heart Of The Sun/Atom Heart Mother (announced as 'The Amazing Pudding', with the Philip Jones Brass Ensemble and the John Aldiss Choir, conducted by John Aldiss).
This huge three-day event (26–28.6.70), which inspired Michael Eavis to stage the first Glastonbury Festival attracted twice the anticipated audience. A rough estimate put the attendance at 150,000 and the traffic generated by the festival caused the biggest jams in Somerset's history.
'We were into the early hours of Sunday morning before Pink Floyd made it on stage. They took a very long time to set up but their act was worth it. People were getting tired but the spectacular close to their set

woke everyone up. After laying down some good sounds they were joined by a choir, about 12 strong, and a brass section and went into a 20 minute thing which will be one side of their new album. It was a heavenly sound. The finale saw three flares bursting open the sky with a galaxy of colours – smoke and the light show flooded the stage. It was amazing.' (*Disc & Music Echo*)
■ 28.6.70
The Holland Pop Festival 70, Kralingse Bos, Rotterdam, Netherlands.
With Jefferson Airplane, Santana, Flock, Canned Heat, Hot Tuna, Quintessence, East of Eden, The Byrds, Family, Dr John, Country Joe, Tyrannosaurus Rex, Renaissance, The Third Ear Band, Al Stewart, Soft Machine, The Chicago Art Ensemble, John Surman, Caravan, Fairport Convention, Fotheringay and others.
Set list: Astronomy Dominé/ Green Is The Colour – Careful With That Axe Eugene/Atom Heart Mother/Set The Controls

For The Heart Of The Sun/A Saucerful Of Secrets/encore: Interstellar Overdrive. Sponsored by Coca-Cola, the three-day Holland Pop Festival (26–28.6.70) had a reciprocal agreement with the Bath Festival that enabled many of the artists to perform at both. Pink Floyd took to the stage late in the evening of the last day without the special effects, light-show and orchestra. A film was made of the event that included the band's performance of 'Set The Controls For The Heart Of The Sun' and 'A Saucerful Of Secrets'. Released at the cinema as *Stamping Ground*, this has also appeared on video under this title and their performance has also featured on many 'various artists' video compilations, including a recent Australian release entitled *Psychomania!* (Music World Video GEMTV-474)

■ **12.7.70**
1st Open Air Pop Festival, Reiterstadion Soers, Aachen, West Germany.
With Taste, Hardin and York, Keef Hartley, If, Fat Mattress, Champion Jack Dupree, Quintessence, Caravan, Golden Earring, Amon Düül II, Kevin Ayres And The Whole World, Traffic, The Edgar Broughton Band, Tyrannosaurus Rex, Deep Purple and others. Pink Floyd headlined on the final day of this three-day festival (10–12.7.70). Set list: Astronomy Dominé/Green Is The Colour – Careful With That Axe Eugene/ Atom Heart Mother/ Set The Controls For The Heart Of The Sun/A Saucerful Of Secrets/encore: Interstellar Overdrive.

■ **16.7.70**
BBC Paris Cinema, Regent Street, London, England
A live audience recording session for BBC Radio One in which the band performed 'The Embryo', 'Fat Old Sun', 'Green Is The Colour', 'Careful With That Axe Eugene', 'If' and 'Atom Heart Mother' (with the Philip Jones Brass Ensemble and the John Aldiss Choir, conducted by John Aldiss) for Peel's Sunday Concert. It was broadcast on 19.7.70 at 4.00pm and repeated on the *Sounds of The Seventies* on 22.7.70 at 6.00pm.

■ **18.7.70**
Blackhill's Garden Party – Hyde Park Free Concert, Hyde Park, London, England.
With The Third Ear Band, Kevin Ayres And The Whole World, The Edgar Broughton Band and DJ Jeff Dexter.
Set list: The Embryo/Green Is The Colour – Careful With That Axe Eugene/Set The Controls For The Heart Of The Sun/Atom Heart Mother (announced as 'The Atomic Heart Mother', with the Philip Jones Brass Ensemble and the John Aldiss Choir, conducted by John Aldiss). 'Over five

Hyde Park, 18 July 1970

hours of varied and contrasting music was topped by a performance from the Pink Floyd, who treated the gathering to a preview of their forthcoming album…. [They] gave an hour of beautifully mature music, soothing and inspiring to listen to. They kept the numbers short, apart from the finale, and carefully restrained. With the sun glinting on Nick Mason's drums and the clouds breaking up overhead, it seemed as if the sounds were dropping from the sky itself. After a quiet and lazy, bluesy, introduction, they went gently into "Green Is The Colour" and "Careful With That Axe Eugene". Even in the latter the volume was down, and the mood reflective. "Set The Controls For The Heart Of the Sun" was` at its most ethereal, the smooth crescendos flying away over the heads of the captivated audience. To end, a brass section and choir were brought on for the 25-minute finale. The piece began with an arrangement for the brass, and then switched into a lengthy choir pattern, followed by a dash of marvellous Floyd rock-jazz. In came the brass again, pursued by incantations from the choir and swirling special effects in twin-channel stereo. A reprise took up the original theme – based on a simple chord progression akin to the finale of "The Man" – and group, choir and orchestra projected it together in fine combination.' (*Disc & Music Echo*)

■ **26.7.70**
XI Festival International de Jazz, Antibes, Juan-les-Pins, France.
Part of the festival, possibly including Pink Floyd, was reportedly recorded and broadcast on French TV later in the year.

■ **1.8.70**
Festival d'Aix-en-Provence, Aix-en-Provence, France.
Pink Floyd, Derek & The Dominoes, Soft Machine, Traffic and Balls were all booked to appear at this three-day festival but it was abandoned on the first day because of rioting.

■ **5.8.70**
Festival Maudit de Biot, Le Biot, France.
With Soft Machine, Daevid Allen's Gong, Kevin Ayres And The Whole World, Traffic, Joan Baez, Keith Emerson and others. The event was broadcast live in part by France's RTL Radio and may have included Pink Floyd.

■ **6.8.70**
Popanalia, Nice, France.
With Derek & The Dominoes, Soft Machine, Balls, Rare Bird, Country Joe, Joan Baez and others. Planned to last thirty-six hours, this event was abandoned soon after it started. When Soft Machine were told they wouldn't receive their contracted fee, they refused to perform, and as a result disgruntled fans rioted. Victims of the extensive damage included a Yamaha grand piano that was pushed off the stage and two RTL mobile recording trucks that were set on fire. Of the acts due to perform only Rare Bird, Country Joe and Joan Baez went on.

■ **8.8.70**
St Tropez Music Festival, St Tropez, France.
Set list included: Astronomy Dominé/Cymbaline/Atom Heart Mother/The Embryo/Set The Controls For The Heart Of The Sun.
Parts of the festival, including Pink Floyd, were reportedly recorded and broadcast on French TV.

■ **12.8.70**
Fête de St Raphaël, Les Arènas, St Raphaël, France.

■ **15.8.70**
Yorkshire Folk, Blues & Jazz Festival, Krumlin, Barkisland, Halifax, Yorkshire.
With Atomic Rooster, Juicy Lucy, Elton John, The Pretty Things, Alexis Korner, Pentangle, Fairport Convention, Ralph McTell, The Kinks, Taste, Yes and others.
Pink Floyd's headline show on the second day of this three-day

festival (14–16.8.70) was abandoned due to heavy rain. A report was printed in *The Times* of the disappearance of the promoter, who had suffered financial losses.

■ **26–30.8.70**
Isle of Wight Festival, East Afton Farm, Isle of Wight, England.

Pink Floyd provided the PA system for this legendary festival, and their chief engineer, Peter Watts, mixed the front-of-house sound for the whole event and was reportedly lent a hand by David Gilmour, who mixed Jimi Hendrix's performance.

■ **12.9.70**
Fête de L'Humanité, Grand Scène, Bois de Vincennes, Paris, France.

Set list: Astronomy Dominé/ Green Is The Colour – Careful With That Axe Eugene/ Set The Controls For The Heart Of The Sun/Atom Heart Mother (with brass and choir).

Pink Floyd were seen by over 500,000 people – their largest single concert attendance ever and a record that remains unbeaten. The event was recorded by French TV crews but has not been broadcast.

NORTH AMERICAN TOUR
The following shows were advertised but were either rescheduled or cancelled: Philadelphia (25.9), New York (26.9), Spokane (2.10), Seattle (3-5.10) and Boston (25.10).

■ **26.9.70**
Electric Factory, Philadelphia, Pennsylvania, USA..

Pink Floyd were a late addition, replacing Chicken Shack as support for Savoy Brown.

■ **27.9.70**
Fillmore East, Manhattan, New York City, New York, USA.

Two shows, at 6.00pm and 9.00pm.
Set list at late show: Astronomy Dominé/Green Is The Colour – Careful With That Axe Eugene/

Fat Old Sun/Set The Controls For The Heart Of The Sun/A Saucerful Of Secrets/encore: Atom Heart Mother (with brass and choir).

'The Pink Floyd trooped out on stage followed by about ten union horn men (dressed "down" for their gig at the Fillmore!), and a chorus of approximately 20 singers. All of this entourage was fronted by a conductor! They all proceeded to perform a type of rock–classically fused composition that lasted about an hour, and sounded like one of Blood, Sweat and Tears' more ambitious compositions at best. I really feel that if one mixes rock with classical music something more ought to come out of it than merely bad rock or bad classical music.'
(unidentified press report)

■ **1.10.70**
The Memorial Coliseum, Portland, Oregon, USA.

■ **2,3.10.70**
Moore Theatre, Seattle, Washington, USA.

Set list on 2.10.70 included: Set The Controls For The Heart Of The Sun/A Saucerful Of Secrets.

■ **4.10.70**
The Gymnasium, Gonzaga University, Spokane, Washington, USA.

unconfirmed appearance.

■ **6.10.70**
Central Washington University, Ellensburg, Washington, USA.

■ **7.10.70**
Gardens Arena, Vancouver, British Columbia, Canada.

Set list: Astronomy Dominé/Fat Old Sun/Cymbaline/The Embryo/ Atom Heart Mother/Green Is The Colour – Careful With That Axe Eugene/Set The Controls For The Heart Of The Sun/A Saucerful Of Secrets.

■ **8.10.70**
Jubilee Auditorium, Calgary, Alberta, Canada.

■ **9.10.70**
Sales Pavilion Annex,

Edmonton, Alberta, Canada.

■ **10.10.70**
Centennial Auditorium, Saskatoon, Saskatchewan, Canada.

■ **11.10.70**
Centre of The Arts, Regina, Saskatchewan, Canada.

Set list included: Green Is The Colour – Careful With That Axe Eugene/Cymbaline/A Saucerful Of Secrets/Atom Heart Mother.

■ **13.10.70**
Centennial Concert Hall, Winnipeg, Manitoba, Canada.

■ **15.10.70**
Terrace Ballroom, Salt Lake City, Utah, USA.

■ **16,17.10.70**
Pepperland Auditorium, San Raphael, California, USA.

Supported by Kimberley and Osceola.
Set list on 17.10.70: Astronomy Dominé/Fat Old Sun/ Cymbaline/Atom Heart Mother/ The Embryo/Green Is The Colour – Careful With That Axe Eugene/ Set The Controls For The Heart Of The Sun/encore: A Saucerful Of Secrets.

■ **21.10.70**
Fillmore West, San Francisco, California, USA.

Set list: Astronomy Dominé/Fat Old Sun/Green Is The Colour – Careful With That Axe Eugene/ Cymbaline/Set The Controls For The Heart Of The Sun/A Saucerful Of Secrets/Atom Heart Mother (with brass and choir conducted by Peter Philips)/ encore: Ave Maria (choir only).
'That was Pink Floyd on the Fillmore stage October 21st, along with the Roger Wagner Chorale, three French horns, three trombones, three trumpets, and a tuba. They were performing, for the second time ever on stage, the suite from "Atom Heart Mother". For an encore the Chorale did an "Ave Maria" written in 1562. "Atom Heart Mother" got a standing ovation, and bassist Roger

Waters introduced Wagner. But it was too much for some of the more dazed and die-hard Fillmore freaks: as the Chorale neared the "Amen", scattered give-me-back-my-candy shouts of "we want Pink Floyd" came through from the sides of the auditorium. If they didn't understand what Pink Floyd's music is all about in the first place, it is a bit puzzling why they spent $3 and four hours to come to see them. The music of Pink Floyd evokes images of cold, clear, far interstellar regions, of black moving water, of the exhilarating bleakness of the moon.' (*Rolling Stone*)

■ **23.10.70**
Civic Auditorium, Santa Monica, Los Angeles, California, USA.

The last night of the tour.
Set list: Astronomy Dominé/ Green Is The Colour – Careful With That Axe Eugene/Fat Old Sun/Set The Controls For The Heart Of The Sun/Cymbaline/A Saucerful Of Secrets/Atom Heart Mother (with the Roger Wagner Chorale and brass, conducted by Peter Philips)/encore: Interstellar Overdrive.

EUROPEAN TOUR
■ **6.11.70**
Concertgebouw, Amsterdam, Netherlands.

Set list: Astronomy Dominé/Fat Old Sun/Cymbaline/Atom Heart Mother/The Embryo/Green Is The Colour – Careful With That Axe Eugene/Set The Controls For The Heart Of The Sun/ encore: A Saucerful Of Secrets.

■ **7.11.70**
Grote Zaal, De Doelen, Rotterdam, Netherlands.

Set list: Astronomy Dominé/Fat Old Sun/Cymbaline/Atom Heart Mother/The Embryo/Green Is The Colour – Careful With That Axe Eugene/Set The Controls For The Heart Of The Sun/A Saucerful Of Secrets/encore: Blues.

■ **11.11.70**
Konserthuset, Gothenburg, Sweden.

■ **12.11.70**
Falkoner Centret,
Frederiksberg,
Copenhagen, Denmark.
Two evening shows.
Set list at early show: Astronomy
Dominé/Fat Old Sun/
Cymbaline/Atom Heart Mother/
Green Is The Colour – Careful
With That Axe Eugene/Set The
Controls For The Heart Of The
Sun/A Saucerful Of Secrets/
encore: The Embryo.
■ **13.11.70**
Vejlby Risskov Hallen,
Åarhus, Denmark.
Set list: Astronomy Dominé/Fat
Old Sun/Cymbaline/Atom Heart
Mother/The Embryo/Green Is
The Colour – Careful With That
Axe Eugene/Set The Controls
For The Heart Of The Sun/A
Saucerful Of Secrets/encore:
Blues.
■ **14.11.70**
Ernst-Merck Halle,
Hamburg, West Germany.
Set list: Astronomy Dominé/Fat
Old Sun/Cymbaline/improvisations
– The Embryo/Atom Heart
Mother/Green Is The Colour –
Careful With That Axe Eugene/
Set The Controls For The Heart
Of The Sun/encore: A Saucerful
Of Secrets.
■ **21.11.70**
Super Pop '70 VII, Casino
de Montreux, Montreux,
Switzerland.
With Krishna Lights.
Set list: Astronomy Dominé/Fat
Old Sun/Cymbaline/Atom Heart
Mother/The Embryo/Green Is
The Colour – Careful With That
Axe Eugene/Set The Controls
For The Heart Of The Sun/A
Saucerful Of Secrets/encore:
Interstellar Overdrive.
■ **22.11.70**
Super Pop '70 VII, Casino
de Montreux, Montreux,
Switzerland.
With Krishna Lights. Set list:
Astronomy Dominé/Fat Old
Sun/Cymbaline/Atom Heart
Mother/The Embryo/Green Is
The Colour – Careful With That
Axe Eugene/Set The Controls

For The Heart Of The Sun/A
Saucerful Of Secrets /encore:
Just Another 12 Bar/Blues.
This show, added at the last
minute, commenced at 2.30pm.
Both Montreux shows were
recorded and EMI pressed
white-label acetates which
included interviews with Gilmour
in French. However, it is likely
these would have been intended
as promotional tools, not for
commercial release. 'Just
Another 12 Bar' is a title shown
on the acetate and is simply an
improvised blues instrumental.
■ **23.11.70**
Grosser Konzerthaussaal,
Wiener Konzerthaus,
Vienna, Austria.
This show was cancelled when
snowdrifts blocking the roads
out of Montreux prevented the
band's equipment lorry getting
through. A replacement show
was planned for 29.11.70, but
this was also cancelled.
■ **25.11.70**
Friedrich Ebert Halle,
Ebertpark, Ludwigshafen,
West Germany.
Set list: Astronomy Dominé/Fat
Old Sun/Cymbaline/Atom Heart
Mother/The Embryo/Green Is
The Colour – Careful With That
Axe Eugene/Set The Controls
For The Heart Of The Sun/
encore: A Saucerful Of Secrets.
■ **26.11.70**
Killesberg Halle 14,
Stuttgart, West Germany.
Set list included: Fat Old
Sun/Cymbaline/Atom Heart
Mother/Green Is The Colour –
Careful With That Axe Eugene/
The Embryo/encore: A Saucerful
Of Secrets.
■ **27.11.70**
Sartory Saal, Cologne,
West Germany.
Show cancelled.
■ **27.11.70**
Sporthalle, Cologne, West
Germany.
Show cancelled.
■ **28.11.70**
Saarlandhalle, Saarbrücken,
West Germany.

■ **29.11.70**
Zirkus Krone, Munich,
West Germany.
The last night of the tour.
Set list: Astronomy Dominé/Fat
Old Sun/Cymbaline/Atom Heart
Mother/The Embryo/ Green Is
The Colour – Careful With That
Axe Eugene/Set The Controls
For The Heart Of The Sun/
encore: A Saucerful Of Secrets.
■ **4,5.12.70**
ORTF Studios, Buttes
Chaumont, Paris, France.
Recording for French TV.
UK TOUR: 'ATOM HEART
MOTHER IS GOING ON
THE ROAD'
■ **11.12.70**

use more than 30 speakers and
they are certainly loud. But they
obviously go to a lot of trouble
to ensure that every sound is
clearly audible. At times they
were far out, freaky even. For
example they made excellent
use of tape recorded sounds
ranging from crying babies to
galloping horses and
explosions.' (*Sounds*)
■ **12.12.70**
Village Blues Club, The
Roundhouse, Dagenham,
Essex, England.
Set list included: The Embryo/A
Saucerful Of Secrets/Atom Heart
Mother/Blues/encore: Astronomy
Dominé.

Big Apple, Regent Theatre,
Brighton, East Sussex,
England.
Set list included: Atom Heart
Mother/Fat Old Sun/Green Is The
Colour – Careful With That Axe
Eugene/The Embryo/Cymbaline/
Set The Controls For The Heart Of
The Sun/A Saucerful Of Secrets/
encore: Astronomy Dominé.
'The Pink Floyd are brilliant
musicians, but it is undoubtedly
their technical genius that has
made them Britain's No.1 truly
progressive pop band. This was
proved conclusively at Brighton's
Big Apple on Friday night when
the Floyd made one of their rare
club appearances.... Thankfully
the Floyd are one of the few
bands who refuse to be
governed by sheer volume. They

■ **18.12.70**
Town Hall, Birmingham,
Warwickshire, England.
Set list included: Alan's
Psychedelic Breakfast/Fat Old
Sun/A Saucerful Of Secrets//
Atom Heart Mother (with brass
and choir conducted by John
Aldiss/encore: Atom Heart
Mother (reprise)
■ **20.12.70**
Colston Hall, Bristol,
Gloucestershire, England.
Set list included: Alan's
Psychedelic Breakfast/Atom
Heart Mother (with brass and
choir conducted by John Aldiss).
■ **21.12.70**
Free Trade Hall,
Manchester, Lancashire,
England.
Set list: Alan's Psychedelic

Breakfast/The Embryo/Fat Old Sun/Careful With That Axe Eugene/Set The Controls For The Heart Of The Sun/A Saucerful Of Secrets//Atom Heart Mother (with brass and choir conducted by John Aldiss)/encore: Atom Heart Mother (reprise).

■ **22.12.70**
City Hall, Sheffield, Yorkshire, England.
The last night of the tour.
Set list: Alan's Psychedelic Breakfast/The Embryo/Fat Old Sun/Careful With That Axe Eugene/Set The Controls For The Heart Of The Sun/A Saucerful Of Secrets//Atom Heart Mother (with brass and choir conducted by John Aldiss)/encore: Atom Heart Mother (reprise).

1971

■ **17.1.71**
Implosion, The Roundhouse, Chalk Farm, London, England.
Supported by Quiver and Nico with John Cale.
Set list: The Embryo/Astronomy Dominé/Fat Old Sun/Careful With That Axe Eugene/Cymbaline/Set The Controls For The Heart Of The Sun/A Saucerful Of Secrets//Atom Heart Mother (with brass and choir conducted by John Aldiss).

■ **23.1.71**
Refectory Hall, University Union, Leeds University, Leeds, Yorkshire, England.
Set list included: Atom Heart Mother/Careful With That Axe Eugene/Cymbaline/Set The Controls For The Heart Of The Sun/A Saucerful Of Secrets

■ **3.2.71**
Great Hall, Devonshire House, University of Exeter, Exeter, Devon, England.
Set list: Atom Heart Mother/The Embryo/Astronomy Dominé/Fat Old Sun/Careful With That Axe Eugene/Cymbaline/Set The

Controls For The Heart Of The Sun/encore: A Saucerful Of Secrets.

■ **12.2.71**
Lecture Theatre Block 6 & 7, University of Essex, Wivenhoe Park, Colchester, Essex, England
Set list: Atom Heart Mother/The Embryo/Careful With That Axe Eugene/Astronomy Dominé/Cymbaline/Set The Controls For The Heart Of The Sun/encore: A Saucerful Of Secrets.

■ **13.2.71**
Student Union Bar, Farnborough Technical College, Farnborough, Hampshire, England.
Set List: Atom Heart Mother/The Embryo/Careful With That Axe Eugene/Cymbaline/Astronomy Dominé/Set The Controls For The Heart Of The Sun/encore: A Saucerful Of Secrets.

■ **20.2.71**
Student Union, Queen Mary College, Strawberry Hill, Twickenham, London, England.
EUROPEAN TOUR

■ **22.2.71**
Théâtre du Huitième, Lyon, France.
Show cancelled.

■ **24.2.71**
Halle Münsterland, Münster, West Germany.
Set list: The Embryo/Green Is The Colour – Careful With That Axe Eugene/Fat Old Sun/Set The Controls For The Heart Of The Sun/Cymbaline/A Saucerful Of Secrets//Atom Heart Mother (with brass and choir conducted by Jeffrey Mitchell).
The second half of the show nearly didn't happen since the score for 'Atom Heart Mother' had been left behind in London and the mistake wasn't discovered until 6.00pm, when the crew were setting up the equipment. A courier flew out to Düsseldorf and a police Porsche waiting at the airfield raced back to the show, arriving at 10.30.

■ **25.2.71**

Grosser Saal, Musikhalle, Hamburg, West Germany.
Set list: Astronomy Dominé/Green Is The Colour – Careful With That Axe Eugene/Cymbaline/The Embryo/Set The Controls For The Heart Of The Sun/A Saucerful Of Secrets//Atom Heart Mother (with brass and choir conducted by Jeffrey Mitchell).
Hamburg's Staatsoper was the original location for this concert, but the venue was changed at the last minute when the band were given less than two hours to set up their equipment by the venue's management.
The *Hamburger Abendblatt* commented, 'Never before had that many bootleggers and tape recorder microphones been seen in an auditorium.' The concert was also filmed by ZDF German TV, and parts of it were later broadcast, along with a band interview at the venue, on an unidentified arts programme for which we have no details of broadcast dates or times.

■ **26.2.71**
Stadthalle, Offenbach, West Germany.
Set list: Astronomy Dominé, Green Is The Colour – Careful With That Axe Eugene/The Embryo/Set The Controls For The Heart of The Sun/Cymbaline/A Saucerful Of Secrets//Atom Heart Mother (with brass and choir conducted by Jeffrey Mitchell)/encore: Atom Heart Mother (reprise)/Blues.
The Frankfurt Oper was the original location for this show, but, like the Hamburg concert, this was changed at the last minute and for the same reasons.

■ **27.2.71**
ORTF TV Studios, Buttes Chaumont, Paris, France.
The end of this European tour culminated in a live TV broadcast session in which the band performed 'Set The Controls For The Heart Of The Sun' for the

music programme *Pop 2* at 6.25pm.

■ **3.4.71**
Sportpaleis Ahoy, Rotterdam, Netherlands.
Set list: Astronomy Dominé/Careful With That Axe Eugene/Fat Old Sun/Set The Controls For The Heart Of The Sun/Cymbaline/The Embryo/A Saucerful Of Secrets//Atom Heart Mother (with brass and choir conducted by Jeffrey Mitchell).

■ **16.4.71**
Top Rank Suite, Doncaster, Yorkshire, England.
Presented by Doncaster College of Technology. Supported by Quiver and America.
Set list: Atom Heart Mother/A Saucerful Of Secrets/Cymbaline/Fat Old Sun/The Embryo/Green Is The Colour – Careful With That Axe Eugene/Set The Controls For The Heart Of The Sun/encore: Astronomy Dominé.

■ **22.4.71**
Norwich Lads Club, Norwich, Norfolk, England.
Presented by the University of East Anglia.
Set list included: Atom Heart Mother/Fat Old Sun/Set The Controls For The Heart Of The Sun/A Saucerful Of Secrets and the premiere of a new piece, 'Return Of The Son Of Nothing', an early working title for 'Echoes'.

■ **7.5.71**
Central Hall, University of Lancaster, Bailrig, Lancaster, Lancashire, England.
Set list included: Return Of The Son Of Nothing.

■ **15.5.71**
Garden Party, Crystal Palace Bowl, Crystal Palace, London, England.
With Quiver, Mountain, The Faces and compere Pete Drummond.
Set list: Atom Heart Mother/Careful With That Axe Eugene/Fat Old Sun/Return Of

PHILIPS HALLE DÜSSELDORF

Freitag, 4. Juni 71, 20 Uhr
einziges Konzert
In Nordrhein-Westfalen

PINK FLOYD

Vorverkauf in Köln: nur
Theaterkasse Rudolf-
platz, Telefon 24 69 45.

SPORTP...

5. JUNI

MAMA-O...

die progressive...

THE PINK FLOYD
in concert
Vorverkauf Theaterkasse Nagel
am Sportpalast, bek. Stellen und
Abendkasse.
Einheitspreis DM 9.—

Inset photograph: Roger Waters and David Gilmour, backstage at Crystal Palace Bowl, London, 15 May 1971

The Son Of Nothing/Set The Controls For The Heart Of The Sun/The Embryo/A Saucerful Of Secrets/encore: Astronomy Dominé.
'Soon after the Floyd struck up with "Atom Heart Mother" the skies opened. The audience huddled under miles of polythene... revellers swam in the muddy pond... and the band played on... There was also a new work, "The Return Of The

Son Of Nothing", which didn't come across on first hearing as particularly distinguished. Secondly, the absence of the choir and additional orchestration meant that "Atom Heart" suffered in comparison with the LP and came across rather limply. But the performance as a whole underlined the moving, dramatic epic quality of Floyd music, enhanced by the so called

quadraphonic sound, achieved by having speakers at different points on the rim of the arena. Visual aids were effective too: orange smoke bombs misting up the pond and the trees at the end, rockets, and for fun, a giant octopus inflated in the water.' (*Croydon Advertiser*)
■ **18.5.71**
University of Stirling, Stirling, Stirlingshire, Scotland.

Set list: Atom Heart Mother/Set The Controls For The Heart Of The Sun/Fat Old Sun/Careful With That Axe Eugene/Return Of The Son Of Nothing/encore: A Saucerful Of Secrets.
■ **19.5.71**
Caledonian Cinema, Edinburgh, Lothian, Scotland.
■ **20.5.71**
The Ballroom, University of Strathclyde, Glasgow, Lanarkshire, Scotland.
■ **21.5.71**
Trent Polytechnic, Nottingham, Nottinghamshire, England.
EUROPEAN TOUR
■ **4.6.71**
Philips Halle, Düsseldorf, West Germany
Set list: Atom Heart Mother/ Careful With That Axe Eugene/ Fat Old Sun/The Embryo/Return Of The Son Of Nothing/Set The Controls For The Heart Of The Sun/ Cymbaline/encore: A Saucerful Of Secrets.
■ **5.6.71**
Berliner Sportpalast, West Berlin, West Germany.
This show was originally scheduled to take place on 27.5.71, but was postponed. Set list: Careful With That Axe Eugene/Fat Old Sun/The Embryo/Return Of The Son Of Nothing/Set The Controls For The Heart Of The Sun/ Cymbaline/A Saucerful Of Secrets/encore: Astronomy Dominé/Blues
■ **12.6.71**
Palais des Sports, Lyon, France.
Set list included: Careful With That Axe Eugene/Set The Controls For The Heart Of The Sun/Cymbaline/A Saucerful Of Secrets/Atom Heart Mother (with a twenty-voice choir, plus three trombones, three trumpets and one tuba, conducted by John Aldiss). The show was reportedly recorded for radio and broadcast

David Gilmour, Palais des Sports, Lyon, 12 June 1971

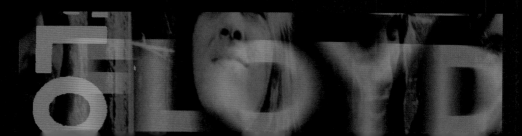

in part by Europe 1, France.

■ **15.6.71**

Abbaye de Royaumont, Royaumont, France.

Set list included: Set The Controls For The Heart Of The Sun/Cymbaline /Atom Heart Mother.

The show was recorded by French TV crews and 'Cymbaline' was later broadcast on ORTF at an unknown date.

■ **19.6.71**

Palazzo Delle Manifestazioni Artistiche, Brescia, Italy.

This show replaced the one scheduled for Palazzo Dello Sport, Bologna, which had in turn replaced the show scheduled for Palasport, Milan. Both shows had been cancelled after failure to obtain licences from the local authorities.

Set list: Atom Heart Mother/ Careful With That Axe Eugene/ Fat Old Sun/The Embryo/Return Of The Son Of Nothing/Set The Controls For The Heart Of The Sun/Cymbaline/encore: A Saucerful Of Secrets.

■ **20.6.71**

Palazzo Dello Sport EUR, Rome, Italy.

The last night of the tour and the band's last performance in Italy for some seventeen years.

Set list: Atom Heart Mother/ Careful With That Axe Eugene/ Fat Old Sun/The Embryo/Return Of The Son Of Nothing/Set The Controls For The Heart Of The Sun/Cymbaline/A Saucerful Of Secrets/encore: Astronomy Dominé.

■ **22.6.71**

Glastonbury Fayre, Worthy Farm, Pilton, Somerset, England.

Pink Floyd were scheduled to appear at 1.00am on the third day of this five-day event (20–24.6.71) – the first Glastonbury festival, now a national institution – but couldn't make it because their equipment was delayed in transit from Italy.

■ **26.6.71**

Free Concert, Amsterdamse Bos, Amsterdam, Netherlands.

With America and Pearls Before Swine.

Set list: Careful With That Axe Eugene/Cymbaline/Set The Controls For The Heart Of The Sun/A Saucerful Of Secrets/The Embryo.

Pink Floyd made a hasty exit from this free rock concert to fly to America.

■ **28.6.71**

Celebration of Life, Cypress Pointe Plantation, McCrea, near Baton Rouge, Louisiana, USA.

With The Amboy Dukes, BB King, The Allman Brothers, Canned Heat, The Chambers Brothers, Chuck Berry, Country Joe McDonald, The Flying Burrito Brothers, Ike & Tina Turner, It's A Beautiful Day, John Lee Hooker, Richie Havens, Roland Kirk and Taj Mahal and others.

This ambitious project saw the promoters of the Toronto Rock & Roll Revival, Atlanta Pop Festival and New Orleans Pop Festival joining forces to stage this huge eight-day festival (21–28.6.71) on a secluded peninsula off the Atchafalaya River. From the outset it was dogged by problems when the promoters could not obtain a licence to open the festival until 23.6. The first live performance was not until the following day and the festival closed down on 27.6 after an all-night show at which Pink Floyd are believed not to have played. The event ended a day early after an invasion by two motorcycle gangs, members of which were charged with attempted murder, inciting a riot and assaulting a law officer.

■ **1.7.71**

Internationale Musikforum Ossiachersee, Stiftshoff, Ossiach, Austria.

Set list: Return Of The Son Of Nothing/Careful With That Axe Eugene/Set The Controls For

The Heart Of The Sun/Atom Heart Mother (with brass and choir).

Pink Floyd appeared at this festival (25.6–5.7.71), which featured a programme of contemporary orchestras – the only other non-classical group to appear was Tangerine Dream. The event was highlighted on Austrian radio and on the Bayerischer Rundfunk TV channel as *Musikforum Ossiachersee*, although it is not known if Pink Floyd were included. A triple LP of the festival, *Ossiach Live* (BASF 4921119-3), was released later in the year but, for contractual reasons, did not feature Pink Floyd.

FAR EAST TOUR

■ **6.8.71**

Aphrodite–Ashinokohan Sheikeigakuen–Jofundai, Hakone, Japan.

Supported by Buffy Sainte Marie & The 1910 Fruit Gum Company.

Set list: Green Is The Colour – Careful With That Axe Eugene/ Atom Heart Mother/Return Of The Son Of Nothing/ Cymbaline/encore: A Saucerful Of Secrets.

■ **7.8.71**

Aphrodite–Ashinokohan Sheikeigakuen–Jofundai, Hakone, Japan.

Supported by Buffy Sainte Marie & The 1910 Fruit Gum Company.

Set list: Green Is The Colour – Careful With That Axe Eugene/ Atom Heart Mother/Return Of The Son Of Nothing/Set The Controls For The Heart Of The Sun/encore: A Saucerful Of Secrets.

■ **9.8.71**

Festival Hall, Osaka, Japan.

Supported by Buffy Sainte Marie & The 1910 Fruit Gum Company.

Set list: Green Is The Colour – Careful with That Axe Eugene/ Fat Old Sun/Atom Heart Mother/ Return Of The Son Of Nothing /Set The Controls For The Heart Of The Sun/Cymbaline/encore: A

Saucerful Of Secrets.

■ **13.8.71**

Festival Hall, Melbourne, Victoria, Australia.

Supported by Lindsay Bourke and Pirana.

Set list: Atom Heart Mother/ Green Is The Colour – Careful With That Axe Eugene/Set The Controls For The Heart Of The Sun/Return Of The Son Of Nothing/Cymbaline/encore: A Saucerful Of Secrets.

■ **15.8.71**

St Leger Stand, Randwick Racecourse, Sydney, New South Wales, Australia.

Supported by Lindsay Bourke and Pirana. 1.00pm show. The last night of the tour and the band's last performance in Australia for seventeen years. Pink Floyd were featured on three separate broadcasts of the local early evening TV show *Get To Know*, which included an interview before the show and part of their performance of 'Careful With That Axe Eugene'.

EUROPEAN TOUR

■ **18.9.71**

Festival de Musique Classique, Pavillon de Montreux, Montreux, Switzerland.

Evening concert.

Set list: Echoes/Careful With That Axe Eugene/Set The Controls For The Heart Of The Sun/Cymbaline/Atom Heart Mother (with members of the London Philharmonic Orchestra and choir)/encore: A Saucerful Of Secrets.

■ **19.9.71**

Festival de Musique Classique, Pavillon de Montreux, Montreux, Switzerland.

Daytime concert.

Set included: Atom Heart Mother (with members of the London Philharmonic Orchestra and choir).

Overleaf: Abbaye de Royaumont, France, 15 June 1971

■ **22.9.71**
Kungliga Tennishallen, Lindingövägen, Stockholm, Sweden.
Set list: Careful With That Axe Eugene/Fat Old Sun/Atom Heart Mother/Set The Controls For The Heart Of The Sun/Cymbaline/Echoes/A Saucerful Of Secrets.

■ **23.9.71**
KB Hallen, Frederiksberg, Copenhagen, Denmark.
The last night of the tour.
Set list: Careful With That Axe Eugene/Fat Old Sun/Set The Controls For The Heart Of The Sun/Atom Heart Mother/Echoes/Cymbaline/A Saucerful Of Secrets/encore: Blues.

■ **30.9.71**
BBC Paris Cinema, Lower Regent Street, London, England.
A live recording session for BBC Radio One's *Sounds of The Seventies* programme in which the band performed 'The Embryo', 'Blues', 'Fat Old Sun', 'One of These Days' and 'Echoes'. The programme was broadcast on 12.10.71 at

10.00pm but omitted 'The Embryo' and 'Blues'. For unexplained reasons these were later broadcast on WNEW radio, New York, which had been sent the tapes by the BBC. Subsequent transcription discs also omitted these two tracks to make a sixty-minute broadcast.

■ **10.10.71**
The Great Hall, Bradford University, Bradford, Yorkshire, England.
Set list: Careful With That Axe Eugene/Fat Old Sun/Set The Controls For The Heart Of The Sun/Atom Heart Mother//Echoes/Cymbaline/One of These Days/A Saucerful Of Secrets/encore: Blues.

■ **11.10.71**
Town Hall, Birmingham, Warwickshire, England.
Set list: Careful With That Axe Eugene/Fat Old Sun/Atom Heart Mother/Set The Controls For The Heart Of The Sun/Echoes/Cymbaline/One of These Days/A Saucerful Of Secrets/encore: Blues.

NORTH AMERICAN TOUR
The following shows were

advertised but were either rescheduled or cancelled: Cincinatti (30.10), Boston (4.11) and Providence (5.11).

■ **15.10.71**
Winterland Auditorium, San Francisco, California, USA.

■ **16.10.71**
Civic Auditorium, Santa Monica, Los Angeles, California, USA.
Set list: Careful With That Axe Eugene/Fat Old Sun/Set The Controls For The Heart Of The Sun/Atom Heart Mother/The Embryo/Cymbaline/Echoes/A Saucerful Of Secrets/encore: Blues.

■ **17.10.71**
Convention Hall, Community Concourse, San Diego, California, USA.
Supported by Mike Finnegan and Jerry Woods.
Set list: Careful With That Axe Eugene/Fat Old Sun/Atom Heart Mother/The Embryo/Set The Controls For The Heart Of The Sun/Cymbaline/Echoes/A Saucerful Of Secrets/encore:

Blues.

■ **19.10.71**
National Guard Armory, Eugene, Oregon, USA.

■ **21.10.71**
Willamette University, Salem, Oregon, USA.
Unconfirmed appearance.

■ **22.10.71**
Paramount Theatre, Seattle, Washington, USA.
Set list included: Atom Heart Mother/Set The Controls For The Heart Of The Sun/A Saucerful Of Secrets/Careful With That Axe Eugene/Cymbaline/One Of These Days/encore: Echoes.

■ **23.10.71**
Gardens Arena, Vancouver, British Columbia, Canada.

■ **26.10.71**
Eastown Theater, Detroit, Michigan, USA.
Set list: The Embryo/Fat Old Sun/Set The Controls For The Heart Of The Sun/Atom Heart Mother/One Of These Days/Careful With That Axe Eugene/Cymbaline/Echoes/encore: A Saucerful Of Secrets/Blues

Publicity shot, 1971

■ **27.10.71**
Auditorium Theater, Chicago, Illinois, USA.
Set list: The Embryo/Fat Old Sun/Set The Controls For The Heart Of The Sun/Atom Heart Mother/One of These Days/Careful With That Axe Eugene/Cymbaline/Echoes/encore: A Saucerful Of Secrets.

■ **28.10.71**
Hill Auditorium, Ann Arbor, Michigan, USA.
Supported by Guardian Angel. Set list: The Embryo/Fat Old Sun/Set The Controls For The Heart Of The Sun/Atom Heart Mother/One of These Days/Careful With That Axe Eugene/Cymbaline/Echoes/encore: Blues.

■ **31.10.71**
Fieldhouse, University of Toledo, Toledo, Ohio, USA.
Set list: The Embryo/Fat Old Sun/Set The Controls For The Heart Of The Sun/Atom Heart Mother/One of These Days/Careful With That Axe Eugene/Cymbaline/Echoes/encore: Blues.

■ **2.11.71**
McCarter Theatre, Princeton University, Princeton, New Jersey, USA.
'The Floyd are something from a different century – rarely smiling, never speaking to their audience except to put down a request with a weary mincingly English, "We'll never play 'Astronomy Dominé' again." Unreceptive as they may be, the Floyd are undeniably good musicians with a unique style of composition. Their main strength, and their claim to the kingship of psychedelia, is their mastery of electronics – they proved perfectly capable of reproducing the synthetic soundstorms and whispery, sibilant, echoing vocals that characterise their albums in concert. In fact, they actually surpassed their studio work by employing a quadraphonic sound system

that, piloted by the organist with a modified joystick control, could seemingly place the group's sound effects anywhere in the theatre. The illusion of movement was sufficiently astonishing that anyone attending the concert drugged must have gotten a far bigger dose of psychedelia than he had bargained for. The magnificent six-ton sound system that accomplished this – the stage was piled ten feet high with amplifiers, while more equipment was set up in the balcony – was also quite sufficient to fill a hall the size of, say, the Spectrum. In McCarter, it was literally painfully loud, and I must admit that sheer volume drove me out halfway through a concert that I was otherwise enjoying very much.' (*Daily Princeton*)

■ **3.11.71**
Central Theatre, Passaic, New Jersey, USA.

■ **4.11.71**
Lowes Theatre, Providence, Rhode Island, USA.

■ **5.11.71**
Assembly Hall, Hunter College, Columbia University of New York, Manhattan, New York City, New York, USA.
Compered by Zach of WPLJ Radio. Set list: The Embryo/Fat Old Sun/Set The Controls For The Heart Of The Sun/Atom Heart Mother/One of These Days/Careful With That Axe Eugene/Cymbaline/Echoes/encore: A Saucerful Of Secrets.

■ **6.11.71**
Emerson Gym, Case Western Reserve University, Cleveland, Ohio, USA.

■ **8.11.71**
Peace Bridge Exhibition Center, Buffalo, New York, USA.

■ **9.11.71**
Centre Sportif, Université de Montréal, Montreal, Quebec, Canada.

■ **10.11.71**
Pavillon de la Jeunesse, Quebec City, Quebec, Canada.
Set list: The Embryo/Fat Old Sun/Set The Controls For The Heart Of The Sun/One of These Days/Atom Heart Mother/Cymbaline/Careful With That Axe Eugene/Echoes/encore: A Saucerful Of Secrets.

■ **11.11.71**
Music Hall, Boston, Massachusetts, USA.

■ **12.11.71**
Irvine Auditorium, Pennsylvania State University, Philadelphia, Pennsylvania, USA.
Set list: The Embryo/Fat Old Sun/Set The Controls For The Heart Of The Sun/Atom Heart Mother/One of These Days/Careful With That Axe Eugene/Cymbaline/encore: Echoes.

■ **13.11.71**
Convention Hall, Asbury Park, New Jersey, USA.

■ **14.11.71**
State University of New York, Stony Brook, Long Island, New York, USA

■ **15.11.71**
Carnegie Hall, Manhattan, New York City, New York, USA.
Set list included: Set The Controls For The Heart Of The Sun/Atom Heart Mother/One Of These Days/ Careful With That Axe Eugene/Cymbaline/ Echoes.

■ **16.11.71**
Lisner Auditorium, The George Washington University, Washington, District of Columbia, USA.
Set list: The Embryo/Fat Old Sun/Set The Controls For The Heart Of The Sun/Atom Heart Mother/One of These Days/Careful With That Axe Eugene/Cymbaline/encore: Echoes.
'This was no ordinary rock show – it was the closest thing that rock music has to show in the way of avant-garde music. Even apart from the strange opening –

in which a fellow gifted as magician, juggler and fire-eater, breathed forth flame so a white-robed lady could light her cigarette – there were other novelties in the Pink Floyd show at Lisner Auditorium last night.... Echo and reverberation units, time delivery devices, synthesisers and taped sound segments were all part of the act. [Pink Floyd] played into a 32 channel mixing panel that relayed the joy into a public address system completely encircling the audience. Any given instrument, by these means could be "placed" at any position in the hall and could be mixed with all kinds of taped wonders such as chirping birds and high volume "white" noise. They did not worry too much with the usual content of music. When they sang, the vocals were not important as words with meanings but rather as aspects of an exciting tension that you could hear in the process of creation. Form and content were replaced by dynamics. The band sounded sometimes like a screaming saw, sometimes like a fleet of intergalactic jets. A guitar, with this group, became a screeching bird. Drums were explosions. "Set The Controls" as they sang (and as the audience did) For The Heart Of The Sun."' (*Washington Post*)

■ **19.11.71**
Syria Mosque Theater, Pittsburgh, Pennsylvania, USA.

■ **20.11.71**
Taft Auditorium, Cincinnati, Ohio, USA.
This show replaced the one scheduled for 30 October at The Music Hall, Cincinnati. The last night of the tour.
Set list: Improvisations – The Embryo/Fat Old Sun/Set The Controls For The Heart Of The Sun/Atom Heart Mother/Careful With That Axe Eugene/Cymbaline/ Echoes/encore: Blues.

5

1972 – 1973

The initial ideas for a new album had been discussed towards the end of 1971 at a band meeting in the usual venue of Nick Mason's kitchen. Waters came up with the specific idea of dealing with all the things that drive people mad. The album would focus on the enormous pressures the band themselves were experiencing on the road: the strains of travelling and the problems of living, often abroad for great stretches at a time, and coping with (and without) money. It would also explore violence, social problems and the comforts of religion – this last theme no doubt prompted by their recent tours through Middle America.

Waters, the main source of inspiration, began furiously writing the lyrics around the beginning of 1972, while Gilmour and Wright concentrated on the music. An album's worth of material would also be of convenient length for the first half of a new stage show, the second half of which could be given over to established favourites. As Waters explained, 'It had to be quick, because we had a tour starting. It might have been only six weeks before we had to have something to perform. We went somewhere in West Hampstead for a couple of weeks and we got a lot of pieces together.'[1]

It all came happened in such a short space of time it is almost unbelievable, as Wright confirmed. 'At the start we only had vague ideas about madness being a theme. We rehearsed a lot just putting down ideas and then in the next rehearsals we used them. It flowed really well. There was a strong thing in it that made it easier to do.'[2]

Lyrically, it was Waters' most profound and focused effort to date, and for the first time he dominated the creative input almost exclusively, conveying a vision all his own. The album's success is probably attributable to the fact that it was kept deliberately simple and as accessible as possible, with strong dynamics and melodies. It was certainly more down to earth than earlier flights of fancy such as 'Echoes'. Indeed, Waters gave some hint of what to expect on the forthcoming tour when he spoke to *Sounds* that January under the headline, 'Pink Floyd Have Gone Mental!': 'In concept it's more literal, not as abstract as the things we've done before.'[3]

Finally, the new work was given the provisional title 'Dark Side Of The Moon'. But said Gilmour, 'At one time, it was called "Eclipse" because Medicine Head did an album called "Dark Side Of The Moon". But that didn't sell well, so what the hell. I was against "Eclipse" and we felt a bit annoyed because we had already thought of the title before Medicine Head came out. Not annoyed at them, but because we wanted to use the title.'[4]

Both on stage and on record the piece would propel the group into the superstar league,

Roger Waters, Rainbow Theatre, London, February 1972

severing their underground roots for ever. As for Waters, it boosted his confidence as a writer – his skills clearly far outstripped anything any of the others could achieve – and he became the self-appointed lyricist of the band.

With their first countrywide UK tour since 1969 about to commence, they were still working out the last few details and intricacies of the piece and booked a few days' rehearsal at the Rolling Stones' warehouse in Bermondsey, south London. Final dress rehearsals would take place at the Rainbow Theatre, where they would return to perform exactly one month later.

Previous page: 'Set The Controls For The Heart Of The Sun', Rainbow Theatre, London, February 1972

To complete the production, the band purchased a brand-new WEM PA with a twenty-eight-channel mixing desk and four-channel 360-degree quadraphonic sound system. They also had a complete light-show, the first to go out on the road with them since early 1968, built to specification by their lighting designer Arthur Max. In addition, specially recorded backing tapes were created to accompany the music on stage. A total of over nine tons of equipment, which required assembly by a crew of seven each afternoon before the performance, was put together and transported by three trucks. Wright himself remarked on the scale of the operation: 'Sometimes I look at our huge truck and tons and tons of equipment and think, "Christ, all I'm doing is playing an organ!"'.5

It was also the first time Pink Floyd had taken an entire album on the road, and although they had been used to previewing material before recording it, 'Dark Side Of The Moon' was a piece that was vastly improved and refined as a result of the decision to tour with it before its release.

It was performed in exactly the same order as

on the finished album but the early shows lacked synthesizers: for example, the track 'On The Run' was merely a keyboard and guitar improvisation. 'The Great Gig In The Sky', on the other hand, widely known to fans at the time as 'The Mortality Sequence', was an electric piano solo backed by pre-recorded tapes of readings from the Book of Ephesians, of the Lord's Prayer and other biblical discourses, along with recordings of the controversial British broadcaster Malcolm Muggeridge in full rant.

Some other tracks had been written already. 'Brain Damage', for example, was written at the time of *Meddle*, but not used, while 'Us And Them' came out of the previously mentioned 'The Violent Sequence' from the *Zabriskie Point* sessions.

Despite first-night hitches at the Brighton Dome, caused by an electrical fault that knocked out the tape playback, and a total power failure in Manchester, the tour was acclaimed, if not fully comprehended, by the press and public. However, the band's pivotal performance was in February at

UK cinema poster for La Vallée

north London's Rainbow Theatre, where the world press sat in attendance to witness 'Dark Side Of The Moon' in all its well-rehearsed glory.

In a series of faultless presentations Pink Floyd were heralded as a triumph of the imagination and for the first time greeted by critical acclaim throughout the national press.

And as if the band didn't have enough on their plate, the French director Barbet Schroeder invited them to write the music for another film for which he had them in mind, *La Vallée*. In two one-week sessions, one before and one after their tour of Japan, they composed and recorded the entire work at the Strawberry Studios, in the Château d'Hérouville near Paris. The album was released in June as *Obscured By Clouds* and once again the film – about a young woman's spiritual awakening in Papua New Guinea – although not a great success elsewhere, was well received in France.

Obscured By Clouds is as striking as it is subtle, with some remarkable music that would feature on later tours. The last true combined effort by the band, the album contains some particularly pensive lyrics by Waters. 'Free Four', for example, deals for the first time with the pressures of touring, well before the subject was taken to a conclusion on *Dark Side Of The Moon*. His father's death is also discussed, perhaps flippantly, but it is a theme that later recurs on *The Wall* with greater vehemence. Significantly, with 'Childhood's End' Gilmour made his last complete lyrical/musical composition in this line-up. The album ends with 'Absolutely Curtains', which includes taped recordings of a religious chant performed by the Mapuga tribe.

The album completed, Pink Floyd continued their extensive tour throughout North America and Europe, playing their largest (and generally sold-out) venues to date on both continents. At one particularly spectacular concert, at the Hollywood Bowl, eight powerful searchlights beamed rays skywards from behind the domed stage of the vast amphitheatre into the night sky, and a colourful fireworks display rounded off the evening. Elsewhere on tours of the time, other impressive effects included sheets of flame shooting from cauldrons at the back of the stage during 'Echoes', and a huge gong that burst into flame at the climax of 'Set The Controls For The Heart Of The Sun'.

It was also the year that Pink Floyd delved into other performing arts to enhance their work. They had already provided incidental music for the Ballet Rambert in 1969 and plans were now approaching fruition to link up with Europe's foremost contemporary ballet school, directed by Roland Petit and based in Marseilles. The band were brought to the attention of Petit by his daughter, a fan, who had suggested marrying a traditional ballet with modern music. The basic idea was discussed by the two parties in the middle of the band's American tours of 1971, when it was suggested that Proust's novel *Remembrance Of Things Past* be adapted for the project. However, this idea floundered almost immediately, having failed to fire anyone's imagination sufficiently, and, after unsuccessful attempts by the band to read the monumental work, the project was abandoned. Petit even considered adapting either *A Thousand And One Nights* or *Carmen*, but again these ideas were dropped.

Waters recalled, with some disbelief, the farcical planning meeting that took place that year: 'First of all it was Proust, then it was Aladdin, then it was something else. We had this great lunch one day, me, Nick and Steve. We went to have lunch with Nureyev, Roman Polanski, Roland Petit, some film producer or other. What a laugh. It was to talk about the projected idea for us doing the music, and Roland choreographing it, and Rudy Bryans being the star, and Roman Polanski directing the film, and making this fantastic ballet

Performing with the Roland Petit Ballet, Marseilles, November 1972

film. It was all a complete joke because nobody had any idea what they wanted to do.

'We all sat around this table until someone thumped the table and said, "What's the idea then?" and everyone just sat there drinking this wine and getting more and more drunk, with more and more poovery going on around the table, until someone suggested "Frankenstein" and then Nureyev started getting a bit worried. And when Polanski was drunk enough he started to suggest we make the blue movie to end all blue movies, and then it all petered out into cognac and coffee and then we jumped in our cars and split. God knows what happened after we left.'6

In what seemed like a sensible conclusion to their encounter it was agreed that the band should compose forty minutes' worth of original material to which Petit would provide choreography. There had even been plans to stage the production at the 10,000-seat Grand Palais in Paris on 10 June 1971, with a 108-piece orchestra, and have it broadcast on Eurovision. This idea was also passed over, this time because of Pink Floyd's touring and recording commitments.

But, still pushed for time, Pink Floyd finally agreed on a forty-minute set of existing material from their current repertoire and the performance was finally staged in Marseilles, at a residency midway through their European tour in November 1972. Waters, for one, approached it with some trepidation: 'Playing live means that we've got to be note-perfect each night, otherwise the dancers are going to get lost, and we won't be using a score, we'll be playing from memory. That might be a bit difficult.'[7]

From here the production moved to Paris for a series of weekend shows in January and February of 1973. Curiously, only four of these featured Pink Floyd performing live: all of the other dates used pre-recorded music. Gilmour even mentioned plans to take the show to Canada, 'but they couldn't because in the Maïakovski ballet that goes before it, there's two pieces both written by the same man, which had something to do with the Russian Revolution and things. In one part of it there's a thing with huge red flags draped on the stage, and the Canadian government wouldn't let them use it.'[8]

The conclusion of this extraordinary project illustrated yet another facet of Pink Floyd's ever-widening talents. Their shows were treated with awe and wonder by fans and critics alike. As Nick Mason had recently said: 'The thing to do is to really move people. To turn them on, to subject them to a fantastic experience, to do something to stretch their imagination.'[9]

Nineteen seventy-three was the first year in the band's career that the UK was largely ignored in favour of North America, which received the full-scale sensory assault of a greatly improved 'Dark Side Of The Moon' on two extensive tours.

Additional vocalists were also recruited for the tour, with backing singers Carlena Williams and Vanetta Fields joining the band on stage to reproduce the deep, soulful harmonies the piece now required. For the London shows of that year Vicki Brown was also added to the entourage.

Such was the scale of the production, the touring machine was akin to a finely tuned military operation and by now Pink Floyd required a small army of technicians to make it all possible. Arthur Max and his assistants Graeme Fleming and Rob Murray were responsible for the lighting, which, beginning with the second US tour of 1973, included a hemispherical mirror

ball which rose above the stage and reflected beams from two batteries of red lasers. Chris Anderson maintained the backline. Mick 'The Pole' Klucznski operated the effects tapes and looked after the quad system. Alan Parsons was the front-of-house engineer and Bobby Richardson was the band's general roadie.

At least one week before a show the tour manager and chief technician Peter Watts (who had started with the band back in late 1967), with the assistance of new recruit Robbie Williams (their present-day production manager), would go to each hall and talk to the promoter and venue staff to ensure that the stage and the electrics would be ready on the show day. Additional house staff were also needed to help deal with the equipment and run the show: two fork-lift drivers, six stage hands, two electricians, two soundmen, eight follow-spot operators and one house electrician.

On a typical day two forty-foot articulated equipment trucks, crewed by two drivers each, would arrive at the venue for ten in the morning, usually after an overnight drive, to be met by the road crew, who would have flown with the band on the show day, to start setting up. This would take until at least four in the afternoon to complete, by which time the band would appear for their customary sound-check. After the show the equipment would take less than half the time to dismantle and, once it was loaded on the trucks, the process would start all over again.

Dark Side Of The Moon was finally released in March – a landmark album in every respect. The press reception was boycotted by Pink Floyd because a quadraphonic mix had not been completed in time. Against the wishes of the band, EMI presented a stereo playback through an inferior PA system.

Waters had commented to the *NME* shortly after the release of *Meddle* that, 'however long you

Earls Court, London, May 1973

go on working on an album I don't think you ever come out thinking, "bugger me, I've done it this time". I don't think it's possible to make an album that you think is definitely all right from begining to end.' Nevertheless, the album successfully combined every element of Pink Floyd's collective ability and, for the first time, was consistent throughout, with strong dynamics and thoughtful lyrics. It also boasted enough FM radio-friendly tracks to make a serious dent in the hard-to-crack American market, thus exposing Pink Floyd for the very first time to a mass audience, propelling them out of the weird cult-band bracket and into a solidly mainstream rock market.

'The thing about "Dark Side",' commented Nick Mason, 'is that I think when it was finished, everyone felt it was the best thing we'd ever done to date, and everyone was very pleased with it, but there's no way that anyone felt it was five times as good as "Meddle", or eight times as good as "Atom Heart Mother", or the sort of figures that it has in fact sold. It was something of a phenomena, and was about not only being a good album, but also about being in the right place at the right time.'[10]

No one could quite explain this meteoric success, which took the band by surprise. As Rick Wright commented: 'We approached the album, I would say, in exactly the same way as any other album we've done. Except that this was a concept album. It was about madness, it was about one's fear, it was about the business – whereas none of the other albums had been about that. They may have been musically tied together, but there hadn't been a theme like that running on both sides.'[11]

The album begins and ends, as did the live shows, with a heartbeat – the simple thread that pulls the whole thing together, the essence of what it is all about and, as Gilmour said, 'It alludes to the human condition and sets the mood for the music which describes the emotions experienced during a lifetime. Amidst the chaos

there is beauty and hope for mankind. The effects are purely to help the listener understand what the whole thing is about.'[12]

The album's sleeve follows the idea through. A centre-spread gatefold repeats the central theme, showing a cardiograph blip, while the stunning front cover has an impressive, yet simple, white-light beam and a full spectrum that fans out from a central prism. The mysticism of the prism image continues in the publicity material, which used shots of the Great Pyramids at Giza in Egypt.

The recorded material itself was significantly altered from the live originals and many tracks featured female backing vocals for the first time, which lent a much softer edge to the overall piece. In addition, 'On The Run' was developed entirely in the studio to replace the comparatively weak guitar and keyboard jams while 'The Mortality Sequence' was changed beyond all recognition with a stunning improvised lead vocal from Clare Torry to form 'The Great Gig In The Sky'. The vastly improved production was also largely a result of the different textures used. 'Time' has a creative use of sound effects and the use of silence as a second instrument to Mason's roto-tom drumming.

Atom Heart Mother had employed taped voices, and now Roger Waters extended this idea much further by devising a system of questions that were written out on a series of cards and presented in such a way as to prevent anticipation and to elicit a definite answer. In all he interviewed about twenty people for this exercise, including Paul and Linda McCartney (although they don't appear on the album), the band's road crew, the Abbey Road engineers and the studio doorman, Gerry Driscoll. All of the questions were delivered on a one-to-one basis with very little repetition, to prevent interviewees benefiting from others who may have told them about their own session. The questions asked about the interviewees' thoughts

Rainbow Theatre, London, 4 November 1973

on life and death, what did the dark side of the moon mean to them, had they ever been violent and, in the case of Henry McCullough, when did you last thump someone? Very noticeble on the finished album is a stream of manic laughter from one of the band's roadies, known as 'Roger the Hat'.

Despite the length of time the music had been on the road, and the time the band had spent in the studio recording it, people still didn't understand its meaning. 'It's amazing,' said Gilmour. 'At the final mixing stage we thought it was obvious what the album was about, but still a lot of people, including the engineers and roadies, when we asked them, didn't know what the LP was about. I really don't know if our things get through, but you have to carry on hoping. Our music is about neuroses. We are able to see it, and discuss it. The "Dark Side Of The Moon" itself is an allusion to the moon and lunacy. The dark side is generally related to what goes on inside people's heads – the subconscious and the unknown.'[13]

By the end of the year sales of *Dark Side Of The Moon* were showing little sign of tailing off on the *Billboard* US Top 100 album chart, and by now over 700,000 copies had been bought in the UK alone. From here it would just continue to sell and sell and sell. It was calculated, some twenty years after its release, that the album had sold in excess of twenty-five million copies worldwide, and it is still in the top five best-selling album titles of all time. Surprisingly, it never made the UK number one spot, being thwarted by Alice Cooper's *Billion Dollar Babies*.

Despite the band's success, Capitol Records in the USA just weren't shaping up to their needs. This was because many other artists on the label were being prioritized, and also because the band felt that the company had insufficient resources to cope with their requirements. Although Pink Floyd was the only act with which the label was

having any real success – it had spent years slogging away with what was basically a cult band but was now finally hitting big – Capitol could do little to prevent Pink Floyd from moving on now that their contract had been fulfilled.

In late 1973 the band's manager, Steve O'Rourke, signed a deal with the mighty CBS, who, like EMI in the UK, were prepared to give them the artistic freedom they wanted and had the financial muscle to successfully market and promote them on a much larger scale. 'We thought they'd be the best for us,' explained Rick Wright, 'largely because of their size. They're well organised. When we left Capitol, they were badly organised. Also, we'll be the only act of our type on CBS. When you're competing against similar acts on the same label, someone is bound to be squeezed out. We didn't want that.'[14] Credit to O'Rourke here, since the band had nothing on offer – no new material or plans for a US tour. He pulled off a deal that ensured them a great deal of breathing space and no doubt a hefty advance to go with it.

With such an exhausting period of their career behind them, Pink Floyd went into semi-retirement, not only to catch up with their families but also to reflect on their new-found wealth and the stardom that had been thrust upon them so suddenly.

Notes
1. *Zig Zag* 32
2. *Disc & Music Echo*, c.1974
3. *Sounds*, 29.1.72
4. *Sounds*, 19.5.73
5. *Sounds*, 3.6.72
6. *Zig Zag* 32
7. Unidentified press article
8. *Beetle*, May 1973
9. *Beat Instrumental*, April 1971
10–11. *Pink Floyd Story*, Capital Radio, 7.1.77
12–13. *Sounds*, 19.5.73
14. *Beetle*, January 1975

1972

UK TOUR
■ **20.1.72.**
The Dome, Brighton, East Sussex, England.
Set list: Dark Side Of The Moon (abandoned at Money due to technical problems)/Atom Heart Mother//Careful With That Axe Eugene/One Of These Days/ Echoes/encore: A Saucerful Of Secrets.
■ **21.1.72**
The Guildhall, Portsmouth, Hampshire, England.
Set list: Dark Side Of The Moon//One Of These Days/Set The Controls For The Heart Of The Sun/Echoes/encore: A Saucerful Of Secrets.
■ **22.1.72**
Winter Gardens, Bournemouth, Hampshire, England.
Set list: Dark Side Of The Moon// One Of These Days/Careful With That Axe Eugene/Echoes/ encore: A Saucerful Of Secrets.
■ **23.1.72**

The Guildhall, Southampton, Hampshire, England.
Set list: Dark Side Of The Moon//One Of These Days/ Careful With That Axe Eugene/ Echoes/encore: A Saucerful Of Secrets.
■ **27.1.72**
City Hall, Newcastle-upon-Tyne, Northumberland, England.
Set list: Dark Side Of The Moon//One Of These Days/ Careful With That Axe Eugene/ Echoes/encore: A Saucerful Of Secrets.
■ **28.1.72**
City Hall, Leeds, Yorkshire, England.
Set list: Dark Side Of The Moon//One Of These Days/ Careful With That Axe Eugene/ Echoes/encore: Set The Controls For The Heart Of The Sun.
■ **3.2.72**
Lanchester Polytechnic Arts Festival, Locarno Ballroom, Coventry, Warwickshire, England.
With The Mandala Lightshow.

Set list: Dark Side Of The Moon//Careful With That Axe Eugene/One Of These Days/ Echoes/encore: Set The Controls For The Heart Of The Sun.
The band's performance at this festival (28.1–4.2.72) turned out to be their last engagement at a college or university in the UK. The show finished at 2.30am, the band having had to set up their show after the Chuck Berry concert had finished.
■ **5.2.72**
Colston Hall, Bristol, Gloucestershire, England.
Set list: Dark Side Of The Moon//One Of These Days/ Careful With That Axe Eugene/ Set The Controls For The Heart Of The Sun/encore: Echoes.
■ **6.2.72**
ABC Theatre, Plymouth, Devon, England.
Show cancelled.
■ **10.2.72**
De Montfort Hall, Leicester, Leicestershire, England.
Set list: Dark Side Of The Moon//One Of These Days/

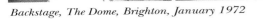
Backstage, The Dome, Brighton, January 1972

Careful With That Axe Eugene/
Echoes/encore: Set The Controls
For The Heart Of The Sun/Blues.

■ **11.2.72**
Free Trade Hall,
Manchester, Lancashire,
England.
Set list: One Of These Days/
Careful With That Axe Eugene.
About twenty-five minutes into
the show, during 'Careful With
That Axe Eugene', there was a
power cut and, despite cries of
'Acoustic!' from the audience,
the concert was abandoned.

■ **12.2.72**
City Hall, Sheffield,
Yorkshire, England.
Set list: One Of These Days/
Careful With That Axe Eugene/
Dark Side Of The Moon/Set The
Controls For The Heart Of The
Sun/encore: Echoes.

■ **13.2.72**
The Empire Theatre,
Liverpool, Lancashire,
England.

■ **17.2.72**
Rainbow Theatre, Finsbury
Park, London, England.
Set list: Dark Side Of The
Moon//One Of These Days/
Careful With That Axe Eugene/
Set The Controls For The Heart
Of The Sun//encore: Echoes.

■ **18.2.72**
Rainbow Theatre, Finsbury
Park, London, England.
Set list: Dark Side Of The
Moon//One Of These Days/
Careful With That Axe Eugene/
Echoes/encore: A Saucerful Of
Secrets/Blues/Set The Controls
For The Heart Of The Sun.

■ **19.2.72**
Rainbow Theatre, Finsbury
Park, London, England.
Set list: Dark Side Of The
Moon//One Of These Days/
Careful With That Axe Eugene/
Echoes/encore: A Saucerful Of
Secrets/Blues/Set The Controls
For The Heart Of The Sun.

■ **20.2.72**
Rainbow Theatre, Finsbury
Park, London, England.
The last night of the UK tour.
Set list: Dark Side Of The

Moon//One Of These Days/
Careful With That Axe Eugene/
Echoes/encore: A Saucerful Of
Secrets/Blues/Set The Controls
For The Heart Of The Sun.
JAPANESE TOUR
■ **6.3.72**
Tokyo-To Taiikukan, Tokyo,
Japan.

Set list: Dark Side Of The
Moon//One Of These Days/
Careful With That Axe Eugene/
Echoes/encore: Set The Controls
For The Heart Of The Sun.

■ **7.3.72**
Tokyo-To Taiikukan, Tokyo,
Japan.
Set list: Dark Side Of The

Moon//One Of These Days/
Careful With That Axe Eugene/
Echoes/encore: A Saucerful Of
Secrets.

■ **8.3.72**
Festival Hall, Osaka, Japan.
Set list: Dark Side Of The
Moon//One Of These Days/
Echoes/Atom Heart Mother/
Careful With That Axe Eugene/
encore: A Saucerful Of Secrets.

■ **9.3.72**
Festival Hall, Osaka, Japan.
Set list included: Dark Side Of
The Moon/One Of These Days/
Careful With That Axe Eugene/
Echoes

■ **10.3.72**
Dai-Sho-Gun Furitsu
Taiikukan, Kyoto, Japan.
Set list: Dark Side Of The
Moon//One Of These Days/
Careful With That Axe Eugene/
Echoes.

■ **11.3.72**
Yokohama, Japan.
Show cancelled.

■ **13.3.72**
Nakajima Sports Centre,
Sapporo, Hokkaido, Japan.
The last night of the tour.
Set list: Dark Side Of The
Moon//One Of These Days/

Rainbow Theatre, London, February 1972

Careful With That Axe Eugene/
Echoes.
UK SHOWS
■ **29,30.3.72**
Free Trade Hall,
Manchester, Lancashire,
England.
These two shows were
arranged to make up for the
aborted show at the same
venue in February.
Set list on 29.3.72: Dark Side Of
The Moon//One Of These Days/
Careful With That Axe Eugene/
Echoes/encore: Set The Controls
For The Heart Of The Sun.
NORTH AMERICAN TOUR
Pink Floyd's uncertainty over the
title for their forthcoming album
was such that for the US tour
Dark Side Of The Moon was
referred to as 'Eclipse' until
September 1972 and their
second US tour of the year.
■ **14.4.72**
Fort Homer Hesterly Armory,
Tampa, Florida, USA.
■ **15.4.72**
The Sportatorium,
Hollywood, Florida, USA.
This show replaced the one
scheduled for Pirates World,
Dania, Hollywood, Florida on
16 4.72.
Set list: Dark Side Of The
Moon//One Of These Days/

Careful With That Axe Eugene/
Echoes/encore: Set The Controls
For The Heart Of The Sun.

■ **16.4.72**
Township Auditorium,
Columbia, South Carolina,
USA.
Set list: Dark Side Of The
Moon//One Of These Days/
Careful With That Axe Eugene/
Atom Heart Mother/encore:
Echoes.
■ **18.4.72**
Symphony Hall, Atlanta
Memorial Arts Center,
Atlanta, Georgia, USA.
■ **20.4.72**
Syria Mosque Theatre,
Pittsburgh, Pennsylvania,
USA.
Set list included: Dark Side Of
The Moon//One Of These Days/
Careful With That Axe Eugene/
Echoes.
■ **21.4.72**
The Lyric Theatre,
Baltimore, Maryland, USA.
■ **22.4.72**
Civic Theatre, Akron, Ohio,

USA.
■ **23.4.72**
Music Hall, Cincinnati,
Ohio, USA.
Set list: Dark Side Of The Moon//One
Of These Days/Careful With That
Axe Eugene/Echoes/encore: A
Saucerful Of Secrets.
■ **24.4.72**
Sports Arena, Toledo,
Ohio, USA.
■ **26,27.4.72**
Ford Auditorium, Detroit,
Michigan, USA.
Set list on 27.4.72: Dark Side Of
The Moon//One Of These Days/
Careful With That Axe Eugene/
Echoes/encore: Blues/Set The
Controls For The Heart Of The Sun.
■ **28.4.72**
Auditorium Theatre, Chicago,
Illinois, USA.
Set list: Dark Side Of The
Moon//One Of These Days/
Careful With That Axe Eugene/
Echoes/encore: Set The Controls

For The Heart Of The Sun.

■ **29.4.72**
Spectrum Theater, Philadelphia, Pennsylvania, USA.

■ **30.4.72**
Toronto, Ontario,Canada.
Although widely advertised, this show never took place.

■ **1,2.5.72**
Main Hall, Carnegie Hall, Manhattan, New York City, New York, USA.
Set list on 2.5.72: Dark Side Of The Moon//One Of These Days/ Careful With That Axe Eugene/ Echoes/encore: A Saucerful Of Secrets.

■ **3.5.72**
Concert Hall, John F Kennedy Center for Performing Arts, Washington, District of Columbia, USA.

■ **4.5.72**
The Orpheum Aquarius Theater, Boston, Massachusetts, USA.
The last night of the tour.
EUROPEAN SHOWS

■ **18.5.72**
Deutschlandhalle, West Berlin, West Germany.
Set list: Dark Side Of The Moon//One Of These Days/ Careful With That Axe Eugene/ Echoes/encore: Set The Controls For The Heart Of The Sun.

■ **21.5.72**
2nd British Rock Meeting, Insel Grün, Germersheim, West Germany.
Set list: Atom Heart Mother/Set The Controls For The Heart Of The Sun/One Of These Days// Careful With That Axe Eugene/ Echoes/A Saucerful Of Secrets.

■ **22.5.72**
The Amsterdam Rock Circus 1972, Olympisch Stadion, Amsterdam, Netherlands.
With Donovan, New Riders of The Purple Sage, Buddy Miles Band with Carlos Santana, Tom Paxton and Memphis Slim, Dr John The Night Tripper, Spencer Davis with Sneeky Pete and Gene

Clark. The last night of the tour. Set list: Atom Heart Mother/ One Of These Days/Careful With That Axe Eugene/Echoes/ encore: A Saucerful Of Secrets.

■ **23–25.6.72**
Bièvres Festival, Bièvres, France.
Pink Floyd's appearance at this festival, which was organized by the French collective group Crium Delirium, is unconfirmed. Also scheduled to appear were Soft Machine, Matching Mole, Amon Düül II, Kevin Ayres, Hawkwind, Third World War, Pink Fairies, Gong, Lard Free, Dagon, Catharis, Komintern, Moving Gelatine Plates, Opus N, Higelin, Fontaine, Areski and Catherine Ribiero with free jazz, Magic Circus and Le Cirque Bonjour.
UK SHOWS

■ **28.6.72**
The Dome, Brighton, East Sussex, England.
Set list: Dark Side Of The Moon//One Of These Days/ Careful With That Axe Eugene/ Echoes/Set The Controls For The Heart Of The Sun/encore: A Saucerful Of Secrets (short version).

■ **29.6.72**
The Dome, Brighton, East Sussex, England.
Set list: Dark Side Of The Moon//One Of These Days/ Echoes/Set The Controls For The Heart Of The Sun/encore: A Saucerful Of Secrets (short version). As at Manchester, two shows were arranged as a replacement for the concert which had been abandoned in January. One of the concerts was professionally filmed and directed by Peter Clifton for inclusion in his film Sounds of The City (also known as Music Power). Clips of this material occasionally appear on television and compilation videos, more recently 'Careful With That Axe Eugene', which appeared on the 'various artists' video Superstars In Concert (Telstar TVE 1003).

■ **26–28.8.72**

Arena Pop Festival, Roman Arena, Verona, Italy.
Pink Floyd, America and Jefferson Airplane, among many other groups, were announced in the music press as scheduled to appear at this three-day festival to be held inside the best-preserved Roman arena in the world. In fact, the event never got beyond the planning stage, and the strong opposition of the Italian press contributed to its cancellation. However, Pink Floyd would perform at this spectacular venue, which is mainly devoted to classical music, some twenty-seven years later.

NORTH AMERICAN TOUR
The working title of 'Eclipse' was finally dismissed altogether and the album's title reverted to Dark Side Of The Moon.

■ **8.9.72**
Municipal Auditorium, Austin, Texas, USA.

■ **9.9.72**
Music Hall, Houston, Texas, USA.

■ **10.9.72**
McFarlin Auditorium, Southern Methodist University, University Park, Dallas, Texas, USA.
Set list: Dark Side Of The Moon//One Of These Days/ Careful With That Axe Eugene/ Set The Controls For The Heart Of The Sun/encore: Echoes.

■ **11.9.72**
Memorial Hall, Kansas City, Missouri, USA.

■ **12.9.72**
Civic Center Music Hall, Oklahoma City, Oklahoma, USA.

■ **13.9.72**
Henry Levitt Arena, Wichita, Kansas, USA.

■ **15.9.72**
Community Center Arena, Tucson, Arizona, USA.

■ **16.9.72**
Golden Hall, Community Concourse, San Diego, California, USA.

■ **17.9.72**

Big Surf, Tempe, Arizona, USA.
Set list: Dark Side Of The Moon//One Of These Days/ Careful With That Axe Eugene/ Echoes.
'Pink Floyd, chief explorers into the music of Space, appeared oddly in Tempe on Sunday night. A crowd entered Big Surf, looked at the speakers on their four sides, the mountain of equipment on-stage surrounded by banks of coloured lights, said "wow" and sat down. Gradually a heartbeat hit them from behind, lights begin to revolve in Mason's clear drums, a dense bank of green fog rolls onto the stage, towers of lights raise themselves high into the air and Pink Floyd begins with words from "Music from the Body". Using loud effects, Pink Floyd played most of their latest album, "Obscured By Clouds" [the reviewer mistakenly referred to Dark Side Of The Moon as this] ending with the appearance of a yellow disc of light above the band. After intermission, they returned with "One Of These Days", which was so engulfing, the audience could not helped but be merged with the flashing lights…. After the stage exploded with light and flame during a piece from "Ummagumma" and Pink Floyd followed with "Echoes", a long super-mellow thing, it was no wonder that the wind started blowing and the rain falling. Roger Waters stopped, said rain could mean instant death to their sound stage. Pink Floyd was over.' (New Times)

■ **19.9.72**
University of Denver Arena, Denver, Colorado, USA.

■ **22.9.72**
The Hollywood Bowl, Hollywood, Los Angeles, California, USA.
Set list: Dark Side Of The Moon//One Of These Days/ Careful With That Axe Eugene/ Set The Controls For The Heart

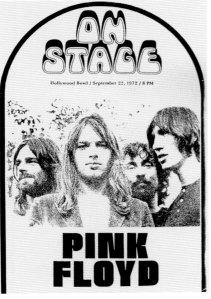

Of The Sun/Echoes/encore: A
Saucerful Of Secrets.

■ 23.9.72
Winterland Auditorium, San
Francisco, California, USA.

This show was originally
scheduled for Santa Clara
Fairgrounds, San Jose but was
moved to Winterland at one
week's notice.
Set list: Dark Side Of The
Moon//One Of These Days/
Careful With That Axe Eugene/
Echoes/encore: Set The Controls
For The Heart Of The Sun.

■ 24.9.72
Winterland Auditorium, San
Francisco, California, USA.

Set list: Dark Side Of The
Moon//One Of These Days/
Careful With That Axe Eugene/
Echoes/encore: A Saucerful Of
Secrets.

■ 27.9.72
Gardens Arena, Vancouver,
British Columbia, Canada.

Set list: Dark Side Of The
Moon//One Of These Days/
Careful With That Axe Eugene
Echoes/encore: Set The Controls
For The Heart Of The Sun.
'Pink Floyd are definitely a band
whose multi-sensory stage
performance lends them open-
air performances; the confines
of the Gardens Arena just don't
do justice to David Gilmour's
brilliant guitar playing – full of
floating shadows – or the
various lighting and theatric

smoke and fire
effects that the
band have
become known
for. After a half-
hour delay
while the stage
crew hassled
with some of
the equipment
needed to run
the
quadraphonic
sound system
that is being
used on this
tour, the crowd
was silenced
by an insistent throbbing beat
that passed around the four
speakers (two of them situated
mid-way back in the audience)
and grew to the guitar
introduction of the first number.
Smoke had poured from outlets
near the back of the stage
during the beginning of this
number and it hung in the air
reflecting various coloured
spotlights as the band worked
into the second piece which
gave the first real glimpses of
Gilmour's brilliance on guitar.
Madcap shouts and laughter
echoed round the sound system
and the music started out once
more in the cosmic zones.
Gently, sawing guitar notes over
wailing organ runs and a
pulsating bass line. Quietly
building creeping up and then
exploding into a solid wall of
sound as smoke and flame
flares up on stage and bright
yellow and red spots blow away
the darkness. There was a lot of
dope doing the rounds and there
were a few tripping initiates to
Pink Floyd concerts that were
heard giving wild shouts at this
juncture – the guy next door to
me shot bolt upright as if
someone had cracked a whole
cluster of amyl nitrates under his
nostrils. After continuing for a
while with the onslaught the
musicians cut back and
developed a series of floaty guitar

runs and breathy scat vocals in
amongst the clouds of smoke
that are reflecting bands of
coloured light. Well received, even
my neighbour seemed to wind
down sufficiently to get his hands
meeting.' (*Vancouver Free Press*)

■ 28.9.72
The Memorial Coliseum,
Portland, Oregon, USA.

■ 29.9.72
Hec Edmundson Pavilion,
University of Washington,
Seattle, Washington, USA.

This show was originally
scheduled for The Seattle Arena.

■ 30.9.72
Gardens Arena, Vancouver,
British Columbia, Canada.

Two shows, at 4.00pm and
9.00pm. The last night of the tour.

■ 21.10.72
A Benefit For War On Want
and Oxfam, Empire Pool,
Wembley, Middlesex, England.

Set list: Dark Side Of The
Moon//One Of These Days/
Careful With That Axe Eugene/
Echoes/encore: Set The Controls
For The Heart Of The Sun/Blues.
'From the word go, they gave
the packed stadium a faultless
demonstration of what
psychedelic music is all about.
There wasn't a note, or a sound,
out of place during the whole
evening... For starters, on
Saturday, we had that lengthy
work entitled "Dark Side Of The
Moon", an eerie title for an
equally eerie piece of music that
takes the listener through a host
of different moods, most of
which are accompanied by
unusual sounds stretching
around his head by way of the
group's quadraphonic sound
system. The effect is quite
stunning. The second half of the
recital was composed of three
more major pieces, and a couple
of encores. The first – the
riveting "Set The Controls For
The Heart Of The Sun" – was
obviously rehearsed, but the
second – a bluesy jam – wasn't.
It served a useful purpose to
show that the group are not

confined to playing science
fiction soundtrack music all the
time. The incendiary gimmicks
from the stage frequently
obliterated the artists. Flash-
bombs erupted here and there
at well timed places, and Roger
Waters gong actually became a
blazing sun during "Set The
Controls". All the time the group
were effectively illuminated by
their imposing lighting tower at
the rear of the stage which
served a dual purpose – at
frequent intervals it belched out
smoke which mingled with the
coloured lights and the dry ice
surface mist to effectively whisk
us all away to Planet Floyd.'
(*Sounds*)

EUROPEAN TOUR
■ 10,11.11.72
KB Hallen, Frederiksberg,
Copenhagen, Denmark.

Set list: Dark Side Of The
Moon//One Of These Days/
Careful With That Axe Eugene/
Echoes/encore: Set The Controls
For The Heart Of The Sun.

■ 12.11.72
Ernst-Merck Halle,
Hamburg, West Germany.

Set list: Dark Side Of The
Moon//One Of These Days/
Careful With That Axe Eugene/
Echoes/encore: Set The Controls
For The Heart Of The Sun.

■ 14.11.72
Philips Halle, Düsseldorf,
West Germany.

Set list: Dark Side Of The
Moon//One Of These Days/
Careful With That Axe Eugene/
Echoes/encore: Set The Controls
For The Heart Of The Sun.

■ 15.11.72
Sporthalle, Böblingen,
West Germany.

Set list: Dark Side Of The
Moon//One Of These Days/
Careful With That Axe Eugene/
Echoes (announced by Roger
Waters as 'Looking Through The
Knotholes In Granny's Wooden
Leg')/encore: Set The Controls
For The Heart Of The Sun.

■ 16.11.72
Festhalle, Frankfurt-am-

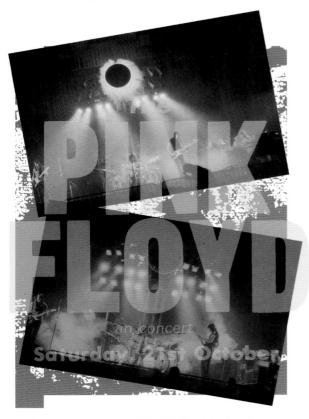

Inset photographs: Philips Halle, Düsseldorf, West Germany, 14 November 1972

Main, West Germany.
Set list: Dark Side Of The Moon//One Of These Days/ Careful With That Axe Eugene/ Echoes (announced by Roger Waters as 'The March of The Dambusters')/encore: Set The Controls For The Heart Of The Sun.

■ **17.11.72**
Festhalle, Frankfurt-am-Main, West Germany.
Set list: Dark Side Of The Moon//One Of These Days/ Careful With That Axe Eugene/ Echoes/encore: Set The Controls For The Heart Of The Sun.

■ **22–26.11.72**
Roland Petit Ballet, Salle Valliers, Marseilles, France.
These five shows, which did not from part of the scheduled European tour, featured the company of Les Ballets de Marseille with Roland Petit as

Choreographer and Artistic Director, and with the participation of Maïa Plissetskaia, a recent addition from Moscow's Bolshoi Theatre.The programme was divided into three sections:
1. Allumez les Étoiles (Light The Stars) – a ballet concerning Mayakovsky (1893–1930), a poet of the Russian Revolution, with extracts of the works of Prokofiev, Shostakovich and Mussorgsky.
2. La Rose Malade (The Sick Rose) – a ballet in three movements based on William Blake's poem with extracts from Mahler's 2nd and 5th Symphonies.
3. The Pink Floyd Ballet – a ballet in four movements, based on

the following set list: One Of These Days/ Careful With That Axe Eugene/Obscured By Clouds – When You're In/Echoes.

■ **28.11.72**
Palais des Sports, Toulouse, France.

■ **29.11.72**
Les Arènas, Poitiers, France.
Set list: Dark Side Of The Moon/ One Of These Days/Careful With That Axe Eugene/Echoes.

■ **1.12.72**
Palais des Sports de L'Ile de la Jatte, St Ouen, France.
Set list: Dark Side Of The Moon//One Of These Days/ Careful With That Axe Eugene/ Blues/Echoes/encore: Set The Controls For The Heart Of The Sun.

■ **2.12.72**
Palais des Sports de L'Ile de la Jatte, St Ouen, France.
Set list: Dark Side Of The Moon//One Of These Days/ Careful With That Axe Eugene/ Echoes/encore: Set The Controls For The Heart Of The Sun.
Some 14,000 people attended the two shows in St Ouen, one of which was recorded and broadcast in a ninety-minute presentation on RTL radio.

■ **3.12.72**
Parc des Expositions, Caen, France.

■ **5.12.72**
Sport Palais Vorst Nationaal, Brussels, Belgium.

■ **7.12.72**
Palais des Sports, Lille, France.
Set list: Dark Side Of The Moon//One Of These Days/ Careful With That Axe Eugene/encore: Echoes.
This show was almost cancelled because the power supply was inadequate to meet Pink Floyd's demands. The show went ahead with a reduced lighting rig.

■ **8.12.72**
Parc des Expositions, Nancy, France.

■ **9.12.72**
Hallenstadion, Zurich, Switzerland.
Set list: Dark Side Of The Moon// One Of These Days/Careful With That Axe Eugene/encore: Echoes.

■ **10.12.72**
Palais des Sports, Lyon, France.
Set list: Dark Side Of The Moon// One Of These Days/Careful With That Axe Eugene/encore: Echoes.
The last night of the tour.
The band were held up by customs authorities at the Swiss border and took the stage two hours later than scheduled, at 8.00pm..

1973

Roland Petit Ballet, Paris, France.
The following series of shows

Salle Valliers, Marseilles, France, November 1972

was identical in presentation to those performed in Marseilles in November 1972 (see above). As *Sounds* reported: 'Dry ice was fuming quietly all over an apron stage and the Pink Floyd, standing above it all amongst their sound equipment and lighting towers, seemed suspended about ten feet up in the blackness. An unsteady, bright shaft of light opened up beneath them and slowly a stiff, bowed figure moved out and, gradually unbending, took command of the stage. Rudy Bryans, star soloist with the Ballets de Marseille, danced to the Pink Floyd's "Echoes". The audience is strange, hardly a typical crush of Floyd devotees, but a mixture of people who obviously came because it was the band, people who obviously came because it was the ballet, and people who didn't look quite sure why they'd come. The opening movement, "One Of These Days" was fairly short, a kind of introduction with the whole troupe dancing, and it struck me at the time that that was what organised dance to rock music should look like, it was essentially rhythmic and fast. "Obscured by Clouds" was a solo for Rudy Bryans and Daniele Jossi, beautifully lit, which had a hesitant, slightly menacing air. "Careful With That Axe" was the troupe again, moving through various tableaux and sequences, featuring the exploding flares. "Echoes" was the finale, a constantly changing sequence of short pieces, the most spectacular of which were Rudy's entrance from the tunnel, and a dance where he pulled Daniele right across the width of the stage with her in the splits position.'

■ **13.1.73**
Palais des Sports de la Porte de Versailles, Paris, France.
Two shows, at 5.00pm and 8.45pm.

■ **14.1.73**
Palais des Sports de la Porte de Versailles, Paris, France.
Two shows, at 2.30pm and 6.00pm.

■ **20.1.73**
Palais des Sports de la Porte de Versailles, Paris, France.
Two shows, at 5.00pm and 8.45pm, with audio playback only.

■ **21.1.73**
Palais des Sports de la Porte de Versailles, Paris, France.
Two shows, at 2.30pm and 6.00pm, with audio playback only.

■ **27.1.73**
Palais des Sports de la Porte de Versailles, Paris, France.
Two shows, at 5.00pm and 8.45pm, with audio playback only.

■ **28.1.73**
Palais des Sports de la Porte de Versailles, Paris, France.
Two shows, at 2.30pm and 6.00pm, with audio playback only.

■ **3.2.73**
Palais des Sports de la Porte de Versailles, Paris, France.
Two shows, at 5.00pm and 8.45pm.

■ **4.2.73**
Palais des Sports de la Porte de Versailles, Paris, France.
Two shows at 2.30pm and 6.00pm – the last night of the ballet season.
Part of the above series of shows was recorded and transmitted on France's Europe 1 radio.

NORTH AMERICAN TOUR
Additional touring personnel:
Venetta Fields: Backing vocals
Dick Parry: Saxophone
Carlena Williams: Backing vocals
(The identity of the third backing vocalist is unknown.)

■ **4.3.73**
Dane County Memorial Coliseum, Madison, Wisconsin, USA.
Set list: Echoes/Obscured by Clouds – When You're In/Careful With That Axe Eugene//Dark Side Of The Moon/encore: One Of These Days.

■ **5.3.73**
Cobo Arena, Detroit, Michigan, USA.
Set list : Echoes/Obscured by Clouds – When You're In/Careful With That Axe Eugene//Dark Side Of The Moon/encore: One Of These Days.
During 'Careful With That Axe Eugene' pyrotechnics damaged the PA system, showering the crowd with debris. The second half was without incident.

■ **6.3.73**
Kiel Opera House, St Louis, Missouri, USA.
Set list: Echoes/Obscured By Clouds – When You're In/Childhood's End/Careful With That Axe Eugene//Dark Side Of The Moon/encore: One Of These Days.

■ **7.3.73**
International Amphitheatre, Chicago, Illinois, USA.
Set list: Echoes/Obscured By Clouds – When You're In/Childhood's End/Careful With That Axe Eugene//Dark Side Of The Moon/encore: One Of These Days.

■ **8.3.73**
University of Cincinatti

Fieldhouse, Cincinnati, Ohio, USA.
Set list: Echoes/Obscured By Clouds – When You're In/Childhood's End/Careful With That Axe Eugene//Dark Side Of The Moon/encore: One Of These Days.

■ **10.3.73**

Kent State University, Kent, Ohio, USA.
Set list: Echoes/Obscured By Clouds – When You're In/Childhood's End/Careful With That Axe Eugene//Dark Side Of The Moon/encore: One Of These Days.

■ **11.3.73**
Maple Leaf Gardens, Toronto, Ontario, Canada.
Set list: Echoes/Obscured By Clouds – When You're In/Set The Controls For The Heart Of The Sun/Careful With That Axe Eugene//Dark Side Of The Moon/encore: One Of These Days.

■ **12.3.73**
The Forum, Montreal, Quebec, Canada.

■ **14.3.73**
Music Hall, Boston, Massachusetts, USA.
Set list: Careful With That Axe Eugene/Obscured By Clouds – When You're In/Set The Controls For The Heart Of The Sun/

Overleaf: Maple Leaf Gardens, Toronto, 11 March 1973

Echoes//Dark Side Of The Moon/
encore: One Of These Days.

■ **15.3.73**
**Spectrum Theater,
Philadelphia, Pennsylvania,
USA.**
■ **17.3.73**
**Radio City Music Hall,
Manhattan, New York City,
New York, USA.**
Set list: Obscured By Clouds –
When You're In/Set The Controls
For The Heart Of The Sun/
Careful With That Axe Eugene/
Echoes//Dark Side Of The Moon/
encore: One Of These Days.
'Radio City Music Hall is one of
the few halls in the States that
were specifically constructed 30
or 40 years ago for live shows,
and in fact four times a day it
normally features the last show
of its kind in America, with
orchestra, dancers and special
sets. It was here that the Pink
Floyd turned out an exciting set
last week with a stage half a
block long, and a 6,200 seat
theatre on four levels as their
basic props. At one-thirty in the
morning the lights dimmed, the
audience stood, clouds of steam
shot upwards from the vents in
the stage, and the Floyd rose
into view on one of the
elevators; three light towers
with a reflecting dish mounted
on the centre one, created a
glowing, hypnotic effect as you
looked at the stage. The
elevated stage section reached
its full height then began to inch
forward, and the crowd roared
approval. Special mention ought
to be made of the Floyd's
lighting and sound crews who
seemed never to miss a cue,
and the 20 speaker quad system
with speakers on all levels of the
hall gave a close almost
headphone sound. The music
started with some of their well
known older pieces with
"Echoes" ending the first half.
The second half was the new
album "Dark Side Of The
Moon" (on which they used
three black singers) with an

encore of "One Of These
Days". The fifteen foot dish
hanging from the centre tower
glowed and steamed in the
lights, and at one point as the
red spots caught it the effect
was of red laser beams flashing
through the dark hall. Other
times when the lights caught it,
it looked like one of those
mirrored globes they had at 30s
balls. The Floyd were at their
best and the stage presentation
was one of the best I've seen in
a hell of a long time.' (*Sounds*)
■ **18.3.73**
**Palace Theatre, Waterbury,
Connecticut, USA.**
■ **19.3.73**
**Providence Civic Center,
Providence, Rhode Island,
USA.**
■ **22.3.73**
**Hampton Coliseum,
Hampton, Virginia, USA.**
■ **23.3.73**
**Charlotte Park Center,
Charlotte, North Carolina,
USA.**
This concert replaced the one
scheduled for the same day at
the Clemson Coliseum,
Clemson, South Carolina.
■ **24.3.73**
**Municipal Auditorium,
Atlanta, Georgia, USA.**
The last night of the tour.
Set list: Obscured By Clouds –
When You're In/Set The
Controls For The Heart Of The
Sun/Careful With That Axe
Eugene/Echoes//Dark Side Of
The Moon/encore: One Of
These Days.
■ **25.3.73**
**Bayfront Center, St
Petersburg, Florida, USA.**
This hastily arranged show was
proposed for the end of the tour
but was cancelled because
Santana were scheduled to
appear at the Tampa Stadium on
the same night and the
promoter considered that this
would reduce the audience for
Pink Floyd.
UK SHOWS
Additional personnel:

Radio City Music Hall, New York City, 17 March 1973

Vicki Brown: Backing vocals
Venetta Fields: Backing vocals
Dick Parry: Saxophone
Carlena Williams: Backing vocals
■ **18,19.5.73**
Earls Court Exhibition Hall,

**Earls Court, London,
England.**
Set list: Obscured By Clouds –
When You're In/Set The Controls
For The Heart Of The Sun/
Careful With That Axe Eugene/

Echoes//Dark Side Of The Moon/ encore: One Of These Days. 'After the reportedly dismal failure of David Bowie's Earls Court fiasco, when he could be seen by a few and heard by fewer, we approached last night with mixed emotions, anticipation and slight apprehension of what was to come. However, from the moment Rick Wright's synthesiser played the droning beginning of "Obscured By Clouds" amidst appropriate clouds of smoke, we knew we need fear no more.... The Floyd have used their vast technical knowledge and financial resources in a good way, and built a PA of such crystal clarity that it may be equalled but never bettered. Of the rest of their brilliant set, "Eugene" and "Set The Controls" are still there, but

PINK FLOYD

Left: Earls Court, London, May 1973.

given a new freshness with the aid of burning gongs and a spaceman whose eyes lit up, and the inevitable smoke bombs after the by now legendary "Careful With That Axe Eugene". Then came "Echoes" when, during the wind and crows sequence, tons of dry ice poured on to the stage and swirled around the feet of the group and into the 18,000 strong audience giving a very effective Macbeth-ian "blasted heath" scene. The second half featured "Dark Side Of The Moon", complete with girl Negro singers, a saxophonist and insane laughter which made full use of the quadraphonic sound system. It has been said that the Floyd have relied too heavily on taped effects to liven up their performances. Now they have integrated them into their performance so well that the tape deck becomes another instrument contributing to a homogenous group sound rather than a group entity.... The end of "Dark Side Of The Moon" came along with rockets being fired into the roof of the hall and the tolling of the iron bell.... All however was not over. To greet us at the door was the Army, complete with wartime-type searchlights which panned across the faces of the people leaving, then raked into the sky to form the all too familiar criss-cross patterns which have not been with us over London since 1945.' (John Baxter and Martin Whicker-Kempton)

NORTH AMERICAN TOUR
Additional touring personnel:
Venetta Fields: Backing vocals
Carlena Williams: Backing vocals
(The identities of the third backing vocalist and the replacement saxophonist in Dick Parry's absence from this tour are not known.)

■ **16.6.73**
Roosevelt Stadium, Jersey City, New Jersey, USA.
Set list at this show and all shows on this tour, except for

Jet Set Enterprises Presents
an evening with
Pink Floyd
Wednesday, June 27   8:00 P.M.   Tickets $5 in advance
Jacksonville Coliseum
Tickets available at Hemming Park, Coliseum, Civic Aud., Regency Square, and Hixon's Surf Shop, Jax. Beach. For more information, call (904) 398-3706

Louisville (25.6), Jonesboro (26.6) and Jacksonville (27.6), for which set lists are unconfirmed: Obscured By Clouds – When You're In/Set The Controls For The Heart Of The Sun/Careful With That Axe Eugene/Echoes//Dark Side Of The Moon/encore: One Of These Days.
■ **17.6.73**
Saratoga Performing Arts New York, USA.
■ **19.6.73**
Civic Center Arena, Pittsburgh, Pennsylvania, USA.
■ **20,21.6.73**
Merriweather Post Pavilion, Columbia, Maryland, USA.
■ **22.6.73**
Buffalo Memorial Auditorium, Buffalo, New York, USA.
This show replaced the one scheduled for 15.6.73.
■ **23.6.73**
Olympia Stadium, Detroit, Michigan, USA.
■ **24.6.73**
Blossom Music Center, Cuyahoga Falls, Ohio, USA.
■ **25.6.73**
Convention Center, Louisville, Kentucky, USA.
■ **26.6.73**

Lake Spivey Park, Jonesboro, Georgia, USA.
■ **27.6.73**
Jacksonville Coliseum, Jacksonville, Florida, USA.

■ **28.6.73**
The Sportatorium, Hollywood, Florida, USA.
This show replaced the one scheduled for the same day at Pirates World, Dania, Hollywood, Florida.
■ **29.6.73**
Tampa Stadium, Tampa, Florida, USA.
The last night of the tour.
EUROPEAN SHOWS
■ **22-23.9.73**
3rd British Rock Meeting, Sandrennbahn Altrip, Ludwigshafen, West Germany.
Pink Floyd were advertised to headline this two-day festival on 23.9.73, but did not perform. Among the scheduled acts were Frank Zappa and The Mothers of Invention, Lou Reed, Wishbone Ash, Lindisfarne, Genesis and ELO.
■ **12.10.73**
Olympiahalle, Munich, West Germany.
Set list: Obscured By Clouds – When You're In/Set The Controls For The Heart Of The Sun/Careful With That Axe Eugene/Echoes//Dark Side Of The Moon/encore: One Of These Days.
■ **13.10.73**
Stadthalle, Vienna, Austria.

The last date of the tour.
Set list: Obscured By Clouds – When You're In/Set The Controls For The Heart Of The Sun/Careful With That Axe Eugene/Echoes//Dark Side Of The Moon/encore: One Of These Days.
UK SHOWS
Additional personnel:
Vicki Brown: Backing vocals
Venetta Fields: Backing vocals
Dick Parry: Saxophone
Carlena Williams: Backing vocals
■ **4.11.73**
Rainbow Theatre, Finsbury Park, London, England.
Two shows, at 5.00pm and 9.00pm. Supported by Soft Machine.
Set list at both shows: Dark Side Of The Moon//Obscured By Clouds – When You're In.
'It was a splendid evening of rock co-operation, in which both groups gave their services in aid of disabled drummer Robert Wyatt, and compere John Peel was pleased to announce that some 10,000 pounds was raised. Heartbeats in fact commenced proceedings, pulsating through the auditorium and stilling the more excitable elements in the crowd. Clocks ticked mysteriously and with perfect precision the Floydmen slotted their live instruments into the recorded sound, combining quadraphonic pre-recorded tapes, lights, smoke and theatrical effects into a kind of rock "Son et Lumiere". Overhead was suspended a huge white balloon to represent the moon, on which spotlights played, and not long after performance began, searchlights began to pierce the gloom, and yellow warning lights began revolving in banks on the speaker cabinets. A choir of ladies cooed like angels of mercy and as a silver ball reflecting myriad beams of light began to revolve and belch more smoke, the audience rose to give them an ovation. They deserved a Nobel prize or at least an Oscar.' (*Melody Maker*)

6

The Pink Floyd's break from both live performance and recording between late 1973 and early 1974 saw Gilmour and Mason, for the first time, involved in projects outside the band. Gilmour had been introduced to a talented young singer-songwriter called Kate Bush, and he eventually influenced EMI's decision to give her her first recording contract. Since then Gilmour has frequently guested on her work.

He had also spotted a band called Unicorn who, in early 1974, were down on their luck. After financing some recording sessions at Olympic studios in London, he produced their debut album, *Blue Pine Trees*. Steve O'Rourke became Unicorn's manager and they quickly signed to the Chrysalis label, for which they went on to make three albums.

Mason, meanwhile, lent his hand to producing Principal Edward's Magic Theatre as well as Robert Wyatt. With Wyatt he later drummed at London's Theatre Royal, as well as on Wyatt's performance on BBC TV's *Top Of The Pops* of his cover of the Monkees' 'I'm A Believer'.

It wasn't very long before Pink Floyd themselves were back in the studio. Despite having promised themselves more leisure time, they found it hard to let go of the routine of constant activity, and by spring they were already working hard on new material. They booked rehearsal time at a studio near King's Cross, London, where many of the songs for the next two albums would emerge, not least a stunning new title, 'Shine On' (later changed to 'Shine On You Crazy Diamond'), an ode to Syd Barrett.

'We started playing together and writing in the way we'd written a lot of things before. In the same way that "Echoes" was written,' Waters remembered. '"Shine On You Crazy Diamond" was written in exactly the same way, with odd little musical ideas coming out of various people. The first one, the main phrase, came from Dave, the first loud guitar phrase you can hear on the album was the starting point and we worked from there until we had the various parts of "Shine On You Crazy Diamond".'[1]

A second number, entitled 'Raving And Drooling', was also worked out, and both tracks were premiered in June during a tour of France – the only country outside the UK where Pink Floyd would perform this year.

The band also re-enlisted the services of backing singers Carlena Williams and Venetta Fields, now labelled The Blackberries, and saxophonist Dick Parry. The entourage was also expanded by the hiring of many extra roadies, including Phil Taylor, who is nowadays the band's chief backline technician, to carry them through both this and the UK shows in the late autumn.

The band had also gone to considerable effort

Palais des Sports, Paris, June 1974

and expense to redesign their stage presentation to create a far greater visual impact than ever before. The show now featured, at the centre rear of the stage, a forty-foot circular screen which was used to back-project specially prepared film and animation sequences. The screen also served as a backdrop at the close of 'Shine On', when a huge rotating mirror ball was raised in front of it and hit with a spotlight to produce blinding shards of white light, under cover of which the band exited. Fireworks and rockets, launched from the stage, also provided some spectacular visual effects.

The French tour was dogged by an enormous amount of problems. A succession of cancelled and rescheduled dates occurred when promoters realized how much electrical power the band's new equipment required and the ceiling height that was needed to accommodate the huge circular screen. However, the shows that did go ahead were complete sell-outs in the five cities in which Pink Floyd performed, setting new records for audience attendance in France.

Whereas problematic dates were eventually straightened out, a sponsorship campaign into which the band had entered with the French soft drinks company Gini, turned decidedly sour. The agreement required a photo-shoot for press adverts and the recording of a song for the TV ads called 'Bitter Love', for which the band was offered the princely sum of £50,000. Although this was a potentially good idea and would go some way to offsetting the high costs of the tour, the band became increasingly wary of the implications it would have for their image – not to mention the fact that Waters was told he wouldn't be allowed to sing on it. Their position was clearly compromised and although nothing could stop the press advertisements coming out, it is not clear whether the TV ad was ever aired. It is an incident that the band have chosen to put down to experience, and all the monies were subsequently donated to charity.

Even so, the episode left a bad taste in Waters' mouth and, after taking a short break in Morocco following the tour, he started writing a new song, which remains unrecorded, expressing his feelings about it: 'How Do You Feel'. It seems strange, therefore, that the band were all seen sporting Guinness T-shirts on stage throughout the year, but no hint of a sponsorship deal has ever been made public. An advertising campaign launched in 1973 by Avis also attracted the band's name, with the inviting slogan 'Make tracks like Pink Floyd – Rent an Avis truck'.

The 1974 British Winter Tour, as it was called, was booked to start in November, and was planned to coincide with important football games in the cities on the itinerary, in order that the band could enjoy watching a good afternoon match before each show.

By now 'Shine On' had become 'Shine On You Crazy Diamond' and, like 'Raving And Drooling', had been knocked into better shape. The band had also added a third new song to the set, 'Gotta Be Crazy', which Waters had penned at home and to which Gilmour added the chord sequence at a later date. All three songs were very harsh in comparison with the softer melodies of *Dark Side Of The Moon* and the lyrics were an unforgiving tirade against society's current values. It certainly laid to rest the last traces of Pink Floyd's psychedelic past.

The choice of films they had projected on to the circular screen for the 'Dark Side Of The Moon' half of the show in France was now extensively refined, with whole new sequences being produced throughout the rest of the summer. In addition, a three-week rehearsal period was booked at the Elstree film studios, north of London, before the tour to allow the band to work out the intricate timings that were required to keep the music in sync with the visual material.

David Gilmour, 1974

Audiences in Britain were treated to a version of 'Dark Side Of The Moon' with greater dimension and visual impact than ever before, including specially commissioned animation by Ian Eames. The piece now began with quadraphonic sound blasting out the taped maniacal laughter that appears on the album and the spoken line of 'I've been mad for fucking years' repeated over and over again at deafening volume. A picture of the moon grew bigger and bigger until it occupied the whole screen and then, with the underlying heart beat now very audible, this gave way to a darting cardiograph blip, allowing the band to launch into 'Breathe'.

Perhaps the most outstanding feature of all was the sequence for 'On The Run' and 'Time'. A series of flashing street, car, airport and aircraft lights, in bewildering and dazzling succession, led the viewer into a tunnel with a planet at the far end. As this image seemed to rush towards the viewer, the film switched to animation, skimming across the planet's surface and then sweeping through urban landscapes to reveal scenes of utter destruction.

The 'Time' sequence, again animated, was equally remarkable: flights of clock faces were seen passing across a cloudy sky, then piling up against one another and peeling away, squadrons of them flying through the air as their hands raced round. The final scene focused on a pendulum sweeping the sky to introduce the opening line of the song.

'The Great Gig In The Sky' featured underwater shots taken from the film *Crystal Voyager* and 'Money' had a series of rapid-fire shots of banknotes, coins, women parading in fur

coats, a lyrically appropriate Lear jet and even copies of *Dark Side Of The Moon* coming off the production line.

'Us And Them', the dreamy blues number from the album, featured slow-motion footage of the rush hour in the City of London in contrast with the miners of South Africa. As 'Dark Side Of The Moon' came to its grand finale with 'Brain Damage', film images of politicians were used to complement the accompanying insane laughter. The eclipse of the sun by the moon concluded the epic piece.

The UK tour was a complete success, with every venue sold out. However, it was also the first time that a noticeable backlash against the band had occurred within the national music press. Throughout the early seventies Pink Floyd had reigned supreme, but the concerts at Wembley's Empire Pool brought disdain from a younger generation of critics, principally Nick Kent of the *NME*, who described their show as 'a pallid excuse for creative music' and not only suggested they lived a bourgeois existence, but also attacked Gilmour's personal appearance.

On Monday 13 January 1975 Pink Floyd entered EMI's newly refitted Studio 3 at Abbey Road to start work on their seventh studio album, *Wish You Were Here.* Because of their touring commitments, the sessions took place either side of and between two tours of the USA. As a result, the recording process became very drawn-out, and ultimately pushed the album's release back to September. One by-product of this delay was that the band were again able to refine new works on stage.

The first US tour of that year was announced

in March and, in a new departure, carried no national advertising. Instead, CBS Records used FM radio to alert fans to a specially prepared Pink Floyd show which was simulcast early that month to the seven major cities where they were booked to play. Within hours, all of the dates had completely sold out, breaking all the venues' box-office records, including those of the Los Angeles Sports Arena, which in a single day sold all of its 67,000 tickets for the band's scheduled four-night run. Even an extra fifth show sold out within hours, and indeed the demand for tickets was so great that the band's residency could easily have been extended still further.

Overall, American fans' response to the tour was so positive that the band's former label, Capitol, was prompted to issue a promotional compilation album, *Tour '75*, to radio stations in order to boost back-catalogue sales.

Pink Floyd chose to play a different set from that of the UK tour of the previous year. 'Dark Side of The Moon' still formed the mainstay of the second half of the show, with 'Echoes' as an encore, but the first half, although still opening with 'Raving And Drooling' and 'Gotta Be Crazy', now divided the lengthy 'Shine On You Crazy Diamond' into two halves which straddled another new composition, 'Have A Cigar', a dig at the corporate music industry.

For the first time American fans witnessed the full visual impact of the new stage show, complete with circular film screen, giant mirror ball, crashing model aircraft and obligatory pyrotechnics – in addition to the trademark quadraphonic sound system. It was a large-scale operation in every sense: over thirty tons of equipment, much of it shipped over from England, was transported around the country, and it took a full-time road crew of seventeen to make the event possible. The band also chartered a private jet to travel between shows, while the road crew moved the gear in a

Former UK Prime Minister Alec Douglas Home on screen during the band's 1975 US tour

convoy of articulated trucks.

Although this vast array of visual effects was spectacular in indoor venues, the band ran into serious trouble when they began their East Coast leg of the tour in June. Their still primitive staging – small-scale compared with the vast scaffolding structures of today's outdoor concerts (although not quite as rudimentary as the Beatles' set-up at Shea) – looked decidedly lost in the vast expanses of the huge sports stadiums in which they were now performing.

In an attempt to boost the visual impact and lend the shows a more impressive scale, Pink Floyd turned to Mark Fisher and Jonathan Park, two accomplished London-based architectural designers with experience of advanced inflatable and mobile pneumatic structures. Their brief was

to construct a huge pyramid that would sail above the stage and radiate light beams in a way that was reminiscent of the cover of *Dark Side Of The Moon*.

Assembled in record time, the structure made its maiden flight at the huge Three Rivers Stadium in Pittsburgh, five dates into the tour, on 20 June. The huge pyramid, its base sixty-six foot square and its height the same, was held by guides and launched from the back of the stage. It rose some distance before the wind blew it over, dislodging the huge helium balloon inside. The balloon was never seen again; nor was the pyramid, which, after crashing into a number of vehicles in the stadium car park, was shredded in minutes by souvenir-hungry fans.

Despite the overall success of the tour, it is also

remembered for the heavy-handed actions of the Los Angeles Police Department, which arrested over 500 fans during the five-night run at the Sports Arena. Police Chief Ed Davis, in a speech to businessmen a week before the concerts, described the forthcoming shows as an 'illegal pot festival' and gave the assurance that his force was committed to bringing the full weight of the law to bear on even the most minor of offences committed at or in the grounds of the venue. Inevitably, many innocent fans were also stopped and questioned.

This confrontation had been brewing for months; the LAPD had been waiting eagerly to deal with the biggest event in the city. *Rolling Stone*, in its June 1975 edition, ran an extensive report that gave evidence that many other venues in the greater Los Angeles area had been subjected to the heavy-handed actions of Chief Davis, who was quoted as saying, 'I'm the meanest chief of police in the history of the United States.' The article also contained an allegation that the 'bust' had been planned well in advance: 'One young man arrested at the Shrine Auditorium's Robin Trower concert of March 16th claimed an officer told him, "If you think this is something, you ought to see what we're going to do at the Sports Arena."'

Officially only seventy-five police officers were deployed at the shows on each of the five nights Pink Floyd played, but the venue management estimated the figure at nearer 200. Of the 511 arrests made in that period, the majority were for possession of marijuana. The police justified their actions by claiming that there were a couple of more serious offences, including cocaine dealing and possession of a loaded gun. This fact made more headline news in the *LA Times* than the concerts themselves.

Despite the tense atmosphere, the fans behaved well in the view of the Arena's management, which later praised them.

Back in Britain, with the US tour just a few days behind them, in July Pink Floyd were due to give their long-awaited 'homecoming' concert at Knebworth Park in rural Hertfordshire. The concert was dogged by problems from the start, among which was the arrival of the road crew, jet-lagged from the US tour, only a day or so beforehand. Because of the scale of the event, Pink Floyd's own PA system had to be used by all the other bands throughout the day and, not surprisingly, by the time they came to use it themselves it had taken a serious pounding.

In addition, their stage entrance had been precisely scheduled to coincide with the fly-past of two Second World War Spitfires, but in the event the fighters buzzed the audience at low level while the roadies were still frantically trying to prepare the stage. As a result the band came on stage unprepared and their set was tired, uninspired and marred throughout by technical breakdowns. The most noticeable of these occurred during 'Raving and Drooling', when the stage-right PA stack failed altogether. This problem was later rectified, but the mains power was not coming through at the correct frequency and this put Rick Wright's Hammond organ out of tune. The instrument couldn't be retuned and Wright was forced to use his Farfisa instead, which gave the rest of show a very hard, mechanical feel.

It may have been a wonderful day out for the estimated 100,000 crowd: the concert had an official licence for 40,000, but so great was the turn-out that the perimeter fencing was eventually removed. And yet, all in all, it was not quite the return the fans had been expecting from Pink Floyd, especially since it was their first British show for seven months.

Predictably, the band again fell foul of the UK music press. Some reviewers accused them of turning in a poor performance and others for playing 'Dark Side of The Moon' yet again; others took them to task for playing in their own country all too infrequently. Whereas Pink Floyd had once been seen as stalwarts of the British rock-underground, regular performers at festivals and small UK venues, the view now was that the industry machine had taken over and the band had overreached themselves. What the journalists failed to realize was that their own overwhelming support over the years had contributed to this massive expansion. The audience had swelled considerably, which prevented the band from playing a small-scale concert ever again. Besides, as much as the band disliked it, they and their management recognized that a US tour was far more lucrative than its UK counterpart could ever be. Underlining this difference, the American tour had ensured enough album sales to propel *Dark Side of The Moon* back into the *Billboard* Top 100 album chart on 12 April 1975, where it resided until 6 March 1977.

Money aside, the US tour had left the band cold. There was a distinct feeling of isolation as the audiences had grown, with the back row getting further and further away. The fans' intense enthusiasm and ability to make plenty of noise meant that attending a Pink Floyd concert in the States was akin to watching an FA Cup Final back home. Such was this sense of alienation, at least in Roger Waters' mind, that it led him to believe there may as well have been a brick wall between band and audience. 'I cast myself back into how fucking dreadful I felt on the last American tour with all those thousands and thousands and thousands of drunken kids smashing each other to pieces. I felt dreadful because it had nothing to do with us – I didn't think there was any contact between us and them.'[2]

It was an idea he would nurture over the next few years, but for the moment there was a deadline looming for the release of *Wish You Were Here*. Their record company and management were now exerting greater pressure than ever before on the band to deliver an album that would equal the massive success of its predecessor. But the truth was, their hearts just weren't in it. In fact, they were very close to splitting up. Indeed Waters has, on many occasions, stated in print that *Dark Side Of The Moon* had more or less finished the group as a creative force, since they had fulfilled at a stroke the shared ambition of fame and fortune.

He spoke quite frankly of these fraught times shortly after the later album's release: 'I definitely think that at the "Wish You Were Here" recording sessions most of us didn't wish we were there at all, we wished we were somewhere else. I wasn't happy being there because I got the feeling we weren't together. The album is about none of us really being there, or being there only marginally. About our non-presence in the situation we had clung to through habit, and are still clinging to through habit – being Pink Floyd.

'We pressed on regardless of the general ennui for a few weeks and then things came to a bit of a head. I felt that the only way I could retain interest in the project was to try to make the album relate to what was going on there and then – i.e. the fact that no one was really looking each other in the eye, and that it was all very mechanical. So I suggested we change it – that we didn't do the other two songs ['Raving And Drooling' and 'Gotta Be Crazy'] but tried somehow to make a bridge between the first and second halves of "Shine On", which is how "Welcome To The Machine", "Wish You Were Here" and "Have A Cigar" came in".'[3]

Speaking of the recording sessions Waters later commented: 'We all sat round and unburdened ourselves a lot, and I took notes on what everybody was saying. It was a meeting about what wasn't happening and why. Dave was always

Roger Waters, Knebworth Park, Hertfordshire, 5 July 1975

clear that he wanted to do the other two songs –
he never quite copped what I was talking about.
But Rick did and Nicky did and he was out-voted,
so we went on.'[4]

The final recording sessions, after Knebworth,
saw much of the same atmosphere. For a start
Waters' vocals on 'Shine On You Crazy Diamond'
were turning into a nightmare: 'It was right on
the edge of my range. I always felt very insecure
about singing anyway because I'm not naturally
able to sing well. I know what I wanna do but I
don't have the ability to do it well. It was
fantastically boring to record, 'cos I had to do it
line by line, doing it over and over again just to
get it sounding reasonable.'[5]

By the time they had reached 'Have A Cigar',
Waters' singing was beyond a joke and as a last
resort their friend Roy Harper was drafted in.
'Roy was recording in the studio anyway,' recalled
Waters, 'and was in and out all the time. I can't
remember who suggested it, maybe I did,
probably hoping everybody would go "oh no Rog,
you do it", but they didn't! They all went, "Oh
yeah that's a good idea". And he did it and
everybody went "oh, terrific!". So that was that.'[6]
It seems to be a decision that Waters has bitterly
regretted to this day, despite successful takes of
Harper and Gilmour duetting the vocals.

Also present on the album's title track was
Stephane Grappelli, who was recording with
Yehudi Menuhin at Abbey Road. It is often
claimed that the tapes were lost or recorded over
but, according to Waters, Grappelli definitely
appears at the very end of the song, although his
contribution is barely audible. He isn't credited on
the sleeve, but he reportedly received a small fee.

One final incident at those sessions has passed
into Pink Floyd lore: the sudden and uncanny
appearance of Syd Barrett in the studio at
precisely the moment the band was going
through the final playbacks of 'Shine On You

Crazy Diamond', their extended tribute to him.
The date was reportedly 5 June 1975, just before
their departure for their second America tour. It
was all the more bizarre because none of them
recognized Barrett at first, assuming he was a
caretaker. His appearance had changed dramatically:
he had a shaven head, was extremely overweight
and was wearing tatty clothes. He hardly spoke a
word and after a short time merely wandered off.
It was the last time the band ever saw him.

'I'm very sad about Syd,' Waters declared. 'I
wasn't for years. For years I suppose he was a
threat because of all that bollocks written about
him and us. Of course he was very important and
the band would never have fucking started
without him but on the other hand it couldn't
have gone on with him. He may or may not be
important in rock 'n' roll anthology terms but
he's certainly not nearly as important say in terms
of Pink Floyd. "Shine On" is not really about Syd,
he's just a symbol for the extremes of absence
some people have to indulge in because it's the
only way they can cope with how fucking sad it is
– modern life, to withdraw completely.'[7]

As on all Pink Floyd's albums, the artwork is
quite unique and again was designed by Storm
Thorgerson and friends at Hipgnosis. It is a very
specific visual representation of the subject matter
and continues the theme of alienation and absence
throughout. Even the sleeve was concealed by a
black shrink-wrapped outer covering which made
the album look appropriately anonymous.

Wish You Were Here was finally released on
15 September and went straight to the top of the
album charts on both sides of the Atlantic. No
doubt CBS in the USA gave a huge sigh of relief
on learning that its investment had paid off.

Notes
1–5.Unidentified press article c.1977
6. *Pink Floyd Story*, Capital Radio, 14.1.77
7. Unidentified press article c.1977

1974

FRENCH TOUR

Many conficting dates for shows were advertised in French music magazines. This situation was caused by the difficulty in locating suitable venues, and the following shows did not take place: Palais des Sports, Cambrai (14.6); Palais des Sports, Lyon (14.6); Strasbourg (16.6); Nancy (16.6); Palais des Sports, Lyon (16.6); Palais des Sports, Cambrai (18.6); Les Arènas, Poitiers (20.6); Palais des Sports, Lyon (21.6) and Parc des Expositions, Toulouse (22.6). Additional touring personnel (to end of year):
Venetta Fields: Backing vocals
Dick Parry: Saxophone
Carlena Williams: Backing vocals

Roger Waters, Palais des Sports, Paris, June 1974

■ **18.6.74**
Parc des Expositions, Toulouse, France.
Set list at this show and all shows on this tour: Shine On*/
Raving And Drooling/Echoes// Dark Side Of The Moon/encore: Careful With That Axe Eugene (except all Paris shows (24–26.6) where the encore was replaced by 'One Of These Days').
*'Shine On' and 'Shine On You Crazy Diamond' are early versions of the later recorded piece 'Shine On You Crazy Diamond Pts.6-9'.
The first date of the tour was recorded along with band interviews by France's Europe 1 radio, and segments were later broadcast.
■ **19.6.74**
Les Arènas, Poitiers, France.
■ **21.6.74**
Palais des Expositions, Dijon, France.
■ **22.6.74**
Parc des Expositions, Colmar, France.
■ **24–26.6.74**
Palais des Sports de la Porte de Versailles, Paris, France.
The show of 26.6.74. was the last night of the tour.
BRITISH WINTER TOUR
■ **4,5.11.74**
Usher Hall, Edinburgh, Lothian, Scotland.
Set list at this show and all shows up to and including the show of 16 11.74.: Shine On You Crazy Diamond/Raving And Drooling/Gotta Be Crazy//Dark Side Of The Moon/encore: Echoes.
■ **8,9.11.74**
The Odeon, Newcastle-upon-Tyne, Tyne and Wear, England.
■ **14.11.74**
Empire Pool, Wembley, Middlesex, England.
'After approximately five minutes of slightly laboured tuning up, the band start their first number of the set – a new composition entitled "Shine On You Crazy Diamond". It is very slow, rather low on melodic inventiveness, each note hanging in that archetypally ominous stunted fashion that tends to typify the Floyd at their most uninspired. This thoroughly unimpressive beginning is duly followed by the second of the three new numbers to be showcased in this section. "Raving And Drooling" is motivated by a rhythm somewhat akin to that of the human heart-beat with further references gathered from numerous Floyd stylised devices. So then there was "Gotta Be Crazy", the magnum opus of this dubious triumvirate, which features a fairly decent melody; a fetching minor chord strummed out by Gilmour who also sings over it. Unfortunately, the Floyd as always, let the song sprawl out to last twice as long as it should. The second half is, of course, taken up by the whole "Dark Side Of The Moon" presentation, to be graced by the projection of a special film made as a visual complement to the music. Finally the set is completed and the band walk off to ecstatic applause. They eventually return for an encore – no "thank-yous" or anything, and the band do "Echoes". Visuals are now relegated to luminous green orbs of circular light projected on the big screen.' (*NME*)
■ **15,16.11.74**
Empire Pool, Wembley, Middlesex, England.
The second half and encore of the show of 16.11.74 was recorded by BBC Radio One. However, only 'Dark Side Of The Moon' – with the line 'I've been mad for fucking years' in 'Speak To Me' removed from the mix – was broadcast,.on the *Alan Freeman Show* on 11.1.75 at 2.00pm.

Backstage with 'Po' Powell of design team Hipgnosis, UK tour 1974

■ **17.11.74**
Empire Pool, Wembley, Middlesex, England.
Set list at this show and all shows until end of tour: Raving And Drooling/Gotta Be Crazy/Shine On You Crazy Diamond// Dark Side Of The Moon/encore: Echoes.
■ **19.11.74**
Trentham Gardens, Stoke-on-Trent, Staffordshire, England.
An unauthorized recording of this concert found its way on to a bootleg album – perhaps the first mass-produced illegal record to date – which reportedly sold well in excess of 100,000 copies. The album, *British Winter Tour '74*, was thought to have been pressed in Germany or the Netherlands, and, had it been an official release, would have gained Gold Record status.
■ **22.11.74**
Sophia Gardens Pavilion, Cardiff, Glamorgan, Wales.
■ **28–30.11.74**
Empire Theatre, Liverpool, Merseyside, England.
■ **3–5.12.74**
The Hippodrome,

Birmingham, West Midlands, England.
■ **9,10.12.74**
The Palace Theatre, Manchester, Greater Manchester, England.
■ **13,14.12.74**
The Hippodrome, Bristol, Avon, England.
The show of 14.12.74. was the last night of the tour.

1975

FIRST NORTH AMERICAN TOUR
Additional touring personnel (to end of year):
Vanetta Fields: Backing vocals
Dick Parry: Saxophone
Carlena Williams: Backing vocals
■ **8.4.75**
Pacific National Exhibition Coliseum, Vancouver, British Columbia, Canada.
Set list at this and all shows on North American tours this year, except San Francisco (12.4), Denver (17.4), Tucson (19.4), Los Angeles (22–25.4), Atlanta (7.6), Philadelphia (13.6) and Detroit (24.6), for which set lists are unconfirmed although were

probably the same as for the other shows: Raving And Drooling/Gotta Be Crazy/Shine On You Crazy Diamond Pts.1-5/ Have A Cigar/Shine On You Crazy Diamond Pts.6-9//Dark Side Of The Moon/encore: Echoes.
■ **10.4.75**
The Coliseum, Seattle, Washington, USA.
■ **12,13.4.75**
Cow Palace, Daly City, San Francisco, California, USA.
■ **17.4.75**
Denver Coliseum, Denver, Colorado, USA.
■ **19.4.75**
Tucson Community Center Arena, Tucson, Arizona, USA.
■ **20.4.75**
University Activity Center, Arizona State University, Tempe, Arizona, USA.
This concert replaced the one scheduled for 15.4.75., which was cancelled because the power supply was deemed to be inadequate and the scaffold stage was considered unsafe. After the concert there were allegations of ticket fraud when head counts by both the promoter and Pink Floyd's

management put the attendance at 1,000 over the 9,000 capacity. Nevertheless it was regarded as a successful concert.
'…the audience went wild when the light show began. Concert-goers were particularly impressed when a parabolic mirror which reflected spots of light on the ceiling and walls of the Activity Center. Smoke rose from the stage. Imitation snow fell from above. A huge screen hung from the ceiling showed scenes of an operating room to accompany cuts from "Dark Side". Hundreds of yellow clock dials were projected moving in time to the music. The crowd liked it, and that should be reason enough. But I think the crowd is wrong. A light show is a good addition to most rock shows, but when special effects are carried to the extreme they can only detract from the music and create a carnival atmosphere. The music was good enough to outweigh the gimmicks,

Right and following spreads: North American tour, June 1975

however. And let it be said that their 32 tons of equipment was enough. My ears were ringing for hours after the show.' (*State Press,* student magazine)

■ **21.4.75**
Sports Arena, San Diego, California, USA.

■ **23–27.4.75**
Sports Arena, Exposition Park, Los Angeles, California, USA.
The show of 27.4.75. was the last night of the tour.

SECOND NORTH AMERICAN TOUR

■ **7.6.75**
Atlanta Stadium, Atlanta, Georgia, USA.

■ **9,10.6.75**
Capital Centre, Landover, Maryland, USA.

■ **12,13.6.75**
Spectrum Theater, Philadelphia, Pennsylvania, USA.

■ **15.6.75**
Garden State Music Fair, Roosevelt Stadium, Jersey City, New Jersey, USA.
This show was originally scheduled for the day before but heavy rain prevented the show from proceeding.

■ **16,17.6.75**
Nassau Veterans Memorial Coliseum, Uniondale, Long Island, New York, USA.

■ **18.6.75**
Boston Garden, Boston, Massachusetts, USA.

■ **20.6.75**
Three Rivers Stadium, Pittsburgh, Pennsylvania, USA.

■ **22.6.75**
County Stadium, Milwaukee, Wisconsin, USA.
Set list: Dark Side Of The Moon/Echoes.
The set was abbreviated because of heavy rain.

■ **23,24.6.75**
Olympia Stadium, Detroit, Michigan, USA.
'Just about everything was working against Pink Floyd

at its Monday night [23.6] concert at Olympia Stadium. Fortunately, the one thing that was perfectly right was the music. Pink Floyd is not nearly as well known to the general public as some groups that attract legions of hard-core rock fans, but nevertheless it has been hugely successful since 1964. Monday,

the four members of Floyd were put to the test. Could their music, without many of their infamous special effects, make 17,000 people forget the misery of being crammed into a building that felt like a steam-bath gone mad? As part of the contract with Pink Floyd, Olympia used festival-style seating for the Floyd's Monday and Tuesday concerts, and the result was sweaty thigh jammed against sweaty thigh on the main floor where fans sat cross-legged like sweltering Indians. As if the heat weren't enough, Monday's audience was denied a special film by Peter

Medak, director of "Ruling Class". The film, an interpretation of Floyd's "Dark Side Of The Moon", was on the premises, but the projector was soaked during a downpour at an outdoor date in Milwaukee Sunday, and was out of commission. The group turned the old ballroom mirrored globe to its own use, bathing the crowd in a swirl of stars. Pink Floyd's futuristic but never garish music shows the polish over 10 years together, with only one personnel change, and the group proved Monday that its music, nothing more, is the foundation of its long success.' (*Detroit Free Press*)

■ **26.6.75**
Autostade, Montreal, Quebec, Canada.

■ **28.6.75**
Ivor Wynne Stadium, Hamilton, Ontario, Canada.
The last night of the tour.

UK SHOW

■ **5.7.75**
Knebworth Park, Stevenage, Hertfordshire, England.
With The Steve Miller Band, Captain Beefheart & His Magic Band, Roy Harper, Linda Lewis and Monty Python. Compered by John Peel and Pete Drummond.
Set list: Raving And Drooling/ Gotta Be Crazy/Shine On You Crazy Diamond Pts.1-5/Have A Cigar/Shine On You Crazy Diamond Pts. 6-9//Dark Side Of The Moon/encore: Echoes.

Knebworth, 5 July 1975

David Gilmour with Roy Harper on Trigger, backstage at Knebworth

7

PINK FLOYD IN CONCERT

SOUTH DOOR ENTRANCE

Pink Floyd's 1977 album *Animals* was recorded entirely in the seclusion of their newly acquired and purpose built twenty-four-track recording complex in a renovated church hall in Britannia Row, Islington, north London. Recording commenced in the spring of 1976 and was completed in November – a relatively short space of time for the band. The recording of the album was marked by Waters' exercise of an ever-increasing power over the three other members. This led to a noticeable rift in the working unit, which in any case was by now merely serving as a vehicle for his lyrical output.

Wright, being less assertive than the others, was more susceptible to such divisive pressure. It is only in recent years that he has spoken of this fraught period at all: 'I didn't really like a lot of the music on the album. I have to say I didn't fight very hard to put my stuff on, and I didn't have anything to put on. I played on it. I think I played well, but I didn't contribute to the writing of it but I think also Roger was kind of not letting me do that. This was the start of the whole ego thing in the band.'[1]

Waters' dominance would, according to his fellow members of the band, reduce it to a mere shadow of its former self. His ability to write cutting lyrics expressing sheer hatred and blind fury was faultless. But excluding others from the process to pursue his own vision – a trend that would continue over the next two studio albums –

ultimately worked to the detriment of both Waters himself and the band itself.

It was also during the recording of *Animals* that Waters slowly developed a collection of unconnected songs into a conceptual piece that described the apparent social and moral decay of modern society, likening the human condition to that of mere animals. Surprisingly, the two previously ditched songs that had formed the mainstay of the band's 1974–5 tour were revived and extensively reworked for the album. 'Raving And Drooling' and 'Gotta Be Crazy' mutated into the tracks 'Sheep' and 'Dogs' respectively. As Waters explained: 'Sometime during the middle of recording it, it seemed like the right thing to tie it all together. It gave me the lead to re-write the lyrics to "Raving And Drooling" and turn it into "Sheep", 'cos "Raving And Drooling" was just another shout, but it was a rather incoherent shout of abuse in a way that "Pigs" is a kind of fairly compassionate scream of abuse. I've had the idea of "Animals" in the back of my mind for years… many years. It's a kind of old chestnut, really.'[2]

Despite the tensions within the band, *Animals* contains one of their best recorded performances. It is is a dark and powerful album, even violent at times. 'Sheep', for example, bastardizes Psalm 23 and 'Pigs' makes a scathing attack on, in particular, Mary Whitehouse, the self-appointed protector of the nation's morals (another verse was later revealed by Waters as a sideswipe at the rising Margaret Thatcher MP). It is a work that matched the air of depression and gloom of the times. Despite a strong economy and high employment, there was a growing social unrest in England. Street violence was increasing, partially fuelled by rampaging gangs of punks and skinheads, and so was the racial violence initiated by

right-wing organizations such as the National Front; both expressions of discontent contributed to a feeling of unease, even oppression. It is surprising how well *Animals* fared with the music press, considering its attempts to push rock supergroups like Pink Floyd out of the window once and for all now that it had the Sex Pistols to fawn over. Perhaps the sheer vehemence of the attack on society won over the more radical critics, although some reviewers thought it was simply just too much to stomach.

By complete contrast, part of the album is also benevolent. 'Pigs On The Wing', with which it opens and closes, is a very personal message of love from Waters to his then wife Carolyne.

At Waters' suggestion, the sleeve depicted a large inflatable pink pig hovering between two of the four towering chimneys of London's Battersea power station. Hipgnosis, again commissioned to provide the artwork, suggested that an inflatable pig could be photographed in any location and the shot then 'stripped into' a separate photograph of the power station. However, the band insisted that the shoot be done for real and a forty-foot inflatable pig was shipped over from its designers, Eventstructure Research Group in

Amsterdam. (The pig was actually made in Germany by Ballon Fabrik, which had constructed the original Zeppelin airships.) Once it had been inflated with helium and raised on cables, it would be tethered in position and eleven stills photographers and an eight-man film crew (including one in a helicopter) who had been assembled at the location would capture it for posterity on launch day, 2 December. A marksman had also been hired: to shoot the pig down should it break free from its moorings and escape. However, for one reason or another the creature couldn't be inflated. The following day, a bright, sunny morning, a successful launch was made, only for a freak gust of wind to snap the pig's mooring cables. Unfortunately, nobody had told the marksman to return that day.

Later that morning the pig, having been spotted by an astonished commercial pilot, was tailed by a police helicopter as far as Crystal Palace, south-east London. By mid-afternoon it was seen at 18,000 feet over Chatham, in Kent, by which time everybody concerned assumed it was heading for home. Eventually it deflated and crashed, rather appropriately, into a farmer's field at Chilham near Canterbury.

In a final, ironic twist the pictures of the power station on the first day were thought to be more interesting because of the contrasting skies – it had been rather overcast that morning – and the pig ended up being stripped in after all.

Many of the photos taken during the shoot were used for the subsequent tour publicity, programme, song book and, much later, for the remastered CD booklet. However, the film footage has, except for the occasional TV clip, only ever been seen as a backdrop film for Waters' much later solo tours, which incorporated material from the album.

An extensive tour of much of Europe and North America followed, in support of the album, and as a result the band's concert entourage needed to be expanded. Sax player Dick Parry was re-employed and a new support guitarist, Terence 'Snowy' White, was brought in. 'I hadn't heard of "Dark Side Of The Moon" even,' Snowy recalled. 'I must have been the only person in England that hadn't heard it – so I went down to the studio to see the boys and that was right at the end of the "Animals" album. It was funny, when I walked in the atmosphere was terrible… I thought, "fucking hell!" but I discovered that they'd accidentally rubbed out one of Dave Gilmour's favourite solos they were really pleased with and they'd just lost it – and that's when I walked in! Dave took me in the office and told me what the gig was all about and asked me if I fancied doing it and I said, "can we have a bit of a play or a jam or something?", and he said, "well you wouldn't be here if you couldn't play would you?" and I replied, "well, no not really." So he said, "well that's all right then. You start in November for rehearsals" – and that was it.'[3]

And on that same day Waters said, 'Well as you're here you might as well play something,'[4], so Snowy turned in the delicate guitar solo that was used to bridge the two parts of 'Pigs On The Wing'. Although this was only ever used on the eight-track cartridge release, it completed the tape loop that brought the album back to its starting point.

The album was released on the day of the opening show of the tour, in Dortmund, West Germany on 23 January 1977. Each show consisted of the whole of *Animals* and, for the first time, the complete *Wish You Were Here*, as first and second-half performances. On stage, a transistor radio was placed on a stand and miked up ready for Waters to scan the airwaves randomly, often with hilarious results, for the introduction of the title track of the latter album. The encores, which depended to a great extent on the collective mood of the band, varied between 'Money' and

'Us And Them', although on occasion both were performed and always featured the familiar back-projected films of the previous tours.

A large part of the rehearsals had taken place at Britannia Row in early November and the final dress rehearsals at the Olympia Exhibition Hall in London, from where the production was shipped out to Germany. For the first time, Pink Floyd now truly tackled the problem of the stadium environment. Conscious of the fact that many of the larger venues would tend to isolate the audience, they attempted to make the back row feel as involved as the front – to increase the element of spectacle for everyone.

In order to realize this ideal, again largely conceived by Waters, the Fisher–Park design team were once more mobilized and set to work on the design and construction of various large-scale inflatables to symbolize the typical 'nuclear-age' family. This consisted of a businessman, his wife reclining on a sofa and, as the statistics would have it, 2.5 children. These characters were inflated by industrial fans and hoisted into position by hydraulic rigging halfway through 'Dogs', to be quickly deflated at the end of the song. They were first used at the shows in

Pink Floyd's inflatable 'nuclear-age' family, Empire Pool, Wembley, 16 March 1977

Previous page: Pavillon de Paris, Porte de Pantin, Paris, France, February 1977. Right: Empire Pool, Wembley, March 1977

London, but by the time the tour had reached America a Cadillac, a fridge and a TV set, all in relative scale, had also been added.

Appropriately, the tour motif and newly acquired mascot, the giant inflatable pig, was also used. Not as benign as the Battersea model, the helium-filled balloon sported an ugly snarl as it poked its head from out behind the stage through a massive burst of smoke during 'Pigs'. In indoor shows it would travel the length of the auditorium suspended by steel cables. At outdoor shows it was floated on a cable to a position high above the stage, where the propane charge it carried was detonated to dramatic effect.

Another new element was a compressed-air 'sheep-cannon' that fired small sheep made from tea-bag material deep into the audience. But the most striking addition was the awe-inspiring animation film designed by the English satirical cartoonist Gerald Scarfe which was shown to 'Welcome To The Machine'. The band had

spotted Scarfe's work as early as 1972, when he was sent to Los Angeles by BBC TV to try out a new cartoon animation method. This resulted in the *Long-Drawn-Out-Trip*, a parody which let rip at every cliché of American life and is best remembered for its depiction of Mickey Mouse whacked out on drugs. His first work for Pink Floyd, however, had been his caricature of the band for the centrespread of their 1974–5 tour programmes.

Scarfe's film for Pink Floyd was every bit as heart-warming as the song itself and featured a constantly changing series of environments which included a huge, lizard-like metallic creature roaming a geometric landscape; a head that is brutally severed and slowly decays; and a city enveloped by a sea of blood whose lapping waves transform into a sea of bloody, outstretched hands worshipping a huge monolithic structure.

It was reported in *Melody Maker* that the band had allocated a budget of around £100,000 to produce the animation sequence for the concerts alone and that Scarfe had taken some six months to produce it. The result was certainly amazing when seen on the big screen.

Another piece of Scarfe animation was used for the closing section of 'Shine On You Crazy Diamond', the number which ended the show. This depicted a naked, faceless and sexless body somersaulting through the air as it transformed into a falling leaf and back again until the screen was slowly blanked out by a huge mirror ball, revived from the previous tour. American shows also featured a waterfall of fireworks that stretched the full width of the stage and provided a spectacular conclusion to the extravaganza.

When the UK tour went ahead, the only real technical problems occurred at Wembley, where their series of concerts kicked off. Incidentally, the band were disappointed at having to play this venue again rather than Earls Court, where they had had better success on previous occasions. The tour then progressed to the New Bingley Hall, Stafford – an unusual choice of venue as no other bands had been known to play there. But it was not altogether inappropriate, since it was formerly a livestock market. (Similarly, the shows in Paris were held in a converted abattoir.)

The following month, as the show laboured across America, it was dubbed 'Pink Floyd – In The Flesh?'. It is now that it all started to go wrong. Overexcited fans were yelling and screaming throughout the performances, a habit which destroyed the rapt atmosphere that had hitherto existed at live shows. This, along with the fact that firecrackers were being hurled about in abundance, contributed to a growing frustration in Waters that no one was actually listening to his songs, and eventually he came to nurse a hatred for the impersonal nature of stadium touring.

The crunch came at the final show, in Montreal, where the crowd were unusually rowdy: 'I was on stage and there was one guy in the front row shouting and screaming all the way through everything. In the end I called him over and, when he got close enough, spat in his face. I shocked myself with that incident enough to think: "hold on a minute. This is all wrong. I'm hating this."'[5]

But while the incident struck a devastating chord in Waters' psyche, Gilmour recalled that neither he nor the others had been aware at the time of the effect on their band mate. 'I just thought it was a great shame to end up a six-month tour with a rotten show. In fact, I remember going off stage for the encore and going back to the sound mixing board in the middle of the audience to watch the encore while Snowy played guitar.'[6] 'It was quite a long jam,' Snowy recalls. 'I was enjoying myself, and then the crew started dismantling the equipment as we were playing. In the end Nick was just left with a bass drum!'[7]

Close to nervous collapse after the tour, Waters felt that the best therapy would be to write about his own experiences. He would attempt to trace his feelings of alienation back to his childhood; his sense of solitude as a consequence of his father's death during the war; the tyranny of his schooling; and the break-up of his first marriage.

Leaving Waters to his own devices, Gilmour, Wright and Mason each recorded a solo album, the former two of which were released a year later. It was only then that they began thinking about his proposal for a new Pink Floyd album.

Notes
1. *Omnibus*, BBC TV, 15.11.94
2. *Pink Floyd Story*, Capital Radio, 21.1.77
3–4. Authors' interview with Terence 'Snowy' White, September 1996
5. Unidentified press article c.1982
6. *Musician*, c.1982
7. Authors' interview with Terence 'Snowy' White, September 1996

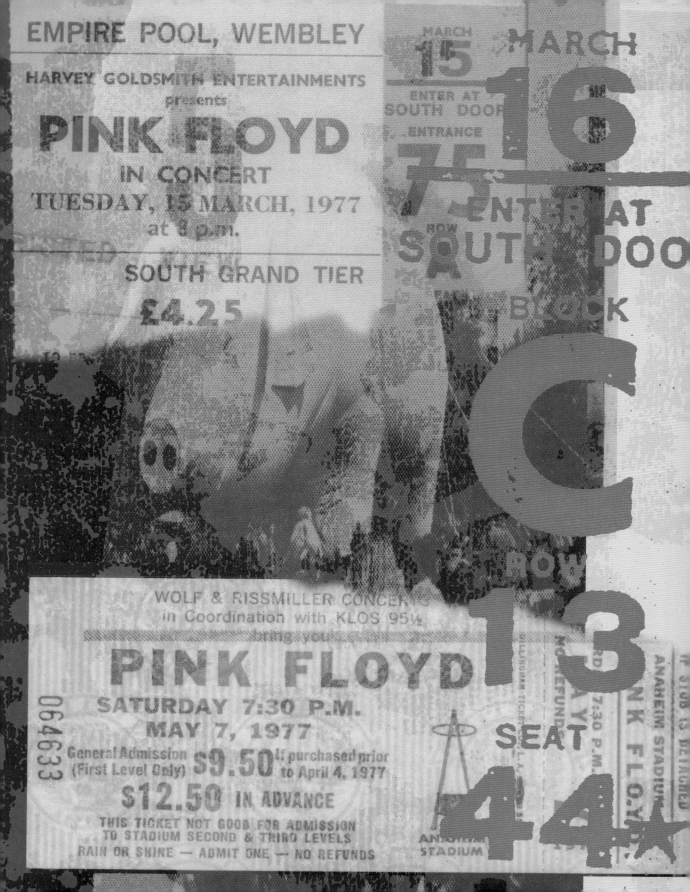

1976

Pink Floyd gave no concerts in 1976.

1977

EUROPEAN TOUR

Additional touring personnel (to end of year):

Dick Parry: Saxophone
Snowy White: Rhythm guitar, bass guitar

■ **23.1.77**
Westfalenhalle, Dortmund, West Germany.

Set list: Sheep/Pigs On The Wing Pt.1/Dogs/Pigs On The Wing Pt.2/Pigs//Shine On You Crazy Diamond Pts.1-5/Welcome To The Machine/Have A Cigar/Wish You Were Here/Shine On You Crazy Diamond Pts.6-9/ encore: Money/Us And Them.

■ **24.1.77**
Westfalenhalle, Dortmund, West Germany.

Set list: Sheep/Pigs On The Wing Pt.1/Dogs/Pigs On The Wing Pt.2/Pigs/ Shine On You Crazy Diamond Pts.1-5/Welcome To The Machine/Have A Cigar/Wish You Were Here/Shine On You Crazy Diamond Pts.6-9/ encore: Money.

■ **26.1.77**
Festhalle, Frankfurt-am-Main, West Germany.

Set list: Sheep/Pigs On The Wing Pt.1/Dogs/Pigs On The Wing Pt.2/Pigs//Shine On You Crazy Diamond Pts.1-5/Welcome To The Machine/Have A Cigar/Wish You Were Here/Shine On You Crazy Diamond Pts.6-9/ encore: Money/Us And Them.

■ **27.1.77**
Festhalle, Frankfurt-am-Main, West Germany.

Set list: Sheep/Pigs On The Wing Pt.1/Dogs/Pigs On The Wing Pt.2/Pigs//Shine On You Crazy Diamond Pts.1-5/Welcome To The Machine/Have A Cigar/Wish You Were Here/Shine On You Crazy Diamond Pts.6-9/ encore: Money.

'It had been an evening totally

Inset photographs: Antwerp, 20 February 1977

without mishaps. The 12,000 natives packed into Frankfurt's Festhalle for the second successive night on Thursday were in a generally friendly mood, for the Floyd hardly attract the standard aggro crowd of people like Zep or Purple. But in an audience that size, it is a statistical certainty there are bound to be some nutters, like those who were throwing cans and bottles during the first set. An announcement in the first interval asked them to desist, bitte, because delicate equipment was getting damaged. I saw another bottle smash on Nick Mason's Hokusai painted drum kit - evidently a full one, for it sprayed his face with foam. in the shadow of the PA columns, a group of "plain clothes" polizei, about as inconspicuous as a panzer armoured division in their uniform anoraks and regulation length haircuts, took photographs of the crowd to see if anyone was smoking dope. Their American counterparts in the Military Police also ranged through the crowd, checking the IDs of hapless GIs out of camp for a little night music, searching if they were AWOL or carrying exotic substances. The bands special effects departament still hadn't got the highpoint of their contribution to the show quite right yet. In the middle of the "Pigs" section, which closed the first half, a gigantic inflated porker is meant to fly over the PA, emerging out of a cloud of smoke, clearing the stacks by a few inches, and making a circuit of the hall over the heads of the audience. well, Mr. Pig made it over the stack all right without toppling the driver horns on the top, but the trouble was the smoke. The first three nights of the tour they couldn't get enough product out of the rented fog-machine, so they tried a smoke-bomb instead. that worked rather too well for comfort, filling the hall with

billowing clouds of acrid, throat strangling murk, through which it was barely possible to see that something was happening on stage.' (*Melody Maker*)

■ **29,30.1.77**
Deutschlandhalle, West Berlin, West Germany.
Set list at both shows: Sheep/Pigs On The Wing Pt.1/ Dogs/Pigs On The Wing Pt.2/ Pigs//Shine On You Crazy Diamond Pts.1-5/Welcome To The Machine/Have A Cigar/Wish You Were Here/Shine On You Crazy Diamond Pts.6-9/encore: Money.

■ **1.2.77**
Stadthalle, Vienna, Austria.
Set list: Sheep/Pigs On The Wing Pt.1/Dogs/Pigs On The Wing Pt.2/Pigs//Shine On You Crazy Diamond Pts.1-5/Welcome To The Machine/Have A Cigar/ Wish You Were Here/Shine On You Crazy Diamond Pts.6-9/ encore: Money/Us And Them.

■ **3,4.2.77**
Hallenstadion, Zurich, Switzerland.
Set list at both shows: Sheep/Pigs On The Wing Pt.1/ Dogs/Pigs On The Wing Pt.2/ Pigs/ Shine On You Crazy Diamond Pts.1-5/Welcome To The Machine/Have A Cigar/Wish You Were Here/Shine On You Crazy Diamond Pts.6-9/encore: Money.

■ **17–19.2.77**
Sportpaleis Ahoy, Rotterdam, Netherlands.
Set list: Sheep/Pigs On The Wing Pt.1/Dogs/Pigs On The Wing Pt.2/Pigs//Shine On You Crazy Diamond Pts.1-5/ Welcome To The Machine/ Have A Cigar/Wish You Were Here/ Shine On You Crazy Diamond Pts.6-9 encore: Money.

■ **20.2.77**
Sportpaleis, Antwerp, Belguim
Set list: Sheep/Pigs On The Wing Pt.1/Dogs/Pigs On The Wing Pt.2/ Pigs//Shine On You Crazy Diamond Pts.1-5/ Welcome To The

Machine/Have A Cigar/Wish You Were Here/Shine On You Crazy Diamond Pts.6-9/encore: Money.

■ **22–25.2.77**
Pavillon de Paris, Porte de Pantin, Paris, France.
Set list: Sheep/Pigs On The Wing Pt.1/Dogs/Pigs On The Wing Pt.2/Pigs//Shine On You Crazy Diamond Pts.1-5/Welcome To The Machine/Have A Cigar/ Wish You Were Here/Shine On You Crazy Diamond Pts.6-9/ encore: Money.

■ **27,28.2.77 and 1.3.77**
Olympiahalle, Munich, West Germany.
Set list on 27, 28.2.77: Sheep/Pigs On The Wing Pt.1/ Dogs/Pigs On The Wing Pt.2/ Pigs//Shine On You Crazy Diamond Pts.1-5/Welcome To The Machine/Have A Cigar/Wish You Were Here/Shine On You Crazy Diamond Pts.6-9/encore: Money. The show of 1.3.77. was the last night of the tour.

UK TOUR

■ **15,16.3.77**
Empire Pool, Wembley, Middlesex, England.
The original series of dates was 17–20.3.77, but for unspecified reasons a date on 16.3. was substituted for 20.3. A further show, on 15.3, was added to cope with the vast excess of ticket applications already received for the other shows. Set list: Sheep/Pigs On The Wing Pt.1/Dogs/Pigs On The

Wing Pt.2/Pigs//Shine On You Crazy Diamond Pts.1-5/Welcome To The Machine/Have A Cigar/ Wish You Were Here/Shine On You Crazy Diamond Pts.6-9/ encore: Money.
'The time has come for the Pink Floyd to completely re-think their stage act. They play in vast, windy auditoria and do nothing to turn their concerts into human events: the ambience they encourage is that of a few thousand robots responding to a computer. Last Wednesday evening at Wembley's Empire Pool was no exception. It was rather like sitting at home in the dark listening to their albums a lot louder than the neighbours would permit, with more treble than anyone would wish and a giant inflatable pig hanging over your head. And this is rock? A band playing though their two latest albums, with as little variation as possible? It was all so cold, clean and clinical. The Floyd have altered the whole concept of rock; they've turned the stage into a one-take recording studio, dispensing with the human bond between artist and audience.' (*Melody Maker*)

Right: Snowy White, performing with Pink Floyd, Empire Pool, Wembley, March 1977
Overleaf: Wembley, 1977

■ **17,18.3.77**
Empire Pool, Wembley, Middlesex, England.
Set list: Sheep/Pigs On The Wing Pt.1/Dogs/Pigs On The Wing Pt.2/Pigs//Shine On You Crazy Diamond Pts.1-5/Welcome To The Machine/Have A Cigar/ Wish You Were Here/Shine On You Crazy Diamond Pts.6-9/ encore: Us And Them.

■ **19.3.77**
Empire Pool, Wembley, Middlesex, England.
Set list: Sheep/Pigs On The Wing Pt.1/Dogs/Pigs On The Wing Pt.2/Pigs//Shine On You Crazy Diamond Pts.1-5/Welcome To The Machine/Have A Cigar/ Wish You Were Here/Shine On You Crazy Diamond Pts.6-9/ encore: Money.

■ **28–31.3.77**
New Bingley Hall, Stafford, Staffordshire, England.
Set list: Sheep/Pigs On The Wing Pt.1/Dogs/Pigs On The Wing Pt.2/Pigs//Shine On You Crazy Diamond Pts.1-5/Welcome To The Machine/Have A Cigar/ Wish You Were Here/Shine On You Crazy Diamond Pts.6-9/ encore: Money.
The show of 31.3.77. was the last night of the tour.

PINK FLOYD IN THE FLESH – FIRST NORTH AMERICAN TOUR

■ **22.4.77**
Miami Baseball Stadium, Miami, Florida, USA.
Set list: Sheep/Pigs On The Wing Pt.1/Dogs/Pigs On The Wing Pt.2/Pigs//Shine On You Crazy Diamond Pts.1-5/Welcome To The Machine/Have A Cigar/ Wish You Were Here/Shine On You Crazy Diamond Pts.6-9/ encore: Money/Us And Them.
Because of technical problems, the circular film screen couldn't be lowered and the pig, tethered to a flag pole throughout the show, caught fire, rather than simply exploded, when detonated.

■ **24.4.77**
Tampa Stadium, Tampa, Florida, USA.

Set list: Sheep/Pigs On The Wing Pt.1/Dogs/Pigs On The Wing Pt.2/Pigs//Shine On You Crazy Diamond Pts.1-5/Welcome To The Machine/Have A Cigar/ Wish You Were Here/Shine On You Crazy Diamond Pts.6-9/ encore: Money.

■ **26.4.77**
The Omni Coliseum, Atlanta, Georgia, USA.
Set list: Sheep/Pigs On The Wing Pt.1/Dogs/Pigs On The Wing Pt.2/Pigs//Shine On You Crazy Diamond Pts.1-5/Welcome To The Machine/Have A Cigar/ Wish You Were Here/Shine On You Crazy Diamond Pts.6-9/ encore: Money.

■ **28.4.77**
Assembly Center, Louisiana State University, Baton Rouge, Louisiana, USA.
Set list: Sheep/Pigs On The Wing Pt.1/Dogs/Pigs On The Wing Pt.2/Pigs//Shine On You Crazy Diamond Pts.1-5/Welcome To The Machine/Have A Cigar/ Wish You Were Here/Shine On You Crazy Diamond Pts.6-9/ encore: Money.

■ **30.4.77**
Jeppesen Stadium, Houston, Texas, USA.
Set list: Sheep/Pigs On The Wing Pt.1/Dogs/Pigs On The Wing Pt.2/Pigs//Shine On You Crazy Diamond Pts.1-5/Welcome To The Machine/Have A Cigar/ Wish You Were Here/Shine On You Crazy Diamond Pts.6-9/ encore: Money/Us And Them.

■ **1.5.77**
Tarrant County Convention Center, Fort Worth, Texas, USA.
Set list: Sheep/Pigs On The Wing Pt.1/Dogs/Pigs On The Wing Pt.2//Shine On You Crazy Diamond Pts.1-5/Welcome To The Machine/Have A Cigar/ Wish You Were Here/Shine On You Crazy Diamond Pts.6-9/ encore: Money/Us And Them.

■ **4.5.77**
Phoenix Coliseum, Phoenix, Arizona, USA.

■ **6,7.5.77**

Anaheim Stadium, Anaheim, Los Angeles, California, USA.
Set list: Sheep/Pigs On The Wing Pt.1/Dogs/Pigs On The Wing Pt.2/Pigs//Shine On You Crazy Diamond Pts.1-5/Welcome To The Machine/Have A Cigar/ Wish You Were Here/Shine On You Crazy Diamond Pts.6-9/ encore: Money.

■ **9.5.77**
Oakland Coliseum Arena, Oakland, California, USA.
Set list: Sheep/Pigs On The Wing Pt.1/Dogs/Pigs On The Wing Pt.2/Pigs//Shine On You Crazy Diamond Pts.1-5/Welcome To The Machine/Have A Cigar/ Wish You Were Here/Shine On You Crazy Diamond Pts.6-9/ encore: Money/Us And Them/ second encore: Careful With That Axe Eugene.

■ **10.5.77**
Oakland Coliseum Arena, Oakland, California, USA.
Set list: Sheep/Pigs On The Wing Pt.1/Dogs/Pigs On The Wing Pt.2/Pigs//Shine On You Crazy Diamond Pts.1-5/Welcome To The Machine/Have A Cigar/ Wish You Were Here/Shine On You Crazy Diamond Pts.6-9/ encore: Money.

■ **12.5.77**
The Memorial Coliseum, Portland, Oregon, USA.
Set list included: Sheep/Pigs On The Wing Pt.1/Dogs/Pigs On The Wing Pt.2/Pigs//Shine On You Crazy Diamond Pts.1-5/Welcome To The Machine/Have A Cigar/ Wish You Were Here/Shine On You Crazy Diamond Pts.6-9.
The last night of the tour.

PINK FLOYD IN THE FLESH – SECOND NORTH AMERICAN TOUR

■ **15.6.77**
County Stadium, Milwaukee, Wisconsin, USA.
Set list: Sheep/Pigs On The Wing Pt.1/Dogs/Pigs On The Wing Pt.2/Pigs//Shine On You Crazy Diamond Pts.1-5/Welcome To The Machine/Have A Cigar/ Wish You Were Here/Shine On

You Crazy Diamond Pts.6-9/ encore: Money.

■ **17.6.77**
Freedom Hall, Louisville, Kentucky, USA.
Set list included: Sheep/Pigs On The Wing Pt.1/Dogs/Pigs On The Wing Pt.2/Pigs//Shine On You Crazy Diamond Pts.1-5/ Welcome To The Machine/Have A Cigar/Wish You Were Here/ Shine On You Crazy Diamond Pts.6-9.
'A 30 by 15 foot helium-filled pig with glowing amber eyes. Two human counterparts in a helium husband and wife. Billowing green smoke and fireworks. A spell-binding animation film in which a raw nerve is strung up on a meat-hook only to be ripped off by a wild animal, who is then devoured himself. That and more made up the spectacular fusion of music and theatre that was the Pink Floyd concert at Freedom Hall last night…' (*Louisville Courier Journal*)

■ **19.6.77**
The Super Bowl of Rock 'n' Roll, Soldier Field, Chicago, Illinois, USA.
Set list: Sheep/Pigs On The Wing Pt.1/Dogs/Pigs On The Wing Pt.2/Pigs//Shine On You Crazy Diamond Pts.1-5/Welcome To The Machine/Have A Cigar/ Wish You Were Here/Shine On You Crazy Diamond Pts.6-9/ encore: Money.
Despite the success of the concert, a Federal Grand Jury investigated allegations of mail fraud, wire fraud, kickbacks and other financial irregularities connected with this concert. On the day itself, the official box-office figure showed attendance of about 67,000, but Pink Floyd, doubting its accuracy, hired a helicopter, with a photographer and an attorney on board, to carry out a head count. The aerial estimate was around 95,000, which meant a shortfall in the takings of several hundred thousand dollars.

■ **21.6.77**
Kemper Arena, Kansas City, Missouri, USA.
■ **23.6.77**
Cincinnati Gardens, Cincinnati, Ohio, USA.
■ **25.6.77**
World Series of Rock, Municipal Stadium, Cleveland, Ohio, USA.
Supported by Mother's Finest.
Set list: Sheep/Pigs On The Wing Pt.1/Dogs/Pigs On The Wing Pt.2/Pigs//Shine On You Crazy Diamond Pts.1-5/Welcome To The Machine/Have A Cigar/ Wish You Were Here/Shine On You Crazy Diamond Pts.6-9/

Wing Pt.1/Dogs/Pigs On The Wing Pt.2/Pigs//Shine On You Crazy Diamond Pts.1-5/Welcome To The Machine/Have A Cigar/ Wish You Were Here/Shine On You Crazy Diamond Pts.6-9/ encore: Money.
■ **29.6.77**
Spectrum Theater, Philadelphia, Pennsylvania, USA.
Set list: Sheep/Pigs On The Wing Pt.1/Dogs/Pigs On The Wing Pt.2/Pigs//Shine On You Crazy Diamond Pts.1-5/Welcome To The Machine/Have A Cigar/ Wish You Were Here/Shine On You Crazy Diamond Pts.6-9/

Manhattan, New York City, New York, USA.
Set list: Sheep/Pigs On The Wing Pt.1/Dogs/Pigs On The Wing Pt.2/Pigs//Shine On You Crazy Diamond Pts.1-5/Welcome To The Machine/Have A Cigar/ Wish You Were Here/Shine On You Crazy Diamond Pts.6-9/ encore: Money/Us And Them.
■ **3.7.77**
Madison Square Garden, Manhattan, New York City, New York, USA.
Set list: Sheep/Pigs On The Wing Pt.1/Dogs/Pigs On The Wing Pt.2/Pigs//Shine On You Crazy Diamond Pts.1-5/Welcome

equivalent to November 5th – it's when all the fireworks go off. Quite a few had brought them to the Garden, and even before the concert began fire-crackers were spluttering in the upper tiers.... [One] set fire to the T-shirt of a guy five seats away while on stage Roger Waters was playing "Pigs On The Wing". The fireworks were making the audience a bit edgy – those of them that could still feel anything – and it was a while before the Floyd were able to pull together the 20,000 sell-out crowd and get them involved. Gilmour seemed able to use the tension to put an edge on his guitar licks, but Waters was obviously not happy. Roger's lyrics came through clearer and louder than any others of the evening: "You stupid mother-fucker!" he bellowed. "And anyone else in here with fireworks – just fuck off and let us get on with it."' (*NME*)
■ **4.7.77**
Madison Square Garden, Manhattan, New York City, New York, USA.
Set list: Sheep/Pigs On The Wing Pt.1/Dogs/Pigs On The Wing Pt.2/Pigs//Shine On You Crazy Diamond Pts.1-5/Welcome To The Machine/Have A Cigar/ Wish You Were Here/Shine On You Crazy Diamond Pts.6-9/ encore: Money/Us And Them.
■ **6.7.77**
Stade Du Parc Olympique, Montreal, Quebec, Canada.
The last night of the tour.
Set list: Sheep/Pigs On The Wing Pt.1/Dogs/Pigs On The Wing Pt.2/Pigs//Shine On You Crazy Diamond Pts.1-5/Welcome To The Machine/Have A Cigar/Wish You Were Here/Shine On You Crazy Diamond Pts.6-9/encore: Money/Us And Them/Blues.

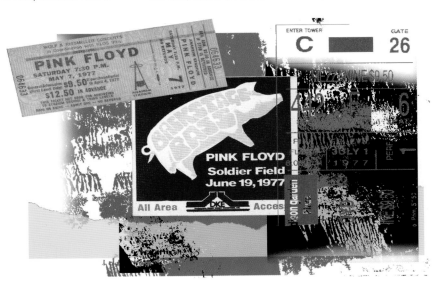

encore: Money/Us And Them.
■ **27.6.77**
Boston Garden, Boston, Massachusetts, USA.
Set list: Sheep/Pigs On The Wing Pt.1/Dogs/Pigs On The Wing Pt.2/Pigs//Shine On You Crazy Diamond Pts.1-5/Welcome To The Machine/Have A Cigar/ Wish You Were Here/Shine On You Crazy Diamond Pts.6-9/ encore: Money/Us And Them.
■ **28.6.77**
Spectrum Theater, Philadelphia, Pennsylvania, USA.
Set list: Sheep/Pigs On The

encore: Money/Us And Them (this song performed without Roger Waters).
■ **1.7.77**
Madison Square Garden, Manhattan, New York City, New York, USA.
Set list: Sheep/Pigs On The Wing Pt.1/Dogs/Pigs On The Wing Pt.2/Pigs//Shine On You Crazy Diamond Pts.1-5/Welcome To The Machine/Have A Cigar/ Wish You Were Here/Shine On You Crazy Diamond Pts.6-9/ encore: Money.
■ **2.7.77**
Madison Square Garden,

To The Machine/Have A Cigar/ Wish You Were Here/Shine On You Crazy Diamond Pts.6-9/ encore: Money/Us And Them. 'Not only was it the eve of July 4th, but also it was the week that marijuana had been decriminalised in New York State. The surprisingly young audience was thus inevitably out of it. Blitzed young men from the Bronx would periodically rise to their feet, extend their clenched fist and bellow "Floiiiiid!" before sinking exhausted back to their seats. July 4th is, of course, the US

Overleaf: Nick Mason, Madison Square Garden, New York City, July 1977

8

Despite massive box-office and album sales in recent years, Pink Floyd were very much in the red in the late 1970s. They had teamed up with City investment brokers Norton Warburg to invest in various high-risk ventures in order to reduce their own tax liability, which, under the Labour government, stood at some 83 per cent. The scheme had backfired.

It wasn't until March 1981 that the full extent of their losses became apparent. At a creditors' meeting it was claimed that Norton Warburg had managed to lose the band some £2.5 million and as a company had only £800,000 in remaining assets to pay off their debtors, of whom Pink Floyd was only one. In short, almost everything Pink Floyd had earned from their record sales over the past few years was wiped out in an instant and they were effectively flat broke – as well as facing a huge tax bill.

However, using this misfortune as a convenient lever, the ever-resourceful Waters proposed bailing the band out with one of two possible album projects he had envisaged and part written since the 'Animals' tour: 'Bricks In The Wall' (later known simply as 'The Wall') and 'The Pros And Cons Of Hitch-Hiking', one of which he expected to complete as a solo album at a later date. However, as Gilmour recalled, 'the demos for both "The Wall" and "Pros and Cons" were unlistenable, a shitty mess. [They] sounded exactly alike, you couldn't tell them apart. We thought of recording "Pros and Cons" at a later date, but as it turned out Roger preferred to go off and do it as a solo project.'[1]

In the end it was decided that 'The Wall' was the better prospect. As a result the band received a hefty advance from their record company which temporarily stabilized their finances. It was an ambitious project by any stretch of the imagination. From its inception Waters envisaged a three-pronged attack: album, tour and film. Initially it was hoped that all three would be in simultaneous production, but almost at once it became evident that the sheer magnitude of effort the recording process alone would require would make this plan unfeasible.

The album came first and recording began at the Superbear studios in France, followed by CBS in New York and finally, for the largest part, the Producers Workshop in Los Angeles. The whole process lasted from November 1978 until just before the release of the double album in November 1979.

Because of the complexity of the project, an outside producer was brought in to co-ordinate efforts in the studio, and, for the first time in many years, the band opted for an assistant to help realize Waters' vision: the Canadian-born producer Bob Ezrin. In addition, Michael Kamen was brought in as a composer and arranger for the orchestrations. A host of other musicians and performers were engaged and, at one stage, it was even hoped to include all the Beach Boys on vocal harmonies.

The album told a desperate story of isolation and fear, far more complex than anything previously tackled by Waters. Inevitably the work is seen as partly autobiographical: Pink, the central character, played by Waters, is a successful rock star facing the break-up of his marriage while on tour. This leads him to review his whole

life and to begin to build a protective wall around himself, each brick representing the things that have caused him to suffer: suffocating, protective mothers, vicious schoolteachers, faithless wives and stupid groupies. Pink imagines himself elevated to the position of a fascist dictator, with the audience his obedient followers. Hitler-like, he wields his power to persecute the 'unclean'. At the story's climax he faces up to his tormentors and the wall finally crumbles. However, as soon as this wall has fallen, so another slowly begins to rise, suggesting, in a bleak conclusion, a perpetual cycle of imprisonment.

Many of the scenes in the album also represented actual events in Waters' or the band's personal history. There are obvious references to Syd Barrett and Pink Floyd's hippie heyday; the loss of Waters' father in the war; and rioting at the LA Sports Arena in 1975. The trashing of a motel room recalls an all too common aspect of the seventies rock star's lifestyle. There are even – and this was to start a Pink Floyd tradition – a few backward messages concealed in the mix.

Bob Ezrin's task was a formidable one, but he succeeded in moulding the sorry story into a workable shape. Much later he said, 'in an all night session I re-wrote the record. I used all of Roger's elements, but I rearranged their order and put them in a different form. I wrote "The Wall" out in 40 pages, like a book, telling how the songs segued. From that the stage show grew. It wasn't so much rewriting as redirecting.'[2] This explains why the album sleeve lists a different running order from that on the two discs and also why there are lyrics to tracks (for example, the 'Empty Spaces'/'What Shall We Do Now' sequence that later appeared in the film) that are not included on the records. Indeed it is often

Overleaf: 'The Wall' performed live, Dortmund, West Germany, February 1981

said that the recorded material would have filled three discs before it was carefully edited down.

Ezrin's thankless task was repaid by Waters' indignant remark: 'You can write anything you want, just don't expect a credit for it.'[3] Gilmour was determined not to suffer the same fate. In exchange for providing Waters with the music for the album's three outstanding compositions, he received the only shared credits on the album: for 'Young Lust', 'Run Like Hell' and perhaps the finest track of all, 'Comfortably Numb', derived from an unused demo from his solo album.

By the late stages of recording, Waters' impatience was such that he finally gave vent to his complete intolerance of Wright, effectively dismissing him before the recording process was over. Reports later suggested that Wright had a rampant cocaine habit and that it was because of the effects of this on his role in the band that Gilmour and Mason did little to prevent his departure. It was also rumoured that his lack of commitment was made worse by marital problems.

'It's quite simple,' Wright explained. 'It started because Roger and I didn't get on. There was a lot of antagonism during "The Wall" and he said either you leave or I'll scrap everything we've done and there won't be an album. Normally I would have told him to get lost, but at that point we had to earn the money to pay off the enormous back-taxes we owed. Anyway, Roger said that if I didn't leave he would re-record the material. I couldn't afford to say no, so I left.'[4]

It would appear that their differences went back right to the start. Wright went on to say, in an interview with *Mojo* magazine, that the situation started during their student days at the Regent Street Polytechnic in the sixties: 'The two of us didn't really get on. Being the kind of person he is, Roger would try to… rile you, if you like, try to make you crack. Definitely mental things going on between us and big political

disagreements. Him being an armchair socialist.' And on stage? 'Never, the only time I'd ever get angry with Roger on stage was when he'd be playing out of tune; we'd be in D and he was still banging away in E because he couldn't hear it. I had to tune his bass on-stage, you know. In those days there were no strobe tuners, so after every number he'd stick the head of the bass guitar over my keyboards and I'd tune it up for him.'

In leaving, Wright may have made the correct decision. Not only was he assured royalties from the album sales but he also came back to receive a wage for the tour, something the remaining band members had to forfeit to help pay off the massive debt they would accumulate in touring 'The Wall'.

Much of the planning of the live shows was carried out in an intensive effort during the Christmas period, when Pink Floyd were enjoying a number one chart placing with the album across the globe and a surprise top position in the UK with the preceding single, 'Another Brick In The Wall Pt.2'. This number was controversial in every respect, having been banned by the less than tolerant governments of South Africa and Korea, among others, for its anti-establishment message, as well as attracting accusations in the UK media of exploiting children from a school near their Britannia Row complex for the chorus.

On stage 'The Wall' was Pink Floyd's most overwhelming spectacle to date; presented exclusively at indoor arenas, it skilfully combined every aspect of the rock-theatre genre. A wall was literally constructed from hundreds of cardboard bricks before the audience's eyes, and by the close of the first half it spanned the entire width of the auditorium to a height of some forty feet.

The band again went to the Fisher–Park team with the problem of the wall's design, construction and eventual on-stage collapse. The show also incorporated a crashing Stuka dive-bomber for

DORTMUND
WESTFALENHALLE

13.2.–20.2.1981
jew. 20.00 Uhr

local Transport
by Mercedes Benz

Kartenversand ab sofort zu DM 49,–, 39,– + 34,– zzgl. DM 8,– Bearb.-Gebühr gegen Übersendung eines
Euroschecks, PschKto.- oder Bankeinzahlung per Einschreiben. Bitte deutlich lesbare Absenderangaben.
PINK FLOYD SONDERKASSEN:
1) Westfalenhalle, Rheinlanddamm 200, 46 Dortmund, Tel.: 0231/1 20 45 96 – PschKto Nr. Dortmund
215540-461 – Bank Kto. Nr. BfG Bank Dortmund 1023267800, BLZ 440 101 11
2) Sonderkasse Peter Rieger, Linzer Str. 35, 5 Köln 41, Tel.: 0221/42 77 97. Versand nur gegen Übersendung von Euroscheck
3) Sonderkasse Willy Sandrock, Verkehrsverein im Hauptbahnhof, 6 Frankfurt/Main, Tel.: 0611/23 11 08,
PschKto. Nr. Frankfurt 303363-604, Bank Kto. Nr. Deutsche Bank Sonderkonto Pink Floyd 4062162-01,
BLZ 500 700 10
4) Pink Floyd Sonderkasse, Sendlinger Str. 51, 8 München 2, Tel.: 089/26 34 07, Bank Kto. Nr. Bayerische
Vereinsbank 2719525, BLZ 700 202 70 oder Übersendung von Euroschecks
5) Pink Floyd Sonderkasse, Leipnitzstr. 33, 1 Berlin 12, Tel.: 030/3 13 77 77. Versand nur gegen Übersendung von Euroschecks
6) PINK FLOYD Sonderkasse ABR, Am Stachus, 8 München, Tel.: 089/5 90 43 34, PschKto. Nr. München
3020-806 oder Übersendung von Euroschecks

PINK FLOYD REISEN
Im Sonderzug der Deutschen Bundesbahn direkt zum Bahnhof Westfalenhalle und im Anschluß an das Konzert zurück.
Sonderzug 1: München – Augsburg – Nürnberg – Würzburg – Aschaffenburg – Frankfurt – Gießen – Dortmund (Westfalenhalle)
Sonderzug 2: Ulm – Stuttgart – Heidelberg – Mainz – Koblenz – Dortmund
Sonderzug 3: Basel – Freiburg – Offenburg – Karlsruhe – Kaiserslautern – Saarbrücken – Trier – Dortmund
Sonderzug 4: Kiel – Lübeck – Hamburg – Bremen – Osnabrück – Dortmund
Sonderzug 5: Braunschweig – Hannover – Minden – Dortmund
Sonderzug 6: Köln – Düsseldorf – Essen – Dortmund
Preise ab: München, Augsburg, Nürnberg, Basel, Freiburg/Offenburg/Ulm – DM 199,– inkl. Karte
Würzburg, Aschaffenburg, Stuttgart, Freiburg, Offenbach, Karlsruhe, Kaiserslautern, Saarbrucken/Trier – DM 179,– inkl. Karte
Frankfurt/Main – Heidelberg – Mainz – Kiel – Lübeck – Braunschweig – Hamburg – DM 169,– inkl. Karte
Hannover – Osnabrück – Bremen – Koblenz – Gießen – DM 149,– inkl. Karte
Eintrittskarten und Rückfahrten werden gegen Übersendung eines Euroschecks oder Postscheckkonto-Einzahlung per Einschreiben übersandt.
Pink Floyd Reisen, Große Bockenheimer Str. 44, 6000 Frankfurt/Main 1, Tel.: 0611/20110 – Sonderkonto Pink Floyd Reisen
Postscheckkonto-Nr. Frankfurt 159572-600
Sonderflüge zum Pink Floyd Konzert aus München, Berlin, Hamburg und Frankfurt mit Hotelübernachtung, Pick-Up, Konzertkarte etc. Spezielles
Premierenarrangement für den 13. Februar 1981. Anfragen Pink Floyd Reisen, Tel.: 0611/20110
Zentraler Vorverkauf für die Schweiz: Good News Productions, Tel.: 0041/1/251 1168, Carmenstr. 25, 8001 Zürich, Schweiz
Zentraler Vorverkauf für Österreich: Promota, Tel.: 0043/222/65 47 81-4, Prinz-Eugen-Str. 1, 1030 Wien, Österreich
Zentraler Vorverkauf für Holland: Mojo Concerts, Tel.: 0031/12 19 80, Po. Box. 3035, Delft, Holland

the culmination of 'In The Flesh'; a circular screen on to which hideous and newly designed animations by Gerald Scarfe were projected; and three 35mm projectors, used in a horizontal configuration, to throw animated images on to the wall itself.

In addition, three giant puppets, further products of Scarfe's twisted imagination, made appearances at key points, representing the villains of the piece. These were a twenty-five-foot high model of the Schoolteacher, a smaller one of the Wife and an inflatable Mother. Even the familiar helium-filled pig made a mad dash around the hall during 'Run Like Hell', which Waters regularly introduced as their 'disco' number.

There was even a set built into the face of the wall itself, depicting the motel room where Pink sits comatose before a TV showing an old war film. But one of the most visually striking elements was Gilmour atop the wall playing his guitar solo in 'Comfortably Numb'.

As for the sound, the system was by far the band's best yet, producing 106 decibels of clean sound in perfect quadraphonic arrangement. An unexpected feature was additional speaker cabinets under the tiered seating to accentuate the rumbling collapse of the wall itself – the show's grand finale – and give the impression that the very arena itself was crumbling.

But what pleased Waters most about the whole production was that it was pleasantly removed from the stadium environment he so hated. 'I went and walked all the way around the top row of seats at the back of the arena. And my heart was beating furiously and I was getting shivers right up and down my spine. And I thought it was so fantastic that people could actually see and hear something from everywhere they were seated. Because after the 1977 tour I became seriously deranged – or maybe arranged – about stadium gigs. Because I do think they are awful.'[5]

The whole production called for massive effort to punishing deadlines and it is a miracle it ever happened at all: 'We were all working furiously up until the first night,' Waters recalled. 'And the first time we had the wall up across the arena with some film on it was four days before the first show!'[6]

And that task itself was a nightmare because the editors employed to cut the animation film had the additional job of transforming the projections from a single screen to three in order to project the film across the full width of the auditorium. Peter Hearn, who was working on this, recalled: 'Just before the show he [Waters] decided it should be on three screens. Quite a task. A screaming hurry to do that... We also had something went wrong with the time code and they went into rehearsal in Los Angeles and the picture and sound went out, and I tell you what happened was we were having this conversation over the phone from London with this guy in Los Angeles who was sitting in a hotel bedroom spilling film all over the floor telling him what to cut and what to look for!'[7]

There were further problems. Because of dissatisfaction with the existing lighting designer, Marc Brickman was hired to rectify the situation only twenty-four hours before the opening night in Los Angeles. He recalls this as 'one of the most shocking experiences of my life'.[8] Before that day he hadn't even heard the album.

With immediate sell-outs in both locations and an oversubscribed attendance it was hardly surprising that the promoter offered to extend the band's residency in New York, but this was turned down. In addition, an offer to take the show elsewhere prompted yet another bust-up within the band, as Waters explained: 'Larry Maggid, a Philadelphia promoter, offered us a guaranteed million dollars a show plus expenses to go and do two dates at JFK Stadium with "The Wall". To truck straight from New York, to

*This page and overleaf:
performing 'The Wall' live,
Nassau Veterans Memorial
Coliseum, Long Island,
New York, February 1980*

Philadelphia. And I wouldn't do it. I had to go through the whole story with the other members. I said, "You've all read my explanations of what 'The Wall' is about. It's three years since we did that last stadium and I saw then that I'd never do one again. And 'The Wall' is entirely sparked off by how awful that was and how I didn't feel that the public or the band or anyone got anything

out of it that was worthwhile. And that's why we've produced this show strictly for arenas where everybody does get something out of it that is worthwhile. Blah-blah-blah. And, I ain't fuckin' going!' So there was a lot of talk about whether Andy Bown could sing my part. Oh, you may laugh, and in the end they bottled out. They didn't have the balls to go through with it.'[9]

With the US tour over without further incident, a string of London 'Wall' shows were scheduled for 9–13 June at the Empire Pool, Wembley. In the event, the tour reached its conclusion at London's Earls Court in August 1980 because the band had learned in the meantime that, for tax reasons, they would have to delay returning to the UK. In addition, a one-off production of the piece at the Milton Keynes National Bowl on 26 May was announced in the music press, as well as a 'greatest hits' show at the same venue in August, but neither got beyond the initial stages of planning.

Shortly after the end of the tour, EMI began work on a compilation of material to be culled from the band's archive. However, the efforts of the Harvest label's A&R head, Colin Miles, to provide fans with an interesting and varied package of rarities were thwarted when both band and EMI opted for an inferior greatest hits collection in the shape of 1981's *A Collection of Great Dance Songs*. The only unusual item this contained was a re-recording of 'Money', carried out for the express purpose of the album and prompted, it would appear, by some dispute with Capitol Records in the USA.

Pressure was now mounting on the band to start work on the full-length movie adaptation – the third and final instalment – of 'The Wall' and Waters began planning out the script with Gerald Scarfe and Michael Seresin as directors and film-maker Alan Parker as producer. However, Seresin was soon ousted in favour of Parker, who was

prepared to invest part of the $12 million it was going to cost to produce the film, the bulk of the remainder being financed by the band.

The announcement of a further string of 'Wall' shows, in Dortmund in February and London in June 1981, came as a big surprise to fans. But the band had an ulterior motive: they intended to use the events to film themselves in concert, as called for by the original script.

Production began at Pinewood Film Studios in September that same year. However, Parker was not satisfied with the results of the filming at the UK shows, although he captured a competent (as yet unreleased) concert movie. Having decided on a change of plan, he persuaded a reluctant Waters to both drop the live scenes and relinquish his lead role as Pink. Parker's change of plan also upset Scarfe in that his stage-show puppets would be sacrificed to the creation of an entirely new piece of work separate from the stage presentation, although about twenty minutes of his animation would be retained.

It is well documented that the three men were given to lengthy rows and walk-outs during the filming. Parker resolved the matter by forcing Waters to take a six-week holiday so that he could work unhindered. 'In that period I was allowed to develop my vision,' he said, 'and I really made that film with a completely free hand. I had to have that. I couldn't be second-guessed by Roger, and he appreciated that. The difficulty came when I'd finished. I'd been shooting for sixty days, fourteen hours a day – that film had become mine. And then Roger came back to it, and I had to go through the very difficult reality of having it put over to me that actually it was a collaborative effort.'[10]

Waters was exceptionally pragmatic about the situation, describing it as 'The most unnerving, neurotic period of my life – with the possible exception of my divorce in 1975. Parker is used to sitting at the top of his pyramid, and I'm used to sitting at the top of mine. We're both pretty much used to getting our own way. If I'd have directed it – which I'd never have done – it would have been much quieter than it is. But that's one of the reasons I liked Parker doing it. He paints in fairly bold strokes, he is very worried about boring his audience. It suits us very well, because we did want a lot of this to be a punch in the face.'[11]

The film, which had had its world premiere at the Cannes Film Festival on 23 May 1982, opened in London on 14 July. It surprised many by featuring Bob Geldof, the leader of the post-punk band The Boomtown Rats, as Pink, ranting the parts of 'In The Flesh?' to great effect.

The band had also re-recorded some of their works for the soundtrack, using new Michael Kamen orchestrations on 'Mother', 'Bring The Boys Back Home' (with Welsh choir) and an expanded 'Empty Spaces', which this time, like the stage shows, included the segue of 'What Shall We Do Now'. In addition, a completely new track was introduced to act as an overture to the film. 'When The Tigers Broke Free' was inspired by the death of Waters' father on the Anzio bridgehead in the Second World War.

When it opened in London, the film was generally seen as a powerful piece of celluloid rock music, but it did receive a few unfavourable reviews. Some of the more sensitive writers felt they had been subjected to a battering from start to finish, while a few, misreading it completely, accused of it of being neo-Nazi propaganda – a view no doubt inspired by the scenes in which menacing gangs of specially recruited Tilbury skinheads paraded as Pink's 'Hammer Guard'.

Soon after the film's release, the band announced the release of additional material used on the soundtrack, as well as some that had been cut from both the album and film. As Waters explained: 'We were contracted to make a soundtrack album but there really wasn't enough

new material in the movie to make a record that I thought was interesting. The project then became "Spare Bricks", and was meant to include some of the film music, like "When The Tigers Break Through" [the working title of 'When The Tigers Broke Free'] and the much less ironic version of "Outside The Wall" which finishes the movie, the sequence with the kids playing with the milk bottles, plus some music written for the movie but left on the cutting room floor. I decided not to include the new version of "Mother" from the movie because it really is film music and it doesn't stand up. It's a very long song, and besides, I'm bored with all that now. I've become more interested in the remembrance and requiem aspects of the thing, if that doesn't sound too pretentious. Anyway, it all seemed a bit bitty then I came up with a new title for the album: "The Final Cut".'[12]

When the album of this name was eventually released, in the spring of 1983, it was very different from what had been predicted. Waters, inspired by the British Government's military retaliation against Argentina's invasion of the Falkland Islands in the South Atlantic, had composed and recorded new pieces of music that related to the Falklands conflict, almost without consulting the rest of the band. It was a decisive departure from their normal policy and, in the light of Wright's recent exit, it seemed that Waters had assumed unilateral responsibility for the direction of the band.

As a result, this was Pink Floyd's most turbulent period, with arguments raging constantly over band policy, and album quality and content. 'It got to the point on "The Final Cut",' said Gilmour, 'that Roger didn't want to know about anyone else submitting material.'[13] It seemed that much of what the rest of band had cherished as a democracy was fast disappearing, as Gilmour went on to explain: 'There was at one time a great spirit of compromise within the group. If someone couldn't get enough of his vision on the table to convince the rest of us, it would be dropped. "The Wall" album, which started off unlistenable and turned into a great piece, was the last album with this spirit of compromise. With "The Final Cut", Waters became impossible to deal with.'[14]

Waters himself admitted that it was a highly unpleasant time, but his overriding feeling was frustration at the others' unwillingness – and this applied to Gilmour in particular – to submit to his complete control. 'We were all fighting like cats and dogs. We were finally realising – or accepting, if you like – that there was no band. It was really being thrust upon us that we were not a band and had not been a band in accord for a long time. Not since 1975, when we made "Wish You Were Here". Even then there were big disagreements about content and how to put the record together. I had to do it more or less single handed, with Michael Kamen, my co-producer. That's one of the few things that the "boys" and I agreed about.'[15]

Gilmour submitted in the sense that he refused to have anything more to do with the album's production, agreeing merely to perform, as required, opting for an easy life in preference to endless rows. 'I came off the production credits because my ideas weren't the way Roger saw it. It is not personally how I would see a Pink Floyd record going.'[16] The power this granted Waters gratified his now tremendous ego, leaving him free to act as if his band mates were no more than mere hired hands. Gilmour later recalled how Waters, at the end of recording, told him that 'the only way he'd ever consider doing another Pink Floyd album was on that basis'.[17]

Even the sleeve, under Waters' artistic control, carried the subtitle 'A Requiem for The Post War Dream by Roger Waters – *performed* by Pink Floyd'.

The obvious lack of Wright's name gave fans their first indication of his departure, confirmation of which did not emerge until some three years after the album's release.

The *Final Cut* was dedicated to Waters' late father, Eric Fletcher Waters, and at last laid his ghost to rest. It was Pink Floyd's worst-selling record in recent years, scraping the top five, a point which Gilmour has gleefully raised time and again to underline the fact that the material was exceptionally weak in comparison with previous albums and obviously lacked a cohesive band effort.

If Pink Floyd's history was to come to an end with this album – and every indication was that it would – it was hardly the offering to be best remembered by. Waters' lyrics were at his scathing best, to be sure, but musically it was merely a soundtrack to his vicious dialogue, its subject matter little more than a political rant. It is therefore hardly surprising that many fans regard the aptly titled album as marking Waters' departure from the band.

With absolutely no intention of touring the album, the band were now on permanent holiday, and this state of affairs, along with solo albums and extensive tours from both Waters and Gilmour during early the early part of 1984, furthered the growing belief that Pink Floyd had all but split up.

Notes
1. Glenn Povey interview with David Gilmour, 25.9.87
2–3. *Circus*, 15.4.80
4. *South China Sunday Morning Post*, 17.1.88
5–6. *Q*, August 1987
7. Glenn Povey interview with Peter Hearn, 2.7.86
8. *Q*, August 1987
9–10. *Rolling Stone*, 16.9.82
11. Unidentified press article c.1982
12. Unidentified press article c.1988
13. Washington Post, 19.10.1987
14–15. *Q*, August 1987
16. *Sun*, 27.4.83
17. *Washington Post*, 19.10.87

LONDON
Court Tube Station)
BLOCK
A
ENTRANCE
ROW
D
SEAT
33
TO BE RETAI

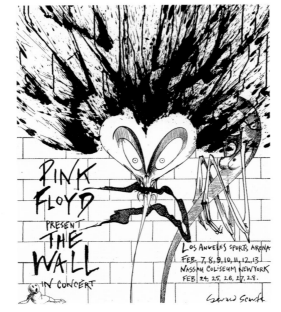

1978–9

Pink Floyd gave no concerts in 1978–9.

PINK FLOYD
(1979–85)
Personnel:
David Gilmour
Nick Mason
Roger Waters

1980

PINK FLOYD – THE WALL PERFORMED LIVE
Additional touring personnel:
The Surrogate Band:
Andy Bown: Bass guitar
Snowy White: Guitars
Willie Wilson: Drums
Peter Wood: Keyboards
Richard Wright: Keyboards
Backing vocalists:
Joe Chemay: Backing vocals
Jim Farber: Backing vocals
Jim Haas: Backing vocals
John Joyce: Backing vocals
Master of Ceremonies:
Cynthia Fox: 7,9,12,13.2.80
Jim Ladd: 10,11.2.80
Identity of MC on 8.2.80 unknown
Gary Yudman: All New York and London shows
■ **7–13.2.80**
Sports Arena, Exposition Park, Los Angeles, California, USA.
Set list at this and all subsequent stage performances of *The Wall*:
In The Flesh?/The Thin Ice/ Another Brick In The Wall Pt.1/ The Happiest Days Of Our Lives/Another Brick In The Wall Pt.2/Mother/Goodbye Blue Sky/ What Shall We Do Now – Empty Spaces/Young Lust/One Of My Turns/Don't Leave Me Now/ Another Brick In The Wall Pt.3/ 'Improvisations'*/Goodbye Cruel World//Hey You/Is There Anybody Out There?/Nobody Home/Vera/ Bring The Boys Back Home/ Comfortably Numb/The Show Must Go On/In The Flesh/Run Like Hell/Waiting For The Worms/ Stop/The Trial/Outside The Wall.
*'Improvisations' is a title we

have used to describe an instrumental filler, usually lasting about five minutes. At the first few shows this was primarily a blues instrumental with the melody of 'Another Brick' coming through. In later shows it developed into an atmospheric synthesizer-based instrumental with elements of 'Another Brick', 'Young Lust' and 'Empty Spaces'.
■ **24–28.2.80**
Nassau Veterans Memorial Coliseum, Uniondale, Long Island, New York, USA.
■ **4–9.8.80**
Earls Court Exhibition Hall, Earls Court, London, England.

1981

PINK FLOYD – THE WALL PERFORMED LIVE
Additional touring personnel:
The Surrogate Band:
Andy Bown: Bass guitar
Andy Roberts: Guitars

Willie Wilson: Drums
Peter Wood: Keyboards
Backing vocalists:
Joe Chemay: Backing vocals
Jim Farber: Backing vocals
Jim Haas: Backing vocals
John Joyce: Backing vocals
Master of Ceremonies:
Wili Tomsik: All Dortmund shows
Gary Yudman: All London shows
■ **13–18.2.81**
Westfalenhalle, Dortmund, West Germany.
■ **13–17.6.81**
Earls Court Exhibition Hall, Earls Court, London, England.
It was reported in the music press that second drummer Willie Wilson was taken ill just before the opening show. Clive (nobody seems to know his surname), a Floyd roadie who happened to also be a drummer, was given a crash course in the set's requirements by Nick Mason and replaced Wilson for that one concert.
The show of 17.6.81 marked the last night of the 'Wall Shows' tour and, significantly, the last time Waters played with Pink Floyd.

1982–5

Pink Floyd gave no concerts in 1982–5.

*This and following spread:
'The Wall' performed live,
Dortmund, 1981*

WALL
'PERFORMED LIVE

9

RAIN OR SHINE AND 2DAY

27 20.00 FRI OCTOBER 30,1987 8PM 27

GATE 3 AISLE

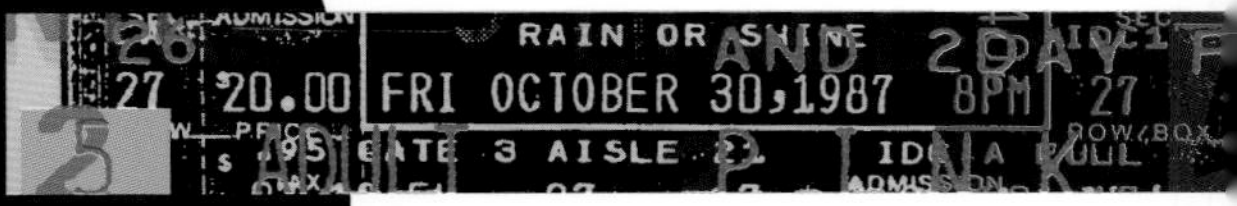

Unbeknown to the general public, Waters had technically dismissed himself from Pink Floyd in late 1985, after his final Pros And Cons Of Hitch-Hiking tour. He had issued a statement to EMI and CBS Records saying that he considered the band a 'spent force' and that he wouldn't record with Gilmour and Mason ever again, or with anyone else as Pink Floyd. When he declared this he had apparently not believed that the others had the necessary qualities to carry on under that name.

However, about a year later, at a routine board meeting of Pink Floyd Music Ltd, he learnt that Gilmour and Mason were about to open a bank account to pay out and receive money on what was being termed 'the new Pink Floyd project'. He was outraged, and in a much-publicized chain of events, including plenty of mud-slinging, he claimed that the group was defunct and that the band's pursuit, with or without his involvement, of any further projects was simply not acceptable.

As a result, Waters instigated High Court proceedings to legally determine the nature of the Pink Floyd partnership. Therefore, on 31 October 1986, exactly twenty years after the band first entered a recording studio, there began a court case which, he hoped, would uphold his belief that, since he had written the bulk of its songs, he was entitled to prevent others' commercial exploitation of the name 'Pink Floyd'.

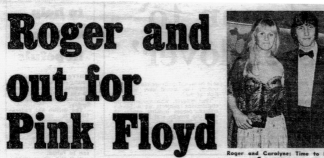

The Daily Mail *announces the departure of Roger Waters from Pink Floyd in October 1985*

Within days, every UK national newspaper was carrying headlines saying that Pink Floyd had split up, but Gilmour and Mason countered with a statement issued by their record company, saying 'Pink Floyd are alive, and well, and recording in England', which gave some hope to their fans at the same time as increasing their puzzlement.

For his part, Gilmour reluctantly countered Waters' legal action. Speaking to Nicky Horne on London's Capital Radio in early 1987, he said: 'I think it's rather unnecessary. There's been many many years together when we have achieved a lot together, and it's a shame when anyone wants to leave of course. But, everyone has to do what they want to do, and of course that's their decision. What is sad and unnecessary about it is trying to

prevent anyone else from carrying on with their legitimate artistic and business endeavours.'

Waters eventually dropped his legal action, conceding that Gilmour could continue to use the name 'Pink Floyd'. As Gilmour explained: 'The situation is that Virgin wanted to release his soundtrack [Waters' 'When The Wind Blows'] and in order to do so, EMI made him sign a piece of paper on the case saying, essentially, if you want to put this soundtrack out on another label, not to interfere with Pink Floyd being Pink Floyd, or pursue any activities in the name of Pink Floyd – which Roger signed and agreed to.'[1]

Gilmour and Mason, who had been recording together since the autumn of 1986, had long been convinced that a new album was a better idea than just taking a greatest hits show out on the road. It was a shrewd gamble and, although over the next few months the going was tough, the result was an album that was a worldwide best-seller.

A Momentary Lapse Of Reason, recording of which was completed in March 1987, followed by three months post-production in Los Angeles, was released in September of that year. The album was mainly recorded at Gilmour's Thames studio houseboat *Astoria*, with Bob Ezrin producing (much to Waters' consternation, since he had hoped Ezrin would work on the Radio KAOS album for him). Significantly, it was the first Pink Floyd album in some fourteen years that didn't follow a conceptual path.

Not that a concept album wasn't attempted. Eric Stewart, formerly of 10cc, had been drawn in via Nick Mason's second solo album, and recalled: 'Dave Gilmour and I got together around August or September 1986 to work on a concept that was definitely intended for the next Pink Floyd album. We sat around writing for a period of time, but we couldn't get the different elements to gel. The song-writing itself was acceptable in certain parts, but not as a whole, so the concept was eventually scrapped.'[2]

Also drafted in were the English poet Roger McGough and Canadian songwriter Carole Pope. 'The idea to contact me came from Bob Ezrin,' explained Pope. 'It was January 1987, and they were looking for somebody to rewrite a batch of Dave Gilmour's material, so I went over to England for a few weeks to lend assistance. Bob and David asked me if I had suggestions for concept albums in the Pink Floyd style. By the time I left England in February, they still couldn't decide what to do.'[3]

Eventually, however, the idea of a concept album was abandoned in favour of a conventional approach, with songs not linked thematically.

To help him and Mason make *A Momentary Lapse of Reason* Gilmour selected musicians whom he had met in recent years. He had become a highly respected session player himself and had performed at many charity events including Live Aid (where he was the only Floyd member in attendance), and The Secret Policeman's Ball, where he had recruited some talented individuals.

As for Rick Wright, the chance to return to the band was very welcome, particularly since he had all but given up playing, his confidence, like Mason's, having been shattered during Waters' rule. For legal reasons, however, Wright couldn't officially rejoin the band and, in any case, the album was almost complete by the time he made contact with Gilmour and Mason.

When *A Momentary Lapse Of Reason* appeared, much of Waters' expected criticism focused on the amount of supporting musicians used, which infuriated Gilmour. 'Roger never used to credit anyone. Yet he was always fussy about the credit for himself. I never had the time to worry about it, that sort of thing. On "Animals" for instance Roger took the credits for everything. Let's say that I wrote 70% of "Sheep". At least half of that album I played bass on and Roger was hardly ever in the studio during its recording. I played bass on almost all of the Pink Floyd albums, which is where Roger forgets that other people had huge, vast amounts of input, but at the time I never worried, so long as the product was completed. On "The Wall" there was a song that Bob Ezrin never got credited for, "Is There Anybody Out There", Roger never credited him for that.'[4]

The album came over as a strange cross between the cold and sterile aspects of *Wish You Were Here* and the bleakness of *Animals*. Although it is basically a dolled-up Gilmour solo album, it is, as a first effort with a new line-up, an accomplished piece. At the least it offered a chance for the post-Waters band to gain self-confidence and start touring again, in addition to recording.

In order to make the comeback complete in this respect, Gilmour wanted to re-create the spectacle of the world-renowned Pink Floyd shows with a breathtaking production. With Mason, he invested some $3 million of his personal wealth in the project. But finding a promoter and agent willing to take on an almost equal risk was proving to be a bigger problem than they had first reckoned. No one could estimate Pink Floyd's pulling power since they had been redundant for so long. It had been over six years since they had performed live and even longer since they had given a nationwide tour in either Europe or America. In addition, Waters' absence was at the forefront of their minds.

But for Michael Cohl, of the CPI agency in Canada, there was little doubt about the band's potential and he gauged the box-office reaction by placing on sale, on 27 April 1987, tickets for a

Madison Square Garden, New York City, October 1987

single show at the CNE Stadium in Toronto on
21 September. The result was that all 60,000
tickets sold out as fast as they could be printed –
the fastest sell-out in the history of the CNE.
Hardly believing it, he put a second show on sale,
with exactly the same result, then a third show,
which was also a sell-out, and thus secured a gross
income of over US$3 million.

In no time at all local promoters were queuing
up to take on the show, well before the album was
released to radio or the public, and a massive
North American tour was set in motion to run
until the end of the year. In almost every location
box-office records fell, making it the most
successful US tour, by any band, that year.

To complicate matters further, Waters, who
was still attempting to obstruct his former band
mates at every turn, issued a threat of legal action
to any US promoter if they dared put a Pink
Floyd show on sale. Heavyweight US promoters
aren't easily discouraged, but Gilmour and Mason
played safe by having a team of expert lawyers
on hand at every city they played in.

The bankability of the name Pink Floyd had
become increasingly apparent, and the tour
simply snowballed. Tours of Australia, Japan,
Europe and the UK followed, with two more tours
of the US thrown in for good measure, and the
band sold out at almost every venue.

For Waters, by contrast, the going was tough.
He had released *Radio KAOS* slightly ahead of *A
Momentary Lapse Of Reason* and decided to tour
the US simultaneously. Whereas his former band
mates succeeded in selling out huge auditoria, he
was struggling to pull a crowd even a third the
size. Overall, however, fans benefited from seeing
and hearing twice as much Floyd music as they
had anticipated, and a strong debate raged
between hard-core fans over who was the rightful
heir to the name. Waters fuelled much of this by
having T-shirts printed for his tour with the

Top: Rotterdam, June 1988. Above: Lille, July 1988

defiant motif 'Which One's Pink?' emblazoned
on the front. Even the media was confused. The
only certainty was that Pink Floyd's success was
enduring, if baffling – a twenty-year-old rock band
outstripping any other artist for sales and concert
attendances the world over.

But putting Pink Floyd on the road was
another matter entirely. A great deal had
happened in the world of stadium touring, from
stage designs through to PA and lighting
technology, since they had last hit the road and a
massive investment had to be made to bring the
show up to and beyond the fans' expectations.

The Fisher–Park design team declined to design the stage show, favouring the confines of Waters' 'Radio KAOS', and the task was given to theatre set designer Paul Staples and 'Wall' lighting man Marc Brickman. Whereas in Waters' day the band had employed a handful of technicians, a crew of about a hundred was now required to maintain three separate stages which leap-frogged across continents to keep the show moving.

The concerts themselves incorporated many of the old trademarks: the giant circular film screen displayed much of the vintage footage, a flowering mirror ball, green and red lasers and over a hundred other lights. All of this was housed within a vast steel stage framework which measured some eighty feet high, a hundred and sixty-eight feet wide and ninety-eight feet deep. Suspended from this were 'pods' of lights and smoke machines attached to four moving units that were suspended from tracks above the stage, as well as smaller 'Floyd Droids', as they became known, reminiscent of R2-D2 in *Star Wars*, that rose from the stage to throw out light into the audience. Quadraphonic sound was also used, with some 240 speaker units making up the system, a crashing aeroplane during 'On The Run' (later replaced by a crashing bed to make further use of the tour motif), an inflatable pig and a strange winged creature that launched skywards in 'Learning To Fly'.

It all made for a visually striking comeback, so much so that many reports suggested that the spectacle distracted from the music, which combined the old and new. It came as a huge surprise that 'Echoes' opened the show, albeit only in the early concerts, followed by selections of the new album in the first half and a 'greatest hits' package in the second. The only frustrating aspect was that the set list remained unchanged throughout the tour, despite a rich heritage of numbers to choose from.

On 22 November 1988, after the US tour, Pink Floyd released an album derived from recordings made at their New York concerts. *Delicate Sound Of Thunder* also appeared as a video, in June the following year, and acted as a promotional tool for the current round of European dates.

A few days after the album's release, Gilmour and Mason accompanied President François Mitterand of France to the Baykonur Cosmodrome, in Kazakhstan, USSR, to attend the launch of the Soyuz-7 space rocket, which was piloted by a Franco-Soviet crew. The cosmonauts had requested a cassette of the album to listen to when they rendezvoused with the orbiting MIR station. Pink Floyd thus made history as the first rock band to be played in space.

The comeback tour finally came to its official conclusion with a one-off show at Knebworth Park, north of London, in September 1990. There had been some 200 shows, attracting over 4.25 million fans and taking more than £60 million at the box office alone (merchandising revenues were separate). It certainly rammed the point home to a retreating Waters. Gilmour later summed up their return quite simply: 'we wanted to leave no one in any doubt that we were still in business and meant business – and no one was going to stop us.'[5]

Completing the reunion, Wright was now playing full time with the band. In this role he contributed substantially to the soundtrack for Gilmour, Mason and O'Rourke's self-produced film of their vintage motor-car racing exploits across Mexico, *La Carrera Panamericana*, which was released on video in April 1992.

Notes

1. Glenn Povey interview with David Gilmour, 25.9.87
2–3. Unidentified press reports
4. Glenn Povey interview with David Gilmour, 25.9.87
5. *Q*, September 1990

David Gilmour, London Arena, 8 July 1989

1986

Pink Floyd (1986–93)
Personnel:
David Gilmour
Nick Mason

Pink Floyd gave no concerts in
1986.

1987

**A MOMENTARY LAPSE OF
REASON – WORLD TOUR
(1987–88)**
Additional touring personnel:
Jon Carin: Keyboards and vocals
Rachel Fury: Backing vocals
Scott Page: Saxophones and
guitars
Guy Pratt: Bass guitar and vocals
Tim Renwick: Guitars
Margaret Taylor: Backing vocals
Gary Wallis: Percussion
Richard Wright: Keyboards and
vocals

■ **7.9.87**
**Buffalo Memorial
Auditorium, Buffalo, New
York, USA.**
Before this first show, which
was cancelled because the
album release was put back,
Pink Floyd made four weeks'
use of a bonded warehouse, at a
reported cost of $70,000, to
rehearse their stage show. A
huge flying saucer, hovering
over the audience's heads, was
intended to have been a feature
of the special effects for the
outdoor shows, but insurance
difficulties prevented its use.

■ **9.9.87**
**Lansdowne Park Stadium,
Ottawa, Ontario, Canada.**
Set list: Echoes/Signs Of
Life/Learning To Fly/A New
Machine Pt.1/Terminal Frost/A
New Machine Pt.2/Yet Another
Movie/Round and Around/
Sorrow/The Dogs Of War/On
The Turning Away//One Of
These Days/Time/On The Run/
Wish You Were Here/Welcome
To The Machine/Us And
Them/Money/Another Brick
In The Wall Pt.2/
Comfortably Numb
encore: One Slip/Run
Like Hell.

■ **12–14.9.87**
**The Forum, Montreal,
Quebec, Canada.**
Set list: Echoes/Signs Of
Life/Learning To Fly/A New
Machine Pt.1/Terminal Frost/A
New Machine Pt.2/Yet Another
Movie/Round and Around/
Sorrow/The Dogs Of War/On
The Turning Away//One Of
These Days/Time/On The
Run/Wish You Were Here/
Welcome To The Machine/Us
And Them/Money/Another Brick
In The Wall Pt.2/Comfortably
Numb/encore: One Slip/Run Like
Hell/second encore: Shine On
You Crazy Diamond Pts.1-5.

■ **16.9.87**
**Municipal Stadium,
Cleveland, Ohio, USA.**
Set list: Echoes/Signs Of
Life/Learning To Fly/Yet Another
Movie/Round and Around/A
New Machine Pt.1/Terminal
Frost/A New Machine Pt.2/
Sorrow/The Dogs Of War/On
The Turning Away//One Of
These Days/Time/On The Run/
Wish You Were Here/Welcome
To The Machine/Us And Them/
Money/Another Brick In The Wall
Pt.2/Comfortably Numb/encore:
One Slip/Run Like Hell.

■ **17.9.87**
**Municipal Stadium,
Cleveland, Ohio, USA.**
Set list: Echoes/Signs Of
Life/Learning To Fly/Yet Another
Movie/Round and Around/A

New Machine Pt.1/Terminal
Frost/A New Machine Pt.2/
Sorrow/The Dogs Of War/On
The Turning Away//One Of
These Days/Time/On The Run/
Wish You Were Here/Welcome
To The Machine/Us And Them/
Money/Another Brick In The
Wall Pt.2/Comfortably Numb/
encore: One Slip/Run Like Hell/
second encore: Shine On You
Crazy Diamond Pts.1-5.

■ **19.9.87**
**John F. Kennedy Stadium,
Philadelphia, Pennsylvania,
USA.**
Set list: Echoes/Signs Of
Life/Learning To Fly/Yet Another
Movie/Round and Around/A
New Machine Pt.1/Terminal
Frost/A New Machine Pt.2/
Sorrow/The Dogs Of War/On
The Turning Away//One Of
These Days/Time/On The Run/
Wish You Were Here/Welcome
To The Machine/Us And Them/
Money/Another Brick In The
Wall Pt.2/Comfortably Numb/
encore: One Slip/Run Like Hell.

■ **21–23.9.87**
**Canadian National
Exhibition Stadium,
Toronto, Ontario, Canada.**
Set list: Echoes/Signs Of
Life/Learning To Fly/Yet Another
Movie/Round and Around/A
New Machine Pt.1/Terminal
Frost/A New Machine Pt.2/
Sorrow/The Dogs Of War/On
The Turning Away//One Of
These Days/Time/On The Run/
Wish You Were Here/Welcome
To The Machine/Us And Them/
Money/Another Brick In The
Wall Pt.2/Comfortably Numb/
encore: One Slip/Run Like Hell.

■ **25.9.87**
**Rosemont Horizon, Rosemont,
Chicago, Illinois, USA.**
Set list: Echoes/Signs Of
Life/Learning To Fly/Yet Another
Movie/Round and Around/A
New Machine Pt.1/Terminal
Frost/A New Machine Pt.2/
Sorrow/The Dogs Of War/On
The Turning Away//One Of
These Days/Time/On The
Run/Wish You Were Here/

Welcome To The Machine/Us And Them/Money/Another Brick In The Wall Pt.2/Comfortably Numb/ encore: One Slip/Run Like Hell.

■ **26–28.9.87**
Rosemont Horizon, Rosemont, Chicago, Illinois, USA.
Set list at these shows and all shows until the end of the year, unless otherwise noted: Shine On You Crazy Diamond Pts.1-5/ Signs Of Life/Learning To Fly/Yet Another Movie/Round and Around/A New Machine Pt.1/

a large bed. In addition, the huge scaffolding stage carried revolving radar dishes, flashing beacons and radio masts which were not present at the later shows.

■ **3.10.87**
Carrier Dome, Syracuse University, Syracuse, New York, USA.

■ **5–7.10.87**
Madison Square Garden, Manhattan, New York City, New York, USA.

■ **10–12.10.87**

■ **19–22.10.87**
Capital Centre, Landover, Maryland, USA.

■ **25,26.10.87**
Dean E. Smith Student Activities Center, University of North Carolina, Chapel Hill, North Carolina, USA.

■ **30.10.87**
Tampa Stadium, Tampa, Florida, USA.

■ **1.11.87**
Orange Bowl, Miami,

for international use. In addition, tracks from this concert, including 'Run Like Hell', 'The Dogs Of War' and 'On The Turning Away', were used as B-sides of a number of singles.

■ **7,8.11.87**
Rupp Arena, Civic Center, Lexington, Kentucky, USA.

■ **10.11.87**
Pontiac Silverdome, Pontiac, Detroit, Michigan, USA.

■ **12.11.87**
Hoosier Dome, Indianapolis, Indiana, USA.

■ **15,16.11.87**
St Louis Arena, St Louis, Missouri, USA.

■ **18.11.87**
Astrodome, Houston, Texas, USA.

■ **19,20.11.87**
Frank Erwin Center, University of Texas, Austin, Texas, USA

■ **21–23.11.87**
Reunion Arena, Reunion Park, Dallas, Texas, USA.

■ **26–30.11.87 and 1.12.87**
Sports Arena, Los Angeles, California, USA.

■ **3–6.12.87**
Oakland Coliseum Arena, Oakland, California, USA.

■ **8.12.87**
Kingdome, Seattle, Washington, USA.

■ **10,11.12.87**
Pacific National Exhibition Coliseum, Vancouver, British Columbia, Canada.

Terminal Frost/A New Machine Pt.2/Sorrow/The Dogs Of War/On The Turning Away// One Of These Days/Time/On The Run/Wish You Were Here/ Welcome To The Machine/Us And Them/Money/Another Brick In The Wall Pt.2/Comfortably Numb/ encore: One Slip/Run Like Hell.

■ **30.9.87**
County Stadium, Milwaukee, Wisconsin, USA.
The show featured, for the last time until the end of the European 1989 tour, a crashing replica Stuka dive-bomber for the culmination of the 'On The Run' sequence. In this period it was replaced by

Brendan Byrne Meadowlands Arena, East Rutherford, New Jersey, USA.
After the show of 11.12.87. Gilmour, Mason, Scott Page, Rachel Fury, Margaret Taylor, Guy Pratt and Tim Renwick made an impromptu appearance at The World Club in New York, where they performed a forty-minute set of R&B standards.

■ **14,15.10.87**
Hartford Civic Center, Hartford, Connecticut, USA.

■ **16,17.10.87**
Providence Civic Center, Providence, Rhode Island, USA.

Florida, USA.
Heavy rainfall at the concert prevented the inflatable pig from making an appearance.

■ **3–5.11.87**
The Omni Coliseum, Atlanta, Georgia, USA.
The entire show of 5.11.87. was filmed using twenty-three Panavision video cameras. The entire concert was due to be screened on various European networks, but was withdrawn at the last minute for unknown reasons. Promotional videos comprising 'The Dogs Of War', 'On The Turning Away' and 'One Slip' were made from the film

1988

Additional touring personnel:
Jon Carin: Keyboards and vocals
Rachel Fury: Backing vocals
Durga McBroom: Backing vocals
Scott Page: Saxophones and guitars
Guy Pratt: Bass guitar and vocals
Tim Renwick: Guitars
Margaret Taylor: Backing vocals
Gary Wallis: Percussion
Richard Wright: Keyboards and vocals

■ **23,24.1.88**
Western Springs,

Auckland, New Zealand.
Set list at these shows and all Australian shows on this tour: Shine On You Crazy Diamond Pts.1-5/Signs Of Life/Learning To Fly/Yet Another Movie/Round And Around/A New Machine Pt.1/Terminal Frost/A New Machine Pt.2/Sorrow/The Dogs Of War/On The Turning Away// One Of These Days/Time/On The Run/The Great Gig In The Sky/Wish You Were Here/ Welcome To The Machine/Us And Them/Money (extended version)/Another Brick In The Wall Pt.2/Comfortably Numb/ encore: One Slip/Run Like Hell.
■ **27–31.1.88 and 1–4.2.88 Entertainment Centre, Sydney, New South Wales, Australia.**
Members of Pink Floyd and their band made an impromptu appearance at the Round Midnight club in King's Cross, Sydney after one of their many shows in the city.
■ **7,8.2.88 Entertainment Centre, Brisbane, Queensland, Australia.**
■ **11.2.88 Thebarton Oval, Thebarton, Adelaide, South Australia, Australia.**
■ **13–17.2.88 Tennis Centre, Melbourne, Victoria, Australia.**
Members of the touring party, including Gilmour, Pratt, Wallis, Renwick, Page, Taylor, Fury, McBroom and Carin, performed under the name The Fishermen on two occasions in after-show gigs at the Corner Hotel in Richmond, Melbourne to crowds of about 200. The first show also featured Roy Buchanan and seventies Floyd backing vocalist Vanetta Fields, who reportedly sang an amazing version of 'Little Red Rooster'. The second show saw The Fishermen perform a set that included 'Respect', 'I Shot The Sheriff', 'Unchain My Heart', 'Superstition', 'Reeling In The

Years', 'Good Lovin' Gone Bad' and 'Pick Up The Pieces'.
■ **24.2.88 Subiaco Oval, Perth, Western Australia, Australia.**
■ **2,3.3.88 Budokan Grand Hall, Tokyo, Japan.**
Set list at these shows and all Japanese shows on this tour: Shine On You Crazy Diamond Pts.1-5/Signs Of Life/Learning To Fly/Yet Another Movie/Round And Around/A New Machine Pt.1/ Terminal Frost/A New Machine Pt.2/Sorrow/The Dogs Of War/ On The Turning Away//One Of These Days/Time/The Great Gig In The Sky/Wish You Were Here/ Welcome To The Machine/ Us And Them/Money (extended version)/Another Brick In The Wall Pt.2/Comfortably Numb/ encore: One Slip/Run Like Hell.
■ **4–6.3.88**

Yoyogi Olympic Pool, Tokyo, Japan.
■ **8,9.3.88 Joh Hall, Osaka, Japan.**
■ **11.3.88 Rainbow Hall, Sogo Taiikukan, Nagoya, Japan.**
■ **15.4.88 Los Angeles Memorial Coliseum, Los Angeles, California, USA.**
Set list at this show and all North American shows on this tour, unless otherwise noted: Shine On You Crazy Diamond Pts.1-5/Signs Of Life/Learning To Fly/Yet Another Movie/Round And Around/A New Machine Pt.1/Terminal Frost/A New Machine Pt.2/Sorrow/The Dogs Of War/On The Turning Away// One Of These Days/Time/On The Run/The Great Gig In The Sky/Wish You Were Here/ Welcome To The Machine/Us And Them/Money (extended

version)/Another Brick In The Wall Pt.2/Comfortably Numb/ encore: One Slip/Run Like Hell.
■ **18.4.88 Mile High Stadium, Denver, Colorado, USA.**
■ **20.4.88 Hughes Stadium, California State University at Sacramento, Sacramento, California, USA.**
■ **22,23.4.87 Oakland Coliseum Stadium, Oakland, California, USA.**
■ **25,26.4.88 Municipal Stadium, Phoenix, Arizona, USA.**
■ **28.4.88 Texas Stadium, Irving, Dallas, Texas, USA.**
■ **30.4.88 Citrus Bowl, Orlando, Florida, USA.**
Torrential rain prevented the performance of 'Shine On You Crazy Diamond Pts.1-5' and 'Welcome To The Machine'.
■ **4.5.88 Carter-Finley Stadium, North Carolina State University, Raleigh, North Carolina, USA.**
■ **6,7.5.88 Foxboro Stadium, Foxboro, Boston, Massachusetts, USA.**
■ **11.5.88 Stade du Parc Olympique, Montreal, Quebec, Canada.**
■ **13.5.88 Canadian National Exhibition Stadium, Toronto, Ontario, Canada.**
■ **15,16.5.88 Veterans Stadium, Philadelphia, Pennsylvania, USA.**
■ **18.5.88 University of Northern Iowa

Dome, Cedar Falls, Iowa, USA.
■ 20.5.88
Camp Randall Stadium, University of Madison–Wisconsin, Madison, Wisconsin, USA.
■ 21,22.5.88
Rosemont Horizon, Rosemont, Chicago, Illinois, USA.
■ 24.5.88
Hubert H Humphrey Metrodome, Minneapolis, Minnesota, USA.
■ 26.5.88
Arrowhead Stadium, Kansas City, Missouri, USA.
■ 28.5.88
Ohio State University Stadium, Colombus, Ohio, USA.
■ 30.5.88
Three Rivers Stadium, Pittsburg, Pennsylvania, USA.
■ 1.6.88
Robert F Kennedy Stadium, Washington, District of Columbia, USA.
■ 3,4.6.88
Giants Stadium, East Rutherford, New Jersey, USA.
■ 10.6.88
Stade de la Beaujoire, Nantes, France.
Set list at this show and all shows until the end of 1988, unless otherwise noted: Shine On You Crazy Diamond Pts.1-5/Signs Of Life/Learning To Fly/Yet Another Movie/Round And Around/A New Machine Pt.1/Terminal Frost/A New Machine Pt.2/Sorrow/The Dogs Of War/On The Turning Away//One Of These Days/Time/On The Run/The Great Gig In The Sky/Wish You Were Here/Welcome To The Machine/Us And Them/Money (extended version)/Another Brick In The Wall Pt.2/Comfortably Numb/encore: One Slip/Run Like Hell.
■ 13,14.6.88
Stadion Feyenoord, Rotterdam, Netherlands.
'A New Machine Pt.1', 'Terminal

Above: Versailles, France, June 1988

Frost' and 'A New Machine Pt.2' were not performed at these shows.
■ 16.6.88
Reichstagsgelände, West Berlin, West Germany.
■ 18.6.88
Maimarktgelände, Mannheim, West Germany.
■ 21,22.6.88
Place d'Armée, Château de Versailles, France.
Both shows were filmed for use on the *Delicate Sound of Thunder* concert video, but only a small segment of 'The Great Gig In The Sky' was included.
■ 25.6.88
Niedersachsenstadion, Hannover, West Germany.
■ 27–29.6.88
Westfalenhalle, Dortmund, West Germany.
■ 1.7.88
Praterstadion, Vienna, Austria.
'A New Machine Pt.1', 'Terminal Frost' and 'A New Machine Pt.2' were not performed at this show.
■ 3.7.88
Olympiastadion, Munich, West Germany.
'A New Machine Pt.1',

'Terminal Frost' and 'A New Machine Pt.2' were not performed at this show.
■ 6.7.88
Stadio Comunale, Turin, Italy.

Stade du Municipal, Grenoble, France.
This show replaced the one scheduled for the same day at the Stade Gerland, Lyon.

■ 8,9.7.88
Stadio Comunale Braglia, Modena, Italy
■ 11,12.7.88
Stadio Flaminio, Rome, Italy.
■ 15.7.88

■ 17.7.88
Stade de l'Ouest, Nice, France.
■ 20.7.88
Estadio Sarria Español FC, Barcelona, Spain.

■ **22.7.88**
Estadio Vincente Calderón,
Madrid, Spain.
■ **24.7.88**
Espace Richter,
Montpellier, France.
■ **26.7.88**
Fussballstadion St Jakob,
Basle, Switzerland.
■ **28.7.88**
Stadium du Nord, Villeneuve
d'Ascq, Lille, France.
■ **31.7.88**
Gentofte Stadium,
Gentofte, Copenhagen,
Denmark.
■ **2.8.88**
Valle Hovin Stadion, Oslo,
Norway.
This show replaced the one
scheduled for 19.8.88. 'A New
Machine Pt.1', 'Terminal Frost'
and 'A New Machine Pt.2' were
not performed.
■ **5,6.8.88**
Wembley Stadium, Wembley,
Middlesex, England.
 'A New Machine Pt.1',
'Terminal Frost' and 'A New
Machine Pt.2' were not
performed at these shows.
■ **8.8.88**
Maine Road Football Club,
Moss Side, Manchester,
England.
This show replaced those
scheduled for 1,2.8.88. 'A New
Machine Pt.1', 'Terminal Frost'
and 'A New Machine Pt.2' were
not performed.
■ **10.8.88**
Jumping Arena, Royal
Dublin Showgrounds,
Dublin, Republic of Ireland.
This show, Pink Floyd's first visit
to the Republic of Ireland since
1967, was cancelled because of
poor ticket sales.
■ **12–14.8.88**
The Coliseum, Richfield,
Cleveland, Ohio, USA.
■ **16,17.8.88**
The Palace of Auburn Hills,
Auburn Hills, Detroit,
Michigan, USA.
■ **19–21 and 23.8.88**
Nassau Veterans Memorial
Coliseum, Uniondale, Long

Island, New York, USA.
All four concerts were recorded
and filmed for the concert video
and album *Delicate Sound of*
Thunder.
The show of 23.8.88 was the
last night of the world tour.

1989

ANOTHER LAPSE –
EUROPEAN TOUR
Additional touring personnel:
Jon Carin: Keyboards and vocals
Rachel Fury: Backing vocals
Durga McBroom: Backing vocals
Lorelei McBroom: Backing vocals
Scott Page: Saxophones and
guitars
Guy Pratt: Bass guitar and vocals
Tim Renwick: Guitars
Gary Wallis: Percussion
Richard Wright: Keyboards and
vocals
■ **9,10.5.89**
London Arena, Isle of
Dogs, London, England.
The band rehearsed before
setting off on tour.
■ **12.5.89**
Festivalweise, Werchter,
Belgium.
A final dress rehearsal took
place, to the delight of nearby
campers waiting for the following
night's show, although they
weren't allowed into the arena.
■ **13.5.89**
Festivalweise, Werchter,
Belgium
Set list at this show and all other
shows on this tour: Shine On
You Crazy Diamond Pts.1-5/
Signs Of Life/Learning To Fly/Yet
Another Movie/Round And
Around/A New Machine Pt.1/
Terminal Frost/A New Machine
Pt.2/ Sorrow/The Dogs Of
War/On The Turning Away/ One
Of These Days/Time/On The
Run/ The Great Gig In The Sky/
Wish You Were Here/ Welcome
To The Machine/ Us AndThem/
Money (extended version)/
Another Brick In The Wall Pt.2/
Comfortably Numb/encore: One
Slip/Run Like Hell.
■ **16–18.5.89**

Roman Arena, Verona, Italy.
■ **20.5.89**
Arena Concerti - Autodromo
Di Monza, Monza, Italy.
■ **22,23.5.89**
Stadio Comunale Ardenza,
Livorno, Italy.
■ **25,26.5.89**
Stadio Simonetta Lamberti,
Cava De' Tirreni, Italy.
■ **31.5.89**
Olympic Stadium, Athens,
Greece.
■ **3–7.6.89**
Bol'aja Sportivnaja Arena,
Lushniki, Moscow, USSR.
■ **10.6.89**
Lahden Surhali, Lahti, Finland.
■ **12–14.6.89**
Globe Arena, Stockholm,
Sweden.
■ **16.6.89**
Festweisse Im Stadtpark,
Hamburg, West Germany.
■ **18.6.89**
Mungersdorfer Stadion,
Cologne, West Germany.
■ **20,21.6.89**
Festhalle, Frankfurt-am-
Main, West Germany.
■ **23.6.89**
Stadion Linz, Linz, Austria.
■ **25.6.89**
Neckarstadion, Stuttgart,
West Germany.
■ **27–30.6.89 and 1.7.89**
Palais Omnisports de
Bercy, Paris, France.
■ **4–9.7.89**
London Arena, Isle of
Dogs, London, England.
All evening shows, except the
final one, which began at
3.00pm.
■ **10.7.89**
Goffertpark, Nijmegen,
Netherlands.
■ **12.7.89**
Stade Olympique de la
Pontaise, Lausanne,
Switzerland.
■ **15.7.89**
Canale di San Marco,
Piazza San Marco, Venice,
Italy.
Set list: Shine On You Crazy
Diamond Pts.1-5/Learning To
Fly/Yet Another Movie/Sorrow

/The The Dogs Of War/On The
Turning Away/Time/The Great
Gig In The Sky/Wish You Were
Here/Money/Another Brick In
The Wall Pt.2/Comfortably
Numb/Run Like Hell.
An abbreviated ninety-minute
show was staged on a huge
barge moored off Piazza San
Marco and broadcast to over
twenty countries, to be seen by
an estimated 100 million people.
In the UK it was broadcast live on
BBC2 at 10.45pm.
■ **18.7.89**
Stade Vélodrome,
Marseilles, France.
The last night of the tour.

1990

■ **30.6.90**
The Silver Clef Award
Winners Show, Knebworth
Park, Stevenage,
Hertfordshire, England.
With Tears For Fears, Status
Quo, Cliff Richard, Robert Plant
with Jimmy Page, Phil Collins,
Genesis, Eric Clapton, Dire
Straits, Elton John and Paul
McCartney.
Set list: Shine On You Crazy
Diamond Pts.1-5/The Great Gig
In The Sky/Wish You Were Here/
Sorrow/Money/Comfortably Numb/
Run Like Hell.

*Previous page: David
Gilmour, London Arena,
8 July 1989
Right: Sound check,
Cowdray Ruins Concert,
18 September 1993, with
Mike Rutherford and David
Gilmour in foreground*

This charity event in aid of the
Nordoff–Robbins Music Therapy
Centre featured eleven hours of
continuous entertainment. Pink
Floyd closed the day with a brief
set in torrential rain without their
circular screen. During a heavy
storm earlier in the day, it had

collected water and ripped while
suspended above the stage.
Pink Floyd were supplemented
by Guy Pratt (bass guitar), Candy
Dulfer (saxophone), Sam Brown,
Vicki Brown, Claire Torry and
Durga McBroom (backing vocals)
and Michael Kamen (keyboards
on 'Comfortably Numb').
BBC Radio One broadcast the
entire event live and Castle
Music Pictures released a three-
video set of highlights, entitled
Knebworth – The Event, and
featuring 'Comfortably Numb'
and 'Run Like Hell', on 6.8.90.
Polydor released an album of
highlights, including these two
tracks, at the same time.

1991–2

Pink Floyd gave no concerts in
1991–2.

1993

**18.9.93
Cowdray Ruins Concert
1993, Cowdray Castle,
Midhurst, East Sussex,
England.**
Set list: Run Like Hell/Wish You
Were Here/Comfortably Numb.
This was a celebrity charity
event sponsored by Virgin Radio
to raise £200,000 for the King
Edward VII hospital in Midhurst.
With a ticket price of £140 for
the main arena and £80 the
outer picnic zones, it was an
exclusive gathering, out of the
reach of the band's
usual fans. The
concert opened with
a set from Queen,
comprising on this
occasion Roger
Taylor (lead vocals),
John Deacon
(bass), Tim
Renwick (guitar)
and Gary Wallis
(drums). Also
appearing were
Genesis, made up
of Phil Collins
(lead vocals),
Mike Rutherford
(bass), Tony Banks (keyboards),
Tim Renwick (guitar) and Gary
Wallis and Roger Taylor (drums).
Pink Floyd headlined with a fairly
standard set but with the
unusual addition of Mike
Rutherford (bass), Paul Young of
Mike & The Mechanics (vocals
on 'Run Like Hell') Tim Renwick
(guitar) and Gary Wallis (drums).
Nick Mason sat
behind Roger
Taylor's drum kit,
complete with the
famous Queen
emblem. The last
act to appear was
Eric Clapton playing
lead guitar on a
two-song encore
with Gilmour,
Taylor, Young,
Collins and
Renwick.

10

1994 -

The previous year's soundtrack material provided a solid base for Gilmour when, beginning in January 1993, he recorded a new Pink Floyd album at his studio aboard the *Astoria*. It was not nearly as painstaking a task as making the last album, especially now that Mason and Wright were, in theory, back on form.

The Division Bell, released in March 1994, took its title from the bell located in the UK's House of Commons that summons Members of Parliament to debate. (The idea was suggested to Gilmour by his friend the science-fiction writer Douglas Adams, in exchange for a £5000 charity donation to the Environmental Investigation Agency.) Many took the title to be a final message to the doubters: it's time to make your mind up. The phenomenal success of the album suggested that the vote had gone decisively in Gilmour, Mason and Wright's favour: it was one of the most successful in Pink Floyd's near-thirty-year history.

The Division Bell, with its distinctive artwork by Storm Thorgerson, saw a classic return to form, and the result was a much warmer and inviting work than the previous one. Moreover, it had stronger lyrics which took listeners back to the classic seventies album feel – almost in the tradition of *Dark Side Of The Moon*. The reason for the regained sense of shared purpose that characterizes the album, Gilmour suggested, was 'because we're all playing and functioning much better than we were after the trials and tribulations of the late Roger years. Recording "A Momentary Lapse Of Reason" was a very, very difficult process. We were all sort of catatonic. Unfortunately, we didn't really work together an awful lot. But the success of that album, and the success of the supporting tour and the enjoyment that we got out of working together meant that this one could be made in a different way.'[1]

And in another interview he explained: 'On this album both Nick and Rick are playing all the stuff they should be playing which is why it sounds much more like a genuine Pink Floyd record to me than anything since "Wish You Were Here". It has a sort of theme about non-communication, but we're not trying to bash anybody over the head with it. We went out last time with the intention of showing the world, look we're still here, which is why we were so loud and crash-bangy. This is a much more reflective album.'[2]

Indeed, using communication as a general theme enabled Gilmour to lay many ghosts to rest. Chief among these were the recent breakdown of his marriage and his personal recovery, in 'Coming Back To Life'; the collapse of his relationship with Waters, in 'Lost For Words' – in which he buries the hatchet and offers a (refused) olive branch; and the hopelessness of Barrett's condition in 'Poles Apart'. But the album also had a deep focus of the problem of communication, on a global as well as personal level, and this theme is explored to great effect in 'A Great Day For Freedom', 'Keep Talking' and the upbeat 'Take It Back'. But, without doubt, the highlight is the anthemic and highly emotive 'High Hopes', a nostalgic return by Gilmour to his Cambridge roots and the passing of the years.

Although Anthony Moore and Nick Laird-Clowes made some contribution to the writing of the album, it is particularly apt that Gilmour's present wife, ex-journalist Polly Samson, should have co-written much of the material, for it was she who performed wonders in hauling Gilmour out of the mire of depression after his battles with Waters. Gilmour, given his admitted diffidence as a wordsmith, greatly valued her close reading of his work. 'After I would write some lyrics, it just seemed natural to have her look through them. In the beginning she tried not to interfere at all, and tried to encourage me to do it on my own. But, of course, that isn't the way things stay. And as time went by, she got more and more involved with the process that was beginning to absorb me 24 hours a day. Her involvement with the lyric writing process – and, in fact, with the music – grew. Her assistance was invaluable.'[3]

Since the band now had a sizeable repertoire to choose from for the inevitable tour, a new strategy was employed. Now, they presented a pot-pourri of songs, some new and some dating right back to their first album, discarding the usual format of playing the whole of the current album during one half of the show. In addition, a system was adopted whereby the band changed their set list constantly, making it less rigid and thus reducing the risk of boredom for themselves and their fans alike – many of whom, they realized, were seeing them at more than one location throughout the tour.

In staging the show Pink Floyd welcomed back on board designer Mark Fisher, who, along with Marc Brickman, came up with what will inevitably be seen as the band's most impressive stage show to date. (An unwritten Floyd tradition demands that each tour should be more spectacular than the previous one). A large semicircular shell now housed the production, replacing a monolithic square steel frame, and this was equipped with a

Overleaf: Estádio de Alvalade, Lisbon, Portugal, July 1994

much larger circular projection screen. Overall the design was strongly reminiscent of the Hollywood Bowl, while the lighting effects and the fantastical newly generated film sequences – both live-action and computer-generated – were nothing short of awe-inspiring.

It is therefore not surprising that band manager Steve O'Rourke announced to the press that 'David, Rick and Nick have put no limit on the budget. It is a matter of however much it takes to create the best show we can possibly do.'[4] And it certainly showed: a much-improved Turbosound PA system provided the best quadraphonic sound available, using some 300 speakers, a raised forty-foot circular projection screen with a 35mm back-projector, a 70mm IMAX front screen projector, a vast mirror ball that raised from the centre of the now giant slug-like construction that housed the front-of-house soundboard and projectors, and an array of lighting that included 400 Vari-Lites and two copper-vapour pulse lasers that, for the first time, induced a variety of colours, including emerald green, lime green, gold, yellow and blood red – this last innovation originally developed for NASA by the Hughes Corporation. The band even recalled their sixties lighting man Peter Wynne-Wilson to re-create liquid-oil patterns to illuminate the revival of the classic Barrett-era anthem 'Astronomy Dominé'.

The new projection films, which alone cost a small fortune, were spectacular. The most impressive were those used for 'Shine On You Crazy Diamond' and 'Time', a computer-generated masterpiece that seemed to suck viewers into the vast workings of a hugely intricate mechanical timing device. Reworked scenes also accompanied the classic footage used during 'Us And Them', and the renditions of 'Dark Side Of The Moon' were updated with appropriate inserts of modern-day politicians for the 'Brain Damage'/'Eclipse'

finale. Also, much greater attention to detail was given to the lighting effects, with the Vari-Lite production being the largest ever taken on the road. Then there was the usual battery of fireworks and props, including a crashing plane for 'On The Run' and two massive comic hogs that launched out of the tops of the twin speaker columns during 'One Of These Days'. It was a show to please every type of Pink Floyd fan, with its visuals that were a mixture of both mainstream rock lighting and full-on psychedelia. With these complemented by a more creative use of the quad system and mind-mashing sound effects, it was a total sensory bombardment calculated to blow the fans right out of their seats.

The statistics of such a large-scale touring machine are mind-boggling, and the amount of materials and manpower required to take the band on the road simply too fantastic, to be ignored: 200 crew members, three separate touring stages (although only one set of lights was carried on tour, since it was the most expensive single element to hire), forty-nine container trucks, 700 tons of steel to build the set – a task which took four days – and a daily running cost of some $500,000. Two Boeing 747 cargo planes and a chartered Russian Antonov freight plane were used to transfer the equipment from the USA for the European tour.

Robbie Williams, once the band's roadie and now Production Manager, looked on this complexity with a mixture of awe and disbelief. 'We used to get away with a main lighting effect that consisted of four Genie towers, which came up with flashing police beacons on top and 24 par cans – and that was seen as absolutely astonishing. Now, to get the same effect on an audience you have to have 20 million dollars' worth of stuff out there. It sometimes amazes me, going back into stadiums that we played in the '70's, when it was a lot more basic. Fax machines? We didn't even have telephones on some of those gigs yet we did stadium tours. Sometimes I look around and think, we're ordering 21 phone lines at every venue, and as for computers – we didn't even have calculators!'[5]

At a press conference held in London on 30 November 1993 to announce the European tour, Pink Floyd said they would be performing in Greece, Turkey and Israel in addition to the shows already announced, but none of these locations was confirmed. Plans for a show in front of the Great Pyramids at Giza in Egypt and shows in Australasia in 1995 were also shelved.

To assist with the spiralling costs of the tour the band, perhaps rather hastily, struck a sponsorship deal with the German car manufacturer Volkswagen. (The company even went so far as to produce a special limited-edition 'Pink Floyd' VW Golf with interiors part-designed by Nick Mason.) Although it seemed like a good idea at the time, Gilmour regretted this, 'not having thought it through entirely. Meeting and greeting Volkswagen people. I was not a popular chappy with Volkswagen. I don't want them to be able to say they have a connection with Pink Floyd, that they are part of our success. We will not do it again. I didn't like it, and any money I made from it went to charity. We should remain proudly independent, that's my view, and we will in the future.'[6] Little, it seems, had been learnt from the Gini episode some twenty years earlier.

If one thing set *The Division Bell* and the related stage show apart from all others, it was the sheer power of their delivery – and such an audio and visual feast are they that it would be difficult to imagine Pink Floyd topping this achievement. While whole families attended their concerts, most striking

was the fact that the band had captured the imagination of a new generation. A huge number of teenagers who might well have been steeping themselves in rave or grunge were committing themselves to Pink Floyd. As one industry observer put it, 'it's hard to tell how they attract a younger demographic. Unlike Neil Young or Aerosmith, they have no connection to '90s music. I can't even think of an act that has caught younger consumers' favour that would even lead them to Pink Floyd. This is a unique situation.'[7]

At the close of the tour it was calculated that over 5.3 million tickets had been sold, grossing some $100 million for the band.

Finally, to commemorate their efforts, a live album and video, both entitled *Pulse*, were released. These not only gave a balanced and well-recorded picture of Pink Floyd's then current repertoire but, for the first time, contained a complete official rendition of the whole of 'Dark Side Of The Moon', which they had revived towards the close of the US tour and performed as a complete second half in shows throughout Europe.

'We were bitterly disappointed that we didn't make a proper record of "Dark Side Of The

Special 'Pink Floyd' Volkswagen Golf, Germany, 1994

Above and right: Earls Court, London, October 1994

Moon" at Earls Court in '73 – or "The Wall" show,'[8] said Nick Mason recently. Inevitably, though, critics would have much preferred that they had done this in the first place rather than present a rehashed latter-day performance for their hi-fi pleasure. After all, while the last two tours are now fully documented, there remains an unforgivable void between 1969's *Ummagumma* and 1988's *Delicate Sound of Thunder*. Not even the BBC sessions have been released (although they're not hard to find on bootleg) and although an 'Anthology' set, similar to the recent trawl of The Beatles' archive, would be a wonderful treat for fans, the prospect seems remote.

Once again, however, Pink Floyd have stepped out of the limelight, as they always have done after an extensive bout of recording or touring. In fact, despite the surprise release of a solo album by Rick Wright in 1996, they have remained more than usually inactive – even Gilmour has been curiously absent from the session circuit.

At the time of writing, strong rumours persist among the more optimistic fans that Pink Floyd will one day reunite with Roger Waters and put their differences behind them. Gilmour, however, does not share their dream. 'There's absolutely no likelihood of that happening at all. A lot of very good work came out of our time together. Roger wrote a lot of very, very good words. It's understandable that people would have an affection for some possibility of us going back to the heyday – if you like – of our career, but it is irrelevant to me.'[9]

But then with Pink Floyd it never turns out the way you think it will...

Notes
1. *Guitar World*, September 1994
2. *Mojo*, May 1994
3. *Guitar World*, September 1994
4. *Evening Standard* (London), 30.11.93
5. *Live*, September 1994
6. *Mojo*, July 1995
7. *USA Today*, c.July 1994
8. *Mojo*, July 1995
9. *Access*, July 1994

EARLS COURT OLYMPIA

PINK FLOYD

17/10/94   19:45

ROW 10

SEAT 59

NOT FOR RESALE

1994

PINK FLOYD (1994–)
Personnel:
David Gilmour
Nick Mason
Richard Wright

THE DIVISION BELL –
WORLD TOUR
Additional touring personnel:
Sam Brown: Backing vocals
Jon Carin: Keyboards and vocals
Claudia Fontaine: Backing vocals
Durga McBroom: Backing vocals
Dick Parry: Saxophones
Guy Pratt: Bass guitar and vocals
Tim Renwick: Guitars
Gary Wallis: Percussion

■ **29.3.94**
**Joe Robbie Stadium,
Miami, Florida, USA.**

Final dress rehearsals for the world tour, which was to begin the following day. MTV filmed segments and interviewed the band and crew for broadcast.

■ **30.3.94**
**Joe Robbie Stadium,
Miami, Florida, USA.**
Set list: Astronomy Dominé/ Learning To Fly/What Do You Want From Me/Take It Back/Lost For Words/Sorrow/A Great Day For Freedom/Keep Talking/One Of These Days//Shine On You Crazy Diamond Pts.1-5/Breathe/ Time/Breathe (reprise)/High Hopes/Wish You Were Here/ Another Brick In The Wall Pt.2/ The Great Gig In The Sky/Us And Them/Money/Comfortably Numb/encore: Hey You/Run Like Hell.

■ **3.4.94**
**Alamo Dome, San Antonio,
Texas, USA.**
Set list: Astronomy Dominé/ Learning To Fly/What Do You Want From Me/Poles Apart/ Sorrow/Take It Back/Lost For Words/Keep Talking/On The Turning Away//Shine On You Crazy Diamond Pts.1-5/Breathe/ Time/Breathe (reprise)/High Hopes/Wish You Were Here/One Of These Days/The Great Gig In The Sky/Us And Them/Money/ Comfortably Numb/encore: Hey You/Run Like Hell.

■ **5.4.94**
**Rice University Stadium,
Houston, Texas, USA.**
Set list: Astronomy Dominé/ Learning To Fly/What Do You Want From Me/Take It Back/Lost

The Rose Bowl, Pasadena, Los Angeles, 16 April 1994

For Words/Sorrow/A Great Day For Freedom/Keep Talking/One Of These Days/Another Brick In The Wall Pt.2//Shine On You Crazy Diamond Pts.1-5/Breathe/Time/Breathe (reprise)/High Hopes/Wish You Were Here/The Great Gig In The Sky (part)/Money/encore: Run Like Hell (part).

Heavy rain seriously damaged the electrics, curtailing the second set.

■ **9–10.4.94**

Autodromo Hermanos Rodríguez, Mexico City, Mexico.

Set list on 9.4.94: Astronomy Dominé/Learning To Fly/What Do You Want From Me/A Great Day For Freedom/Sorrow/Take It Back/Keep Talking/One Of These Days//Shine On You Crazy Diamond Pts.1-5/Breathe/Time/Breathe (reprise)/High Hopes/Another Brick In The Wall Pt.2/The Great Gig In The Sky/Us And Them/Money/Comfortably Numb/encore: Hey You/Run Like Hell.

■ **14.4.94**

Jack Murphy Stadium, San Diego, California, USA.

Set list: Astronomy Dominé/Learning To Fly/What Do You Want From Me/A Great Day For Freedom/Sorrow/Take It Back/On The Turning Away/Keep Talking/One Of These Days//Shine On You Crazy Diamond Pts.1-5/Breathe/Time/Breathe (reprise)/High Hopes/Wish You Were Here/Another Brick In The Wall Pt.2/Us And Them/Money/Comfortably Numb/encore: Hey You/Run Like Hell.

■ **16.4.94**

The Rose Bowl, Pasadena, Los Angeles, California, USA.

Set list: Astronomy Dominé/Learning To Fly/What Do You Want From Me/Poles Apart/Sorrow/On The Turning Away/Keep Talking/Take It Back/One Of These Days//Shine On You Crazy Diamond Pts.1-5/Breathe/Time/Breathe (reprise)/

High Hopes/Wish You Were Here/Another Brick In The Wall Pt.2/The Great Gig In The Sky/Us And Them/Money/Comfortably Numb/encore: Hey You/Run Like Hell.

■ **17.4.94**

The Rose Bowl, Pasadena, Los Angeles, California, USA.

Set list: Astronomy Dominé/Learning To Fly/What Do You Want From Me/A Great Day For Freedom/Sorrow/Take It Back/On The Turning Away/Keep Talking/One Of These Days//Shine On You Crazy Diamond Pts.1-5/Breathe/Time/Breathe (reprise)/High Hopes/Wish You Were Here/Another Brick In The Wall Pt.2/The Great Gig In The Sky/Us And Them/Money/Comfortably Numb/encore: Hey You/Run Like Hell.

■ **20.4.94**

Oakland Coliseum Stadium, Oakland, California, USA.

Set list: Astronomy Dominé/Learning To Fly/What Do You Want From Me/On The Turning Away/Poles Apart/Sorrow/Take It Back/Keep Talking/One Of These Days//Shine On You Crazy Diamond Pts.1-5/Breathe/Time/Breathe (reprise)/High Hopes/Wish You Were Here/Another Brick In The Wall Pt.2/The Great Gig In The Sky/Us And Them/Money/Comfortably Numb/encore: Hey You/Run Like Hell.

■ **21.4.94**

Oakland Coliseum Stadium, Oakland, California, USA.

Set list: Astronomy Dominé/Learning To Fly/What Do You Want From Me/On The Turning Away/A Great Day For Freedom/Sorrow/Take It Back/Keep Talking/One Of These Days//Shine On You Crazy Diamond Pts.1-5/Breathe/Time/Breathe (reprise)/High Hopes/Wish You Were Here/Another Brick In The Wall Pt.2/The Great Gig In The Sky/Us And Them/Money/Comfortably Numb/encore: Hey You/Run Like Hell.

■ **22.4.94**

Oakland Coliseum Stadium, Oakland, California, USA.

Set list: Astronomy Dominé/Learning To Fly/What Do You Want From Me/On The Turning Away/Poles Apart/Sorrow/Take It Back/Keep Talking/One Of These Days//Shine On You Crazy Diamond Pts.1-5/Breathe/Time/Breathe (reprise)/High Hopes/The Great Gig In The Sky/One Slip/Us And Them/Wish You Were Here/Money/Another Brick In The Wall Pt.2/Comfortably Numb/encore: Hey You/Run Like Hell.

■ **24.4.94**

Sun Devil Stadium, Arizona State University, Tempe, Arizona, USA.

Set list: Astronomy Dominé/Learning To Fly/What Do You Want From Me/On The Turning Away/Lost For Words/Sorrow/Take It Back/Keep Talking/One Of These Days//Shine On You Crazy Diamond Pts.1-5/Breathe/Time/Breathe (reprise)/High Hopes/The Great Gig In The Sky/Wish You Were Here/Us And Them/Money/Another Brick In The Wall Pt.2/Comfortably Numb/encore: Hey You/Run Like Hell.

■ **26.4.94**

Sun Bowl, El Paso, Texas, USA.

Set list: Astronomy Dominé/Learning To Fly/What Do You Want From Me/On The Turning Away/Lost For Words/Sorrow/Take It Back/Keep Talking/One Of These Days//Shine On You Crazy Diamond Pts.1-5/Breathe/Time/Breathe (reprise)/High Hopes/The Great Gig In The Sky/Wish You Were Here/Us And Them/Money/Another Brick In The Wall Pt.2/Comfortably Numb/encore: Hey You/Run Like Hell.

■ **28.4.94**

Texas Stadium, Irving, Dallas, Texas, USA.

Set list: Astronomy Dominé/Learning To Fly/What Do You Want From Me/On The Turning

Away/Poles Apart/Sorrow/Take It Back/Keep Talking/One Of These Days//Shine On You Crazy Diamond Pts.1-5/Breathe/Time/Breathe (reprise)/High Hopes/The Great Gig In The Sky/Wish You Were Here/Us And Them/Money/Another Brick In The Wall Pt.2/Comfortably Numb/encore: Hey You/Run Like Hell.

■ **29.4.94**

Texas Stadium, Irving, Dallas, Texas, USA.

Set list: Astronomy Dominé/Learning To Fly/What Do You Want From Me/On The Turning Away/Coming Back To Life/Sorrow/Take It Back/Keep Talking/One Of These Days//Shine On You Crazy Diamond

Pts.1-5/Breathe/Time/Breathe (reprise)/High Hopes/The Great Gig In The Sky/Wish You Were Here/Us And Them/Money/Another Brick In The Wall Pt.2/Comfortably Numb/encore: Hey You/Run Like Hell.

■ **1.5.94**
Legion Field, Birmingham, Alabama, USA.

Set list: Astronomy Domine/Learning To Fly/What Do You Want From Me/On The Turning Away/Take It Back/Lost For Words/Sorrow/Coming Back To Life/Keep Talking/One Of These Days//Shine On You Crazy Diamond Pts.1-5/Breathe/Time/Breathe (reprise)/High Hopes/The Great Gig In The Sky/Wish

You Were Here/Us And Them/Money/Another Brick In The Wall Pt.2/Comfortably Numb/encore: Hey You/Run Like Hell.

■ **3.5.94**
Bobbie Dodd Stadium, Georgia Institute of Technology, Atlanta, Georgia, USA.

Set list: Astronomy Dominé/Learning To Fly/What Do You Want From Me/On The Turning Away/Take It Back/Lost For Words/Sorrow/Coming Back To Life/Keep Talking/One Of These Days//Shine On You Crazy Diamond Pts.1-5/Breathe/Time/Breathe (reprise)/High Hopes/The Great Gig In The Sky/Wish You Were Here/Us And Them/

Money/Another Brick In The Wall Pt.2/Comfortably Numb/encore: Hey You/Run Like Hell.

■ **4.5.94**
Bobbie Dodd Stadium, Georgia Institute of Technology, Atlanta, Georgia, USA.

Set list: Astronomy Dominé/Learning To Fly/What Do You Want From Me/On The Turning Away/Coming Back To Life/Sorrow/Take It Back/Keep Talking/One Of These Days//Shine On You Crazy Diamond Pts.1-5/Breathe/Time/Breathe (reprise)/High Hopes/The Great Gig In The Sky/Wish You Were Here/Us And Them/Money/Another Brick In The Wall

The Rose Bowl, Pasadena, Los Angeles, April 1994

Pt.2/Comfortably Numb/encore: Hey You/Run Like Hell.

■ **6.5.94 Tampa Stadium, Tampa, Florida, USA.**

Set list: Astronomy Dominé/Learning To Fly/What Do You Want From Me/On The Turning Away/Take It Back/A Great Day For Freedom/Sorrow/Keep Talking/One Of These Days//Shine On You Crazy Diamond Pts.1-5/Breathe/Time/Breathe (reprise)/High Hopes/The Great Gig In The Sky/Wish You Were Here/Us And Them/Money/Another Brick In

The Wall Pt.2/Comfortably Numb/ encore: Hey You/Run Like Hell.

■ 8.5.94
Vanderbilt University Stadium, Nashville, Tennessee, USA.

Set list: Astronomy Dominé/ Learning To Fly/What Do You Want From Me/On The Turning Away/Take It Back/A Great Day For Freedom/Sorrow/Keep Talking/One Of These Days// Shine On You Crazy Diamond Pts.1-5/Breathe/Time/Breathe (reprise)/High Hopes/The Great Gig In The Sky/Wish You Were Here/Us And Them/Money/ Another Brick In The Wall Pt.2/Comfortably Numb/encore: Hey You/Run Like Hell.

■ 10.5.94
Carter-Finley Stadium, North Carolina State University, Raleigh, North Carolina, USA.

Set list: Astronomy Dominé/ Learning To Fly/What Do You Want From Me/A Great Day For Freedom/Sorrow/Take It Back/ On The Turning Away/Keep Talking/One Of These Days// Shine On You Crazy Diamond Pts.1-5/Breathe/Time/Breathe (reprise)/High Hopes/Wish You

Were Here/Another Brick In The Wall Pt.2/The Great Gig In The Sky/Us And Them/Money/ Comfortably Numb/encore: Hey You/Run Like Hell.

■ 12.5.94
Death Valley Stadium, Clemson University, Clemson, South Carolina, USA.

Set list: Astronomy Dominé/ Learning To Fly/What Do You

Want From Me/On The Turning Away/Take It Back/Poles Apart/ Keep Talking/One Of These Days//Shine On You Crazy Diamond Pts.1-5/Breathe/Time/ Breathe (reprise)/High Hopes/ The Great Gig In The Sky/Wish You Were Here/Us And Them/ Money/Another Brick In The Wall Pt.2/Comfortably Numb/ encore: Hey You/Run Like Hell.

■ 14.5.94
Louisiana Superdrome, New Orleans, Louisiana, USA.

Set list: Astronomy Dominé/ Learning To Fly/What Do You Want From Me /On The Turning Away/Take It Back/Coming Back To Life/Sorrow/Keep Talking/One Of These Days//Shine On You Crazy Diamond Pts.1-5/Breathe/ Time/Breathe (reprise)/High Hopes/ The Great Gig In The Sky/Wish You Were Here/Us And Them/ Money/Another Brick In The Wall Pt.2/Comfortably Numb/ encore: Hey You/Run Like Hell

■ 18.5.94
Foxboro Stadium, Foxboro, Boston, Massachusetts, USA.

Set list: Astronomy Dominé/ Learning To Fly/What Do You Want From Me/On The Turning Away/Coming Back To Life/ Sorrow/ Take It Back/Keep Talking/One Of These Days// Shine On You Crazy Diamond Pts.1-5/Breathe/Time/Breathe (reprise)/High Hopes/The Great Gig In The Sky/Wish You Were Here/Us And Them/Money/ Another Brick In The Wall Pt.2/ Comfortably Numb/encore: Hey You/Run Like Hell.

■ 19.5.94
Foxboro Stadium, Foxboro,

Boston, Massachusetts, USA.

Set list: Astronomy Dominé/ Learning To Fly/What Do You Want From Me/On The Turning Away/Take It Back/Poles Apart/ Sorrow/Keep Talking/One Of These Days//Shine On You Crazy Diamond Pts.1-5/Breathe/Time/ Breathe (reprise)/High Hopes/ The Great Gig In The Sky/Wish You Were Here/Us And Them/ Money/Another Brick In The Wall Pt.2/Comfortably Numb/ encore: Hey You/Run Like Hell.

■ 20.5.94
Foxboro Stadium, Foxboro, Boston, Massachusetts, USA.

Set list: Astronomy Dominé/ Learning To Fly/What Do You Want From Me/On The Turning Away/Take It Back/A Great Day For Freedom/Sorrow/Keep Talking/One Of These Days// Shine On You Crazy Diamond Pts.1-5/Breathe/Time/Breathe (reprise)/High Hopes/The Great Gig In The Sky/Wish You Were Here/Us And Them/Money/ Another Brick In The Wall Pt.2/Comfortably Numb/encore: Hey You/Run Like Hell.

■ 22.5.94
Stade du Parc Olympique, Montreal, Quebec, Canada.

Set list: Astronomy Dominé/Learning To Fly/What Do You Want From Me/Poles Apart/Sorrow/On The Turning Away/Take It Back/Keep Talking/One Of These Days// Shine On You Crazy Diamond Pts.1-5/Breathe/Time/Breathe (reprise)/High Hopes/The Great Gig In The Sky/Wish You Were Here/Us And Them/ Money/Another Brick In The Wall Pt.2/Comfortably Numb/encore: Hey You/Run Like Hell.

■ 23.5.94
Stade du Parc Olympique, Montreal, Quebec, Canada.

Set list: Astronomy Dominé/ Learning To Fly/What Do You Want From Me /On The Turning Away/A Great Day For Freedom/ Take It Back/Sorrow/Keep Talking/One Of These Days//

Shine On You Crazy Diamond Pts.1-5/Breathe/Time/Breathe (reprise)/High Hopes/The Great Gig In The Sky/Wish You Were Here/Us And Them/Money/ Another Brick In The Wall Pt.2/Comfortably Numb/ encore: Hey You/Run Like Hell

■ 24.5.94
Stade du Parc Olympique, Montreal, Quebec, Canada.

Set list: Astronomy Dominé/ Learning To Fly/What Do You Want From Me /On The Turning Away/Coming Back To Life/ Sorrow/Take It Back/A Great Day For Freedom/Keep Talking/One Of These Days//Shine On You Crazy Diamond Pts.1-5/Breathe/ Time/Breathe (reprise)/High Hopes/The Great Gig In The Sky/ Wish You Were Here/Us And Them/Money/Another Brick In The Wall Pt.2/Comfortably Numb/ encore: Hey You/Run Like Hell.

26.5.94
Municipal Stadium, Cleveland, Ohio, USA

Set list: Astronomy Dominé/ Learning To Fly/What Do You Want From Me /On The Turning Away/Take It Back/Poles Apart/ Sorrow/Keep Talking/One Of These Days//Shine On You Crazy Diamond Pts.1-5/Breathe/Time/ Breathe (reprise)/High Hopes/ The Great Gig In The Sky/Wish You Were Here/Us And Them/ Money/Another Brick In The Wall Pt.2/Comfortably Numb/ encore: Hey You/Run Like Hell.

■ 27.5.94
Municipal Stadium, Cleveland, Ohio, USA.

Set list: Astronomy Dominé/ Learning To Fly/What Do You Want From Me/On The Turning Away/Sorrow/Take It Back/Keep Talking/One Of These Days// Shine On You Crazy Diamond Pts.1-5/Breathe/Time/Breathe (reprise)/High Hopes/The Great Gig In The Sky/Wish You Were Here/Us And Them/Money/ Another Brick In The Wall Pt.2/Comfortably Numb/encore: Hey You/Run Like Hell.

■ 29.5.94

Ohio State University Stadium, Columbus, Ohio, USA.

Set list: Astronomy Dominé/ Learning To Fly/What Do You Want From Me/On The Turning Away/Coming Back To Life/ Sorrow/Take It Back/Keep Talking/ One Of These Days//Shine On You Crazy Diamond Pts.1-5/ Breathe/Time/Breathe (reprise)/ High Hopes/The Great Gig In The Sky/Wish You Were Here/Us And Them/Money/Another Brick In The Wall Pt.2/Comfortably Numb/ encore: Hey You/Run Like Hell.

■ **31.5.94**
Three Rivers Stadium, Pittsburgh, Pennsylvania, USA.

Set list: Astronomy Dominé/ Learning To Fly/What Do You Want From Me/On The Turning Away/Coming Back To Life/ Sorrow/Take It Back/Keep Talking/One Of These Days// Shine On You Crazy Diamond Pts.1-5/Breathe/Time/Breathe (reprise)/High Hopes/The Great Gig In The Sky/Wish You Were Here/Us And Them/Money/ Another Brick In The Wall Pt.2/Comfortably Numb/encore: Hey You/Run Like Hell.

■ **2.6.94**
Veterans Stadium, Philadelphia, Pennsylvania, USA.

Set list: Astronomy Dominé/ Learning To Fly/What Do You Want From Me/On The Turning Away/Take It Back/Poles Apart/ Sorrow/Keep Talking/One Of These Days//Shine On You Crazy Diamond Pts.1-5/Breathe/Time/ Breathe (reprise)/High Hopes/ The Great Gig In The Sky/Wish You Were Here/Us And Them/ Money/Another Brick In The Wall Pt.2/Comfortably Numb/ encore: Hey You/Run Like Hell.

■ **3.6.94**
Veterans Stadium, Philadelphia, Pennsylvania, USA.

Set list: Astronomy Dominé/ Learning To Fly/What Do You Want From Me/On The Turning

Away/Take It Back/A Great Day For Freedom/Sorrow/Keep Talking/One Of These Days// Shine On You Crazy Diamond Pts.1-5/Breathe/Time/Breathe (reprise)/High Hopes/The Great Gig In The Sky/Wish You Were Here/Us And Them/Money/ Another Brick In The Wall Pt.2/Comfortably Numb/encore: Hey You/Run Like Hell.

■ **4.6.94**
Veterans Stadium, Philadelphia, Pennsylvania, USA.

Set list: Astronomy Dominé/ Learning To Fly/What Do You Want From Me/On The Turning Away/Coming Back To Life/ Sorrow/Take It Back/Keep Talking/One Of These Days// Shine On You Crazy Diamond Pts.1-5/Breathe/Time/Breathe (reprise)/High Hopes/The Great Gig In The Sky/Wish You Were Here/Us And Them/Money/ Another Brick In The Wall Pt.2/ Comfortably Numb/encore: Hey You/Run Like Hell.

■ **6.6.94**
Carrier Dome, Syracuse University, Syracuse, New York, USA.

Set list: Astronomy Dominé/ Learning To Fly/What Do You Want From Me/Take It Back/On The Turning Away/Coming Back To Life/Sorrow/Keep Talking/One Of These Days//Shine On You Crazy Diamond Pts.1-5/Breathe/ Time/Breathe (reprise)/Wish You Were Here/Us And Them/High Hopes/Money/The Great Gig In The Sky/Another Brick In The Wall Pt.2/Comfortably Numb/ encore: Hey You/Run Like Hell.

■ **10.6.94**
Yankee Stadium, New York City, New York, USA.

Set list: Astronomy Dominé/ Learning To Fly/What Do You Want From Me/On The Turning Away/Poles Apart/Take It Back/ Sorrow/Keep Talking/One Of These Days//Shine On You Crazy Diamond Pts.1-5/Breathe/ Time/Breathe (reprise)/High Hopes/The Great Gig In the

Sky/Wish You Were Here/Us And Them/Money/Another Brick In The Wall Pt.2/Comfortably Numb/ encore: Hey You/Run Like Hell.

■ **11.6.94**
Yankee Stadium, New York City, New York, USA.

Set list: Astronomy Dominé/ Learning To Fly/What Do You Want From Me/On The Turning Away/Take It Back/Coming Back To Life/Sorrow/Keep Talking/One Of These Days//Shine On You Crazy Diamond Pts.1-5/Breathe/ Time/Breathe (reprise)/High Hopes/The Great Gig In The Sky/ Wish You Were Here/Us And Them/ Money/Another Brick In The Wall Pt.2/Comfortably Numb/ encore: Hey You/Run Like Hell.

■ **14.6.94**
Hoosier Dome, Indianapolis, Indiana, USA.

Set list: Astronomy Dominé/ Learning To Fly/What Do You Want From Me/On The Turning Away/Take It Back/A Great Day For Freedom/Sorrow/Keep Talking/One Of These Days// Shine On You Crazy Diamond Pts.1-5/Breathe/Time/Breathe (reprise)/High Hopes/The Great Gig In The Sky/Wish You Were Here/Us And Them/Money/ Another Brick In The Wall Pt.2/ Comfortably Numb/encore: Hey You/Run Like Hell.

■ **16.6.94**
Cyclone Stadium, Iowa State University, Ames, Iowa, USA.

Set list: Astronomy Dominé/ Learning To Fly/What Do You Want From Me/On The Turning Away/Take It Back/A Great Day For Freedom/Sorrow/Keep Talking/One Of These Days// Shine On You Crazy Diamond Pts.1-5/Breathe/Time/Breathe (reprise)/High Hopes/The Great Gig In The Sky/Wish You Were Here/Us And Them/Money/ Another Brick In The Wall Pt.2/Comfortably Numb/encore: Hey You/Run Like Hell.

■ **18.6.94**
Mile High Stadium, Denver, Colorado, USA.

Set list: Astronomy Dominé/ Learning To Fly/What Do You Want From Me/On The Turning Away/Take It Back/Coming Back To Life/Sorrow/Keep Talking/One Of These Days//Shine On You Crazy Diamond Pts.1-5/Breathe/ Time/Breathe (reprise)/ High Hopes/The Great Gig In The Sky/Wish You Were Here/ Us And Them/Money/Another Brick In The Wall Pt.2/ Comfortably Numb/encore: Hey You/Run Like Hell.

■ **20.6.94**
Arrowhead Stadium, Kansas City, Missouri, USA.

Set list: Astronomy Dominé/ Learning To Fly/What Do You Want From Me/On The Turning Away/Poles Apart/Take It Back/ Sorrow/Keep Talking/One Of These Days//Shine On You Crazy Diamond Pts.1-5/Breathe/Time/ Breathe (reprise)/High Hopes/ The Great Gig In The Sky/Wish You Were Here/Us And Them/ Money/Another Brick In The Wall Pt.2/Comfortably Numb/ encore: Hey You/Run Like Hell.

■ **22.6.94**
Hubert H Humphrey Metrodome, Minneapolis, Minnesota, USA.

Set list: Astronomy Dominé/ Learning To Fly/What Do You Want From Me/On The Turning Away/Take It Back/Coming Back To Life/Sorrow/Keep Talking/One Of These Days//Shine On You Crazy Diamond Pts.1-5/Breathe/ Time/Breathe (reprise)/High Hopes/The Great Gig In The Sky/Wish You Were Here/Us And Them/Money/Another Brick In The Wall Pt.2/Comfortably Numb/encore: Hey You/Run Like Hell.

■ **25.6.94**
British Columbia Place Stadium, Vancouver, British Columbia, Canada.

Set list: Astronomy Dominé/ Learning To Fly/What Do You Want From Me/Coming Back To Life/Sorrow/On The Turning Away/Take It Back/Keep Talking/ One Of These Days//Shine On

Performing beneath the rain covers during the US tour, 1994

You Crazy Diamond Pts.1-5/ Breathe/Time/Breathe (reprise)/ High Hopes/Wish You Were Here/Another Brick In The Wall Pt.2/The Great Gig In The Sky/ Us And Them/Money/ Comfortably Numb/encore: Hey You/Run Like Hell.

■ **26.6.94**
British Columbia Place Stadium, Vancouver, British Columbia, Canada.
Set list: Astronomy Dominé/ Learning To Fly/What Do You Want From Me/A Great Day For Freedom/Sorrow/On The Turning Away/Take It Back/Keep Talking/ One Of These Days//Shine On You Crazy Diamond Pts.1-5/ Breathe/Time/Breathe (reprise)/ High Hopes/Wish You Were Here/Another Brick In The Wall Pt.2/The Great Gig In The Sky/ Us And Them/Money/ Comfortably Numb/encore: Hey You/Run Like Hell.

■ **28.6.94**
Commonwealth Stadium, Edmonton, Alberta, Canada.
Set list: Astronomy Dominé/ Learning To Fly/What Do You Want From Me/Sorrow/On The Turning Away/Take It Back/Keep Talking/One Of These Days// Shine On You Crazy Diamond Pts.1-5/Breathe/Time/Breathe (reprise)/High Hopes/The Great Gig In The Sky/Wish You Were Here/Money/Us And Them/ Another Brick In The Wall Pt.2/ Comfortably Numb/encore: Hey You/Run Like Hell.

■ **1.7.94**
Winnipeg Stadium, Winnipeg, Manitoba, Canada.
Set list: Astronomy Dominé/

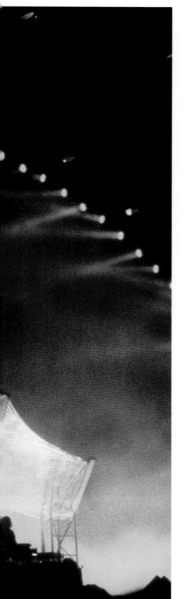

Camp Randall Stadium, University of Madison–Wisconsin, Madison, Wisconsin, USA.
Set list: Astronomy Dominé/ Learning To Fly/What Do You Want From Me/On The Turning Away/Take It Back/A Great Day For Freedom/Sorrow/Keep Talking/One Of These Days// Shine On You Crazy Diamond Pts.1-5/Breathe/Time/Breathe (reprise)/High Hopes/The Great Gig In The Sky/Wish You Were Here/Us And Them/Money/ Another Brick In The Wall Pt.2/ Comfortably Numb/encore: Hey You/Run Like Hell.
■ **5.7.94**
Canadian National Exhibition Stadium, Toronto, Ontario, Canada.
Set list: Astronomy Dominé/ Learning To Fly/What Do You Want From Me/On The Turning Away/Take It Back/Coming Back To Life/Sorrow/Keep Talking/One Of These Days//Shine On You Crazy Diamond Pts.1-5/Breathe/ Time/Breathe (reprise)/High Hopes/The Great Gig In The Sky/ Wish You Were Here/Us And Them/Money/Another Brick In The Wall Pt.2/Comfortably Numb/encore: Hey You/Run Like Hell.
■ **6.7.94**
Canadian National Exhibition Stadium, Toronto, Ontario, Canada.
Set list: Astronomy Dominé/ Learning To Fly/What Do You Want From Me/On The Turning Away/Take It Back/ Sorrow/Keep Talking/One Of These Days//Shine On You Crazy Diamond Pts.1-5/ Breathe/Time/Breathe (reprise)/High Hopes/The Great Gig In The Sky/Wish You Were Here/Us And Them/Money/Another Brick In The Wall Pt.2/ Comfortably Numb/encore: Hey You/Run Like Hell.
■ **7.7.94**
Canadian National

Exhibition Stadium, Toronto, Ontario, Canada.
Set list: Astronomy Dominé/ Learning To Fly/What Do You Want From Me/On The Turning Away/Take It Back/A Great Day For Freedom/Sorrow/Keep Talking/One Of These Days// Shine On You Crazy Diamond Pts.1-5/Breathe/Time/Breathe (reprise)/High Hopes/The Great Gig In The Sky/Wish You Were Here/Us And Them/Money/ Another Brick In The Wall Pt.2/ Comfortably Numb/encore: Hey You/Run Like Hell.
■ **9.7.94**
Robert F Kennedy Stadium, Washington, District of Columbia, USA.
Set list: Astronomy Dominé/ Learning To Fly/What Do You Want From Me/On The Turning Away/Poles Apart/Take It Back/ Sorrow/Keep Talking/One Of These Days//Shine On You Crazy Diamond Pts.1-5/Breathe/Time/ Breathe (reprise)/High Hopes/ The Great Gig In The Sky/Wish You Were Here/Us And Them/ Money/Another Brick In The Wall Pt.2/Comfortably Numb/

encore: Hey You/Run Like Hell.
■ **10.7.94**
Robert F Kennedy Stadium, Washington, District of Columbia, USA.
Set list: Astronomy Dominé/ Learning To Fly/What Do You Want From Me/On The Turning Away/Take It Back/Coming Back To Life/Sorrow/Keep Talking/One Of These Days//Shine On You Crazy Diamond Pts.1-5/Breathe/ Time/Breathe (reprise)/High Hopes/ The Great Gig In The Sky/Wish You Were Here/Us And Them/ Money/Another Brick In The Wall Pt.2/Comfortably Numb/encore: Hey You/Run Like Hell.
■ **12.7.94**
Soldier Field, Chicago, Illinois, USA.
Set list: Astronomy Dominé/ Learning To Fly/What Do You Want From Me/On The Turning Away/Lost For Words/Sorrow/ Take It Back/Keep Talking/One Of These Days//Shine On You Crazy Diamond Pts.1-5/Breathe/ Time/Breathe (reprise)/High Hopes/The Great Gig In The Sky/ Wish You Were Here/Us And Them/Money/Another Brick In

Learning To Fly/What Do You Want From Me/On The Turning Away/Poles Apart/Take It Back /Sorrow/Keep Talking/One Of These Days//Shine On You Crazy Diamond Pts.1-5/Breathe/Time/ Breathe (reprise)/High Hopes/ Wish You Were Here/The Great Gig In The Sky/Us And Them/ Money/Another Brick In The Wall Pt.2/Comfortably Numb/ encore: Hey You/Run Like Hell.
■ **3.7.94**

The Wall Pt.2/Comfortably Numb/
encore: Hey You/Run Like Hell.

■ **14.7.94**

**Pontiac Silverdome, Pontiac,
Detroit, Michigan, USA.**

Set list: Astronomy Dominé/
Learning To Fly/What Do You
Want From Me/On The Turning
Away/Poles Apart/Take It Back/
Sorrow/Keep Talking/One Of
These Days//Shine On You Crazy
Diamond Pts.1-5/Breathe/Time/
Breathe (reprise)/High Hopes/
The Great Gig In The Sky/Wish
You Were Here/Us And Them/
Money/Another Brick In The
Wall Pt.2/Comfortably Numb/
encore: Hey You/Run Like Hell.

■ **15.7.94**

**Pontiac Silverdome, Pontiac,
Detroit, Michigan, USA.**

Set list: Shine On You Crazy
Diamond Pts.1-5/Learning To
Fly/High Hopes/Coming Back To
Life/Take It Back/Sorrow/Keep
Talking/Another Brick In the Wall
Pt.2/One Of These Days//Dark
Side Of The Moon/encore: Wish
You Were Here/Comfortably
Numb/Run Like Hell.

In a surprise change to the
expected programme Pink Floyd
performed 'Dark Side Of The
Moon' in its entirety for the first
time since their show at
Knebworth in July 1975.

■ **17.7.94**

**Giants Stadium, East
Rutherford, New Jersey,
USA.**

Set list: Shine On You Crazy
Diamond Pts.1-5/Learning To
Fly/High Hopes/Take It Back/
Coming Back To Life/Sorrow/
Keep Talking/Another Brick In
the Wall Pt.2/One Of These
Days//Dark Side Of The Moon/
encore: Wish You Were Here/
Comfortably Numb/Run Like Hell.

■ **18.7.94**

**Giants Stadium, East
Rutherford, New Jersey, USA.**

Set list: Shine On You Crazy
Diamond Pts.1-5/Learning To
Fly/High Hopes/Take It Back/
Coming Back To Life/Sorrow/
Keep Talking/Another Brick In
the Wall Pt.2/One Of These

*Estádio de Alvalade,
Lisbon, Portugal, July 1994*

Days//Dark Side Of The Moon/
encore: Wish You Were Here/
Comfortably Numb/Run Like Hell.

■ **22.7.94**

**Estádio de Alvalade,
Lisbon, Portugal.**

Set list: Astronomy Dominé/
Learning To Fly/What Do You
Want From Me/On The Turning
Away/Take It Back/Coming Back
To Life/Lost For Words/Sorrow/
Keep Talking/One Of These Days//
Shine On You Crazy Diamond
Pts.1-5/Breathe/Time/Breathe
(reprise)/High Hopes/The Great
Gig In The Sky/Wish You Were
Here/Us And Them/Money/
Another Brick In The Wall
Pt.2/Comfortably Numb/
encore: Hey You/Run Like Hell.

■ **23.7.94**

**Estádio de Alvalade,
Lisbon, Portugal.**

Set list: Shine On You Crazy
Diamond Pts.1-5/Learning To
Fly/What Do You Want From
Me/On The Turning Away/Poles
Apart/Take It Back/Sorrow/Keep
Talking/One Of These Days//
Astronomy Dominé/Breathe/
Time/Breathe (reprise)/High
Hopes/The Great Gig In The Sky/
Wish You Were Here/Us And
Them/Money/Another Brick In The
Wall Pt.2/Comfortably Numb/
encore: Hey You/Run Like Hell.

■ **25.7.94**

**Estadio Anoeta, San
Sebastián, Spain.**

Set list: Shine On You Crazy
Diamond Pts.1-5/Learning To
Fly/What Do You Want From
Me/On The Turning Away/
Take It Back/A Great Day For
Freedom/Sorrow/Keep
Talking/One Of These Days//
Astronomy Dominé/Breathe/
Time/Breathe (reprise)/High
Hopes/The Great Gig In The
Sky/Wish You Were Here/Us
And Them/Money/Another
Brick In The Wall Pt.2/

Comfortably Numb/
encore: Hey You/Run Like Hell.

■ **27.7.94**

**Estadio Olímpico,
Barcelona, Spain.**

¿ Un elefante ?

¿ Un cerdo ?

¿ Dos peces comiéndose un
gusano ?

¿ Una mariposa ?

¿ Un hipopótamo ?

Set list: Shine On You Crazy
Diamond Pts.1-5/Learning To
Fly/What Do You Want From
Me/On The Turning Away/Take It
Back/Coming Back To Life/
Sorrow/Keep Talking/One Of
These Days//Astronomy
Dominé/Breathe/Time/Breathe
(reprise)/High Hopes/The Great
Gig In The Sky/Wish You Were
Here/Us And Them/Money/
Another Brick In The Wall
Pt.2/Comfortably Numb/encore:
Hey You/Run Like Hell.

■ **30.7.94**

**Château de Chantilly,
Chantilly, France.**

Set list: Shine On You Crazy
Diamond Pts.1-5/Learning To
Fly/What Do You Want From
Me/On The Turning Away/Take

It Back/Lost For Words/Sorrow/ Keep Talking/One Of These Days//Astronomy Dominé/ Breathe/Time/Breathe (reprise)/ High Hopes/The Great Gig In The Sky/Wish You Were Here/Us And Them/Money/Another Brick In The Wall Pt.2/Comfortably Numb/ encore: Hey You/Run Like Hell.

■ **31.7.94**
Château de Chantilly, Chantilly, France.
Set list: Shine On You Crazy Diamond Pts.1-5/Learning To Fly/What Do You Want From Me/On The Turning Away/Poles Apart/Take It Back/Sorrow/Keep Talking/One Of These Days// Astronomy Dominé/Breathe/ Time/Breathe (reprise)/High Hopes/The Great Gig In The Sky/

Wish You Were Here/Us And Them/Money/Another Brick In The Wall Pt.2/Comfortably Numb/ encore: Hey You/Run Like Hell.

■ **2.8.94**
Mungersdorfer Stadion, Cologne, Germany.
Set list: Astronomy Dominé/ Learning To Fly/What Do You Want From Me/On The Turning Away/Take It Back/A Great Day For Freedom/Sorrow/Keep Talking/One Of These Days// Shine On You Crazy Diamond Pts.1-5/Breathe/Time/Breathe (reprise)/High Hopes/The Great Gig In The Sky/Wish You Were Here/Us And Them/Money/ Another Brick In The Wall Pt.2/ Comfortably Numb/encore: Hey You/Run Like Hell.

■ **4.8.94**
Olympiastadion, Munich, Germany.
Set list: Astronomy Dominé/ Learning To Fly/What Do You Want From Me/On The Turning Away/Take It Back/A Great Day For Freedom/Keep Talking/ Sorrow/One Of These Days// Shine On You Crazy Diamond Pts.1-5/Breathe/Time/Breathe (reprise)/High Hopes/The Great Gig In The Sky/Wish You Were Here/Us And Them/Money/ Another Brick In The Wall Pt.2/Comfortably Numb/ encore: Hey You/Run Like Hell.

■ **6.8.94**
Fussballstadion St Jakob, Basle, Switzerland.
Set list: Shine On You Crazy Diamond Pts.1-5/Learning To Fly/High Hopes/Take It Back/ Coming Back To Life/Sorrow/ Keep Talking/Another Brick In the Wall Pt.2/One Of These Days//Dark Side Of The Moon/ encore: Wish You Were Here/ Comfortably Numb/Run Like Hell.

■ **7.8.94**
Fussballstadion St Jakob, Basle, Switzerland.
Set list: Astronomy Dominé/ Learning To Fly/What Do You Want From Me/On The Turning Away/Poles Apart/Take It Back/ Sorrow/Keep Talking/One Of These Days//Shine On You Crazy Diamond Pts.1-5/Breathe/Time/ Breathe (reprise)/High Hopes/ The Great Gig In The Sky/Wish You Were Here/Us And Them/ Money/Another Brick In The Wall Pt.2/Comfortably Numb/encore: Hey You/Run Like Hell.

■ **9.8.94**
Espace Grammont, Montpellier, France.
Set list: Astronomy Dominé/ Learning To Fly/What Do You Want From Me/On The Turning Away/Take It Back/Coming Back To Life/Sorrow/Keep Talking/One Of These Days//Shine On You Crazy Diamond Pts.1-5/Breathe/ Time/Breathe (reprise)/High Hopes/The Great Gig In The Sky/ Wish You Were Here/Us And

Them/Money/Another Brick In The Wall Pt.2/Comfortably Numb/ encore: Hey You/Run Like Hell.

■ **11.8.94**
Esplanade des Quinconces, Bordeaux, France.
Set list: Astronomy Dominé/ Learning To Fly/What Do You Want From Me/On The Turning Away/Take It Back/Coming Back To Life/Sorrow/Keep Talking/One Of These Days//Shine On You Crazy Diamond Pts.1-5/Breathe/ Time/Breathe (reprise)/High Hopes/ The Great Gig In The Sky/Wish You Were Here/Us And Them/ Money/Another Brick In The Wall Pt.2/Comfortably Numb/ encore: Hey You/Run Like Hell.

■ **13.8.94**
Hockenheimring, Hockenheim, Germany.
Set list: Astronomy Dominé/ Learning To Fly/What Do You Want From Me/On The Turning Away/Take It Back/Sorrow/A Great Day For Freedom/Keep Talking/One Of These Days// Shine On You Crazy Diamond Pts.1-5/Breathe/Time/Breathe (reprise)/High Hopes/The Great Gig In The Sky/Wish You Were Here/Us And Them/Money/ Another Brick In The Wall Pt.2/Comfortably Numb/encore: Hey You/Run Like Hell.

■ **16.8.94**
Neidersachsenstadion, Hannover, Germany.
Set list: Shine On You Crazy Diamond Pts.1-5/Learning To Fly/Take It Back/Sorrow/High Hopes/Keep Talking/Another Brick In the Wall Pt.2/One Of These Days//Dark Side Of The Moon/encore: Wish You Were Here/Comfortably Numb/Run Like Hell.

■ **17.8.94**
Neidersachsenstadion, Hannover, Germany.
Set list: Astronomy Dominé/ Learning To Fly/What Do You Want From Me/On The Turning Away/Take It Back/A Great Day For Freedom/Sorrow/Keep Talking/One Of These Days// Shine On You Crazy Diamond

PINK FLOYD

Pts.1-5/Breathe/Time/Breathe (reprise)/High Hopes/The Great Gig In The Sky/Wish You Were Here/Money/Another Brick In The Wall Pt.2/Comfortably Numb/ encore: Hey You/Run Like Hell.

■ **19.8.94**

Lufthafen Wiener Neustadt, Vienna, Austria.

Set list: Shine On You Crazy Diamond Pts.1-5/Learning To Fly/What Do You Want From Me/ On The Turning Away/Take It Back/ Coming Back To Life/Sorrow/ Keep Talking/One Of These Days//Astronomy Dominé/ Breathe/Time/Breathe (reprise)/ High Hopes/The Great Gig In The Sky/Wish You Were Here/Us And Them/Money/ Another Brick In The Wall Pt.2/Comfortably Numb/encore: Hey You/Run Like Hell.

■ **21.8.94**

Maifeld am Olympiastadion, Berlin, Germany.

Set list: Astronomy Dominé/ Learning To Fly/What Do You Want From Me/On The Turning Away/Take It Back/A Great Day For Freedom/Sorrow/Keep Talking/One Of These Days// Shine On You Crazy Diamond Pts.1-5/Breathe/Time/Breathe (reprise)/High Hopes/The Great Gig In The Sky/Wish You Were Here/Money/Another Brick In The Wall Pt.2/Comfortably Numb/ encore: Hey You/Run Like Hell.

■ **23.8.94**

Parkstadion, Gelsenkirchen, Germany.

Set list: Astronomy Dominé/ Learning To Fly/What Do You Want From Me/On The Turning Away/Poles Apart/Take It Back/ Sorrow/Keep Talking/One Of These Days//Shine On You Crazy Diamond Pts.1-5/Breathe/ Time/Breathe (reprise)/High Hopes/The Great Gig In The Sky/ Wish You Were Here/Us And Them/Money/Another Brick In The Wall Pt.2/Comfortably Numb/ encore: Hey You/Run Like Hell.

■ **25.8.94**

Parken, Copenhagen, Denmark.

Set list: Shine On You Crazy Diamond Pts.1-5/Learning To Fly/What Do You Want From Me/On The Turning Away/Take It Back/Coming Back To Life/ Sorrow/Keep Talking/One Of These Days//Astronomy Dominé/Breathe/Time/Breathe (reprise)/High Hopes/The Great Gig In The Sky/Wish You Were Here/Us And Them/Money/ Another Brick In The Wall Pt.2/Comfortably Numb/ encore: Hey You/Run Like Hell.

■ **27.8.94**

Ullevi Stadion, Gothenburg, Sweden.

Set list: Astronomy Dominé/ Learning To Fly/What Do You Want From Me/On The Turning Away/Take It Back/Sorrow/Keep Talking/One Of These Days// Shine On You Crazy Diamond Pts.1-5/Breathe/Time/Breathe (reprise)/High Hopes/The Great Gig In The Sky/Wish You Were Here/Us And Them/Money/ Another Brick In The Wall Pt.2/Comfortably Numb/

encore: Hey You/Run Like Hell.

■ **29.8.94**

Valle Hovin Stadion, Oslo, Norway.

Set list: Astronomy Dominé/ Learning To Fly/What Do You Want From Me/On The Turning Away/Take It Back/Coming Back To Life/Sorrow/Keep Talking/One Of These Days//Shine On You Crazy Diamond Pts.1-5/Breathe/ Time/Breathe (reprise)/High Hopes/ The Great Gig In The Sky/Wish You Were Here/Us And Them/

Money/Another Brick In The Wall Pt.2/Comfortably Numb/ encore: Marooned/Run Like Hell.

■ **30.8.94**

Valle Hovin Stadion, Oslo, Norway.

Set list: Astronomy Dominé/ Learning To Fly/What Do You Want From Me/On The Turning Away/Take It Back/Poles Apart/ Sorrow/Keep Talking/One Of These Days//Shine On You Crazy Diamond Pts.1-5/Breathe/Time/ Breathe (reprise)/High Hopes/ The Great Gig In The Sky/Wish

You Were Here/Us And Them/ Money/Another Brick In The Wall Pt.2/Comfortably Numb/ encore: Marooned/Run Like Hell. The two Oslo shows were the only occasions on which 'Marooned' was performed on the whole tour. A new projection film accompanied the track which featured whales – clearly a dig at Norway's whaling policy. Incidentally, Gilmour's habit of inserting riffs from The Beatles' 'Norwegian Wood' into the intro sequence to 'Run Like Hell' dates from this time.

■ **1.9.94**

Olympiastadion, Helsinki, Finland.

Show cancelled.

■ **2.9.94**

Festivalweise, Werchter, Belgium.

Set list: Shine On You Crazy Diamond Pts.1-5/Learning To Fly/What Do You Want From Me/On The Turning Away/Take It Back/A Great Day For Freedom/ Sorrow/Keep Talking/One Of These Days//Astronomy Dominé/ Breathe/Time/Breathe (reprise)/ High Hopes/The Great Gig In The Sky/Wish You Were Here/ Money/Another Brick In The Wall Pt.2/Comfortably Numb/ encore: Hey You/Run Like Hell.

■ **3.9.94**

Stadion Feyenoord, Rotterdam, Netherlands.

Set list: Astronomy Dominé/Learning To Fly/What Do You Want From Me/On The Turning Away/Poles Apart/Take It Back/Sorrow/Keep Talking/One Of These Days//Shine On You Crazy Diamond Pts.1-5/Breathe/ Time/Breathe (reprise)/High Hopes/The Great Gig In The Sky/ Wish You Were Here/Us And Them/Money/Another Brick In The Wall Pt.2/Comfortably Numb/ encore: Hey You/Run Like Hell

■ **4.9.94**

Stadion Feyenoord, Rotterdam, Netherlands.

Set list: Shine On You Crazy Diamond Pts.1-5/Learning To Fly/Take It Back/Sorrow/Keep

Talking/Wish You Were Here/ Another Brick In The Wall Pt.2/ One Of These Days/Dark Side Of The Moon/High Hopes/encore: Comfortably Numb/Run Like Hell.

■ **5.9.94**
Stadion Feyenoord, Rotterdam, Netherlands.
Set list: Shine On You Crazy

Diamond Pts.1-5/Learning To Fly/Take It Back/Sorrow/High Hopes/Keep Talking/Another Brick In The Wall Pt.2/One Of These Days//Dark Side Of The Moon/Comfortably Numb/ encore: Wish You Were Here/ Run Like Hell.

■ **7.9.94**
Strahov Stadion, Prague, Czech Republic.
Set list: Shine On You Crazy Diamond Pts.1-5/Learning To Fly/What Do You Want From Me/On The Turning Away/Take It Back/A Great Day For Freedom/ Sorrow/Coming Back To Life/ One Of These Days//Astronomy Dominé/Breathe/Time/Breathe (reprise)/High Hopes/The Great Gig In The Sky/Wish You Were Here/Us And Them/Money/ Another Brick In The Wall Pt.2/Comfortably Numb/encore: Hey You/Run Like Hell.

■ **9.9.94**
Stade de la Meinau, Strasbourg, France.
Set list: Astronomy Dominé/ Learning To Fly/What Do You Want From Me/On The Turning Away/Take It Back/Coming Back To Life/Sorrow/Keep Talking/One

Of These Days//Shine On You Crazy Diamond Pts.1-5/Breathe/ Time/Breathe (reprise)/High Hopes/The Great Gig In The Sky/ Wish You Were Here/Us And Them/Money/Another Brick In The Wall Pt.2/Comfortably Numb/ encore: Hey You/Run Like Hell.

■ **11.9.94**
Stade de Gerland, Lyon, France.
Set list: Shine On You Crazy Diamond Pts.1-5/Learning To Fly/What Do You Want From Me/On The Turning Away/Poles Apart/Take It Back/Sorrow/Keep Talking/One Of These Days// Astronomy Dominé/Breathe/Time/ Breathe (reprise)/High Hopes/ The Great Gig In The Sky/Wish You Were Here/Us And Them/ Money/Another Brick In The Wall Pt.2/Comfortably Numb/ encore: Hey You/Run Like Hell.

■ **13.9.94**
Stadio Delle Alpi, Turin, Italy.
Set list: Astronomy Dominé/ Learning To Fly/What Do You Want From Me/On The Turning Away/Take It Back/A Great Day For Freedom/Sorrow/Keep Talking/One Of These Days// Shine On You Crazy Diamond Pts.1-5 & 7/Breathe/Time/ Breathe (reprise)/High Hopes/ The Great Gig In The Sky/Wish You Were Here/Us And Them/ Money/Another Brick In The Wall Pt.2/Comfortably Numb/ encore: Hey You/Run Like Hell.

■ **15.9.94**
Stadio Friuli, Udine, Italy.

Set list: Shine On You Crazy Diamond Pts.1-5 & 7/Learning To Fly/What Do You Want From Me/On The Turning Away/ Coming Back To Life/Take It Back/Sorrow/Keep Talking/One Of These Days//Astronomy Dominé/Breathe/Time/Breathe (reprise)/High Hopes/The Great Gig In The Sky/Wish You Were Here/Us And Them/Money/ Another Brick In The Wall Pt.2/ Comfortably Numb/encore: Hey You/Run Like Hell.

■ **17.9.94**
Festa Nazionale del Unità, Modena, Italy.
Set list: Shine On You Crazy Diamond Pts.1-5 & 7/Learning To Fly/High Hopes/Take It Back/Coming Back To Life/Sorrow/Keep Talking/ Another Brick In The Wall Pt.2/ One Of These Days//Dark Side Of The Moon/encore: Wish You Were Here/Comfortably Numb/ Run Like Hell.

■ **19.9.94**
Cinecittà, Rome, Italy.
Set list: Shine On You Crazy Diamond Pts.1-5 & 7/Learning To Fly/High Hopes/Take It Back/ Coming Back To Life/Sorrow/ Keep Talking/Another Brick In The Wall Pt.2/One Of These Days//Dark Side Of The Moon/ encore: Wish You Were Here/ Comfortably Numb/Run Like Hell.

■ **20.9.94**
Cinecittà, Rome, Italy.
Set list: Shine On You Crazy Diamond Pts.1-5 & 7/Learning To Fly/High Hopes/Take It Back/ Coming Back To Life/Sorrow/ Keep Talking/Another Brick In The Wall Pt.2/One Of These Days//Dark Side Of The Moon/ encore: Wish You Were Here/ Comfortably Numb/Run Like Hell.

■ **21.9.94**
Cinecittà, Rome, Italy.
Set list: Astronomy Dominé/ Learning To Fly/What Do You Want From Me/On The Turning Away/Take It Back/A Great Day For Freedom/Sorrow/Keep Talking/One Of These Days// Shine On You Crazy Diamond

Pts.1-5 & 7/Another Brick In The Wall Pt. 2/High Hopes/Wish You Were Here/Dark Side Of The Moon/encore: Comfortably Numb/Run Like Hell.

■ **23.9.94**
Stade de Gerland, Lyon, France.
Set list: Shine On You Crazy Diamond Pts.1-5 & 7/Learning To Fly/High Hopes/Take It Back/ Coming Back To Life/Sorrow/ Keep Talking/Another Brick In The Wall Pt.2/One Of These Days//Dark Side Of The Moon/ Wish You Were Here/encore: Comfortably Numb/Run Like Hell.

■ **25.9.94**
Stade de la Pontaise, Lausanne, Switzerland.
Set list: Shine On You Crazy Diamond Pts.1-5 & 7/Learning To Fly/What Do You Want From Me/On The Turning Away/Take It Back/Coming Back To Life/ Sorrow/Keep Talking/One Of These Days//Astronomy Dominé/ Breathe/Time/Breathe (reprise)/ High Hopes/The Great Gig In The Sky/Wish You Were Here/ Us And Them/Money/Another Brick In The Wall Pt.2/ Comfortably Numb/encore: Hey You/Run Like Hell.

■ **12.10.94**
Earls Court Exhibition Hall, London, England.
The opening night of Pink Floyd's record-breaking run at Earls Court was marred by the unfortunate collapse of a 1,200-capacity seating stand at the rear of the hall immediately after the lights went down and the band took the stage. No one was seriously hurt, although eight people were rushed to hospital with spinal injuries, cuts, bruises and shock, some having fallen almost twenty feet to the ground. The show was rescheduled to 17.10.94 on what was supposed to be a day off for the band. A free T-shirt as well as a note of apology from the band was given to everyone who had been sitting in the collapsed stands.

13.10.94

Earls Court Exhibition Hall, London, England.

Set list: Astronomy Dominé/ Learning To Fly/What Do You Want From Me/On The Turning Away/Take It Back/Coming Back To Life/Sorrow/Keep Talking/One Of These Days//Shine On You Crazy Diamond Pts.1-5 & 7/ Breathe/Time/Breathe (reprise)/ High Hopes/The Great Gig In The Sky/Wish You Were Here/Us And Them/Money/Another Brick In The Wall Pt.2/Comfortably Numb/ encore: Hey You/Run Like Hell.

■ **14.10.94**

Earls Court Exhibition Hall, London, England.

Set list: Shine On You Crazy Diamond Pts.1-5 & 7/Learning To Fly/High Hopes/Take It Back/A Great Day For Freedom/ Sorrow/Keep Talking/Another Brick In The Wall Pt.2/One Of These Days//Dark Side Of The Moon/Wish You Were Here/ encore: Comfortably Numb/Run Like Hell.

■ **15.10.94**

Earls Court Exhibition Hall, London, England.

Set list: Astronomy Dominé/ Learning To Fly/What Do You Want From Me/On The Turning Away/Take It Back/Coming Back To Life/Sorrow/Keep Talking/One Of These Days//Shine On You Crazy Diamond Pts.1-5 & 7/Breathe/Time/Breathe (reprise)/High Hopes/The Great Gig In The Sky/Wish You Were Here/Us And Them/Money/ Another Brick In The Wall Pt.2/Comfortably Numb/encore: Hey You/Run Like Hell.

■ **16.10.94**

Earls Court Exhibition Hall, London, England.

Set list: Shine On You Crazy Diamond Pts.1-5 & 7/Learning To Fly/High Hopes/Take It Back/ Coming Back To Life/Sorrow/ Keep Talking/Another Brick In The Wall Pt.2/One Of These Days//Dark Side Of The Moon/ Wish You Were Here/ encore:

Comfortably Numb/Run Like Hell.

■ **17.10.94**

Earls Court Exhibition Hall, London, England.

Set list: Astronomy Dominé/ Learning To Fly/What Do You Want From Me/On The Turning Away/Poles Apart/Take It Back/ Sorrow/Keep Talking/One Of These Days//Shine On You Crazy Diamond Pts.1-5 & 7/Breathe/ Time/Breathe (reprise)/High Hopes/The Great Gig In The Sky/ Wish You Were Here/Us And Them/Money/Another Brick In The Wall Pt.2/Comfortably Numb/ encore: Hey You/Run Like Hell.

■ **19.10.94**

Earls Court Exhibition Hall, London, England.

Set list: Shine On You Crazy Diamond Pts.1-5 & 7/Learning To Fly/High Hopes/Lost For Words/ A Great Day For Freedom/Keep Talking/Coming Back To Life/ Sorrow/Another Brick In The Wall Pt.2/One Of These Days// Dark Side Of The Moon/Wish You Were Here/encore: Comfortably Numb/Run Like Hell.

■ **20.10.94**

Earls Court Exhibition Hall, London, England.

Set list: Shine On You Crazy Diamond Pts.1-5 & 7/Learning To Fly/High Hopes/Take It Back/ Coming Back To Life/Sorrow/ Keep Talking/Another Brick In The Wall Pt.2/One Of These Days//Dark Side Of The Moon/ Wish You Were Here/encore: Comfortably Numb/Run Like Hell. The entire concert was recorded and filmed for the official release of the tour video, *Pulse. Earls Court 20.10.94*. A slightly different edition of this was broadcast in the UK on BBC1 on 15.11.94 at 10.55pm.

■ **21.10.94**

Earls Court Exhibition Hall, London, England.

Set list: Astronomy Dominé/ Learning To Fly/What Do You Want From Me/On The Turning Away/Poles Apart/Take It Back/ Sorrow/Keep Talking/One Of

These Days//Shine On You Crazy Diamond Pts.1-5 & 7/Breathe/ Time/Breathe (reprise)/High Hopes/The Great Gig In The Sky/ Wish You Were Here/Us And Them/Money/Another Brick In The Wall Pt.2/Comfortably Numb/ encore: Hey You/Run Like Hell.

■ **22.10.94**

Earls Court Exhibition Hall, London, England.

Set list: Astronomy Dominé/ Learning To Fly/What Do You Want From Me/On The Turning Away/Take It Back/A Great Day For Freedom/Sorrow/Keep Talking/One Of These Days// Shine On You Crazy Diamond Pts.1-5 & 7/Breathe/Time/ Breathe (reprise)/High Hopes/ The Great Gig In The Sky/Wish You Were Here/Us And Them/ Money/Another Brick In The Wall Pt.2/Comfortably Numb/ encore: Hey You/Run Like Hell.

■ **23.10.94**

Earls Court Exhibition Hall, London, England.

Set list: Shine On You Crazy Diamond Pts.1-5 & 7/Learning To Fly/High Hopes/Take It Back/ Coming Back To Life/Sorrow/ Keep Talking/Another Brick In The Wall Pt.2/One Of These Days// Dark Side Of The Moon/Wish You Were Here/encore: Comfortably Numb/Run Like Hell.

■ **26.10.94**

Earls Court Exhibition Hall, London, England.

Set list: Astronomy Dominé/ Learning To Fly/What Do You Want From Me/On The Turning Away/Take It Back/Coming Back To Life/Sorrow/Keep Talking/One Of These Days//Shine On You Crazy Diamond Pts.1-5 & 7/ Breathe/Time/Breathe (reprise)/ High Hopes/The Great Gig In The Sky/Wish You Were Here/Us And Them/Money/Another Brick In The Wall Pt.2/Comfortably Numb/ encore: Hey You/Run Like Hell.

■ **27.10.94**

Earls Court Exhibition Hall, London, England.

Set list: Shine On You Crazy

Diamond Pts.1-5 & 7/Learning To Fly/What Do You Want From Me/ On The Turning Away/Take It Back/ A Great Day For Freedom/ Sorrow/Keep Talking/One Of These Days//Astronomy Dominé/ Breathe/Time/Breathe (reprise)/ High Hopes/The Great Gig In The Sky/Wish You Were Here/Us And Them/Money/Another Brick In The Wall Pt.2/Comfortably Numb/ encore: Hey You/Run Like Hell.

■ **28.10.94**

Earls Court Exhibition Hall, London, England.

Set list: Shine On You Crazy Diamond Pts.1-5 & 7/Learning To Fly/High Hopes/Take It Back/ Poles Apart/Sorrow/Keep Talking/Another Brick In The Wall Pt.2/One Of These Days//Dark Side Of The Moon/Wish You Were Here/encore: Comfortably Numb/Run Like Hell.

David Gilmour's friend the science-fiction author Douglas Adams joined Pink Floyd on stage during 'Brain Damage' to play acoustic guitar. It was a birthday present to Adams, although his participation was unannounced and he remained in the background.

■ **29.10.94**

Earls Court Exhibition Hall, London, England.

Set list: Shine On You Crazy Diamond Pts.1-5 & 7/Learning To Fly/High Hopes/Take It Back/ Coming Back To Life/Sorrow/ Keep Talking/Another Brick In The Wall Pt.2/One Of These Days//Dark Side Of The Moon/ encore: Wish You Were Here/ Comfortably Numb/Run Like Hell.

■ **15.11.94**

BBC TV Broadcast, London, England.

BBC1 broadcast a forty-minute official history of the band on its *Omnibus* documentary programme. It featured previously unseen archive footage and interviews with members of the band. The programme was followed by a broadcast of the Earls Court concert, filmed on 20.10.94.

David Gilmour, European tour, 1994

1995

Pink Floyd gave no concerts in 1995.

1996

■ 17.1.96
11th Annual Rock And Roll Hall of Fame, Waldorf-Astoria Hotel, New York

City, New York, USA.
Pink Floyd were inducted into the prestigious Hall of Fame at a ceremony also celebrating the induction of David Bowie, Jefferson Airplane, Little Willie John, Gladys Knight and The Pips, The Shirelles, The Velvet Underground, Pete Seeger and Tom Donahue. The band were presented with the award by Billy Corgan of the Smashing

Pumpkins, after which Gilmour and Wright (Mason stood down) were joined on stage by Corgan for a rendition of 'Wish You Were Here', in 'Unplugged' fashion. Gilmour remained on stage for the presentation finale, joining Arlo Guthrie, members of Jefferson Airplane, Stevie Wonder and David Byrne for a rendition of Pete Seeger's 'Goodnight Irene'. A twenty-nine-track promotional CD (EMI DPRO 10467) to mark the event, and including Pink

Floyd's 'Wish You Were Here', 'Money' and 'See Emily Play', was presented to guests.

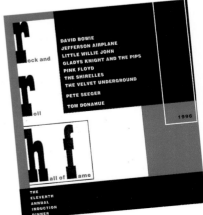

Syd Barrett's brief solo career after leaving Pink Floyd was hampered by his continuing emotional problems. Throughout the 1970s he remained in London, where he was the subject of many press reports, or 'Syd sightings' as they became known. None of these suggested any improvement in his mental health. In the late seventies Barrett retired to his native Cambridge, where he continued to lead a reclusive life, spending much of his time painting. In 1992 Atlantic Records offered him an advance of around £75,000 to record absolutely anything, regardless of content or length. His close relatives respectfully declined on his behalf.

DISCOGRAPHY

■ **14.11.69**

Octopus/Golden Hair.
Harvest (HAR) 5009 (7-inch single).

■ **3.1.70**

The Madcap Laughs.
Harvest (EMI) SHVL 765 (album).
Terrapin/No Good Trying/Love You/No Man's Land/Dark Globe/Here I Go//Octopus/Golden Hair/Long Gone/She Took A Long Cold Look/Feel/If It's In You/Late Night.
Barrett's solo career began on 13.5.68, when Peter Jenner took him to the EMI studios at Abbey Road, north London, to start work on a new album. The initial results were disappointing and recording was suspended, but when sessions resumed on 10.4.69 the work proved good enough to compile a first solo album, The Madcap Laughs. Members of Soft Machine also

played on the album: Elton Dean (alto, saxello, electric piano), Mike Ratledge (organ, electric piano), Hugh Hopper (bass guitar) and Robert Wyatt (drums). It was produced in part by Barrett himself, with the aid of Malcolm Jones (Harvest's label manager), Peter Jenner, David Gilmour and Roger Waters. Interviewed in Melody Maker in early 1970, Barrett announced he would be doing a solo tour in May of that year, but this never materialized.

■ **14.11.70**

Barrett.
Harvest (EMI) SHSP 4007 (album).
Baby Lemonade/Love Song/Dominoes/It Is Obvious/Rats/Masie//Gigolo Aunt/Waving My Arms In The Air/I Never Lied To You/Wined And Dined/Wolfpack/Effervescing Elephant.
Barrett's second solo album was less bleak than its predecessor, and even incorporated the whimsical 'Effervescent Elephant', written in his youth. The album was produced entirely by David Gilmour and Rick Wright, who also played bass and keyboards respectively. Drummer Jerry Shirley, of Humble Pie, and bassist Willie Wilson were also drafted in. Sadly, this was to be Barrett's last original release despite Peter Jenner's efforts in summer 1974 to get him back in the studio. The sessions were aborted after four days when it became obvious that nothing of any value would come of them.

■ **??.11.74**

Syd Barrett.
Harvest (EMI) SHDW 404 (double album). Reissue of The Madcap Laughs and Barrett with new artwork.

■ **??.2.88**

Syd Barrett – The Peel Session.
Strange Fruit SFPSCD 043 (CD EP)/Strange Fruit SFPS 043 (12-inch EP of BBC session of 24.2.70)

Terrapin/Gigolo Aunt/Baby Lemonade/Effervescing Elephant/Two Of A Kind

■ **17.10.88**

Opel.
Harvest (EMI) CZ 144 (CD)/Harvest (EMI) SHSP 4126 (album).
Opel/Clowns & Jugglers (Octopus)/Rats/Golden Hair/Dolly Rocker/Word Song/Wined And Dined//Swan Lee (Silas Lang)/Birdie Hop/Let's Split/Lanky Pt.1/Wouldn't You Miss Me (Dark Globe)/Milky Way/Golden Hair (instrumental).
Interest in Syd Barrett continues to the present day and many recording artists cite him as a major inspiration. One aspect of this adulation was a huge public demand for EMI to release additional archive material. In response, the company eventually issued a collection of rarities on a single album, Opel, which comprised alternate takes and previously unavailable tracks.

■ **26.4.93**

Crazy Diamond – The Complete Syd Barrett.
Harvest (EMI) SYDBOX 1 (CD box set).
Reissue as box set of The Madcap Laughs, Barrett and Opel, with additional out-takes. The sleeves and booklet feature new artwork based on Barrett's lyrics. With this release all the usable solo work is ostensibly now available. However, it is rumoured that David Gilmour holds many more unreleased tracks.

1. The Madcap Laughs:
Terrapin/No Good Trying/Love You/No Man's Land/Dark Globe/Here I Go/Octopus/Golden Hair/Long Gone/She Took A Long Cold Look/Feel/If It's In You/Late Night/Octopus (Takes 1&2)/It's No Good Trying (Take 5)/Love You (Take 1)/Love You (Take 3)/She Took A Long Cold Look At Me (Take 4)/Golden Hair (Take 5).

2. Barrett:
Baby Lemonade/Love Song/Dominoes/It Is Obvious/Rats/Masie/Gigolo Aunt/Waving My

Arms In The Air/I Never Lied To You/Wined And Dined/Wolfpack/Effervescing Elephant/Baby Lemonade (Take 1)/Waving My Arms In The Air (Take 1)/I Never Lied To You (Take 1)/Love Song (Take 1)/Dominoes (Take 1)/Dominoes (Take 2)/It Is Obvious (Take 2).

3. Opel:

Opel/Clowns & Jugglers (Octopus)/Rats/Golden Hair/Dolly Rocker/Word Song/Wind And Dined/Swan Lee (Silas Lang)/Birdie Hop/Let's Split/Lanky Pt.1/Wouldn't You Miss Me (Dark Globe)/Milky Way/Golden Hair (instrumental)/Gigolo Aunt (Take 9)/It Is Obvious (Take 3)/It Is Obvious (Take 5)/Clowns & Jugglers (Take 1)/Late Night (Take 2)/Effervescing Elephant (Take 2)

The three above CDs were later released separately.

FILMS

■ **19.7.93**

Syd's First Trip.

UFO/Vex Films (video).
A limited-edition release on video of poor-quality home movies. The silent film, which lasts only a few minutes, shows a teenage Barrett in the Cambridgeshire countryside with friends; some clips of the Pink Floyd and their multicoloured tour bus outside Abbey Road studios, London, in late 1967; and material from around 1970 shot on the balcony of his London flat.

LIVE PERFORMANCE

If Barrett's solo material is any indication of his mental condition in the years after he left Pink Floyd, it is hardly surprising that he made few public appearances.

■ **27.12.69**

BBC Broadcasting House, London, England.

Syd's appearance on Pete Drummond's end-of-year show on BBC Radio One can be regarded as one of his classic performances. He remained silent throughout the show,

even when questioned.

■ **24.2.70**

BBC Maida Vale Studios, Maida Vale, London, England.

A live recording session in which Barrett and David Gilmour (organ, bass guitar and guitar) and Jerry Shirley (drums) performed 'Baby Lemonade', 'Effervescing Elephant', 'Gigolo Aunt', 'Terrapin' and 'Two Of A Kind' for BBC Radio One. It was broadcast on Top Gear on 14.3.70 at 3.00pm, except 'Two Of A Kind', which was broadcast on Top Gear on 30.5.70 at 3.00pm. The complete session was officially released on vinyl and CD in 1988 (see Discography).

■ **6.6.70**

Extravaganza 70 – Music and Fashion Festival, The Grand Hall, Olympia Exhibition Hall, Olympia, London, England.

With Colosseum, Mungo Jerry, The Move, Mike Raven, The Pretty Things, Rare Bird, Steamhammer, Jackson Heights with Lee Jackson and Fairfield Parlour.
Barrett's first major performance was as a late addition on the last evening of this four-day festival (3–6.6.70). He was joined on stage by David Gilmour (bass guitar) and Jerry Shirley (drums) and played a rushed set that included 'Gigolo Aunt', 'Effervescing Elephant' and 'Octopus'. His vocals were barely audible throughout and even before the last track was finished he left the stage to scattered applause.

■ **16.2.71**

BBC Transcription Service Studios, Kensington House, Shepherd's Bush, London, England.

Barrett's second and final radio session, for BBC Radio One, in which he performed 'Baby Lemonade', 'Dominoes' and 'Love Song'. It was broadcast on Bob Harris – Sounds Of The Seventies on 1.3.71 at 6.00pm.

■ **27.1.72**

The Corn Exchange, Cambridge, Cambridgeshire, England.

Hawkwind, Pink Fairies and The Last Minute Put Together Boogie Band.
Over the years there have been many references to a legendary performance in the King's College Cellar, Cambridge, in

which Eddie 'Guitar' Burns is said to have invited Barrett on stage to perform with himself, drummer Twink and bassist Jack Monck as The Last Minute Put Together Boogie Band. This was the band's only performance and Barrett's inclusion is unconfirmed.

■ **24.2.72**

The Corn Exchange, Cambridge, Cambridgeshire,

England.
Supporting MC5 and Skin Alley.
Following the above-mentioned performance, Barrett, Twink and Monck made a single public performance, as Stars.
Set list: Octopus/Dark Globe/Baby Lemonade/Waving My Arms In The Air/Lucifer Sam.
Stars' only appearance, which closed the show, was a complete disaster and the situation was not improved when the house lights were accidentally switched on to reveal an audience of no more than thirty. Roy Hollingsworth wrote a fair account of the show in the

following week's Sounds. Barrett is said to have been so upset by it that he refused to perform live ever again.

■ **26.2.72**

The Corn Exchange, Cambridge, Cambridgeshire, England.

Supporting Nektar. Stars were scheduled to perform, but their appearance remains unconfirmed.

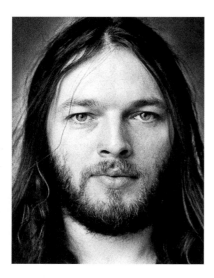

DAVID GILMOUR

Of all the members, past and present, of Pink Floyd, David Gilmour has long been the most active as a solo artist. As well as playing on the albums of many other musicians, he has acted as producer on a number of albums. In addition, he has performed widely, in many cases for charity, and has written and recorded soundtrack material for television.

DISCOGRAPHY
■ **25.5.78**
David Gilmour.
Harvest (EMI) SHVL 817 (album).
Mihalis/There's No Way Out Of Here/Cry From The Street/So Far Away//Short And Sweet/Raise My Rent/Deafinitely/I Can't Breathe Anymore.
■ **4.8.78**
There's No Way Out Of Here (edit)/Deafinitely.
Harvest (EMI) HAR 5226 (7-inch single).
This well-received guitar-based album was the product of a regrouping of his former Cambridge band mates Rick Wills (bass) and Willie Wilson (drums). Recorded at the Super Bear Studios in Miravel, France, it was self-produced and featured Carlena Williams, Debbie Moss and Shirley Roden (backing vocals) and Mick Weaver (piano on 'So Far Away').
All the songs were written by Gilmour, except for 'Cry From The Street', which was by Gilmour and E. Stuart and 'Short And Sweet', which was by Gilmour and Roy Harper.
'There's No Way Out Of Here' was a re-recording of 'No Way Out Of Here', written by K. Baker of Unicorn, which first

appeared on that band's album *Too Many Crooks.*
■ **13.2.84**
Blue Light (edit)/Cruise.
Harvest (EMI) HAR 5226 (7-inch single).
Blue Light (album version)/Cruise.
Harvest (EMI) 12 HAR 5226 (12-inch single).
Blue Light (extended US remix)/Blue Light (instrumental).
Harvest (EMI) DG1 A/B (promotional 12-inch single).
■ **5.3.84**
About Face.
Harvest (EMI) SHSP 24-0079-1 (album).
Until We Sleep/Murder/Love On The Air/Blue Light/Out Of The Blue//All Lovers Are Deranged/You Know I'm Right/Cruise/Let's Get Metaphysical/Near The End.
■ **27.4.84**
Love On The Air/Let's Get Metaphysical.
Harvest (EMI) HAR 5229 (7-inch single) and Harvest (EMI) HARP 5229 (radio-shaped picture-disc single).
Many of the songs on this album leaned towards middle-of-the-road adult pop-rock as opposed to the guitar rock of *David Gilmour.* It was co-produced by Bob Ezrin and featured an array of guest musicians, including Jeff Porcaro (drums and percussion), Pino Palladino (bass guitar), Ian Kewley (Hammond organ and piano), Steve Winwood (piano and organ), Anne Dudley and Jon Lord (synthesizers), Bob Ezrin (keyboards), Louis Jardine and Ray Cooper (percussion), The Kick Horns: Roddy Lorimer, Barbara Snow, Tim Sanders and Simon Clark (brass), Vicki Brown, Sam Brown, Mickey Feat and Roy Harper (backing vocals), Steve Rance (Fairlight programming) and The National Philharmonic arranged by Michael Kamen and Bob Ezrin. Both Pete Townshend and Nick Laird-Clowes co-wrote many tracks.

GUEST APPEARANCES AND PRODUCTION
■ **1969**
Syd Barrett – Octopus/No Good Trying.
Harvest (HAR) 5009 (7-inch single). Produced by Gilmour, Waters and others.
■ **1970**
Syd Barrett – *The Madcap Laughs.*
Harvest (EMI) SHVL 765 (album). Produced by Gilmour, Waters and others.
■ **1970**
Syd Barrett – *Barrett.*
Harvest (EMI) SHSP 4007 (album). Produced by Gilmour, who plays bass throughout.
■ **1974**
Unicorn – *Blue Pine Trees.*
Charisma CAS 1092 (album). Produced by Gilmour, who played pedal steel guitar throughout. In 1993 the track 'Oooh Mother' was included on the four-CD Charisma retrospective *The Famous Charisma Box* (Charisma CASBOX1).
■ **1975**
David Courtney – *First Day.*
United Artists UA LA553-G (album). Gilmour played guitars on 'When Your Life Is Your Own'.
■ **1975**
Roy Harper – *HQ.*
Harvest (EMI) SHSP 4046 (album). Gilmour played guitars on 'The Game Pts.1-5'. Produced by Peter Jenner.
■ **1975**
Sutherland Brothers & Quiver – *Reach For The Sky.*
CBS 69191 (album). Gilmour played pedal steel guitar on 'Ain't Too Proud'.
■ **1976**
Unicorn – *Too Many Crooks.*
Harvest (EMI) SHSP 4054 (album). Gilmour produced the album and played pedal steel guitar on the title track. He covered 'No Way Out Of Here' on his debut solo album as 'There's No Way Out Of Here'.
■ **1977**

Rachid Bahri – *Rachid Bahri*.
EMI France 2C068-14398 (album). Gilmour played guitars on 'Olivier de Cromwell Road' and 'Il Survivra'.
■ 1977

Unicorn – *One More Tomorrow*.
Harvest (EMI) SHSP 4067 (album). Gilmour produced all tracks except the first four.
■ 1977

Unicorn – Slow Dancing/Give And Take.
Harvest (EMI) HAR 5126 (7-inch single). Gilmour produced and engineered the non-album B-side.
■ 1979

Wings – *Back To The Egg*.
MPL PLTC 257 (album). Gilmour played guitars on 'Rockestra Theme' as part of the supergroup Rockestra, and on 'So Glad To See You Here'.
■ 1980

Kate Bush – Army Dreamers/Passing Through Air.
EMI 5106 (7-inch single). Gilmour played guitars on the B-side. Also available exclusively on CD as part of the Kate Bush box set *This Woman's Work* (EMI CDKBBX 1).
■ 1980

Roy Harper – *The Unknown Soldier*.
Harvest (EMI) SHVL 820 (album). Gilmour co-wrote and played guitars on 'Playing Games', 'True Story', 'Short And Sweet', 'Old Faces' and 'You (The Game Pt.II)'. Peter Jenner was executive producer.
■ 1982

Kate Bush – *The Dreaming*.
EMI EMC 3419 (album). Gilmour provided backing vocals on 'Pull Out The Pin'.
■ 1982

Doll By Doll – *Grand Passion*.
MAGL 5047 (album). Gilmour played guitars on 'Boxers Hit Harder When Women Are Around'.
■ 1983

Atomic Rooster – *Headline News*.
Towerbell TOW LP4 (album). Gilmour played guitars on 'Hold Your Fire', 'Metal Minds', 'Land Of Freedom' and 'Time'.
■ 1984

Paul McCartney – *Give My Regards To Broad Street*.
Parlophone (EMI) UK-PCTC-2 (album). Gilmour played guitars on 'No More Lonely Nights (Ballad)' and on the 12-inch single of the same title (Parlophone (EMI) 12-R-6080).
■ 1985

Arcadia – *So Red The Rose*.
Parlophone (EMI) PCSD 101 (album). Gilmour played Guitars on 'The Promise' and 'Missing' and on the 12-inch single of 'Promise' (Parlophone (EMI) 12 NSR 2).
■ 1985

John 'Rabbit' Bundrick – *The Rabbit Archive Vol.5*.
Private release on cassette. Gilmour produced the track 'Rabbit Gets Loose'. The cassette was available only through the Free Appreciation Society.
■ 1985

Dream Academy – Life In A Northern Town.
Blanco Y Negro NEG 10T (7-inch single). Co-produced by Gilmour.
■ 1985

Dream Academy – Please, Please, Please Let Me Get What I Want.
Blanco Y Negro NEG 20T (7-inch single). Non-album track co-produced by Gilmour.
■ 1985

Dream Academy – Dream Academy.
Blanco Y Negro BYN6 (album). Gilmour played guitars on 'Bound To Be' and 'The Party'. All tracks except one were co-produced by Gilmour.
■ 1985

Bryan Ferry – *Boys And Girls*.
EG LC3098 (album). Gilmour played guitars on the title track, 'The Chosen One', 'Sensation' and possibly others.
■ 1985

Grace Jones – *Slave To The Rhythm*.
Island GRACE 1 (album). Gilmour played guitars on the title track and 'The Fashion Show' but was not credited. Also 12-inch single of the title track (Island 1215 206).
■ 1985

Mason & Fenn – *Profiles*.
Harvest (EMI) MAF 1. Gilmour provided vocals on 'Lie For A Lie'. Also 12-inch single of the same title (Harvest (EMI) 12HAR 5238).
■ 1985

Supertramp – *Brother Where You Bound*.
A&M AMA 5014 (album).

Gilmour played guitar solo on the title track.
■ 1985

Pete Townshend – *White City*.
ATCO 252 392-1 (album). Gilmour played guitars on the title track and 'Give Blood' and wrote music for the title track. Also 12-inch single of the same title (WEA U8744T).
■ 1986

Berlin – *Count 3 And Pray*.
Mercury LP 830 586-1 (album). Gilmour played guitars on 'Pink And Velvet' and on the 12-inch promotional single of the same track (Mercury PRO-A-2632).
■ 1986

Liona Boyd – *Persona*.
CBS FM 42120 (album). Gilmour

played guitars on 'L'Enfant', 'Sorceress' and 'Persona'.

■ **1986**

Bryan Ferry – Is Your Love Strong Enough.

EG FERRX 4 (12 -inch and 7-inch single). Gilmour played guitars on the A-side. The track was also used for the soundtrack of the film *Legend* and Gilmour also appeared in the promotional video for the single. The video is also included on *Bryan Ferry and Roxy Music – Video Collection* (Virgin VID 2791).

■ **1987**

Dalbello – She.

EMI CDP 564-7482862 (album). Gilmour played guitars on 'Immaculate Eyes'.

■ **1987**

Bryan Ferry – Bête Noire.

Virgin V2474 (album). Gilmour played guitars on 'Seven Deadly Sins', 'Day For Night', 'New Town', 'Kiss And Tell', 'Limbo' and possibly 'The Right Stuff'. Also 12-inch singles of 'Kiss And Tell' (Virgin VST 1034) and 'Limbo' (Virgin VST 1066).

■ **1988**

Samantha Brown – Stop! A&M 395195-1 (album).

Gilmour played guitars on 'This Feeling' and 'I'll Be In Love'. Also 12-inch single of 'This Feeling' (A&M AMY 440).

■ **1988**

John 'Rabbit' Bundrick – Dream Jungle.

Lumina Music LUM CD2 (album). Gilmour played guitars on 'Through The Clouds' and 'Conquest' and is credited as 'Studio Visitor'.

■ **1988**

Peter Cetera – One More Story.

Warner Brothers WB 925 704-1 (album). Gilmour played guitars on 'You Never Listen To Me' and 'Body Language (There In The Dark)'. Also 12-inch promotional single of 'You Never Listen To Me' WB PRO-A-3216.

■ **1989**

Vicki Brown – Lady Of Time.

RCA PL 74522 (album). Guitars on 'Can't Let Go' credited as 'Mr. E. Guest'.

■ **1989**

Kate Bush – The Sensual World.

EMI EMD 1010 (album). Gilmour played guitars on 'Love And Anger' and 'Rocket's Tail (For Rocket)'. Also 12-inch single of 'Love And Anger' (EMI EM 134). This track also appears on the video *Sensual World* (Music Club MC 2114) and the video CD *The Whole Story* (PMI PMCD 4912882).

■ **1989**

Kirsty MacColl – Kite.

Virgin KMLP1 (album). Gilmour played guitars on 'You And Me Baby' and 'No Victims'. Also 12-inch of 'You And Me Baby (Guitar Heroes Mix)' (Virgin KMAT 3).

■ **1989**

Paul McCartney – Flowers In The Dirt.

Electrola (EMI) 064-7916531 (album). Gilmour played guitars on 'We Got Married'.

■ **1989**

Various Artists – Spirit Of The Forest.

Virgin VS 1191 (7-inch single). Gilmour provided vocals. This track was included on the *Earthrise* album (Polygram TV 515 419-1) and video (Weinnerworld WNR 2027). Gilmour was interviewed and filmed recording his contribution for BBC2 TV's *Nature* programme, which was broadcast in the UK on 2.5.89.

■ **1989**

Warren Zevon – Transverse City.

Virgin America VUS LP 9 (album). Gilmour played guitars on 'Run Straight Down'.

■ **1990**

Blue Pearl – Naked.

Big Life BLR LP4 (album). Gilmour played guitars on 'Running Up That Hill' and 'Alive'. Also 12-inch single of 'Alive' (Big Life BLR T44).

■ **1990**

Samantha Brown – April Moon.

A&M AMA 9014 (album). Gilmour provided backing vocals on 'Troubled Soul'.

■ **1990**

Vicki Brown – About Love And Life.

Polydor 847 266-2 (album). Gilmour played guitars on 'I'll Always Be Waiting'.

■ **1990**

Dream Academy – Love.

Blanco Y Negro NEG46T (12-inch single). Non-album track produced by Gilmour.

■ **1990**

Dream Academy – A Different Kind Of Weather.

Blanco Y Negro BYN 23 (album). All tracks co-produced by Gilmour, who also played guitars on 'Mercy Killing' and 'Forest Fire'; bass guitar and guitars on 'It'll Never Happen Again'; and bass synthesizers on 'Twelve-Eight Angel', which he also sings on and co-wrote. Also 12-inch single of 'Angel Of Mercy', a retitled version of 'Mercy Killing' (Blanco Y Negro NEG 50T).

■ **1990**

Roy Harper – Once.

Awareness AWL 1018 (album). Gilmour played guitars on 'Once', 'Once In The Middle Of Nowhere' and 'Berliners (A Better World)'.

■ **1990**

Michael Kamen – Concerto For Saxophone.

Warner Brothers WB 7599-26157-2. Gilmour played guitars on 'Sasha'.

■ **1990**

Propaganda – 1234.

Virgin V2625 (album). Gilmour played guitars on 'Only One Word'. Also 12-inch single of this track (Virgin VST 1271).

■ **1990**

Andres Roé – Roé.

Barclay 841 628-2 (album, released in France only). Gilmour played guitars on 'Como El Agua'.

■ **1990**

Various Artists – One World, One Voice.

Virgin V2632 (album). Gilmour contributed one short, untitled piece to this musical chain letter recorded for 'One World Week'. This piece also appears in the Howard Jones segment of the video of the same title (BMG 74321-1054-3). The segment was broadcast on BBC TV in the UK before the video's release.

■ **1990**

Various Artists – Rock Aid Armenia/The Earthquake Album.

Carrere 30004 (album). Gilmour played guitars on 'Smoke On The Water'. Also 7-inch single (Carrere ARMEN 001), 12-inch single (Carrere ARMEN T001) and 12-inch single (Mega-Rock Remix) (Carrere ARMEN T001) of this track. A video compilation derived from the album featured Gilmour (Virgin Music Video VVD 636).

■ **1990**

Paul Young – Other Voices.

CBS 4669171 (album). Gilmour played guitars on 'Heaven Can Wait' and 'A Little Bit Of Love'. Also 12-inch single of 'Heaven Can Wait' (CBS Young T6).

■ **1991**

All About Eve - Touched by Jesus.

Vertigo 510 146-1 (album). Gilmour played guitars on 'Wishing The Hours Away' and 'Are You Lonely'.

■ **1991**

Donovan – Living On Love.

Gilmour played guitars on 'Lover, O Lover', 'Everlasting Sea' and 'I Love The Way You Rock Me'. The album remains unreleased.

■ **1991**

The Law – The Law.

Atlantic 7567-82195-1 (album). Gilmour played guitars on 'Stone'.

■ **1991**

Various Artists/Comic Relief - The Stonk.

London LONX 296 (12-inch single). Gilmour played guitars and appeared on the promotional video.

1992
Elton John – *The One.*
Rocket (Phonogram) 512 360-1
(album). Gilmour played guitars
on 'Understanding Women',
which was originally recorded
for the box set *To Be
Continued...* (Rocket
(Phonogram) 848 236-2).

1992
**John Martyn – *Couldn't
Love You More.***
Permanent CD9 (album).
Gilmour played guitars on 'One
World', 'Could've Been Me' and
'Ways To Cry'

1992
**Jimmy Nail – *Growing Up
In Public.***
East-West 4509-90144-1 (album).
Gilmour played guitars on
'Waiting For The Sunshine' and
'Only Love (Can Bring Us Home)'.

1993
**John Martyn – *No Little
Boy.***
Permanent PERM 14 (album).
Gilmour played guitars on 'One
World', 'Could've Been Me' and
'Ways To Cry', which all
previously appeared the album
Couldn't Love You More.

1993
**Paul Rodgers – *Muddy
Water Blues.***
Victory 383 480 013-2 (album).
Gilmour played guitars on
'Standing Around Crying'.

1994
Chris Jagger – *Atcha.*
Sequel NEX CD 258 (album).
Gilmour played guitars on 'Steal
The Time'.

1994
**Snowy White – *Highway To
The Sun.***
Bellaphon 290-07-205 (album).
Gilmour played guitars on 'Love,
Pain And Sorrow'.

1995
Snowy White – *Goldtop.*
RPM 154 (album). Gilmour
played guitars on 'Love, Pain
And Sorrow'. This retrospective
collection also includes the only
official release of Pink Floyd's
'Pigs On The Wing Pts.1 and 2',
on which Snowy played guitars.

SOUNDTRACKS
27.5.90
**ITV TV broadcast, London,
England.**
Soundtrack music composed
and performed by Gilmour was
featured in the documentary film
Endangered Species, which also
included music by Kate Bush,
Soul II Soul, Peter Gabriel, Elton
John and Seal.

??.??.91
The Cement Garden.
Gilmour composed and
performed the song 'Me And J.C.'
for the soundtrack of this film.

27.5.92
**ITV TV broadcast, London,
England.**
Soundtrack music composed
and performed by Gilmour was
featured in ITV TV's *The Last
Show on Earth*, which dealt with
ecological issues.

??.??.92
**BBC TV broadcast, London,
England.**
Soundtrack music composed
and performed by Gilmour was
featured in the BBC2 TV series
Ruby Wax Goes To California.

23.2.93 and 2.3.93
**Channel 4 TV broadcast,
London, England.**
Soundtrack music composed
and performed by Gilmour was
featured in a two-part edition of
the documentary series *Without
Walls* entitled 'The Art Of
Tripping'. The programme,
devised by Storm Thorgerson,
dealt with mind-bending drugs
and their influence on artists,
performers and composers.

??.??.94
**TV broadcast, London,
England.**
Soundtrack music composed
and performed by Gilmour was
featured in a TV programme on
fractal geometry, *Colours of
Infinity*, hosted by Arthur C Clarke.

FILMS
??.??.78.
**Super Bear Studios,
Miravel, France.**
Six tracks from the album *David*

Gilmour were filmed for
promotion on TV: So Far
Away/There's No Way Out Of
Here/Mihalis/I Can't Breathe
Anymore and No Way. Gilmour
was joined by his brother Mark
(guitar) for the session, which
also featured Ricky Wills and
Willie Wilson. The track 'No
Way' was broadcast on BBC2
TV's contemporary rock music
programme *The Old Grey
Whistle Test* on 9.12.78.

LIVE PERFORMANCE
ABOUT FACE – WORLD TOUR
30.3.84
**Channel 4 TV broadcast,
London, England.**
Gilmour previewed his world
tour on the live music programme
The Tube, performing two tracks,
'Until We Sleep' and 'Blue Light'.
His band for this show and the
rest of the tour were Mick Ralphs
(guitar and vocals), Raphael
'Raff' Ravenscroft (saxophone),
Mickey Feat (bass guitar), Gregg
Dechart (keyboards), Chris Slade
(drums) and Jodi Linscott
(percussion).

31.3.84
**National Stadium, Dublin,
Republic of Ireland.**
The tour was an uncomplicated
presentation in comparison with
Waters' full-scale assault of the
same year. Gilmour preferred a
simple stage set and lighting,
concentrating on musicianship
rather than the spectacle.
Set list for this show and all
shows up to and including that
of 1.5.84: Until We Sleep/All
Lovers Are Deranged/Love On
The Air/Mihalis/There's No Way
Out Of Here/Run Like Hell/Out
Of The Blue/Let's Get
Metaphysical/Cruise/Short And
Sweet/You Know I'm Right/Blue
Light/Murder/Near The End/
encore: Comfortably Numb. At
some shows 'I Can't Breathe
Anymore' was performed as an
additional encore.
2.4.84
**Whitla Hall, Belfast, County
Antrim, Northern Ireland.**

5.4.84
**Muziekcentrum
Vredenberg, Utrecht,
Netherlands.**
6.4.84
**Salle de la Vreij Universität
van Brussel (Campus),
Etterbeek, Brussels, Belgium.**
8.4.84
**Parc des Expositions,
Nancy, France.**
9.4.84
**Hall Tivoli, Strasbourg,
France.**
10,11.4.84
**Le Zénith, Parc de Villettte,
Paris, France.**
The show of 10.4.84 was
recorded by RTL Radio, which
later broadcast Run Like
Hell/Out Of The Blue/Cruise/
Blue Light/Near The End/
Comfortably Numb.
12.4.84
**Bourse du Travail, Lyon,
France.**
13.4.84
**Kongresshaus, Zurich,
Switzerland.**
14.4.84
**Circus Krone, Munich,
West Germany.**
15.4.84
**Alte Oper, Frankfurt-am-
Main, West Germany.**
16.4.84
**Musensaal, Mannheim,
West Germany.**
18.4.84
**International Congress
Centre, West Berlin, West
Germany.**
19.4.84
**Congress Centrum
Hamburg, Hamburg, West
Germany.**
21.4.84
**Philipshalle, Düsseldorf,
West Germany.**
24.4.84
**Johanneshovs Isstadion,
Sandstuvägen, Stockholm,
Sweden.**
25.4.84
**Bröndbyhallen,
Copenhagen, Denmark**
28–30.4.84
Hammersmith Odeon,

Hammersmith, London, England.
Nick Mason played drums on 'Comfortably Numb' and Roy Harper sang vocals for 'Short And Sweet' at all three shows. Rick Wright attended the last show, but did not perform. The support band on the first night, the notorious Television Personalities, played a version of 'See Emily Play' before reciting Syd Barrett's home address to the audience. They were instantly dismissed from the remaining two dates by Gilmour and the opening slot was replaced by Billy Bragg, who was (and still is) managed by one of Pink Floyd's former

Lovers Are Deranged/There's No Way Out Of Here/Short And Sweet/Run Like Hell/Out Of The Blue/Blue Light/Murder/Comfortably Numb. The video footage was later combined with behind-the scenes material from the European tour in an MTV documentary entitled *Beyond The Floyd*.

■ **1.5.84**
The Odeon, Birmingham, West Midlands, England.
■ **9.5.84**
Colisée de Québec, Quebec City, Quebec, Canada.
Set list at this show and all shows until the end of the tour: Until We Sleep/All Lovers Are Deranged/Love On The Air/

Anymore' was performed as an additional encore.
Shows scheduled for Chicoutimi, Canada (8.5) and Rimouski, Canada (10.5) were cancelled.
■ **10, 11.5.84**
The Forum, Montreal, Quebec, Canada.
■ **12.5.84**
Ottawa Civic Centre, Ottawa, Ontario, Canada.
■ **14,15.5.84**
Massey Hall, Toronto, Ontario, Canada.
■ **16.5.84**
Shea's Buffalo Theatre, Buffalo, New York, USA.
■ **17.5.84**
Landmark Theatre, Syracuse, New York, USA.

Beacon Theatre, Manhattan, New York City, New York, USA.
■ **25,26.5.84**
The Orpheum Theatre, Boston, Massachusetts, USA.
■ **27.5.84**
Veterans Memorial Coliseum, New Haven, Connecticut, USA.
■ **29–31.5.84**
Tower Theatre, Philadelphia, Pennsylvania, USA.
■ **1.6.84**
Daughters of The American Revolution Constitution Hall, Washington, District of Columbia, USA.
■ **3.6.84**
Public Hall, Cleveland, Ohio, USA.
■ **4.6.84**
Veterans Memorial Hall, Columbus, Ohio, USA.
■ **6.6.84**
Pine Knob Music Theatre, Clarkston, Michigan, USA.
■ **7.6.84**
Cincinnati Gardens, Cincinnati, Ohio, USA.
■ **8.6.84**
Chicago Pavilion, Chicago, Illinois, USA.
■ **10.6.84**
Kiel Opera House, St Louis, Missouri, USA.
■ **11.6.84**
Starlight Theatre, Kansas City, Missouri, USA.
■ **13.6.84**
The Summit Sports Arena, Houston, Texas, USA.
■ **14.6.84**
Frank Erwin Center, University of Texas, Austin, Texas, USA.
■ **15.6.84**
Majestic Theatre, San

managers, Peter Jenner. The concerts were recorded for a simulcast on the USA's MTV and Westwood One radio network on 26.5.84. The broadcast show, which was later released as a video in the USA, comprised: Until We Sleep/All

Mihalis/There's No Way Out Of Here/Run Like Hell/Out Of The Blue/Let's Get Metaphysical/Cruise/Short And Sweet/You Know I'm Right/Money/Blue Light/Murder/Near The End/encore: Comfortably Numb. At some shows 'I Can't Breathe

■ **18.5.84**
Mid-Hudson Civic Center, Poughkeepsie, New York, USA.
■ **20.5.84**
Bushnell Auditorium, Hartford, Connecticut, USA.
■ **22–24.5.84**

Antonio, Texas, USA
■ 16.6.84
Reunion Arena, Reunion Park, Dallas, Texas, USA.
■ 19.6.84
The Amphitheatre, Mesa, Arizona, USA.
■ 20.6.84
Open Air Theatre, San Diego State University, San Diego, California, USA.
■ 21,22.6.84
Universal Amphitheatre, Universal City, Los Angeles, California, USA.
■ 23,24.6.84
Irvine Meadows Amphitheatre, Irvine, California, USA.
■ 26,27.6.84
Kabuki Theatre, San Francisco, California, USA.
■ 28.6.84
California Exposition Amphitheatre, Sacramento, California, USA.
■ 29.6.84
Greek Theatre, University of California, Berkeley, California, USA.
■ 5.7.84
Sunrise Music Theatre, Sunrise, Florida, USA.
■ 6.7.84
Civic Centre Arena, Lakeland, Florida, USA.
■ 11.7.84
Syria Mosque Theater, Pittsburgh, Pennsylvania, USA.
■ 12.7.84
Stabler Arena, Lehigh University, Allentown, Pennsylvania, USA.
This show was recorded and the following tracks were broadcast on the Westwood One radio network in the USA: Until We Sleep/All Lovers Are Deranged/Money/Love On The Air/Short And Sweet/You Know I'm Right/Run Like Hell/Blue Light/Murder/Comfortably Numb.
■ 13.7.84
Jones Beach Theatre, Babylon, Long Island, New York, USA.
■ 14.7.84

Merriweather Post Pavilion, Columbia, Maryland, USA.
■ 15.7.84
Saratoga Performing Arts Centre, Saratoga Springs, New York, USA.
■ 16.7.84
NYC Convention Pier, Manhattan, New York City, New York, USA.
The last night of the tour.

GUEST APPEARANCES
■ 31.8.74
Hyde Park, London, England.
Gilmour appeared with the Roy Harper Band at one of the last Hyde Park free concerts. The event started at midday and featured Roger McGuinn, Julie Felix, Toots & The Maytals, Chilli Willi & The Red Hot Peppers and Kokomo.
■ 10.11.74
Newcastle Polytechnic, Newcastle-upon-Tyne, Tyne and Wear, England.
Gilmour shared lead guitar with Tim Renwick, and Rick Wright guested on keyboards, at this Sutherland Brothers & Quiver show.
■ 20.11.84
Capitol Theatre, Passaic, New Jersey, USA.
As part of an all-star event sponsored by MTV, 'The Guitar Greats', Gilmour performed 'You Know I'm Right' and 'Murder'. He was later joined by yet more musicians for a blues number and a rendition of 'Johnny B. Goode' with Chuck Leavell (bass), Kenny Aaronson (drums), La Bamba, Stanley Harrison, Ed Manion, Mike Spengler and Steven Groppen (horns), Johnny Winter, Link Wray, Dave Edmunds and Neal Schon (guitars).
■ 13.7.85
Live Aid, Wembley Stadium, Wembley, Middlesex, England.
Gilmour was the only member of Pink Floyd to appear at this landmark event, playing guitar with Bryan Ferry's band, which

consisted of Neil Hubbard (guitars), Chester Kamen (guitars), Jimmy Maelen (percussion), Andy Newmark (drums), Marcus Miller (bass), Jon Carin (keyboards) and Michelle Cobbs, Ednah Holt and Fonzi Thornton (backing vocals). The set comprised: 'Sensation', 'Boys And Girls', 'Slave To Love' and 'Jealous Guy'. Gilmour was also participated in the grand finale, 'Feed The World'. The event was broadcast globally. 'Slave To Love' appears on the Bryan Ferry and Roxy Music video *Total Recall* (Virgin Music Video VVD649).

■ 11.10.85
Channel 4 TV broadcast, London, England.
Gilmour performed on the live music programme *The Tube* with Pete Townshend's Deep End, which he had formed to raise money for the Double 0 charity, in aid of victims of drug abuse. The band comprised Simon Philips (drums), John 'Rabbit' Bundrick (keyboards), Jodi Linscott (percussion), Pete Hope-Evans (harmonica), Billy Nichols, Chris Staines, Ian Ellis, Gina Foster and Coral Gordon (backing vocals) and also included The Kick Horns: Roddy Lorimer, Peter Thoms, Dave Plews, Tim Sanders and Simon

Clarke (brass). Deep End performed 'Give Blood', 'Face The Face' and 'Second Hand Love' – all from Townshend's album *White City*.
■ 1,2.11.85
The Academy, Brixton, London, England.
Deep End performed two shows in London (a third show was booked but poor ticket sales forced its cancellation).
Set list at show of 1.11.85:
Mary-Anne With The Shaky Hands/Won't Get Fooled Again/Little Is Enough/Second

Deep End, Brixton Academy, London, November 1985

Hand Love/It's Alright/Behind Blue Eyes/The Shout/Harlem Shuffle/
Barefooting/After The Fire/Love On The Air/Midnight Lover/Blue Light/I Put A Spell On You/I'm One/Magic Bus/Save It For Later/Eyesight For The Blind/Walking/Stop Hurting People/The Sea Refuses No River/Boogie Shoe Shuffle/Face The Face/Pinball Wizard/Give Blood/Night Train. (The show of 2 November also included 'I'm Drifting'.)
Film of the band's rehearsals, including a segment of 'Give Blood', were broadcast in the UK as part of an ITV *South Bank*

Colombian Volcano Appeal concert, Royal Albert Hall, London, 9 February 1986

Show documentary on Pete Townshend. In addition, the USA's King Biscuit Flower Hour radio network recorded and broadcast highlights of the second show.

A video of the full eighty-seven-minute concert was also released (Virgin Music Video VVD318).An album of the concerts was released in the USA only (ATCO 790553-1), as well as a 7-inch single (ATCO U8744) and a 12-inch single (ATCO U8744T) of Give Blood/Won't Get Fooled Again/ Magic Bus (live) from the Brixton show of 1.11.85.

■ 23.1.86
Rockpalast, Gala du Midem, Cannes, France.
This show was the last performance by Deep End. It was broadcast on many European TV networks on 29.1.86.
Set list: Won't Get Fooled Again/Second Hand Love/Give Blood/Behind Blue Eyes/After The Fire/Slit Skirts/Blue Light/I Put A Spell On You/Hiding Out/ The Sea Refuses No River/Face The Face/Pinball Wizard/Little Is

Enough/Rough Boys/Night Train.

■ 9.2.86
Colombian Volcano Appeal, The Royal Albert Hall, Kensington, London, England.
With Pete Townshend and Peter Hope-Evans, Annie Lennox, Jaki Graham, Chrissie Hynde and Robbie McIntosh, The Communards, Working Week, and The London School of Samba. At the request of Deep End musician Chucho Merchan, Gilmour assembled a band to perform at this fund-raising concert. The line-up comprised Sam Brown and Paul Carrack (vocals), Simon Philips (drums), Mick Ralphs (guitar), Jodi Linscott (percussion), Chucho Merchan (bass guitar) and John 'Rabbit' Bundrick (keyboards). Highlights of the show were later released on video as *The Colombian Volcano Concert* (Hendring Video HEN2086) and broadcast on Channel 4 TV in the UK on 20.7.88. Numerous American radio networks have also broadcast highlights of the concert.

■ 15.2.87
The London Jam, The Town & Country Club, Kentish Town, London, England.
At this fund-raiser organized by *Guitar* magazine on behalf of the Childline charity Gilmour performed alongside many other musicians, including Albert Lee, James Burton, Geoff Whitehorn, Seymour Duncan, Tony Muschamp, Robbie Gladwell, Esmond Selwyn, Phil Hilborne, Andy Powell and Neil Murray.

■ 28,29.3.87
The Secret Policeman's Third Ball, The London Palladium, London, England.
Gilmour joined Kate Bush on stage with a band comprising Tony Franklin (bass), Stuart Elliot (drums) and Kevin McAlea (keyboards) for renditions of 'Running Up That Hill' and 'Let It Be' for Amnesty International's occasional fund-raiser. The all-star line-up for the finale of 'I Shall Be Released' included Gilmour on bass, and, on the second night, Nick Mason on drums. Highlights of the event, including 'Running Up That Hill',

were released on video (Virgin Music Video VVD 270) and on CD (Virgin CDV 2458).

■ 12.12.87
NBC TV broadcast, New York, USA.
Gilmour made an appearance on the US TV show *Saturday Night Live*, performing two guitar instrumentals with the house band.

■ 18.8.88
Majestic Theater, Brooklyn Academy of Music, Brooklyn, New York City, New York, USA.
Gilmour performed 'How High The Moon' at this commemorative gala for guitar guru Les Paul alongside Tony Levin (bass) and others. Additional sets were performed by BB King, The Stray Cats and Eddie Van Halen and the all-star finale was a rendition of 'Blue Suede Shoes'. A video of the concert, *Les Paul – He Changed The Music*, was released the following year (Magnum MMGV 023).

■ 27.4.89
The Dinosaur Room, The Natural History Museum, Kensington, London, England.
Gilmour played 'A Whiter Shade of Pale' with Mark Knopfler, Gary Brooker, Chris Rea, Gary Moore and Sam Brown at this fund-raising concert for The Lung Foundation charity. The track was recorded and broadcast the following day in the UK on BBC Radio One's *Friday Rock Show*.

■ 18.9.89
Hysteria 2, Sadlers Wells Theatre, London, England.
Gilmour joined comedian Lenny Henry and musicians Jools Holland (piano) and Eddie Reader (vocals) at this AIDS charity benefit, performing 'My Girl'. A video of the event, *Hysteria 2 – The Second Coming* (Palace PVC 2173A), was later released.

■ 30.9.89
Soho Jazz Festival, Soho, London, England.

Gilmour performed at this Friends Of The Earth benefit concert with Louise Goffin.

■ 15.11.89
Metropolis Studios, Chiswick, London, England.

Gilmour played 'Smoke On The Water' at the media launch of the Rock Aid Armenia single. Other musicians who performed the song with him included Richie Blackmore, Tony Iommi, Alex Lifeson, Brian May, Bryan Adams, Bruce Dickinson, Ian Gillan, Paul Rodgers, Chris Squire, Keith Emerson, Geoff Downes and Roger Taylor.

■ 31.3.90
The Shaw Theatre, London, England.

Gilmour guested at this second of two solo shows by John Martyn, playing on 'The Apprentic', 'John Wayne' and 'One World'. A video of the performance, *John Martyn – The Apprentice Tour*, was released on Virgin in the UK later that year. A CD album, *John Martyn Live* (Permanent PERM CD33), captured the whole show. Gilmour and Martyn were also interviewed at this show as part of the Channel 4 documentary *Rock Steady*, which was broadcast in the UK on 1.5.90.

■ 19.4.90
BBC 2 TV broadcast, London, England.

Gilmour appeared with Ralph McTell, Mark Knopfler, Lemmy, Gary Moore and Mark King in an edition of the comedy show *French and Saunders*. The sketch illustrated the pitfalls of learning to play the guitar without tabulature. Gilmour pretended to be defeated by the riff from 'Another Brick', complaining that there were no 'little pictures that show you where to put your fingers'.

■ 1.2.91
Rock-a-Baby, Hackney Empire Theatre, Hackney, London, England.

Gilmour performed at this charity performance as part of

the all-star band on the second of a three-day event (31.1.–2.2.91) that also featured Paul Young and Paul Carrack (vocals), Andy Fairweather-Low (guitars), Pino Palladino (bass guitar) and Andy Newmark (drums). The set included 'Wish You Were Here' and 'Comfortably Numb'. Support was provided by the group Five Easy Pieces.

■ 24.2.91
The Bloomsbury Theatre, London, England.

Gilmour guested for part of this concert by Dream Academy.

■ 30.6.91
Hysteria 3, The London Palladium, London, England.

At this charity fund-raiser, Gilmour joined the Jools Holland Band on 'Together Again', which also featured vocals by Sam Brown. The all-star finale was led by Elton John. A CD of highlights, *The Best Of Hysteria 3* (EMI CDP 7980212), and a video (PMI MVN 9913183) were later released.

■ 28.12.91
Central TV broadcast, Nottingham, Nottinghamshire, England.

Gilmour and Jools Holland were installed as musical directors of a pre-recorded show entitled Amnesty International – Big 3-0. They were joined by, among many other musicians, Tim Renwick (guitars), Jon Carin (keyboards), Pino Palladino (bass), Jodi Linscott (percussion) and Sam Brown (vocals) on 'On The Turning Away'. Gilmour also joined Tom Jones to play Jones's single 'Kiss' and 'I Can't Turn You Loose'; played lead guitar on Seal's rendition of 'Hey Joe'; performed 'Hard To Handle' and 'What's Going On' with Andrew Strong of The Commitments; and played bass guitar with Spinal Tap on 'Big Bottom'. A video of the show was later released (Video Collection VC6198).

■ ??.6.92

Stars Ball, The Cafe Royal, Soho, London, England.

Gilmour joined Nick Mason and Eric Stewart on stage to raise money for The Anthony Nolan Research Centre.

■ 6.6.92
Channel 4 TV broadcast, London, England.

Gilmour appeared on an edition of the Jools Holland series *Mister Roadrunner* in which Jools goes biking across America in search of 'The Lost Chord', stopping off at suitable locations en route, with appropriate musical interludes. The band, which comprised Gilmour (guitar), Jools Holland (piano), Mica Paris (vocals), Pino Palladino (bass guitar), Gilson Lavis (drums) and Matt Irving (keyboards), performed 'I Put A Spell On You'.

■ 21.6.92
ITV TV broadcast, London, England.

Gilmour joined Tom Jones on stage for a programme in his series *The Right Time*, performing 'Purple Rain' with Tim Renwick (guitar), Gary Wallis (drums) and Jodi Linscott (percussion).

■ 22.6.92
Town & Country Club, Kentish Town, London, England.

Gilmour played guitar at this Tom Jones concert..

■ 11.10.92
Chelsea Arts Ball, Royal Albert Hall, Kensington, London, England.

At this high-society AIDS fund-raiser Gilmour joined the house band – Guy Pratt (bass), Jon Carin (keyboards), Jodi Linscott (percussion), Tim Renwick (guitars), Gary Wallis (drums) and Sam Brown (vocals) – and guest musicians Nick Mason, Rick Wright, Tom Jones, Hugh Cornwell, Mica Paris, Elvis Costello and Sam Moore. Set list: River Deep Mountain High/The Sun Ain't Gonna Shine Anymore/Golden Brown/Stone

Free/I Put A Spell On You/Can't Stand Up For Falling Down/ Another Brick In The Wall Pt.2/ Wish You Were Here/ Comfortably Numb/ Superstition/Knock On Wood/ Kiss.

■ 7.11.92
Channel 4 TV broadcast, London, England.

Gilmour performed 'Such A Night', 'Wide-Eyed And Legless' and 'Movin' On' with Andy Fairweather-Low and Jools Holland in a programme in the latter's series *The Happening*, recorded at the Astoria Theatre, London.

■ 2.6.94
Bop For Bosnia, BBC Television Centre, Wood Lane, London, England.

Gilmour guested at this exclusive fund-raiser organized by Chris Jagger which also featured a band comprising Dave Stewart, Leo Sayer, Simon Kirke and Jon Newey. As well as performing material mainly from Jagger's album *Atcha*, they performed several blues numbers.

■ 29.6.96
Hyde Park, London, England.

Gilmour guested on the last four numbers of The Who's reworked version of *Quadrophenia* for the Prince's Trust' all-day concert, which also featured Bob Dylan, Eric Clapton and Alanis Morissette.

■ 20.7.96
A Day For Tibet, Alexandra Palace, Muswell Hill, London, England.

Gilmour performed for the Dalai Lama of Tibet at a benefit concert which also featured Sinead O'Connor, Andy Summers and The Chris Jagger Band. Gilmour performed with the latter, gave a surprise solo acoustic rendition of Syd Barrett's 'Terrapin' and played 'On The Turning Away', 'Wish You Were Here' and 'Coming Back To Life' with Chucho Merchan (bass) and other musicians.

Nick Mason has made no solo recordings in the strict sense of the term. However, he has collaborated on two albums which were released under his name. He has also co-written and performed much soundtrack material for films and television advertisements. In addition, he has acted as producer and played on several albums for other artists.

DISCOGRAPHY

■ ??.5.81
Nick Mason's Fictitious Sports.
Harvest (EMI) SHSP 4116 (album).
Can't Get My Motor To Start/I Was Wrong/Siam/Hot River//Boo To You Too/Do Ya?/Wervin'/I'm A Mineralist.
The first album that Mason worked on outside of Pink Floyd was essentially the work of jazz artist Carla Bley, who composed all the pieces, plays keyboards on all of them and co-produced it with him. In addition to Mason on drums, the album features Robert Wyatt and Karen Kraft (vocals), Chris Spedding (guitar), Steve Swallow (bass guitar), Gary Windo (woodwind instruments), Gary Valente (trombones), Michael Mantler (trumpets), Howard Johnson (tuba), Terry Adams (piano), and Carlos Ward, D. Sharpe, Vincent Chancey and Earl McIntyre (additional vocals). Although the album was recorded in 1978, it was not released until 1981, owing to contractual difficulties.

■ 19.8.85
Mason & Fenn – Profiles.
Harvest (EMI) MAF 1 (album).
Malta/Lie For A Lie/Rhoda/ Profiles Pts.1&2//Israel/And The Address/Mumbo Jumbo/Zip Code/Black Ice/At The End Of The Day/Profiles Pt.3.

■ 22.9.85
Lie For A Lie/And The Address.
Harvest (EMI) HAR 5238 (7-inch single).

■ Lie For A Lie/And The Address/Mumbo Jumbo.
Harvest (EMI) 12 HAR 5238 (12-inch single).
This album was a collaboration with ex-10cc guitarist Rick Fenn. The pair had been introduced by a mutual friend, Eric Stewart, also of 10cc, when Mason was looking for someone to help him with some music for a TV advert. However, Stewart was preoccupied with other matters and suggested Fenn. The pair hit it off and eventually formed a production company, Bamboo Music, to supply music for films and commercials.
Profiles was the first of their commercially available collaborations and was recorded at Mason's Britannia Row studios and Fenn's Basement Studios.
The lyrics on 'Lie For A Lie' and 'Israel' were written by Danny Peyronel, who also sang on the latter. Other musicians were Mel Collins (saxophone), Craig Pruess (emulator bass on 'Malta'), Maggie Reilly and David Gilmour (vocals on 'Lie For A Lie') and Aja Fenn (intro keyboards on 'Malta'). The album was engineered by Nick Griffiths and Rick Fenn.

GUEST APPEARANCES AND PRODUCTION

■ 1971
Principal Edward's Magic Theatre - The Asmoto Running Band.
Dandelion Records DAN 8002 (album). Produced by Mason.

■ 1974
Principal Edward's Magic Theatre – Round One.
Deram SML 1108 (album). Produced by Mason.

■ 1974
Robert Wyatt – Rock Bottom.
Virgin V 2017 (album). Produced by Mason.

■ 1974
Robert Wyatt – I'm A Believer/Memories.
Virgin VS 114 (7-inch single). Produced by Mason.

■ 1975
Robert Wyatt – Ruth Is Stranger Than Richard.
Virgin V 2034 (album). Produced by Mason.

■ 1976
Gong – Shamal.
Virgin V 2046 (album). Produced by Mason.

■ 1976
Michael Mantler – The Hapless Child And Other Stories. Watteau
WATT 4 (album). Engineered and mixed at Britannia Row studios by Mason, who also appears as an additional speaker.

■ 1977
The Damned – Music For Pleasure.
Stiff SEEZ 5 (album). Produced by Mason at Britannia Row studios.

■ 1977
Robert Wyatt – Yesterday Man/Sonia.
Virgin VS 115 (7-inch single). Produced by Mason.

■ 1978
Steve Hillage – Green.
Virgin V 2098 (album). Co-produced by Mason and Hillage. Mason plays on 'Ley Lines To Glassdom'. Also a 7-inch single, Getting Better/Palm Trees on Virgin VS 212, taken from the album

■ 1983
Michael Mantler – Something There.
Watteau WATT 13 (album). Mason plays on this album, which also features Carla Bley (piano), Mike Stern (guitar), Steve Swallow (bass guitar) and the London Symphony Orchestra conducted by Michael Gibbs.

NICK MASON

■ **1987**
Michael Mantler – *Michael Mantler Live.*
Watteau WATT 18 (album). Mason plays on this album recorded at Mantler's concert held on 8.2.87 in Essen, West Germany.

■ **1996**
Gary Windo – *His Master's Bones.*
Mason played on 'Steam Radio Tapes' recorded at Britannia Row in 1976 but not released until 1996 because of contractual difficulties.

SOUNDTRACKS

The composing partnership of Mason and guitarist Rick Fenn led to several collaborations on film soundtracks and music for television commercials, including HMV, Rowenta, Rothmans and Barclays Bank, although a great many more remain undocumented. Their film soundtracks include *White of The Eye* (1987) and *Tank Malling* (1988). Others reportedly by Mason–Fenn include *Body Contact* and *Cresta Run.*
Mason and Fenn also wrote the soundtrack, including a reworking of their 'Lie For A Lie' (from *Profiles*) as well as a new recording of 'Sh-boom' with Eric Stewart on vocals, for *Life Could Be A Dream.* Directed by Mike Shackleton, this film, also known as *One Of These Days,* is a twenty-minute semi-autobiographical account of Mason's motoring and professional career featuring material from his home archive as well as vintage Pink Floyd performances, including 'One Of These Days' from the film *Pink Floyd Live At Pompeii.* It was shown briefly during 1985 as part of Britannia Airways' in-flight film selection during this year.

LIVE PERFORMANCE
■ **8.9.74**
Theatre Royal, Drury Lane, London, England.
With Twickenham (Robert Wyatt, Mike Oldfield, Fred Frith, Mongezi Feza, Gary Windo, Julie Tippet, Dave Stewart, Hugh Hopper, Laurie Allan and Ivor Cutler). Nick formed part of this one-off line-up.
Set list: Opportunity Knocks – Memories/Sea Song/A Last Straw/Little Red Riding Hood Hit The Road – Alifib/The God Song/Mind Of A Child – Behind Blue Eyes/Instant Pussy – Signed Curtain/First Verse/Little Red Robin Hood/I'm A Believer/Laughing Policeman.

■ **13.9.74**
BBC TV Centre, Shepherd's Bush, London, England.
Mason played on Robert Wyatt's performance of The Monkees' 'I'm A Believer' on BBC1's *Top Of The Pops.*

■ **28.11.75**
Maidstone College of Art, Maidstone, Kent, England.
Mason played with Gary Windo's band.

■ **28–30.4.84**
Hammersmith Odeon, Hammersmith, London, England.
Mason joined David Gilmour at his three solo concerts (see page 235).

■ **??.5.84**
Sendesaal, Cologne, West Germany.
Mason played in Michael Mantler and Carla Bley's 'Music For Six Piece Orchestra'.

■ **8.2.87**
1st International Art Rock Festival, Kongresshalle, Frankfurt-am-Main, West Germany.
The Michael Mantler–Nick Mason Projekt, formed for this concert only, also included Rick Fenn (guitars), Don Preston (synthesizers), John Greaves (bass guitar) and Jack Bruce (vocals). Highlights were broadcast on the German TV channel WDF3 on 31.5.87.
Set list: Alien (from Part 3)/Slow Orchestra Piece No.6/Slow Orchestra Piece No.3/Slow Orchestra Piece No. 8/Alien (from Part 1)//For Instance/When I Run/The Remembered Visit/The Doubtful Guest/The Hapless Child/No Answer/Preview/Something There.

■ **28,29.3.87**
The Secret Policeman's Third Ball, The London Palladium, London, England. Mason made a brief appearance at this Amnesty International benefit concer (see page 238).

■ **??.6.92**

Stars Ball, The Cafe Royal, Soho, London, England.
Mason joined David Gilmour and Eric Stewart on stage to raise money for The Anthony Nolan Research Centre.

■ **11.10.92**
Chelsea Arts Ball, Royal Albert Hall, Kensington, London, England.
Mason guested at this high-society fund-raiser on behalf of AIDS sufferers. Other musicians who performed included the house band – David Gilmour (vocals, guitars), Guy Pratt (bass), Jon Carin (keyboards), Jodi Linscott (percussion), Tim Renwick (guitars), Gary Wallis (drums) and Sam Brown (vocals) – and guest musicians Rick Wright, Tom Jones, Hugh Cornwell, Mica Paris, Elvis Costello, Sam Moore.

ROGER WATERS

Both before and after leaving Pink Floyd in 1985, Roger Waters attempted, with varying degrees of success, to emulate the band's extravagant stage shows in his own live concerts. However, perhaps because the band has had a somewhat faceless image throughout its lifetime, the general public have not readily identified Waters the solo artist as being one of the prime movers of the band in its heyday. Consequently, they have not taken to his work with the same enthusiasm, despite some fine achievements, not least a stage presence that many feel is lacking in the current incarnation of Pink Floyd.

DISCOGRAPHY
■ 28.11.70
The Body (with Ron Geesin).
Harvest (EMI) SHSP 4008 (album).
Our Song/Sea Shell And Stone/Red Stuff Writhe/A Gentle Breeze Blew Through Life/Lick Your Partners/Bridge Passage For Three Plastic Teeth/Chain Of Life/The Womb Bit/Embryo Thought/March Past Of The Embryo's/More Than Seven Dwarfs In Penis-Land/Dance Of The Red Corpuscles//Body Transport/Hand Dance - Full Evening Dress/Breathe/Old Folks Ascension/Bed-Time-Dream-Clime/Piddle In Perspex/Embryonic Womb Walk/Mrs. Throat Goes Walking/Sea Shell And Soft Stone/Give Birth To A Smile.(See page 79 for further details.)
■ 9.4.84
5.01am/4.30am.
Harvest (EMI) HAR 5228 (7-inch single).

5.01am/4.30am/4.33am.
Harvest (EMI) 12 HAR 5228 (12-inch single).
■ 8.5.84
The Pros And Cons Of Hitch-Hiking.
Harvest (EMI) SHVL 24-0105-1 (album).
4.30am (Apparently They Were Travelling Abroad)/4.33am (Running Shoes)/4.37am (Arabs With Knives And West German Skies)/4.39am (For The First Time Today Pt.2)/4.41am (Sexual Revolution)/4.47am (The Remains Of Our Love)//4.50am (Go Fishing)/4.56am (For The First Time Today Pt.1)/4.58am (Dunroamin, Duncarin, Dunlivin)/5.01am (The Pros And Cons Of Hitch-Hiking)/5.06am (Every Strangers Eyes)/5.11am (The Moment Of Clarity).
■ ??.6.84
5.06am/4.39am.
Harvest (EMI) HAR 5230 (7-inch single).
Waters' first solo album is a concept piece. Through a series of dreams, it tells the story of a man struggling with a mid-life crisis in a motel room. Waters recruited many well-known session musicians for the album, including Andy Bown (Hammond organ and twelve-string guitar), Ray Cooper (percussion), Eric Clapton (lead guitar), Michael Kamen (piano), Andy Newmark (drums), David Sanborn (saxophone), Raphael Ravenscroft, Kevin Flanigan and Vic Sullivan (horns), Madeline Bell, Katie Kissoon and Doreen Chanter (backing vocals). The National Philharmonic Orchestra was conducted and arranged by Michael Kamen. The album was produced by Waters and Kamen. Gerald Scarfe's album sleeve depicting a naked female hitch-hiker was branded as sexist by many and a large number of sleeves as well as album and concert advertisements were censored in parts of Europe, USA and Japan.
■ 11.5.87

Radio Waves/Going To Live In LA.
Harvest (EMI) EM 6 (7-inch single).
Radio Waves (extended remix)/Going To Live In LA/Radio Waves (7-inch version).
EMI 12 EM 6 (12-inch single) and EMI CD EM 6 (CD single).
■ 15.6.87
Radio KAOS.
EMI KOAS 1 (album) and EMI CD KAOS 1 (CD)
Radio Waves/Who Needs Information/Me Or Him/The Powers That Be//Sunset Strip/Home/Four Minutes/The Tide Is Turning.
Radio KAOS.
EMI KAOS DJ 1 (banded radio album in custom sleeve with music but no dialogue).
Radio Waves/Who Needs Information/Me Or Him/The Powers That Be//Sunset Strip/Home/Four Minutes/The Tide Is Turning.
■ 16.11.87
The Tide Is Turning/Money (live).
EMI EM 37 (7-inch single).
The Tide Is Turning/Money (live)/Get Back To Radio (demo).
EMI 12 EM 37 (12-inch single) and EMI CD EM 37 (CD single).
Waters' next album after *The Pros And Cons Of Hitch-Hiking* was another concept piece. It is the complex story of Billy, an apparent 'vegetable' who accesses government defence computers to simulate a worldwide nuclear conflagration in order to convince the superpowers that they must discuss peace if global destruction is to be averted. Using a voice synthesizer, he communicates on air with a radio DJ, Jim Ladd, whose show becomes a vehicle for spreading his anti-war message.
■ 10.9.90
Another Brick In The Wall Pt.2/Run Like Hell.
Mercury (Phonogram) MER 332

(7-inch single).

Another Brick In The Wall Pt.2 (edit)/Run Like Hell (Potsdamer Mix)/Another Brick In The Wall Pt.2 (full version).

Mercury (Phonogram) MERX 332 (12-inch single) and Mercury (Phonogram) MERCD 332 (CD single).

■ **17.9.90**

The Wall – Live In Berlin.

Mercury (Phonogram) 846611-2 (Double CD)/Mercury (Phonogram) 846611-1 (Double album).

Pieces from The Wall.

Mercury (Phonogram) 878147-2 (promotional CD).

Another Brick In The Wall Pt.2 (edit)/Young Lust (edit)/Run Like Hell/In The Flesh?

The Wall – Live In Berlin.

Mercury (Phonogram). (promotional box set with CD, concert video and illustrated booklet).

■ **??.10.90**

The Tide Is Turning/Nobody Home.

Mercury (Phonogram) MER 336 (7-inch single).

The Tide Is Turning (album version)/Nobody Home/The Tide Is Turning (7-inch version).

Mercury (Phonogram) MERX 336 (12-inch single) and Mercury (Phonogram) MERCD 336 (CD single).

■ **24.8.92**

What God Wants Pt.I (video edit)/What God Wants Pt.1 (album version)

Columbia (Sony) 6581390 (7-inch single).

What God Wants Pt.I (video edit)/What God Wants Pt.I (album version)/What God Wants Pt.III.

Columbia (Sony) 6581395 (CD single) and Columbia (Sony) 6581399 (limited-edition CD box set with prints).

■ **7.9.92**

Amused To Death.

Columbia (Sony) COL 4687612 (CD).

The Ballad Of Bill Hubbard/What

God Wants Pt.I/Perfect Sense Pt.II/Perfect Sense Pt.II/The Bravery Of Being Out Of Range/Late Home Tonight Pt.I/Late Home Tonight Pt.II/Too Much Rope/What God Wants Pt.II/What God Wants Pt.III/Watching TV/Three Wishes/It's A Miracle/Amused To Death.

Amused To Death

Columbia (Sony). Promotional box set containing the CD and cassette.

Amused To Death.

Columbia (Sony) COL 4687610 (album). Limited-edition double album set with sixteen-page booklet, released in early 1993 in response to lobbying by fans.

■ **23.11.92**

The Bravery Of Being Out Of Range/What God Wants Pt.I/Perfect Sense Pt.I.

Columbia (Sony) 6588192 (CD single).

Waters' third solo album, *Amused To Death*, is by far his most accomplished. In this work he continues to vent spleen over subjects dear to his heart. Foremost among these is the futility of warfare: the piece is dedicated to Private William Hubbard, a rifleman remembered by fellow soldier Alf Razzell, who relived the horror of the First World War trenches in a TV documentary and whose words Waters samples for the album. Waters' other bugbears in this work continue to be consumerism and market forces.

His main asset was to secure Jeff Beck as his lead guitarist and Patrick Leonard as his producer but, as with all of his solo albums, this concept-based work is heavy going and best appreciated through headphones.

The album was originally planned for release on EMI, but its extended production time, coupled with contractual difficulties and his ongoing litigation against Pink Floyd, prompted a shift to Sony.

Incidentally, at this time there were strong rumours of an original sleeve design by Gerald Scarfe, showing Waters' three former colleagues floating rather lifelessly in a cocktail glass. To complete the album Waters assembled an extremely varied and impresive line-up which comprised Don Henley, Rita Coolage and PP Arnold (vocals), John Joyce, Jim Haas, N'Dea Davenport, Natalie Jackson, Lynn Fiddmont-Lindsay, Katie Kissoon and Doreen Chanter (backing vocals), Jeff Beck, Andy Fairweather-Low, Tim Pierce, Steve Lukather, B.J. Cole, Rick DiFonzo, Bruce Gaitsch and Geoff Whitehorn (guitar), James Johnson, John Pierce and Randy Jackson (bass guitar), John Patitucci (upright and electric bass), Graham Broad, Denny Fongheiser and Jeff Porcaro (drums), Luis Conte and Brian MacLeod (percussion), Patrick Leonard (keyboards and piano), John 'Rabbit' Bundrick (Hammond organ), Steve Sidwell (cornet), Guo Yi & The Peking Brothers (dulcimer, lute, zhen, oboe and bass), The National Philharmonic Orchestra, arranged and conducted by Michael Kamen, and The London Welsh Chorale, conducted by Kenneth Bowen.

GUEST APPEARANCES AND PRODUCTION

■ **1969**

Syd Barrett – Octopus/No Good Trying.

Harvest HAR 5009 (7-inch single). Produced by Waters, Gilmour and others.

■ **1970**

Syd Barrett – *The Madcap Laughs.*

Harvest (EMI) SHVL 765 (album). Produced by Waters and others.

SOUNDTRACKS

■ **1984**

The Hit.

The unreleased soundtrack to this film starring John Hurt,

Terence Stamp and Tim Roth featured a soundtrack by Paco de Lucia and Eric Clapton. It is rumoured that it included a small contribution from Waters.

■ **1986**

Waters re-recorded the Pink Floyd track 'Is There Anybody Out There?' from *The Wall* for use in a cinema advertisement by The Samaritans. A few years later parts of 'Welcome To The Machine' were used in another advertisement by this charitable organization.

■ **30.10.86**

When The Wind Blows.

Virgin V 2406 (album).

When The Wind Blows (David Bowie)/Facts And Figures (Hugh Cornwell)/The Brazilian (Genesis)/What Have They Done (Squeeze)/The Shuffle (Paul Hardcastle)//Roger Waters: The Russian Missile/Towers Of Faith/Hilda's Dream/The American Bomber/The Anderson Shelter/The British Submarine/The Attack/The Fallout/Hilda's Hair/Folded Flags.

From around the time of this album Waters gave the name The Bleeding Hearts Band to various combinations of backing musicians. The personnel for this album was as follows: Matt Irving and Nick Glenny Smith (keyboards), Jay Stapley (electric guitar), John Linnwood (Linn programming), Freddie KRC (drums), Mel Collins (saxophone), John Gordon (bass guitar), Clare Torry (vocals) and Paul Carrack (guest vocals on 'Folded Flags'). The tracks on the album's second side were all written by Waters and produced by Waters and Nick Griffiths.

FILMS

■ **31.5.88**

Radio KAOS.

PMI MVS KAO5 (video EP). Radio Waves/Sunset Strip/Four Minutes/The Tide Is Turning.

■ **24.9.90**

The Wall – Live In Berlin.

Channel 5 Music Video CFM 2648 (Concert video).

■ **??.11.92**
What God Wants Pt.I/Roger Waters interview/What God Wants Pt.II.
Video Collection SMV 49148-2 (video EP)

LIVE PERFORMANCE
THE PROS AND CONS OF HITCH-HIKING – WORLD TOUR

Waters assembled a touring band that consisted of many of the key players on the album *The Pros and Cons of Hitch-Hiking*, the big surprise being Eric Clapton (reportedly joining the tour against his management's advice). Also included were Mel Collins (saxophones), Michael Kamen (keyboards), Chris Stainton (keyboards and bass guitar), Andy Newmark (drums), Tim Renwick (guitar and bass guitar) and Doreen Chanter and Katie Kissoon (backing vocals).

The first half of the show featured a retrospective of Waters' best-known Pink Floyd songs, complete with vintage films. The songs were performed well, but had been rearranged and given an up-tempo feel, which in some cases didn't work at all well. Clapton, although a competent guitarist, was clearly no match for Gilmour's style on these numbers.

The second half consisted of the entire album. The stage production was very similar to Pink Floyd's 'The Wall' shows, using the same three-projector arrangement to project animation and film on to three screens spanning the full width of the back of the stage. To increase the visual depth, the second half of the show featured three gauze screens suspended in front of the projected images. Live-action film by Nicholas Roeg and animation by Scarfe were

projected on to both the gauze and the screens behind them. One screen depicted the motel window, another a lounge table and the third, a huge TV set. The sets were designed by Mark Fisher and Jonathan Park, who had worked extensively with Pink Floyd, and quadraphonic sound was used.

The following European shows were cancelled due to poor ticket sales: Westfalenhalle, Dortmund, West Germany (29.6), Messehalle, Frankfurt-am-Main, West Germany (1.7) and the latter's replacement, Parc des Expositions, Nice, France (1.7).

■ **16,17.6.84**
Johanneshovs Isstadion, Sandstuvägen, Stockholm, Sweden.
Set list for this show and all shows on this tour: Set The Controls For The Heart Of the Sun/Money/If/Welcome To The Machine/Have A Cigar/Wish You Were Here/Pigs On the Wing Pt.1/In The Flesh?/Nobody Home/Hey You/The Gunners Dream//The Pros And Cons Of Hitch-Hiking/encore: Brain Damage/Eclipse.

■ **19.6.84**
Sportpaleis Ahoy, Rotterdam, Netherlands.

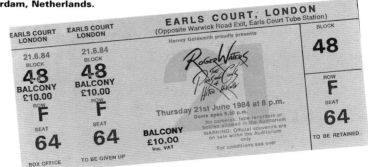

■ **21,22.6.84**
Earls Court Exhibition Hall, Earls Court, London, England.
No encore was performed at the first show.

■ **26,27.6.84**

National Exhibition Centre, Birmingham, West Midlands, England.
■ **3.7.84**
Hallenstadion, Zurich, Switzerland.
■ **6.7.84**
Palais Omnisports de Bercy, Paris, France.
■ **17–19.7.84**
Hartford Civic Center, Hartford, Connecticut, USA.
■ **20–22.7.84**
Brendan Byrne Meadowlands Arena, East Rutherford, New Jersey, USA.
■ **24.7.84**
Spectrum Theater, Philadelphia, Pennsylvania, USA.
■ **26.7.84**
Rosemont Horizon, Rosemont, Chicago, Illinois, USA
■ **28,29.7.84**
Maple Leaf Gardens, Toronto, Ontario, Canada.
■ **31.7.84**
The Forum, Montreal, Quebec, Canada.
The last night of the tour.

PROS AND CONS – PLUS SOME OLD PINK FLOYD STUFF – NORTH AMERICAN TOUR
A second leg of the Pros And Cons Of Hitch-Hiking tour was booked for North America but this time Eric Clapton, Tim Renwick and Chris Stainton didn't participate and were replaced by Andy Fairweather-Low (guitar and bass guitar) and Jay Stapley (guitar)

■ **19.3.85**
Joe Louis Arena, Detroit, Michigan, USA.
Set list at this shows and all shows on this tour: Welcome To The Machine/Set The Controls For The Heart Of The Sun/Money/If/Wish You Were Here/Pigs On The Wing Pt.1/Get Your Filthy Hands Off My Desert/Southampton Dock/The Gunners Dream/In The Flesh?/Nobody Home/Have a Cigar/Another Brick In the Wall Pt.1/The Happiest Days Of Our Lives/Another Brick In The Wall Pt.2//The Pros And Cons Of Hitch-Hiking/encore: Brain Damage/Eclipse.
■ **20.3.85**
The Coliseum, Richfield, Cleveland, Ohio, USA.
■ **21.3.85**
Buffalo Memorial Auditorium, Buffalo, New York, USA.
■ **23.3.85**
Maple Leaf Gardens, Toronto, Ontario, Canada.
■ **26–28.3.85**
Radio City Music Hall, Manhattan, New York City, New York, USA.
The show of 28.3.85 was broadcast in full throughout the USA as a live simulcast with holophonic sound. It was later broadcast on BBC Radio One in the UK on 29.11.85.
■ **29.3.85**
Spectrum Theater, Philadelphia, Pennsylvania, USA.
■ **30.3.85**

The Centrum, Worcester, Massachusetts, USA.
■ 3.4.85
Oakland Coliseum Arena, Oakland, California, USA
■ 4.5.85
The Forum, Inglewood, Los Angeles, California, USA
■ 6.4.85
Veterans Memorial Coliseum, Phoenix, Arizona, USA.
■ 8.4.85
The Summit Sports Arena, Houston, Texas, USA.
■ 9.4.85
Frank Erwin Center, University of Texas, Austin, Texas, USA.
■ 11.4.85
The Omni Coliseum, Atlanta, Georgia, USA.
■ 13.4.85
The Sportatorium, Hollywood, Florida, USA.
■ 14.4.85
Civic Center Arena, Lakeland, Florida, USA.
The last night of the tour.
RADIO KAOS TOUR
Waters' tour was launched at almost exactly the same time as his former band mates revived Pink Floyd. As a result, *Radio KAOS* often reached the same town within days of the Pink Floyd road show, although, as the media was at great pains to point out, Waters usually performed to considerably fewer people.
For this tour The Bleeding Hearts Band were: Andy Fairweather-Low and Jay Stapley (guitars), Paul Carrack (keyboards), Graham Broad (drums), Mel Collins (saxophone) and Doreen Chanter and Katie Kissoon (backing vocals). Jim Ladd played the radio DJ. Sponsored by the Canadian beer maker Moosehead, the show was a simpler production than *The Pros And Cons Of Hitch-Hiking*. Again the sets were designed by Fisher–Park, who used a circular screen on to which were back-projected films

and animations, including some amusing adverts and sketches. A digital message board conveyed Billy's lines and a further innovation was a telephone booth in the audience with a line to the stage, allowing Waters to take fans' questions. As in Waters' previous shows, quadraphonic sound was used.
■ 14.8.87
Providence Civic Center, Providence, Rhode Island, USA.
Set list at this and all shows on this tour (although there was occasional variation in the running order): Audience telephone calls to Jim Ladd/Film advertisement for Club Nowhere/ Audience telephone calls to Jim

Ladd/Tempted (Paul Carrack solo)/Radio Waves/Welcome To The Machine/Who Needs Information/Money/Film advertisement for the Bimbo School/Medley comprising: In The Flesh? – Have a Cigar – Pigs (3 Different Ones) – Wish You Were Here/Mother/Molly's Song/ Me Or Him/The Powers That Be//Film advertisement for Moosehead beer/Audience telephone calls to Waters/Film advertisement for The Shredding Alternative/Going To Live In L.A./ Sunset Strip/Film sketch: Fish Report With A Beat/5.01am (The Pros And Cons Of Hitch-Hiking)/ Get Your Filthy Hands Off My Desert – Southampton Dock/

1967 promotional film of 'Arnold Layne'/If/5.06am (Every Stranger's Eyes)/Not Now John/Another Brick In The Wall Pt.1 – The Happiest Days Of Our Lives – Another Brick In The Wall Pt.2/ Nobody Home/Home – Four Minutes/The Tide Is Turning/ encore: Breathe/Brain Damage/ Eclipse.
■ 15.8.87
Hartford Civic Center, Hartford, Connecticut, USA.
■ 17.8.87
Kingswood Music Theatre, Toronto, Ontario, Canada.
■ 19.8.87
Blossom Music Center, Cuyahoga Falls, Ohio, USA.
■ 20.8.87
Buffalo Memorial Auditorium, Buffalo, New York, USA.
■ 22.8.87
Great Woods, Mansfield, Boston, Massachusetts, USA.
■ 24.8.87
Spectrum Theater, Philadelphia, Pennsylvania, USA.
■ 26.8.87
Madison Square Garden, Manhattan, New York City, New York, USA.
■ 28.8.87
Saratoga Performing Arts Centre, Saratoga Springs, New York, USA.
■ 30.8.87
Capitol Music Theatre, Landover, Maryland, USA.
■ 31.8.87
The Coliseum, Greensboro, North Carolina, USA.
Show cancelled.
■ 2.9.87
The Omni Coliseum, Atlanta, Georgia, USA.
■ 4.9.87
Fox Theatre, St Louis, Missouri, USA.
■ 5.9.87
Market Square Arena, Indianapolis, Indiana, USA.
■ 6.9.87
Ohio Center, Columbus, Ohio, USA.

Roger Waters, Wembley Arena, November 1987

■ **8.9.87**
Pine Knob Music Theatre, Clarkston, Michigan, USA.
■ **9.9.87**
Poplar Creek Music Theatre, Hoffman Estates, Chicago, Illinois, USA.
■ **10.9.87**
MET Center, Minneapolis, Minneapolis, USA.
■ **12.9.87**
McNichols Sports Arena, Denver, Colorado, USA.
■ **14.9.87**
Frank Erwin Center, University of Texas, Austin, Texas, USA.
■ **15.9.87**
Reunion Arena, Dallas, Texas, USA.
■ **17.9.87**
Veterans Memorial Coliseum, Phoenix, Arizona, USA.
■ **20.9.87**
The Forum, Inglewood, Los Angeles, California, USA.
'Wall' show backing vocalists John Joyce, Jim Haas and Joe Chemay joined Waters on stage for a surprise rendition of

'Outside The Wall' at the close of the show.
■ **23.9.87**
The Sports Arena, San Diego, California, USA.
■ **26.9.87**
Oakland Coliseum Arena, Oakland, California, USA.
■ **28.9.87**
Seattle Center Arena, Seattle, Washington, USA.
■ **29.9.87**
Expo Theatre, Vancouver, British Columbia, Canada.
The following shows were cancelled: NBC Arena, Honolulu, Hawaii, USA (3.10); Festival Hall, Brisbane, Queensland, Australia (9.10); Entertainments Centre, Melbourne, Victoria, Australia (15.10); Entertainments Centre, Sydney, New South Wales, Australia (20.10); Entertainments Centre, Perth, Western Australia, Australia (24.10); Osaka, Japan (27.10); NHK Hall, Tokyo, Japan (28,29.10).
With the October engagements cancelled, reportedly due to poor ticket sales, Waters and his colleagues spent time working

on a new album at the Compass Point recording studios in the Bahamas. The tour resumed in November with the same cast and set list.
■ **3.11.87**
Cumberland County Civic Center, Portland, Maine, USA.
■ **4.11.87**
Brendan Byrne Meadowlands Arena, East Rutherford, New Jersey, USA.
■ **6.11.87**
The Forum, Montreal, Quebec, Canada.
■ **7.11.87**
Colisée de Quebec, Quebec City, Quebec, Canada.
The show was recorded and broadcast in an edited eighty-two-minute programme on the Westwood One radio network on 23.11.87. The tracks broadcast were: Radio Waves/ Welcome To The Machine/ Money/In The Flesh/Have A Cigar/Pigs (3 Different Ones)/Wish You Were Here/ Mother/Get Your Filthy Hands

Off My Desert/ Southampton Dock/If/The Powers That Be/Brain Damage/ Eclipse/Another Brick In The Wall Pt.1/The Happiest Days Of Our Lives/Another Brick In The Wall Pt.2.
■ **9.11.87**
The Civic Center, Ottawa, Ontario, Canada.
■ **10.11.87**
Copps Coliseum, Hamilton, Ontario, Canada.
■ **13.11.87**
Mecca Auditorium Arena, Milwaukee, Wisconsin, USA.
■ **14.11.87**
Arie Crown Theatre, Chicago, Illinois, USA.
■ **16.11.87**
The Centrum, Worcester, Massachusetts, USA.
■ **21,22.11.87**
Wembley Arena, Wembley, Middlesex, England.
The last night of the tour. Waters invited *Dark Side Of The Moon* vocalist Clare Torry to sing on 'Great Gig In The Sky' on both nights. However, he was unsuccessful in his efforts to get the Pontardulais Male Voice Choir to perform on stage at this and his earlier show at New York's Madison Square Garden.
The first Wembley show was recorded and edited to make a seventy-one-minute presentation for London's Capital Radio and broadcast on 17.4.88. The tracks broadcast were: Radio Waves/Welcome To The Machine/Who Needs Information/The Powers That Be/ Sunset Strip/If/Every Strangers Eyes/Nobody Home/Home/Four Minutes/The Tide Is Turning.
■ **21.7.90**
The Wall – Live In Berlin, Potsdamerplatz, Berlin, Germany.
This was possibly the most

ambitious outdoor concert event ever staged. At the suggestion of rock merchandiser Mick Worwood, Waters agreed to perform a one-off production of 'The Wall' in order to raise money for the Memorial Fund For Disaster Relief, a charity dedicated to raising five pounds for every life lost in the Second World War, for the relief of natural world catastrophes. It was founded by Leonard Cheshire VC OM DSO DFC, the highly decorated Second World War airman.

There was much talk of staging the concert in other prime locations, but the collapse of the Communist Bloc made the former East Berlin an appropriate location. A twenty-five-acre site formerly occupying the no man's land between East and West was cleared, in order to stage the show. As well as harbouring a vast amount of unexploded armaments from the War, the land had also contained Hitler's bunker. In this climate of unaccustomed reconciliation it took at least six months to establish which of the German governments could give authority to stage the event. The production, designed by Fisher-Park, incorporated a wall eighty-two feet high by 591 feet across, with a stage wide enough and strong enough to carry a marching band, military trucks and trailers, motorbikes and limousines as well as all the necessary mechanisms and scenery. Rehearsals began in Berlin two weeks before the show and there was a final dress rehearsal the night before. It was fortunate that this was filmed, because on the night of the show so many satellite TV stations were linked to the site that power failures occurred repeatedly throughout the performance. For this reason, many scenes were re-shot for the benefit of the video after the crowds had dispersed at the end

of the concert.

An international array of guest musicians complemented Waters on stage, although his own Bleeding Hearts Band formed the core of his musical support. They were: Graham Broad (drums), Snowy White and Rick Di Fonzo (guitars), Andy Fairweather-Low (guitar and bass guitar), Nick Glennie-Smith and Peter Wood (keyboards), Joe Chemay, Jim Haas, Jim Farber and John Joyce (backing vocals).

The show was officially opened by Leonard Cheshire, following the sounding of a First World War army whistle.

Set list for first half (with featured artist): In The Flesh (The Scorpions)/The Thin Ice (Ute Lemper as The Wife)/Another Brick In The Wall Pt.1 (Garth Hudson, saxophone solo)/The Happiest Days Of Our Lives (Joe Chemay, John Joyce, Jim Farber, Jim Haas, vocals)/Another Brick In The Wall Pt.2 (Cyndi Lauper, vocals; Rick Di Fonzo and Snowy White, guitars; Peter Wood, keyboards; Thomas Dolby as The Teacher)/Mother (Sinead O'Connor, vocals with The Band)/Goodbye Blue Sky (Joni Mitchell, vocals; James Galway, flute)/Empty Spaces (Bryan Adams, vocals and guitar)/Young Lust (Bryan Adams, vocals and guitar)/One Of My Turns (Jerry Hall as The Groupie)/Another Brick In The Wall Pt.3/Goodbye Cruel World.

Set list for second half (with featured artist):Hey You (Paul Carrack, vocals)/Is There Anybody Out There? (Snowy White and Rick Di Fonzo, classical guitars; Berliner Rundfunk Orchestra & Choir)/Nobody Home (Snowy White, guitar)/Vera (Berliner Rundfunk Orchestra & Choir)/Bring The Boys Back Home (Berliner Rundfunk Orchestra)/Comfortably Numb (Van Morrison, vocals; The Band; Rick Di Fonzo and Snowy White, guitar solos)/In The Flesh?

(Berliner Rundfunk Orchestra & Choir; Military Orchestra Of The Soviet Army (both to the end of the show)/Run Like Hell/Waiting For The Worms/Stop/The Trial (Tim Curry as The Prosecutor; Thomas Dolby as The Teacher; Ute Lemper as The Wife; Marianne Faithfull as The Mother; Albert Finney as The Judge). Encore: The Tide Is Turning (all). The estimated audience of over 250,000 (many of whom entered free after the collapse of the perimeter fence) must make it one of the biggest single concert attendances ever. But despite the sale of worldwide TV rights and the royalties later realized from the album and video sales, the production costs had spiralled out of control to such an extent that, by May 1992, only an estimated £100,000 had been raised for the Memorial Fund For Disaster Relief – a figure far short of the original target.

■ 18.10.91
The Guitar Legends Festival, Auditorium Expo '92, Seville, Spain.
Set list: In The Flesh/The Happiest Days Of Our Lives/Another Brick In The Wall Pt.2/What God Wants/Brain Damage/Eclipse/Comfortably Numb. This was an unusual event for Waters to take part in, since he is not chiefly known as a guitarist. He performed a set on the fourth of a five-night festival (15–19.10.91) which featured Robert Cray, Steve Cropper, BB King, Bo Diddley, Ricky Lee Jones, John McLaughlin, George Benson, Joe Cocker, Bob Dylan, Keith Richards, Jack Bruce, Steve Vai, Cozy Powell, Paul Rodgers and others. Bruce Hornsby and Robbie Robertson also performed on the night of Waters' appearance.

Waters' backing band for his set included Snowy White and Andy Fairweather-Low (guitar), Tony Levin (bass), Pat Leonard and Peter Wood (keyboards), Graham

Broad (drums) and Doreen Chanter and Katie Kissoon (backing vocals). Bruce Hornsby played keyboards and vocals on 'Comfortably Numb'. Rehearsals took place at Nomis Studios in west London on the two days before the event. Waters' set, which featured a work in progress that would become 'What God Wants' on the *Amused To Death* album, was recorded for TV and broadcast on many worldwide networks, including BBC2 in the UK.

GUEST APPEARANCES
■ 5.12.86
BBC TV Broadcast, London, England.
Waters and Andy Fairweather-Low made a surprise appearance in a special tribute to John Lennon in the BBC2 documentary arts programme *Arena*, and performed a pre-recorded rendition of 'Across The Universe'.

■ ??.6.89
Hard Rock Cafe, London, England.
Waters and his then wife Carolyne attended the opening-day party for Wimbledon fortnight at which a number of tennis players performed, reportedly with Waters, 'Honky Tonk Women' and other R&B numbers.

■ 1.4.92
Walden Woods Benefit Concert, Universal Amphitheatre, Universal City, Los Angeles, California, USA.
Set list: In The Flesh/The Happiest Days Of Our Lives/Another Brick In The Wall Pt.2/Mother/Comfortably Numb. Waters performed at a benefit concert in aid of the preservation of Walden Woods in Massachusetts, at the request of Don Henley. He was joined on stage by Don Henley's band, and additional sets were performed by Neil Young and John Fogerty.

Less active outside Pink Floyd than the other members of the band, Rick Wright has nevertheless made two solo albums, which included contributions from artists previously associated with Pink Floyd.
He has also made an album as one half of the band Zee, the other member being Dave Harris, guitarist and vocalist of Fashion.

DISCOGRAPHY
■ **22.9.78**
Wet Dream.
Harvest (EMI) SHVL 818.
Mediterranean C/Against The Odds/Cat Cruise/Summer Elegy/Waves//Holiday/Mad Yannis Dance/Drop In From The Top/Pink's Song/Funky Deux.
Recorded at the Super Bear Studios in France in record time (10.1.–14.2.78) the album features Snowy White (guitars), Mel Collins (saxophone), Larry Steele (bass guitar) and Reg Isadore (drums/guitars).
■ **12.3.84**
Zee – Confusion (edit)/Eyes Of A Gypsy.
Harvest (EMI) HAR 5227 (7-inch single).
Zee – Confusion (extended version)/Eyes Of A Gypsy (dub mix)/Confusion (7-inch version).
Harvest (EMI) 12 HAR 5227 (12-inch single).
■ **9.4.84**
Zee – *Identity*.
Harvest (EMI) SHSP 24 0101 8 (album).
Confusion/Voices/Private Person/Strange Rhythm//Cuts Like A Diamond/By Touching/How Do You Do It/Seems We Were Dreaming. The cassette release featured the additional track

'Eyes Of A Gypsy'.
Wright recorded the above single and album with Dave Harris of Fashion under the name Zee. The pair had been introduced by mutual friend Raphael Ravenscroft, the instigator of the project, who had just finished working with David Gilmour on his solo album. After several rehearsals and several changes of musician, only Wright and Harris remained, and although all of the music was written by the pair the lyrics were all by Harris. The album, composed and performed almost entirely on the Fairlight computer, was regarded as too clinical by many Pink Floyd fans, who were expecting something more akin to Wright's first solo album. Wright looks back on it as an experiment best forgotten.
■ **7.10.96**
Broken China.
EMI CD EMD 1098 (CD).
Breaking Water/Night Of A Thousand Furry Toys/Hidden Fear/Runaway/Unfair Ground/Satellite/Woman Of Custom/Interlude/Black Cloud/Far From The Harbour Wall/Drowning/Reaching For The Rail/Blue Room In Venice/Sweet July/Along The Shoreline/Breakthrough.
Broken China.
EMI CD EMDJ 1098 (promotional CD).
Night Of A Thousand Furry Toys/Breakthrough/Satellite/Along The Shoreline.
Broken China.
EMI CD RW 101 (promotional CD) and EMI 12 RW 101 (12-inch single).
Runaway (Lemonade Mix)/Runaway (Leggit Dub)/Night Of A Thousand Furry Toys (Inverted Gravy Mix). (Track 1 remixed by The Orb; tracks 2 and 3 remixed by William Orbit with Matt Ducasse.)
Broken China.
EMI CD INT 105 (banded promotional Interview CD - no music)

Wright's third album, his second solo release, was a collaboration with Anthony Moore as sole lyricist. It was written and recorded at Wright's home studio in the south of France shortly after the Pink Floyd's 'Division Bell' tour. While leaning towards a concept piece, it lacks the weight of a Pink Floyd album. Unexpectedly, Sinead O'Connor sings on this album, contributing lead vocals on two tracks, 'Reaching For The Rail' and 'Breakthrough'. Other guest musicians include Tim Renwick, Dominic Miller and Steve Bolton (guitars), Manu Katche (drums), Pino Palladino (bass guitar), Sian Beli (cello), Kate St John (oboe) and Maz Palladino (backing vocals). David Gilmour played guitar on 'Breakthrough' but his performance did not appear on the album.
Although Rick Wright entertained the idea of taking the album on tour, sales were insufficient to justify the cost.

GUEST APPEARANCES
■ **1970**
Syd Barrett – *Barrett*.
Harvest (EMI) SHSP 4007 (album).
Wright played keyboards on Barrett's second solo album.
■ **1971**
BB King – *In London*.
Probe SPB 1041 (album).
Wright reportedly played piano on 'Caledonia'. Although he is credited on the album's sleeve, his appearance is unconfirmed.
■ **1990**
Blue Pearl – *Naked*.
Big Life BLR LP4 (album).
Wright played keyboards on 'Alive' and on the 12-inch single version (Big Life BLR T44).

LIVE PERFORMANCE
■ **10.11.74**
Newcastle Polytechnic, Newcastle-upon-Tyne, Tyne and Wear, England.
Wright played keyboards and David Gilmour shared lead guitar

RICK WRIGHT

with Tim Renwick at this Sutherland Brothers & Quiver show.

■ **11.10.92**
Chelsea Arts Ball, Royal Albert Hall, Kensington, **London, England.** Wright guested at this high-society AIDS fund-raiser. Other musicians who performed included the house band – David Gilmour (vocals, guitars), Guy Pratt (bass), Jon Carin (keyboards), Jodi Linscott (percussion), Tim Renwick (guitars), Gary Wallis (drums) and Sam Brown (vocals) – and guest musicians Nick Mason, Tom Jones, Hugh Cornwell, Mica Paris, Elvis Costello and Sam Moore.

DISCOGRAPHY

This list of Pink Floyd's recordings gives original UK pressings only and does not include re-pressed discs, variations in label design or specialist collectables such as acetates and test pressings. Promotional items of special interest are included. Also listed are videos of Pink Floyd in performance.

We are as sure as we can be of the accuracy of the release dates of recordings, but would emphasize that much of this information comes from contemporary press reports which are known to contain erroneous or contradictory details. Unfortunately, none of the problematic release dates could be verified by EMI Records, who informed us that they do not retain this information. Listed items are formatted as follows, although not all these details appear for every item: original release date where known; the title of the recording; the name of the record company and the item's original catalogue number on release; the format (in brackets); credits for the producer(s) and additional musicians, which remain the same for all subsidiary single releases; track listing (the division between the two sides of a single or album is indicated by a double oblique (//).

■ **10.3.67**

Arnold Layne/Candy & A Currant Bun.
Columbia (EMI) DB 8156 (7-inch single). Produced by Joe Boyd.

■ **16.6.67**

See Emily Play/Scarecrow.
Columbia (EMI) DB 8214 (7-inch single). Produced by Norman Smith.

■ **5.8.67**

The Piper At The Gates Of Dawn.
Columbia (EMI) SCX 6157 (stereo)/SX 6157 (mono) (album). Produced by Norman Smith. Astronomy Dominé/Lucifer Sam/ Matilda Mother/Flaming/Pow R

Toc H/Take Up Thy Stethoscope And Walk//Interstellar Overdrive/ The Gnome/Chapter 24/The Scarecrow/Bike.

■ **18.11.67**

Apples And Oranges/ Paintbox.
Columbia (EMI) DB 8310 (7-inch single). Produced by Norman Smith.

■ **12.4.68**

It Would Be So Nice/Julia Dream.
Columbia (EMI) DB 8410 (7-inch single). Produced by Norman Smith.

■ **1.7.68**

A Saucerful Of Secrets.
Columbia (EMI) SCX 6258 (stereo)/SX 6258 (mono) (album). Produced by Norman Smith. Let There Be More Light/ Remember A Day/Set The Controls For The Heart Of The Sun/Corporal Clegg//A Saucerful Of Secrets/See-Saw/Jugband Blues.

■ **19.7.68**

Tonite Let's All Make Love In London.
Instant INLP 002 (album). This film soundtrack album, featuring 'Interstellar Overdrive', was recorded in early 1967. The release date given here is that of the New York cinema opening of the film, as no exact date can be found. It is generally accepted this opening occurred shortly after the release of *A Saucerful Of Secrets* although the film had been previewed at the New York Film Festival on 26.9.67. See For Miles Records re-issued the Instant album, with the additional track 'Nick's Boogie', on 15.9.90 (SEEG 258). The label also released two CD EPs at the same time. The first (SEA CD4) contained the Pink Floyd material as well as selected interview segments from the film. The second (SFMDP 3) contained the Pink Floyd material and was accompanied by a colour booklet of stills from the band's recording session.

The Pink Floyd tracks were produced by Joe Boyd and Peter Whitehead.

The Pink Floyd – London 66-67.
See For Miles PFVP1 (video). Live footage of the above session and of Pink Floyd's appearance at UFO on 13 January 1967 also appears on this video.

■ **17.12.68**

Point Me At The Sky/ Careful With That Axe Eugene.
Columbia (EMI) DB 8511 (7-inch single). Produced by Norman Smith.

■ **13.6.69**

More.
Columbia (EMI) SCX 6346 (album). Produced by Pink Floyd. Cirrus Minor/The Nile Song/ Crying Song/Up The Khyber/ Green Is The Colour/Cymbaline/ Party Sequence//Main Theme/ Ibiza Bar/More Blues/ Quicksilver/A Spanish Piece/ Dramatic Theme.

■ **1.11.69**

Ummagumma.
Harvest (EMI) SHDW 1/2 (double album). Produced by Pink Floyd and Norman Smith. Astronomy Dominé/Careful With That Axe Eugene//Set The Controls For The Heart Of The Sun/A Saucerful Of Secrets// Sysyphus Pts.1-4/Grantchester Meadows/Several Species Of Small Furry Animals Gathered Together In A Cave And Grooving With A Pict//The Narrow Way Pts.1-3/The Grand Vizier's Garden Party Pt.1 – Entrance; Pt.2 – Entertainment; Pt.3 - Exit. by Syd Barrett.

■ **30.5.70**

Zabriskie Point.
MGM 2315 002 (album). The soundtrack to the Antonioni film of the same name features the previously unreleased Pink Floyd tracks 'Heart Beat Pig Meat', 'Crumbling Land' and 'Come In Number 51 Your Time Is Up'. The remainder of the album features, among others,

The Grateful Dead, The Youngbloods and The Kaleidoscope. Produced by Michelangelo Antonioni and Pink Floyd.

■ **1.10.70**
Atom Heart Mother.
Harvest (EMI) SHVL 781 (album). Produced by Pink Floyd. Atom Heart Mother a) Father's Shout; b) Breast Milky; c) Mother Fore; d) Funky Dung; e) Mind Your Throats Please; f) Remergence// If/Summer '68/Fat Old Sun/ Alan's Psychedelic Breakfast a) Rise And Shine; b) Sunny Side Up; c) Morning Glory.

■ **??.??.70**
Picnic – A Breath Of Fresh Air.
Harvest (EMI) SHSS 1/2 (double album). This sampler features Pink Floyd's 'Embryo'.

■ **14.5.71**
Relics.
Starline (EMI) SRS 5071 (album). Produced by Pink Floyd. Arnold Layne/Interstellar Overdrive/See Emily Play/ Remember A Day/Paintbox//Julia Dream/Careful With That Axe Eugene/Cirrus Minor/The Nile Song/Biding My Time/Bike.

■ **5.11.71**
Meddle.
Harvest (EMI) SHVL 795 (album).
One Of These Days/A Pillow Of Winds/Fearless/San Tropez/ Seamus//Echoes.

■ **3.6.72**
Obscured By Clouds.
Harvest (EMI) SHSP 4020 (album). Produced by Pink Floyd. Obscured By Clouds/When You're In/Burning Bridges/The Gold It's In The.../Mudmen/ Wots... Uh The Deal// Childhood's End/Free Four/Stay/Absolutely Curtains.

■ **Pink Floyd – Live At Pompeii.**
Channel 5 CFV 10422 (video). This is a current edition, with restored interview footage, of the full-length feature film originally released on video by Polygram.

Echoes Pt.1/Careful With That Axe Eugene/A Saucerful Of Secrets/One Of These Days I'm Going To Cut You Into Little Pieces/Set The Controls For The Heart Of The Sun/ Mademoiselle Nobs/Echoes Pt.2.

■ **24.3.73**
The Dark Side Of The Moon.
Harvest (EMI) SHVL 804 (album). Produced by Pink Floyd. Additional musicians: Dick Parry (saxophones on 'Us and Them' and 'Money'), Clare Torry (vocals on 'Great Gig In The Sky'), Doris Troy, Leslie Duncan, Liza Strike, Barry St John (backing vocals). Speak To Me/Breathe/On The Run/Time/The Great Gig In The Sky//Money/Us And Them/Any Colour You Like/Brain Damage/ Eclipse.

■ **18.1.74**
A Nice Pair.
Harvest (EMI) SHDW 403 (double album).
A repackage of *The Piper At The Gates Of Dawn* and *A Saucerful Of Secrets*. Original copies featured a photograph of the window of Dr Phang's dental surgery, but because dentists were at that time not allowed to advertise in the UK, a re-press was made with this picture replaced by that of a gargling monk.

■ **12.9.75**
Wish You Were Here.
Harvest (EMI) SHVL 814 9 (album). Produced by Pink Floyd. Additional musicians: Dick Parry (saxophones on 'Shine on You Crazy Diamond'), Roy Harper (vocals on 'Have A Cigar'), Venetta Fields and Carlena Williams (backing vocals). Shine on You Crazy Diamond Pts.1-5/Welcome To The Machine//Have A Cigar/Wish You Were Here/Shine On You Crazy Diamond Pts.6-9.

■ **23.1.77**
Animals.
Harvest (EMI) SHVL 815 (album). Produced by Pink Floyd. Pigs On The Wing Pt.1/Dogs//

Pigs (3 Different Ones)// Sheep/Pigs On The Wing Pt.2.

■ **??.7.79**
Pink Floyd. First XI.
Harvest (EMI) PF11 (box set). A limited edition of 1,000 box sets containing eleven LPs in their original sleeves: *The Piper At The Gates Of Dawn/A Saucerful Of Secrets/More/ Ummagumma/Atom Heart Mother/Relics/Meddle/Obscured By Clouds/The Dark Side Of The Moon* (issued as a picture disc)/ *Wish You Were Here* (issued as a picture disc)/*Animals*.

■ **23.11.79**
Another Brick In The Wall Pt.2/One Of My Turns.
Harvest (EMI) HAR 5194 (7-inch single).

■ **30.11.79**
The Wall.
Harvest (EMI) SHVL 822 (double album). Produced by Bob Ezrin, David Gilmour and Roger Waters. Additional musicians: Jeff Porcaro (additional drums), Peter Wood (additional keyboards), Freddie Mandell (additional organ), Lee Ritenour (additional guitars), Bruce Johnson, Toni Tennille, Joe Chemay, John Joyce (backing vocals), Children of Islington Green Primary School (backing chorus), Michael Kamen and Bob Ezrin (orchestral arrangements).
In The Flesh/The Thin Ice/ Another Brick In The Wall Pt.1/The Happiest Days Of Our Lives/Another Brick In The Wall Pt.2/Mother//Goodbye Blue Sky/Empty Spaces/Young Lust/ One Of My Turns/Don't Leave Me Now/Another Brick In The Wall Pt.3/Goodbye Cruel World// Hey You/Is There Anybody Out There?/Nobody Home/Vera/Bring The Boys Back Home/ Comfortably Numb//The Show Must Go On/In The Flesh?/Run Like Hell/Waiting For The Worms/ Stop/The Trial/Outside The Wall.

■ **23.11.81**
A Collection Of Great Dance Songs.
Harvest (EMI) SHVL 822

(album). Re-recorded version of 'Money' produced by David Gilmour.
One Of These Days/Money (re-recorded version)/Sheep//Shine On You Crazy Diamond Pts.1-9/ Wish You Were Here/Another Brick In The Wall Pt.2.

■ **23.11.81**
Money (re-recorded version).
Harvest (EMI) HAR 5217 (promotional one-sided pink vinyl 7-inch single).
'Money (re-recorded version)' b/w 'Let There Be More Light' was scheduled for release as a 7-inch single on 7.12.81, but this was cancelled.

■ **26.7.82**
When The Tigers Broke Free/Bring The Boys Back Home.
Harvest (EMI) HAR 5222 (7-inch single issued in both a single and a tri-fold picture sleeve).

■ **Pink Floyd The Wall.**
Channel 5 CFV 08762 (video). This is a current edition of the full-length feature film originally released by MGM/UA.

■ **21.3.83**
The Final Cut.
Harvest (EMI) SHPF 1983 (album). Produced by Roger Waters, James Guthrie and Michael Kamen. Additional musicians: Michael Kamen (piano, harmonium), Andy Bown (Hammond organ), Ray Cooper (percussion), Andy Newmark (drums on 'Two Suns In The Sunset'), Raphael Ravenscroft (tenor sax), uncredited female backing vocalists and the National Philharmonic conducted and arranged by Michael Kamen. The Post War Dream/Your Possible Pasts/One Of The Few/ The Hero's Return/The Gunner's Dream/Paranoid Eyes//Get Your Filthy Hands Off My Desert/The Fletcher Memorial Home/ Southampton Dock/The Final Cut/Not Now John/Two Suns In The Sunset.

■ **24.4.83**
The Final Cut.

Video Music Collection PM0010 (video EP)
The Gunners Dream/Not Now John/The Fletcher Memorial Home/The Final Cut.

■ **30.4.83**

Not Now John/The Hero's Return Pts.I&II.

Harvest (EMI) HAR 5224 (7-inch single).

Not Now John (single version)/The Hero's Return Pts.I&II/Not Now John (album version).

Harvest (EMI) 12 HAR 5224 (12-inch single).

Not Now John/The Hero's Return Pts.I&II.

Harvest (EMI) HAR DJ 5224 (7-inch promotional single).

■ **8.9.87**

A Momentary Lapse Of Reason.

EMI EMD 1003 (album)/EMI CD EMD 1003 (CD). Produced by Bob Ezrin and David Gilmour. A limited-edition reissue of the album (EMI EMDS 1003), with a poster pack and ticket application for the UK shows, was released on 1.2.88. Additional musicians: Bob Ezrin (keyboards, percussion, sequencers), Tony Levin (bass guitar, stick), Jim Keltner (drums), Steve Forman (percussion), Jon Carin (keyboards), Tom Scott (atlo & sopprano saxophone), Scott Page (tenor saxophone), Carmine Appice (drums), Pat Leonard (synthesisers), Bill Payne (Hammond organ), Michael Landau (guitar), John Halliwell (saxophone), Darlene Koldenhaven, Carmen Twillie, Phyllis St James, Donnie Gerrard (backing vocals).
Signs Of Life/Learning To Fly/The Dogs Of War/One Slip/On The Turning Away//Yet Another Movie/Round And Around/A New Machine Pt.1/Terminal Frost/A New Machine Pt.2/Sorrow.■

3.10.87

Learning To Fly (edit)/One Slip (edit).

EMI EM 26 (limited-edition 7-inch

pink vinyl radio promotional single with sleeve labelled as CD tracks below).

Learning To Fly (edit)/One Slip (edit).

EMI EM 26 (limited-edition 7-inch black vinyl promotional single without picture sleeve).

Learning To Fly (edit)/One Slip (edit)/Terminal Frost (album version)/Terminal Frost ('Do Your Own Lead' version).

EMI CD EM 26 (CD single).

■ **12.12.87**

On The Turning Away/Run Like Hell (live).

EMI EM 34/EMI EMP 34 (limited-edition 7-inch pink vinyl single).

On The Turning Away/Run Like Hell (live)/On The Turning Away (live).

EMI 12 EM 34 (12-inch single), EMI 12 EMP 34 (limited-edition 12-inch single in poster sleeve) and EMI CD EM 34 (CD single).

On The Turning Away/Run Like Hell (live).

EMI EM DJ 34(promotional 7-inch single).

■ **13.6.88**

One Slip/Terminal Frost.

EMI EM52 (7-inch single)/EMI EMG 52 (limited-edition 7-inch pink vinyl single in gatefold sleeve).

One Slip/Terminal Frost/The Dogs Of War (live).

EMI 12 EMP 52 (limited-edition 12-inch single in poster sleeve) and EMI CD EM 52 (CD single).

■ **??.6.88.**

Pink Floyd In Europe 1988.

EMI PSLP 1016 (promotional 12-inch mini album).
Money/Shine On You Crazy Diamond Pts.1-5/Another Brick in The Wall Pt.2//One Slip/On The Turning Away/Learning To Fly

■ **22.11.88**

Delicate Sound Of Thunder.

EMI EQ 5009 (double album)/EMI CDEQ 5009 (double CD).Produced by David Gilmour. Recorded at the Nassau Veterans Memorial Coliseum

19–23.8.88. Additional musicians as tour personnel on this leg of the tour.
Shine On You Crazy Diamond Pts.1-5/Learning To Fly/Yet Another Movie/Round And Around/Sorrow/The Dogs Of War/On The Turning Away//One Of These Days/Time/Wish You Were Here/Us And Them (not on vinyl)/Money (not on cassette)/Another Brick In The Wall Pt.2/Comfortably Numb/Run Like Hell.

Delicate Sound of Thunder – Promotional Sample.

EMI 12 PF1 (promotional 12-inch single).
Another Brick in The Wall Pt.2/One of These Days//Run Like Hell.

Delicate Sound of Thunder – Promotional Sample.

EMI CD PINK 1 (promotional CD single). Wish You Were Here/Learning To Fly/Run Like Hell.

■ **5.6.89**

Delicate Sound Of Thunder.

PMI MVN 9911863 (video). Shine On You Crazy Diamond Pts.1-5/Signs Of Life/Learning To Fly/Sorrow/The Dogs Of War/On The Turning Away/One Of These Days/Time/On The Run/The Great Gig In The Sky/Wish You Were Here/Us And Them/Comfortably Numb/One Slip/Run Like Hell/Shine On You Crazy Diamond (reprise for end credits).

■ **13.4.92**

La Carrera Panamericana.

PMI MVN 9913453 (video). New music produced by David Gilmour.
Run Like Hell/Pan Am Shuffle/Yet Another Movie/Sorrow/Signs Of Life/Country Theme/Mexico '78/Big Theme/Run Like Hell/One Slip/Small Theme/Pan Am Shuffle/Carrera Slow Blues.

■ **2.11.92**

Shine On.

EMI PFBOX 1 (box set). A nine-CD box set with postcards and a hardback book: *A Saucerful Of Secrets/Meddle/The Dark Side Of The Moon/Wish You Were Here/Animals/The Wall Pt.1/The

Wall Pt.2/A Momentary Lapse Of Reason.* Bonus CD, *The Early Singles*: Arnold Layne/Candy And A Currant Bun/See Emily Play/Scarecrow/Apples And Oranges/Paint Box/It Would Be So Nice/Julia Dream/Point Me At The Sky/Careful With That Axe Eugene.

Selected Tracks From Shine On.

EMI SHINE 1 (promotional mini-CD).
See Emily Play/Set The Controls For The Heart Of The Sun/One Of These Days/Money/Shine On You Crazy Diamond (radio edit)/Dogs/Comfortably Numb/Another Brick In The Wall Pt.2/One Slip.

■ **24.3.93**

The Dark Side Of The Moon.

EMI 0777 78147923 (CD). Special thirtieth-anniversary CD box set incorporating digitally remastered disc, new artwork and postcards.

■ **30.3.94**

The Division Bell.

EMI EMD 1055 (album)/EMI CD EMD 1055 (CD). Additional musicians: Jon Carin (programming, additional keyboards), Guy Pratt (bass), Gary Wallis (played & programmed percussion), Tim Renwick (guitars), Dick Parry (tenor saxophone), Bob Ezrin (keyboards, percussion), Sam Brown, Durga McBroom, Carol Kenyon, Jackie Sheridan and Rebecca Leigh-White (backing vocals). Orchestrations by Michael Kamen and Edward Shearmur and arranged by Michael Kamen.
Cluster One/What Do You Want From Me/Poles Apart/Marooned/A Great Day For Freedom/Wearing The Inside Out/Take It Back/Coming Back To Life/Keep Talking/Lost For Words/High Hopes.

■ **16.5.94**

Take It Back (edit)/Astronomy Dominé (live).

EMI EM 309 (limited-edition

7-inch red vinyl single).

Take It Back (album version)/Astronomy Dominé (live)/Take It Back (edit).

EMI CD EM 309 (CD single)/EMI CD EMS 309 (limited-edition CD single with poster).

Take It Back.

EMI CD EMDJ 309 (one-track promotion only CD).

■ **17.10.94**

High Hopes (radio edit)/Keep Talking (radio edit).

EMI EM 342 (limited-edition 7-inch clear vinyl single with poster sleeve).

High Hopes (album version)/Keep Talking (album version)/One Of These Days (live).

EMI CD EM 342 (CD single), EMI CD EMS 342 (limited-edition CD single in digipak with

postcards) and EMI 12 EM 342 (12-inch one-sided single in etched coloured vinyl with postcards).

Keep Talking (radio edit)/High Hopes (radio edit).

EMI CD EMDJ 342 (promotional CD).

■ **5.6.95**

Pulse.

EMI CD EMD 1078 (double CD with hardback booklet). Produced by James Guthrie and David Gilmour. Recorded in Europe 1994 with additional musicians as per tour personnel. Shine On You Crazy Diamond Pts.1-6/Astronomy Dominé/ What Do You Want From Me/ Learning To Fly/Keep Talking/ Coming Back To Life/Hey You/ A Great Day For Freedom/ Sorrow/High Hopes/Another Brick In The Wall Pt.2//The

Dark Side of The Moon/Wish You Were Here/Comfortably Numb/Run Like Hell.

Pulse

EMI TC EMD 1078 (double cassette). Shine On You Crazy Diamond Pts.1-6/Astronomy Dominé/ What Do You Want From Me/ Learning To Fly/Keep Talking/ Coming Back To Life/Hey You/A Great Day For Freedom/ Sorrow/High Hopes/Another Brick In The Wall Pt.2/One of These Days//The Dark Side of The Moon/Wish You Were Here/Comfortably Numb/ Run Like Hell/pre-concert sound effects.

Pulse.

EMI LP EMD 1078 (four-album box set with hardback book, released a year later). Shine On You Crazy Diamond Pts.1-6/Astronomy Dominé/

What Do You Want From Me/ Learning To Fly/Keep Talking/ Coming Back To Life/Hey You/A Great Day For Freedom/ Sorrow/High Hopes/Another Brick In The Wall Pt.2/One of These Days//The Dark Side of The Moon (from 'Speak to Me' to 'Money')//The Dark Side of The Moon (from 'Us and Them' to 'Eclipse')/Wish You Were Here/Comfortably Numb/Run Like Hell.

Pulse – Earls Court London 20.10.94.

PMI MVD 4914363 (video). Shine On You Crazy Diamond. Pts.1-5 & 7/Learning To Fly/High Hopes/Take It Back/Coming Back To Life/Sorrow/Keep Talking/Another Brick In The Wall Pt.2/One Of These Days/The Dark Side Of The Moon/Wish You Were Here/Comfortably Numb/Run Like Hell.

Pink Floyd performing 'Money', Empire Pool, Wembley, November 1974

ACKNOWLEDGEMENTS

Most of our research was carried out at the British Newspaper Library, London, England and The Library of Congress, Washington DC, USA. Additional research was completed at The City of London Library, London, England; Kensington Public Library, London, England; Koninklijke Bibliotheek, The Hague, Netherlands; Landes Bibliothek, Berne, Switzerland; Landes Bibliothek, Stuttgart, Germany; The National Sound Archive, London, England; University College of London, London, England; Westminster Public Library, London, England; Zeitungs Museen, Dortmund, Germany. In the course of our research we also sent letters to newspaper and magazine editors all over the world, requesting reader information on Pink Floyd concerts. We would like to thank the editors of the following publications, who kindly responded to our request and, in some cases, duplicated their archives for us: *Apeldoornse Courant, Arizona Daily Star, Bath Chronicle, Berkshire Observer, Bournemouth Evening Echo, Brighton Argus, Brighton & Hove Leader, Bristol Evening Post, Cambridge Evening News, Chichester & Bognor Observer, Cornish Times, Coventry Evening Telegraph, Derby Evening Telegraph, East Anglia Times, Edinburgh Evening News, Exeter Express & Echo, Financial Times, Gazet van Antwerpen, De Gelderlander, Glasgow Herald, Haagsche Courant, Ipswich Evening Star, Kent Today, Lancashire Evening Telegraph, Lancaster Guardian, Leicester Mercury, Malvern Gazette, Oxford Mail, Oxford Star, Oxford Times, Record Collector, St Petersburg Times, South London Press, Swansea Herald, Wantage Herald, Western Evening Herald, Windsor Express, Worthing Herald.* Those whose articles were used with permission have been credited in the text.

We also sent letters to almost every surviving venue, establishment and university that hosted a performance by Pink Floyd and we are most grateful to the following for checking their records: Amsterdam Concertgebouw, Arizona State University, Bristol City Council (on behalf of the Colston Hall), Case Western Reserve University, Clemson University, Edinburgh University, Empire Theatre Liverpool, Fairfield Halls Croydon, Gonzaga University, Hallenstadion Zurich, Keele University, Kent State University, Konzerthaus Vienna, Leicester University, Princeton University, Queen's College Oxford, Royal Albert Hall, Royal Festival and Queen Elizabeth Halls, Royal Holloway College (University of London), Sussex University, Théâtre des Champs Elysées, University of Bradford, University of Denver, University of Essex, University of Montreal, University of Reading, University of Wales, University of Toledo, University of Westminster, Willamette University.

Finally, thanks to everyone who has assisted with contacts, recollections, photos, memorabilia and research: Richard Allen, Nigel Applin, Lesley A. Ashby, Janice Bagwell, D. Bainborough, Rosemary Barbieri, John Baxter, Phil Beckett, Charles Beterams, Sandra J. Blickern, David Boderke, Tony Breen, Mrs Jill Briggs, John Brisbrowne, Danny Burgess, Alastair Cameron, Mrs E. Carmichael, Barry Christian, Mr G. Cook, Ken Cook, Tony Crabtree, Tom Croson, Alan Cross, Eric Cuthbertson, John Delany, Chris Dennis, Mrs Madeline Digby, Rupert Diggens, Steve Edwards, Jean-Manuel Esnault, Alan Felters, Evelyne Fenet, Vic Fledt, Ron Fleischer, M. Fletcher, Dave Ford, Lynn Gardiner, Will Garfitt, Ron Geesin, Ian Gomeche, Elizabeth Gray, Peter R.F. Gunn, Peter Hearn, Malcolm Henderson, Kevin

Hewick, Doug Hext, Mr J. Hopwood, Dave Howells,
Trevor Jeffs, Jeff Jensen, Chris Job, Matt Johns,
Peter Johnson, Vic King, Peter Koks, Alain Lachaud,
Peter Levett, Richard Lawrence, John Lawson,
R.C. Lind, Alastair MacLean, John Mansfield,
Dick Maunders, Steve Millard, Robert Morse,
Gary Murphy, Keith Noble, Sheilagh Noble, Sara
O'Brien, Yoshiko Ogiso, Rosina Osborn, David
Parker, John Parkin, Kevin Peake, Lynda Pearce,
Pete and Tony at Soho Records, John Phillips,
John Phillpott, Darren Powter, Noel Redding,
Larry Reddington, John Revill, Mick Robshaw, Jon
Rosenberg, Veronique Rothwell, Lee Saunders,
Marc Skobac, Dave Scott, Ray Sheppard, Iain
Smith, William Smythe, Henk Snoek, Mark
Solomons, Fraser Speirs, Ron Stewart, Ken
Szymanek, A. Taylor, Caroline Taylor, Greg Taylor,
Elliot Tayman, Stanford Thompson, Bruce
Tippen, Peter Towner, John Tozer, Ivor
Trueman, Chris Varney, Fred Vintner, Lindsay
Wainwright, Ken Waterson, R.J. Webber, Clive
Welham, Bernard White, Snowy White, David
Wickelt, Martin Wicker-Kempton, Roy Wilbraham,
Brian Wilcock, Lindsay Williams, Tony Williams,
Brian Wilson MP, Irene Winsby, A.L. Woodward
and Jim Young.

Our sincere apologies to anyone whom we may
have inadvertently missed.

Further information on Pink Floyd

Pink Floyd fans and collectors may be interested to
receive regular updates on everything connected
with the band. They can do so by subscribing to
Brain Damage, the International Pink Floyd
Magazine. For further details please send a
SAE/IRC to Brain Damage Magazine, PO Box
109, Westmont, Illinois, 60559, USA. E-mail:
BDMag@aol.com

Other recommended publications:
Clowns and Jugglers (Syd Barrett fanzine), c/o
Barry Botatoe, 101 Amersham Road, Terriers,
High Wycombe, Buckinghamshire HP13 5AD, UK.
Eskimo Chain (Syd Barrett/early Pink Floyd
fanzine), c/o Iain Smith, 2 White Cottages, Long
Garth, Durham City DH1 4HL, UK.
REG (the Roger Waters fan club magazine), c/o
Michael Simone, 112 Bennett Road, Aptos, CA
95003, USA.